The Comprehensive ECAA Guide

Written for the New 2021 Specification

By

Sachin Sarin & Thapan Reddibathini

Frontier Education

About the Authors

Sachin Sarin and Thapan Reddibathini are both students from Queen Elizabeth's School, Barnet and are current Economics offer holders at the University of Cambridge.

During our own ECAA preparation, we realised that the amount of quality material on the market was limited. Given that we were the first students to have sat the new exam style, we have unique insight in preparing for and sitting the real ECAA examination.

Therefore, we have written this book in order to provide tailored guidance and practice so that students who complete these questions are in a strong position to be confident and successful on the day.

Contact Us

We are glad that you have chosen the Comprehensive ECAA Guide as a means of providing you with upmost quality guidance in your preparation.

We are aware that university applications are a daunting process and hence at Frontier Education, we offer a range of services to assist, ranging from:

- Personal Statement Guidance
- Mock Interviews
- Tutoring for Mathematics, Further Mathematics and Economics for A and AS level
- General Advice

Whilst attention and care has been dedicated to ensuring that there are no typographical or technical errors in this guide, it may be possible that some mistakes still remain. If you have identified any such errors in this guide or have any queries with regards to the contents of this book, please do not hesitate to contact us at:

frontiereducation2021@gmail.com

Alternatively feel free to connect with Sachin Sarin or Thapan Reddibathini via LinkedIn to direct any similar enquiries or if you require any other assistance regarding the process.

Contents

Introduction to the ECAA

The Economics Admissions Assessment (ECAA) is a written exam undertaken by all applicants applying to study Economics at Cambridge. The exam is usually taken in the first week of November, prior to interviews, which happen later in December.

The ECAA's format from 2020 onwards has changed, with the assessment's previous problem-solving section being replaced by another mathematics section.

The new format of the exam has 2 sections, with the first being split into 2 parts:

Section 1: 1 hour
Section 1A: Mathematics (20 MCQs)
Section 1B: Advanced Mathematics (20 MCQs)

Section 2: 1 hour
Section 2: Essay based on given extract.

General Information

In order to apply for the ECAA, candidates must do so through their school. The exam will have to be sat at a Cambridge authorised testing centre, which in the majority of cases, will be the candidate's school. A list of designated Cambridge centres can be found online on the Cambridge Assessment Admissions Testing website.

The ECAA is marked such that each applicant is given 3 scores for section 1A, 1B and 2. The scores range from 1.0 to 9.0 using a Rausch distribution, such that 4 is made to be the average score. The marking for section 1A and 1B is done using a points-based system, with each correct ANSWER giving 1 mark.

The ECAA is different to certain other entrance exams like the TSA, in that the scores are not released automatically to candidates. However, it is possible to request the results from your college after the results day in January.

The ECAA is essentially used as an indicator for admissions tutors to gauge the mathematical ability of candidates. This is because the Economics course at Cambridge is very maths heavy and therefore, you should use this exam as an opportunity to set yourself apart from other candidates by showing off your mathematical aptitude.

Section 1A mainly encompasses content from the (I)GCSE specification, whilst the majority of section 1B is covered in the first year of the IB SL and A-Level course. However, there are some added topics that may not have been covered in school yet, such as geometric series (AM2.3) and radians (AM4). We would suggest learning these using online resources first before starting practise questions and papers.

The ECAA is a non-calculator exam, meaning that it is imperative that your numerical and mental maths skills are strong. This means being able to estimate sums quickly in your head without wasting valuable time doing working on paper.

How to prepare for the ECAA

Since the ECAA is undertaken in the first week of November, and is of crucial importance, it is recommended to begin preparation in the Summer after Year 12 (July). This should give ample time to go through the specification and practise.

In terms of how to manage preparation, we would suggest to first go through the specification in good detail, and make sure that you are comfortable with each part. After having learnt the content, we'd suggest using this book to its full potential. Having 400 maths questions and 20 essay questions enables candidates to get more and more familiar with the types of questions that they will be getting in the final exam. We would suggest completing the book 2-3 times such that by the final attempt, doing questions quickly has become second nature. The further attempts should be done with a greater focus on time constraint in order to mimic the conditions in the real exam.

Practise papers should be started quickly after you feel you are strong with the content and can do the questions quickly under pressure. These should ideally be started before the new academic year begins in September. It is important not to leave practise papers to late, as many of you will be very busy in September with your UCAS applications.

Fortunately, the ECAA specification overlaps significantly with the maths sections of other entrance exams, and therefore, it is vital you to utilise these resources. Such exams include the NSAA, ENGAA, TMUA and the MAT (multiple choice only). It is not worth practising the problem-solving sections of previous ECAA papers, as these skills will not be required nor tested in the new specification.

When doing the questions in this book, it is important to take a physical or mental note of the areas of weakness. This does not necessarily mean the areas where you went wrong, but also the areas in which you spent longer than you should have.

Practise papers should be run through 2-3 times, with the first time being an indicator to you of your current standard. Do not be disheartened if you start off not doing so well, as it takes a lot of practise before being able to attain a high level of accuracy and speed.

After having completed these three steps of learning, practise and then papers, we believe that you should be in great form to finally do the real exam in November!

Exam Tips

With section 1 containing 40 questions to be finished in 1 hour, it is essential that time is managed efficiently. The University suggests that the 1 hour is split equally between section 1A and 1B. However, given that the advanced mathematics section has harder questions, we would recommend spending 20/25 minutes on section 1A and the rest on 1B. It is crucial for you to plan your timings and adhere to it within the exam.

If you find that a question is taking more than 2 minutes and the answer is not nearby, we recommend to just skip this question and move on. It is pointless to spend too long on one question at the expense of attempting later questions.

Since each question is multiple choice, if you are struggling to find answers, you should make educated guesses. This does not mean picking any random answer, but rather, first ruling out any answers that you know cannot be true. This increases the probability of your guess being right, hence maximising your potential.

It is important to read every question carefully, but at the same time, do not spend too much time on this. We would recommend underlining the key information on the first read, before promptly beginning to solve the problem.

It is very natural to feel under pressure and anxious during the exam, but the key focus is making sure you do not buckle. Do ample practise using this book and past papers, and you will become more and more confident along the way. Stick to your knowledge and you will be fine.

Post Exam

After the exam, it is necessary to realise that it is now out of your control. Please do not be disheartened if you think you did badly, because it is meant to be challenging. The vast majority of applicants in 2021 struggled with the ECAA, indicating that the exam functioned in the way it was supposed to. Ultimately, it is used as an indicator and differentiator by admissions tutors to separate the better candidates from the worse.
Should you be successful in your application, the University will contact you in late November regarding your interview process.

Congratulations if you have made it to this stage, it is a notable feat in itself!

Maths Guide

1A: Maths Guide

M1 Units

M1.1 Using standard units of mass, length, time, money and other measures

- Know metric system for measurements.
- Know SI units and prefixes for measurements.
- Lengths are commonly measured using millimetres, centimetres (1cm = 10mm), metres (1m= 100cm), kilometres (1km= 1000m).
- Times are commonly measured using seconds, minutes (1 minute= 60 seconds), hours (1 hour = 60 minutes).
- Know how compound measures relate to each other.
- $speed = \frac{distance}{time}$.
- $density = \frac{mass}{volume}$.
- $pressure = \frac{force}{area}$.

Prefix	Symbol	10^n	Prefix	Symbol	10^n
deca	da	10^1	deci	d	10^{-1}
hecto	h	10^2	centi	c	10^{-2}
kilo	k	10^3	milli	m	10^{-3}
mega	M	10^6	micro	µ	10^{-6}
giga	G	10^9	nano	n	10^{-9}
tera	T	10^{12}	pico	p	10^{-12}
peta	P	10^{15}	femto	f	10^{-15}
exa	E	10^{18}	atto	a	10^{-18}

M1.2 Be able to switch between related units, e.g. speed, distance and time.

M2 Number

M2.1 Know the common mathematical symbols

- $=$ means "is equal to", indicating two expressions are of equal value.
- $\neq$ means "not equal to", indicating two expressions do not have the same value.
- $>$ means "strictly greater than", indicating that first expression has a value greater than the second.
- $<$ means "strictly less than", indicating the first expression has a value less than the second.
- $\geq$ means "greater than or equal to", indicating the first expression is either greater than or equal to the second.
- $\leq$ means "less than or equal to", indicating the first expression is either less than or equal to the second.
- $\equiv$ represents an identity, meaning the first expression will always be equal to the second, regardless of the value of the unknowns.

M2.2 Apply the four common mathematical operation (addition, subtraction, multiplication and division) to real values and understand how to use place value

- The 4 mathematical operations should be done in the order: multiplication, division, addition subtraction. E.g. $2 - 6 \times 3 + 1 = 2 - 18 + 1 = -15$.
- Place value shows the worth of each digit in a number.
- The order of place value is hundredths, tenths, units, tens, hundreds, thousands etc.
- Every number can be broken down such that it is written as a sum of its individual place values. E.g. 126 is made up of 1 hundred, 2 tens and 6 units. $100 + 20 + 6 = 126$.

M2.3 Understand the concepts and vocabulary relating to prime numbers

- A factor is a number that divides exactly into another number with no remainder.
- A prime number is a number which only has itself and 1 as its factors.
- The unique factorisation theorem states that every natural number can be written as a product of prime factors, and each arrangement is unique to that number.
- Know how to find the highest common factor and lowest common multiples of different numbers. To do this, first write each number as a product of its prime factors.
- To find the HCF, multiply out the factors that are common to both.
- To find the LCM, multiply out each factor once, but do not repeat them. In other words, take the highest power of each prime factor present.

  Example, 12 and 16

$12 = 2^2 \times 3$ $\qquad$ $16 = 2^4$

HCF: Both numbers have 2^2 in common, hence 4 is the HCF

LCM: Take the highest power of each prime factor $= 2^4 \times 3 = 48$

M2.4 Understand how to use more advanced operations and their inverses (brackets, indices etc) and understand how to simplify through cancellation

- The inverse of an operation is one that "nullifies" the outcome of the operation. For example, the inverse of x^2 would be $\sqrt{x}$.
- To simplify (cancel down) a fraction, the numerator and denominator must have a common factor. Then divide, the top and bottom by this factor.
- BIDMAS states the order of which operations should be carried out. Begin with expanding out Brackets, followed by Indices, Division, Multiplication, Addition and finally Subtraction.

M2.5 Understand how to apply systematic listing strategies

- If there are x number of ways of doing one task and y ways of doing another thing, the total number of ways to do both things is xy.
- Additionally, if there are z ways of doing a third task, the number of ways to do all three tasks would be xyz.

M2.6 Index and root notation

- Square is denoted by x^2, which represents one number being multiplied by itself, e.g. $6^2 = 6 \times 6 = 36$.
- Cube is denoted by x^3, which represents one number being multiplied by itself 3 times, e.g. $6^{23} = 6 \times 6 \times 6 = 216$.
- A square root is denoted by $\sqrt{x}$. It is the inverse operation of a square. It is the number that multiplies by itself to receive the input, e.g. $\sqrt{36} = 6$.
- A cube root is denoted by $\sqrt[3]{x}$. It is the inverse operation of a cube. It is the number that multiplies by itself three time to receive the input, e.g. $\sqrt[3]{216} = 6$.
- Square roots always have two solutions, a positive and negative root, e.g. $\sqrt{36} = \pm 6$. This is because when -6×-6, the two negative signs cancel out.

M2.7 Index laws including negative and fractional indices

- Multiplicative law: $a^x \times a^y = a^{x+y}$, e.g. $3^2 \times 3^4 = 3^{2+4} = 3^6 = 729$.
- Dividing law: $a^x \div a^y = a^{x-y}$, e.g. $3^4 \div 3^2 = 3^{4-2} = 3^2 = 9$.
- Bracketed law: $(a^x)^y = a^{xy}$, e.g. $(3^2)^3 = 3^{2\times 3} = 3^6 = 729$.
- Negative power law: $a^{-x} = \frac{1}{a^x}$, e.g. $3^{-3} = \frac{1}{3^3} = \frac{1}{27}$.

- Note, negative powers do not mean the outcome is negative. It means, first take the reciprocal, and then apply the power.
- Fractional law: $a^{\frac{x}{y}} = \left(\sqrt[y]{a}\right)^x$, e.g. $27^{\frac{2}{3}} = \left(\sqrt[3]{27}\right)^2 = 3^2 = 9$.

M2.8 Standard Form

- Standard form is writing any number in the form $a \times 10^b$, where $1 \leq a < 10$, and n can take any positive or negative real value.
- Adding and subtracting numbers in standard form can be done in two ways. Firstly, it may be easy to convert the numbers into their full form and then applying the operations.
- Secondly, the two numbers can be converted such that they have the same order of 10 value. This can be done by adjusting the a value by multiplying or dividing by an order of 10 accordingly. Then add or subtract the two new a values,
  e.g. $2.4 \times 10^2 + 3.6 \times 10^3$
  $= 0.24 \times 10^3 + 3.6 \times 10^3 = 3.84 \times 10^3$
  $= 3{,}840$.
- Multiplying and diving numbers in standard form is relatively easier. Separate the a and 10^b parts and apply the operation to each part. The two a values should be multiplied/divided and then add or subtract the indices using the index laws.
  e.g. $2.4 \times 10^2 \times 3.6 \times 10^3$
  $= (2.4 \times 3.6) \times (10^{2+3})$
  $= 8.64 \times 10^5$
  $= 864{,}000$

M2.9 Decimals, percentages and fractions

- To convert from decimals and fractions into percentages, multiply by 100.
- A terminating decimal is a decimal that is expressed in a finite number of decimals. All terminating decimals can be represented as fractions, with the denominator being a power of 10.
  e.g. $2.341 = 2\frac{341}{1000}$
- A recurring decimal is a decimal which has an infinite number of decimals and is periodic, e.g. 0.192192192192...
- Candidates sometimes think that recurring decimals cannot be represented by fractions, but this is not the case. There are two methods to convert a recurring decimal into a fraction.

Method 1:

- Firstly, let the recurring decimal be represented by x, and we are trying to find the fractional form of x.
- Then, identify the period of the recurrence. This means how many digits the decimal repeats. For example, 0.111111... has period 1, 0.121212... has period 2 and 0.123123... has period 3.
- After identifying the period, p, obtain another term by multiplying x by 10^p. This should now give two terms, $x \text{ and } 10^p x$. It is important to note that both these terms will have the same recurring decimals.
- The penultimate step is to subtract x from $10^p x$, which cancels out the two recurring decimals. This should give $(10^p - 1)x$.
- Then make x the subject of the equation, which should leave a fractional form.

  e.g. 0.121212...
  Let $x = 0.121212\ldots$
  Period = 2, so multiply by 100
  $100x = 12.121212\ldots$
  $100x - x = 12.\dot{1}\dot{2} - 0.\dot{1}\dot{2}$
  $99x = 12$
  $x = \frac{4}{33}$

Method 2:

- Every recurring decimal can be rewritten as a sum of smaller decimals. This sum represents a geometric series. The first step is to rewrite the decimal in this form.
- Then, find the sum to infinity of this geometric series using the formula $\frac{a}{1-r}$, where a is the first term, and r is the common ratio. The r will always be a negative power of 10.

  e.g. 0.121212
  $0.121212\ldots = 0.12 + 0.0012 + 0.000012 + \cdots$
  $a = 0.12$ and $r = 0.01$
  Sum to infinity $= \frac{0.12}{0.99} = \frac{12}{99}$
  $= \frac{4}{33}$

M2.10 Further decimals, percentages and fractions

- Should know the values of basic and common fractions, e.g. $\frac{1}{2}, \frac{1}{3}, \frac{1}{4}, \frac{1}{5}, \frac{1}{6}, \frac{1}{8}, \frac{1}{9}, \frac{1}{10}$.

M2.11 Be able to calculate using fractions, surds and π

- A surd is a nth root of a number which cannot be written as a fraction. It is irrational.
- π is a mathematical term representing the ratio of a circle's diameter to its circumference.
- To multiply surds, multiply the inner numbers together and root the product e.g. $\sqrt{2} \times \sqrt{3} = \sqrt{2 \times 3} = \sqrt{6}$.
- Dividing surds uses the same premise; divide the inner numbers and root the outcome.

  e.g. $\sqrt{28} \div \sqrt{7} = \sqrt{\frac{28}{7}} = 2$
- In simplified fractions, there should not be any surds in the denominator. To simplify these fractions, there are two things that can be done.
- If the denominator is in the form $\sqrt{x}$, multiply the fraction by $\frac{\sqrt{x}}{\sqrt{x}}$,

  e.g. $\frac{2}{\sqrt{3}} = \frac{2}{\sqrt{3}} \times \frac{\sqrt{3}}{\sqrt{3}} = \frac{2\sqrt{3}}{3}$

- If the denominator is in the form $a + b\sqrt{x}$, multiply by the conjugate, $\frac{a-b\sqrt{x}}{a-b\sqrt{x}}$.

  e.g. $\frac{5}{1+\sqrt{2}}$

  $= \frac{5}{1+\sqrt{2}} \times \frac{1-\sqrt{2}}{1-\sqrt{2}}$

  $= \frac{5-5\sqrt{2}}{-1}$

  $= 5\sqrt{2} - 5$

M2.12 Rounding using upper and lower bounds

- Bounds represent the range of numbers an estimated value can take.
- The lower bound is the smallest value that would round up to the estimated value.
- The upper bound is the greatest value that would round down to the estimate value.
- For example, an estimate of 9cm to the nearest cm would have bounds $8.5 \leq x < 9.5$.

M2.13 Rounding using degrees of accuracy

- Numbers can be rounded to various degrees as a method of simplification or estimation.
- Rounding to decimal places involves counting digits to the specified degree after the decimal point. Then, round up or down depending on whether the next number is greater or equal to 5 or less than 5.

- Rounding numbers to significant figures involves the same process but counting digits from the beginning of the number. All digits following the rounding will be 0.
- Truncating a number to a certain degree means cutting off the number after the specified degree. There is no rounding up or down in this case.
- When rounding and truncating, there will always be an error interval. You can use bounds to represent the range of values a rounded number can take.

M2.14 Approximation and estimating involving surds and π

- Should be able to approximate the value of surds to aid calculations. Make sure you know rough values of single digit roots.
- Can approximate pi as 3.14 in calculations.
- When unsure of a method to solve a problem, one solution is to substitute the answer into the question and see which one works quickly using estimation.
- To compare the value of different surds, you can either approximate the surd into a decimal or square both sides. The value with the greater square will be of greater value.
- Reverse percentage problems are when the final value is provided after a percentage change and the initial value needs to be found.
- Again, always take the initial value as "100%", and let the final change be an adjustment of this.
- Then divide by that number to get the value of 1%. Then multiply by 100 to get the initial value.

  e.g. The price of a TV in a sale is reduced by 20% to £240.
  This means that 80% of the original price is £240
  Dividing both by 80 will mean that 1% is £3, and then multiplying by 100 means the original price is £300.

M3 Ratio and Proportion

M3.1 Use of scale factors and diagrams

- Scale factors are used to simplify real life problems by factoring down the values.
- Scale factors are often used to simplify lengths, areas and volumes. It represents the multiplier between two lengths.
- The area scale factor will be the square of the length scale factor. This is because area is a square value (e.g. cm^2).
- The volume scale factor will be the cube of the length scale factor. This is because volume is a cubic value (e.g. cm^3).
- Maps often have keys, showing what a certain length on the map represents in real life. For example, a scale factor of 1:750,000 shows 1cm on the map shows 750,000cm in reality. This means 1cm represents 7.5km.

M3.2 Express one quantity as a fraction of another

- To represent one quantity in ration to another, place the first quantity as the numerator and the second as the denominator. Then, simplify the fraction.
  e.g. to express £2.50 as a fraction of £6, it would be $\frac{2.5}{6} = \frac{5}{12}$
- Depending on which value is greater, the fraction can be either greater or lower than 1.

M3.3 Ratio Notation

- A ratio is a way of comparing two or more quantities.
- The ratio notation is written as A: B, representing the quantity of A compared to the quantity of B in their simplest forms.

M3.4 Splitting a quantity up in different ratios

- In the ratio A: B, the total number of parts is given by A + B.
- Find the value of one part by dividing the quantity by A+B.
- Then to find the split, multiply one part by A and B respectively.
  e.g. to split £120 in the ration 1:2:5
  First, find the total number of parts, which is $1 + 2 + 5 = 8$.
  Then, find the value of one part by doing $120 \div 8 = 15$
  Then multiply 15 by 1, 2 and 5 respectively, giving

  15:30:75

M3.5 Using ratios in real life scenarios

- Ratios are used in exchange rates to represent the value of one currency in terms of another.
- Ratios are also used in scale factors to show how certain lengths are compared to another, e.g. on maps.

M3.6 Proportions, ratios and linear functions

- Proportion represents a part or share of something in relation to the whole.
- A ratio in the form A: B can be represented as a fraction. For example, if A: B = 2: 3, then this means that $\frac{a}{b} = \frac{2}{3}$.
- Similarly, the ratio fraction can allow the ratio to be represented as a linear function. Where A: B is 2: 3, then 3A = 2B.

M3.7 Use fractions in ratio problems

- Converting ratios into fractions makes problems easier to solve as you can then form and manipulate equations accordingly.

M3.8 Use percentages in various problems

- Percentage means "per" "cent", meaning the number of parts for every 100.
- To work out $x\%$ of a value, convert the percentage into a decimal or fraction and multiply.
- To convert fractions into percentages, multiply by 100.
- Percentage change can be calculated by the equation $\frac{difference}{original} \times 100$.

  e.g. the percentage change from £5 to £8 is $\frac{8-5}{5} \times 100 = 60\%$
- To express one quantity as a percentage of another, form a fraction and multiply by 100.
- To increase/decrease a value by a certain percentage, there are two methods.

Method 1:

- Calculate the percentage of the value required.
- Add or subtract this to the original.

e.g. To increase 50kg by 15%

First, to calculate 15%, do $0.15 \times 50 = 7.5$

Then add this to 50 to get 57.5kg

Method 2:

- This method involves only one calculation by using a multiplier.
- Think that all values start at 100%, so to increase or decrease, we are changing from this 100.
- When increasing or decreasing by a percentage, the final value will be either higher or lower. For example, to increase or decrease by 5% would mean the new value is either 105% or 95% respectively.
- Hence you can multiply by 1.05 or 0.95.

e.g. To increase 50kg by 15%

First, identify the final percentage which will be $100 + 15 = 115$

Then multiply 50 by 1.15 giving 57.5kg

- An interest rate is the cost of borrowing and reward for saving. Savers will obtain money whereas borrowers will have to pay more back.
- Simple interest rate means that in each instalment, you gain/lose the same amount.
- The formula for the final value for simple interest rate is $initial\ value\ \times (1 + (interest\ rate \times n))$, where n is the number of years (instalments)
  e.g. the value of a £1,500 investment at a 3% IR after 2 years will be worth $= 1500 \times \left(1 + (0.03 \times 2)\right) = 1{,}590$.
- Alternatively, calculate the value gained each year and multiply by the number of years. Then, add to initial value.

M3.9 Direct and inverse proportion

- Proportion represents two variables and how one affects another.
- Direct proportion means that as one variable increases the other also increases by the same proportion. The notation for this is $y \propto x$, showing y is directly proportionate to x.
- To express this as an equation, it can be written as $y = kx$, where k represents the constant of proportionality.
- The graphical representation is a straight line going through the origin. If the line has a positive gradient, the constant of proportionality is positive. If it has a negative gradient, the constant of proportionality is negative.
- Inverse proportion is when one value increases and the other decreases. The two variables move in opposite directions. The notation for this is $y \propto \frac{1}{x}$.
- This can be written as an equation in the form of $y = \frac{k}{x}$, where k is again the constant of proportionality.
- Graphically, inverse proportion takes the shape of $y = \frac{1}{x}$. The x and y axes are asymptotes.

- As the constant of proportionality increases, the graph will move further away from the origin.

M3.10 Scale factors involving similar shapes

- Scale factors are often used to simplify lengths, areas and volumes. It represents the multiplier between two lengths.
- The area scale factor will be the square of the length scale factor. This is because area is a square value (e.g. cm^2).
- The volume scale factor will be the cube of the length scale factor. This is because volume is a cubic value (e.g. cm^3).
- Similar shapes are shapes that are identical in proportion. This means they have the same scale factor and if it is 1, the two shapes are exactly identical.
- The angles in shapes that are similar will be exactly the same.

M3.11 Compound interest rates, growth, decay and iterative processes

- Unlike simple interest rate, with a compound interest rate, you do not receive the same every instalment. Instead, each instalment gains interest on the previous value.
- The equation for compound interest rate is $A = P(1 + r)^n$, where P is the initial deposit, r is the interest rate and n is the number of time periods.
  e.g. Investing £12,000 in a fund with a yearly rate of return of 3% after 3 years will be worth
  $A = 12{,}000(1 + 0.03)^3$
  $A = £13{,}112.72$.
- With the same principal sum and same interest rate, compound interest rates will always yield a greater final value than a simple interest rate scheme. This is because the interest is gained on the most recent amount which is greater than the initial sum as is the case with simple rates.
- Growth cannot only be limited to interest rate questions but also to bacteria and wildlife. The same concept and equation are used.
- Decay uses the same concept but instead of the multiplier being greater than 1, it will be lower than 1, e.g. 0.95 at 5% decay rate.

M4 Algebra

M4.1 Algebraic notation

- Algebra involves unknowns, which are commonly denoted by letters such as a, b, x and y
- Algebraic expressions are simplified such that there is only one term per unknown. Therefore, unknowns are grouped together. For example, $a + a + a + b + b = 3a + 2b$.
- Algebraic multiplication does not use the ×, symbol but the products of terms are written together. For example, $ab = a \times b$.
- Indices are used to represent unknowns being multiplied by each other. For example $a \times a \times a \times a = a^4$.

M4.2 Algebraic index laws

- Index laws work in the exact same way in algebra.
- Multiplicative law: $a^x \times a^y = a^{x+y}$, e.g. $3^2 \times 3^4 = 3^{2+4} = 3^6 = 729$.
- Dividing law: $a^x \div a^y = a^{x-y}$, e.g. $3^4 \div 3^2 = 3^{4-2} = 3^2 = 9$.
- Bracketed law: $(a^x)^y = a^{xy}$, e.g. $(3^2)^3 = 3^{2\times3} = 3^6 = 729$.
- Negative power law: $a^{-x} = \frac{1}{a^x}$, e.g. $3^{-3} = \frac{1}{3^3} = \frac{1}{27}$.
- Note, negative powers do not mean the outcome is negative. It means, first take the reciprocal, and then apply the power.
- Fractional law: $a^{\frac{x}{y}} = (\sqrt[y]{a})^x$, e.g. $27^{\frac{2}{3}} = (\sqrt[3]{27})^2 = 3^2 = 9$.

M4.3 Substitution and algebraic terminology

- Substituting means inputting an actual numerical value in place of an unknown in a formula or expression.
- An expression is a collection of different terms, e.g. $3a^2 + 2b - c + 1$.
- An equation is when two expressions are set to be equal to each other, e.g. $3a^2 + 2b - c = 10$.
- A formula is a mathematical equation that shows the relationship between two or more variables, e.g. $e = mc^2$, showing the relationship between energy, mass and the speed of light.
- An identity is an equation that is true for all values of the unknown. For example, $x + x \equiv 2x$. This is always true regardless of the value of x.
- A term is either a single number or variable. For example, in the expression $2b - c + 1$, there are three terms.

- A factor is a number or algebraic expression that will divide into an expression or term with no remainder.

M4.4 Simplifying, expanding and factorising

- Expressions are simplified by collecting like terms. This means collecting together the same unknowns. E.g. $a + a + a + b + b = 3a + 2b$.
- Brackets can be expanded by multiplying the number outside the bracket by each individual term inside. E.g.$2(2a + b - 3c) = 4a + 2b - 6c$.
- The opposite of expanding brackets is to factorise an expression. This means taking out a common factor within all of the terms. For example, $2x + 4y - 8z = 2(x + 2y - 4z)$.
- To multiply double brackets and binomials, multiply each term in one bracket by each term in the other. For brackets with two terms, use the FOIL method.
- FOIL stands for First, Outside, Inside and Last, which shows an easy order to multiply brackets out. E.g. $(x + 1)(x + 2) = x^2 + 2x + x + 2 = x^2 + 3x + 2$.
- Note, the order in which the terms inside the brackets are multiplied is not important.

M4.5 Factorising quadratics

- Quadratics are expressions in the form $ax^2 + bx + c$, where a, b and c are numerical constants.
- Factorising quadratics involves splitting them into two brackets, each with an x term and a constant term. E.g. $x^2 + 5x + 6 = (x + 2)(x + 3)$.
- To factorise quadratics where the coefficient of x^2 is 1 is easier. It requires finding two numbers that add up to the c term, and add together to obtain the b term. These two numbers will form the two brackets. E.g. $x^2 + 5x + 6$. Two numbers that multiply to get 6 and add to get 5 are 2 and 3. Hence, $x^2 + 5x + 6 = (x + 2)(x + 3)$.
- Be careful when dealing with negative constants. It is possible that one bracket contains a negative term and the other does not.
- When the coefficient of x^2 is not 1, there are some extra steps involved. This method is called the ac method.
- Firstly, multiply the c term by a to find the value of ac. Then find two numbers that multiply to give ac and sum to give the b term.
- Once these two numbers are identified, split the b term into these two separate terms.
- Then factorise the first two terms and the second two terms such that they have the same factor.
- Then factorise this factor out which should result with the answer.
  Example $6x^2 + 5x + 1$.
  $ac = 6 \times 1 = 6$
  Two numbers that multiply to give 6 and add to give 5 are 2 and 3
  Splitting the b term gives

$6x^2 + 2x + 3x + 1$.
Switch the order if you are unable to factorise at first
Factorising the first two terms and the second two terms gives
$2x(3x + 1) + 1(3x + 1)$
Then, factorise the common $(3x + 1)$ in the two terms giving
$(2x + 1)(3x + 1)$

- Some quadratics may be the difference of two squares, such as $x^2 - 25$.
- Expressions in the form of $a^2 - b^2$ can be factorised into the form $(a + b)(a - b)$
  E.g. $x^2 - 49 = (x + 7)(x - 7)$.

M4.6 Further simplifying fractions

- Expressions can be simplified by cancelling down, or first factorising and then cancelling down.

M4.7 Rearranging formulae

- The subject of a formula is the term that is expressed as an expression of other terms. E.g. x is the subject in the equation $x = 2a + b - 3c$
- Formulae may need to be rearranged to make another unknown the subject. To do this, apply mathematical operators to manipulate the formulae.
- Note that when manipulating equations, it is crucial that whatever operation is done on one side is replicated on the other.

M4.8 Equations and Identities

- An equation is when two expressions have the same value and are equalled to each other. It is true only for certain values of the unknowns. E.g. $2x = 2$ is only true for $x = 1$.
- An identity is when two expressions are equated to each other, but it is true for all values of the unknowns. E.g. $4x - 2x = 2x$ will always be true.
- An equation uses the $=$ sign, whereas identities use the $\equiv$ sign.

M4.9 Coordinate systems

- A graph has two axes. The x axis the horizontal axis and the y axis is the vertical one.
- A point on the graph is written as (x, y), where x and y are the coordinates of the point.
- Graphs have 4 quadrants.
- Quadrant 1 is the top right, where both x and y values are positive.
- Quadrant 2 is top left, where x is negative and y is positive.

- Quadrant 3 is bottom left, where both x and y are negative.
- Quadrant 4 is bottom right, where x is positive and y is negative.

M4.10 Straight line graphs

- Straight lines can be shown on graphs and have the formula $y = mx + c$, where m is the gradient of the line and c is the y intercept.
- The gradient of a line shows how steep the line is. A line with a greater gradient is steeper than a line with a lower gradient.
- When the gradient is positive, it shows that as x increases, y also increases, meaning the line is technically "going up".
- When the gradient is negative, it shows that as x increases, y decreases, meaning the line is technically "going down".
- The y intercept represents the point at which the line crosses the vertical y axis. It is the value of y when $x = 0$.
- The root of a straight line is where the line crosses the x axis, meaning $y = 0$. Therefore, it cuts the x axis at $\frac{-c}{m}$.
- To find the value of the gradient of a line, two known points are required, (x_1, y_1) and (x_2, y_2).
- The gradient can be calculated using $m = \frac{y_2 - y_1}{x_2 - x_1}$.
- The length of a line between two known points is $\sqrt{(y_2 - y_1)^2 + (x_2 - x_1)^2}$. This can be shown graphically and is using Pythagoras by drawing straight lines between the two points vertically and horizontally.
- The midpoint of the two known points is given by $(\frac{y_1 + y_2}{2}, \frac{x_1 + x_2}{2})$.
- If two lines have the same gradient, it means that they are parallel. This is because they have the same steepness, and therefore, will never meet.
- If the gradient of two lines have a product of -1, meaning that one is the negative reciprocal of the other, these two lines are perpendicular. This means that they meet each other at right angles.
- When given a gradient and one point, there are two ways to find the equation of the line.
  1) Substitute the coordinates of the known point and the gradient in the general line equation $y = mx + c$. Then, rearrange to find c and the equation should be obtained.

  2) Some questions may want the equation of the line in another form: $ax + by + c = 0$.
- In this case, use the formula $y - y_1 = m(x - x_1)$, where (x_1, y_1) are the coordinates of the known point and m is the gradient.
- Note that the constants a, b and c do not have any wider meaning (e.g. gradient or intercept) but are simply constants.

M4.11 Quadratic graphs

- Quadratic graphs are written in the form $y = ax^2 + bx + c$.
- They have a parabolic shape.
- The roots of a quadratic graph are where the graph crosses the x axis. This is where $ax^2 + bx + c = 0$.
- Find the roots by solving the quadratic either through factorising, completing the square or using the quadratic formula.
- The y intercept is always the constant value, c, because every other term including x will be 0 on the y axis.
- Quadratic graphs have a turning point, which is known as the maximum or minimum. The coordinates of this turning point can be calculated by completing the square.
- Completing the square would rewrite the quadratic equation in the form $y = a(x + b)^2 + c$. The turning point of this graph would therefore be $(-b, c)$.
- The turning point can either be a maximum or a minimum.
- A maximum is when the parabola is ∩ shaped. It goes up then down. This will be the case when a, the coefficient of x^2 is negative.
- A minimum occurs when the parabola is U shaped. It goes down then up. This will be the case, when a, the coefficient of x^2 is positive.
- To sketch a quadratic curve, first identify the intercepts and any turning points. Then identify the shape it should take.

M4.12 Recognising and sketching various algebraic graphs

- A linear graph is a straight line. It is written in the form $y = mx + c$. Straight line graphs have a constant gradient throughout.

$y = 2x + 1$

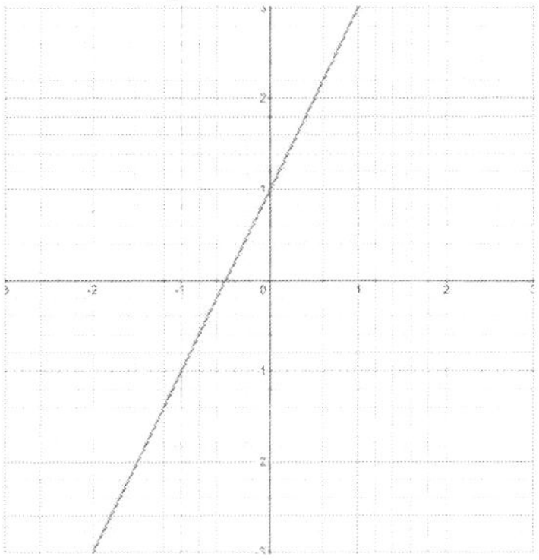

- A quadratic curve has two different distinct shapes. It can either be a ∪ or ∩ shape.
- Positive x^2 coefficient $=$ ∪ shape, graph has minimum
- Negative x^2 coefficient $=$ ∩ shape, graph has maximum
- Quadratic functions can have up to 3 roots

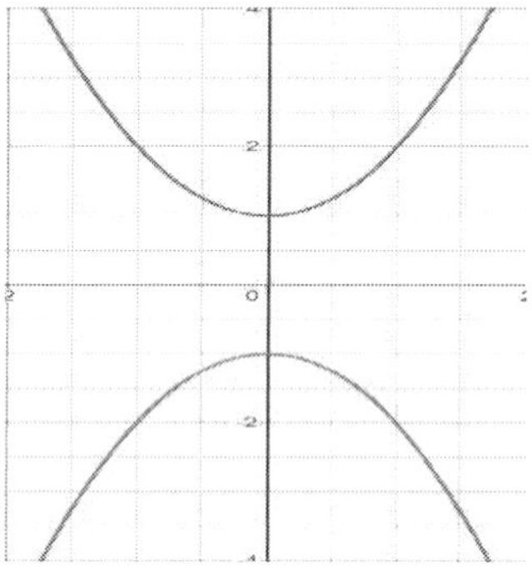

$y = x^2 + 1$

$y = -x^2 - 1$

- Cubic functions are written in the form $y = ax^3 + bx^2 + cx + d$, where d is the y intercept.
- Cubic functions can have up to 3 roots and 2 turning points.
- If the coefficient of x^3 is positive, the graph starts with a positive gradient, and if negative, it will start with a negative gradient.

$y = x^3 + 3x^2 + 1$

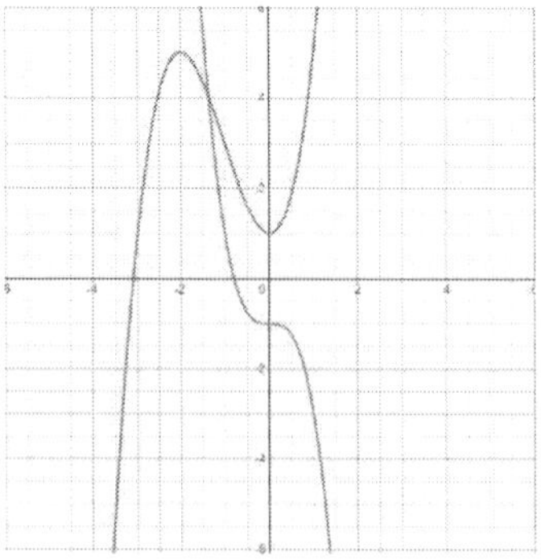

$y = -2x^3 - 1$

- Reciprocal graphs are written in the form $y = \frac{k}{x}$, where $x \neq 0$.
- Note that $x \neq 0$, because the function would be undefined at this point, as the denominator cannot be 0.
- The x and y axes will be asymptotes for $y = \frac{k}{x}$, where $x \neq 0$.
- As k increases, the graph will tend further and further from the origin.

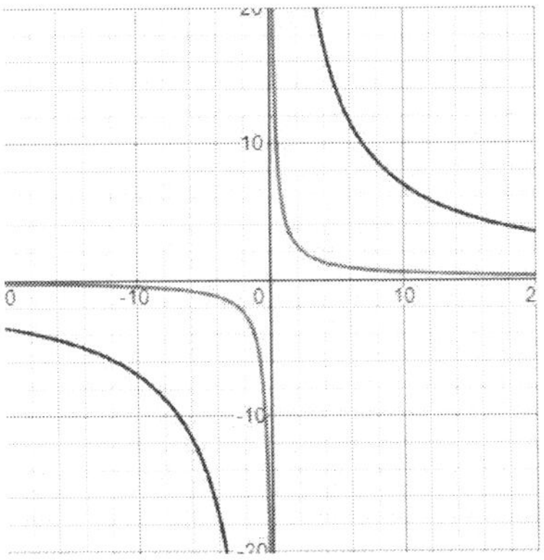

Outer graph: $y = \frac{70}{x}$

Inner graph: $y = \frac{5}{x}$

- Exponential graphs are functions where the value of y changes at ever increasing rates as $x \to \pm\infty$.
- They will have x as the exponent, in the form $y = k^x$.
- The x axis is an asymptote, because it is not possible for k^x to be negative, but will tend towards 0 as $x \to -\infty$.

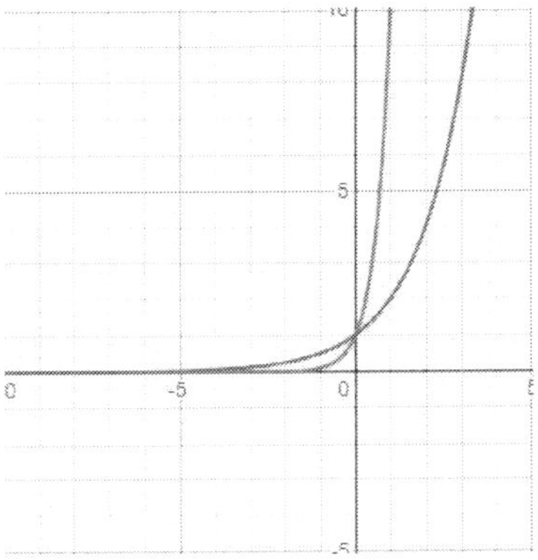

Outer graph: $y = 2^x$

Inner graph: $y = 10^x$

- There are three trigonometric functions which will be covered in more detail in the next section: sin (sin), cosine (cos) and tangent (tan).
- Trigonometric functions are not defined for x, but according to angles, so degrees or radians.
- Defining in terms of degrees, $y = sin\theta$ repeats every $360°$. It has roots at all multiples of $180°$, which is where it cuts the x axis.

- The function has a range of $-1 \leq \ sin\theta \leq 1$.

$y = \sin x$

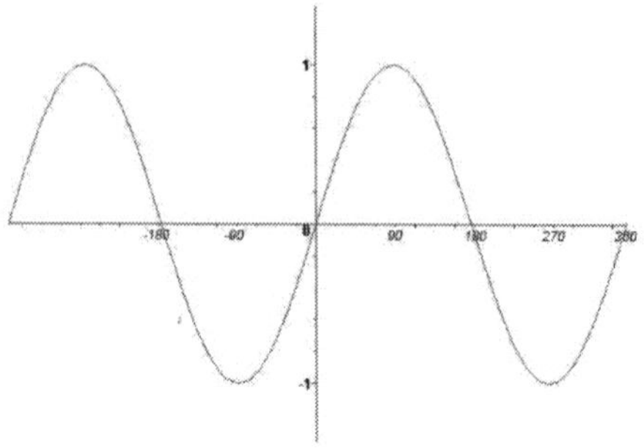

- $y = cos\theta$ also repeats every 360 degrees. It is the same function as $y = sin\theta$, but is translated 90 degrees to the left.
- It has roots at the odd multiples of 90, so -90, 90, 270, 450...
- The function also has range$-1 \leq \ cos\theta \leq 1$.

$y = \cos x$

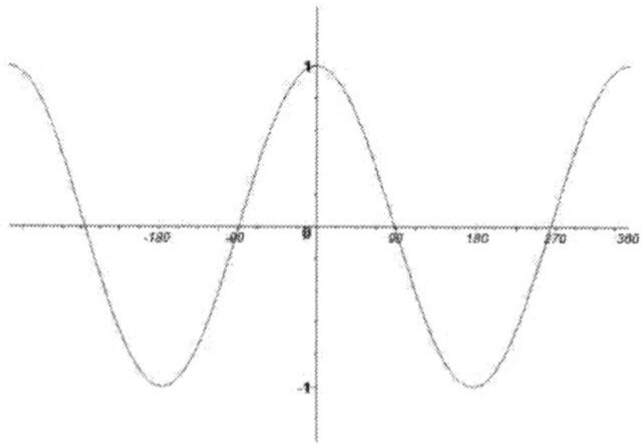

- Unlike the previous two trigonometric functions, $y = tan\theta$ repeats itself every 180 degrees.
- It has roots at the even multiples of 90, so -180,0 180, 360...
- It has asymptotes at the odd multiples of 90, so -90, 90, 270, 450...
- The function is defined for all values of y, so $-\infty < \tan\theta\,\theta < \infty$.

$y = tanx$

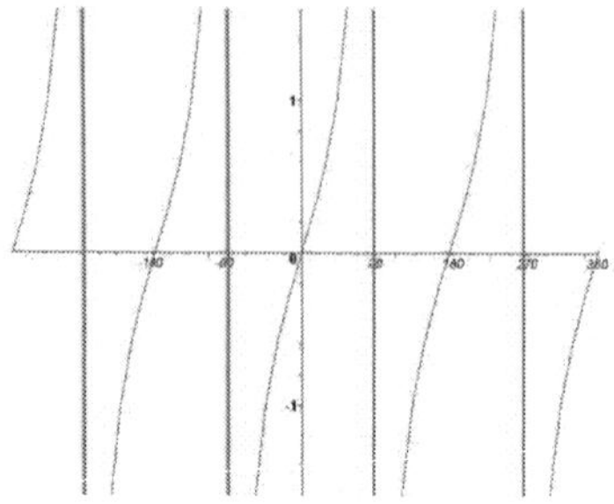

M4.13 Interpreting graphs in real life contexts

- Graphs may be used in kinematic calculations involving distance, velocity and acceleration.

M4.14 Further Interpreting graphs in real life contexts

- To estimate the gradient of a graph, draw a tangent at the point required. Then, take two points on this line and calculate the gradient of it.
- Alternatively, if the equation of the graph is known, differentiate and then substitute the x value at the point the gradient is required.
- Reciprocal and exponential graphs are typically used to model growth and decay. For example, a herd sheep starting with a population of 100 may be modelled using the function, $P = 100 \times (1.05)^t$.
- One type of graph is a displacement- time graph, which shows how far you are from a starting position over time. Since time is the dependent variable, it goes on the x axis, and displacement on the y.
- Velocity is the change in distance over time, which means that the gradient at a point on a displacement-time graph will give the velocity. Therefore, a straight line on the displacement-time graph shows a constant velocity. This would also mean that the acceleration is 0.
- A second type of graph is a velocity-time graph, which shows how velocity changes over time, e.g. during a journey. Since time is the dependent variable, it goes on the x axis, and velocity on the y.
- The total distance under the graph between two time periods represents the total distance travelled in that period.
- Acceleration is the change in velocity over time, which means that the gradient at a point on a velocity-time graph will give the acceleration.
- To find the exact area under the graph, use definite integration.
- Alternatively, an estimate can be obtained by using the trapezium rule. This involves splitting the curve into numerous trapezia and finding the individual area of each before summing them all up.

M4.15 Simultaneous equations

- Linear simultaneous equations can be solved in two ways: elimination and substitution.
- Elimination is when one variable is eliminated by adding or subtracting the two equations which should leave only one variable
  e.g. $x + 2y = 3$ and $x - 2y = -1$
  Adding together the two equations gives $2x = -2$, hence eliminating one variable.
  Then, solve for x and substitute into one of the equations and obtain y

- Substitution involves making one unknown the subject of an equation and substituting this expression into the other equation.
  e.g.
  $x + 2y = 3$
  $x - 2y = -1$
  Rearranging the first equation gives $x = 3 - 2y$, and then substituting this into the second equation gives $3 - 2y - 2y = -1$. Then, solve for y and obtain x by resubstituting into one of the equations.
- To solve simultaneous equations involving one linear and quadratic equation, substitute the linear equation into the quadratic and solve the quadratic.
- There can be up to 2 pairs of solutions depending on the quadratic. To quickly check how many solutions there are, find the value of the discriminant, $b^2 - 4ac$ for the new quadratic after the linear equation has been substituted in.
- To solve simultaneous equations graphically, find the points of intersection between the equations.

M4.16 Solving quadratic equations

- There are three ways to solve quadratic equations: factorising, completing the square and the quadratic formula.
- If the quadratic is factorizable, this is the easiest method. After factorising and equating to 0, one of the brackets must be 0, meaning two solutions can easily be obtained.
  e.g. $(2x + 1)(x + 3) = 0$, equating each bracket to 0 and solving for x gives $x = -\frac{1}{2}$ and $x = -3$.
- Completing the square is a method that involves manipulating the quadratic such that it becomes a squared term and a constant term.
- First half the b term, and square the x term with that, which should make up for the halving. However, we need to account for the extra constant term that will be created, so take away $(\frac{b}{2})^2$.
  e.g. $x^2 + 6x + 2 = 0$
  Halving the b term and taking away this square gives
  $(x + 3)^2 - 9 + 2 = 0$
  This can then be solved by square rooting both sides.
- The quadratic formula is $\frac{-b \pm \sqrt{b^2 - 4ac}}{2a}$. This equation can be obtained from completing the square on the general formula for a quadratic. Substituting the values a, b and c will give up to 2 solutions.
- The discriminant is $b^2 - 4ac$, which is used to determine how many solutions the quadratic will have.
- If $b^2 - 4ac < 0$, there are no solutions.
- If $b^2 - 4ac = 0$, there is one repeated solution (only one distinct solution).

- If $b^2 - 4ac > 0$, there are two solutions.

M4.17 Solving linear inequalities

- To solve inequalities, treat the inequality symbol as an = sign, and solve as you would do normally by applying the same operators on each side to isolate the variable.
- Note that although all operators are the same, when multiplying or dividing by a negative number, the inequality symbol changes sign.
  e.g. $-2x - 2 < 1$
  $2x + 2 > -1$
- The inequality solutions can be represented on a number line. To show strictly greater than or strictly less than, use o, an unshaded circle and if the inequality is not strict, shade in the circle.

M4.18 Basic sequences

- The term-to-term rule shows how to get from one term in the sequence to the next term.
- The nth term is often represented using the notation U_n, and the nth term is shown using a relationship between U_{n+1} and U_n. For example, $U_{n+1} = U_2 + 2$. This shows that the term-to-term rule is to add 2 to the previous term.
- The second possibility is the position-to-term rule. Where the previous point showed how a term is generated using the position before, the position-to-term rule uses a general function, such as $U_n = 3n - 4$.

M4.19 Calculating the nth term of sequences

- The nth term of a linear sequence will have the form $an + b$.
- To calculate the nth term of a linear sequence, there are two pieces of information required. First, find the term-to-term rule, which is what is added or subtracted to get the next term. Second, find the 0th term. This is the term before the start of the sequence. Then add n to the term-to-term rule and add the 0th term as a constant.
  e.g. 3, 7, 11, 15
  The term-to-term rule is $+4$, and the 0th term is -1.
  Therefore, the nth term is $4n - 1$
- The nth term of a quadratic sequence will have the form $an^2 + bn + c$.
- A quadratic sequence will have a changing term to term rule, but you need to find the second difference, which is technically, the term-to-term rule of the first term-to-term rule. After finding this difference, half it, which will be the value of a.
- Just like before, find the 0th term as well, which will be the constant term, c.
- To find the bn term, take any given term in the sequence and equate it to $an^2 + bn + c$, after having substituted the values for a and c.

M5 Geometry

M5.1 Basic geometry terminology

- A point is single coordinate on a graph or location, which is represented using a dot.
- A line is a straight one-dimensional figure that extends infinitely. There are an infinite number of points on any line. Lines have no thickness.
- A line segment is a portion of a line. It is a finite line. It is joined by two distinct points at each side, and still has an infinite number of points on it.
- Vertices are where two or more lines or edges meet on a polygon or 3D shape. For example, a triangle has 3 vertices. Vertices are commonly identified as the "number of points of a shape", e.g. a pentagon has 5 points.
- An edge is a type of line segment that joins up two vertices on a polygon or 3D shape.
- A plan is a flat straight two-dimensional surface that extends infinitely. It is in a way a step up from a line.
- Parallel lines are when two lines will never ever meet regardless of how much they extend by. This will be the case if the two lines have the same gradient, and hence, they will have the same steepness.
- Perpendicular lines are two lines that meet at right angles. This will be the case when the product of the two gradients is -1. In other words, one gradient is the negative reciprocal of the other.
- A right angle is an angle that measures 90°. It is shown using ∟ at a vertex.
- A subtended angle is the angle that is found between either the arc of a curve or between two lines.

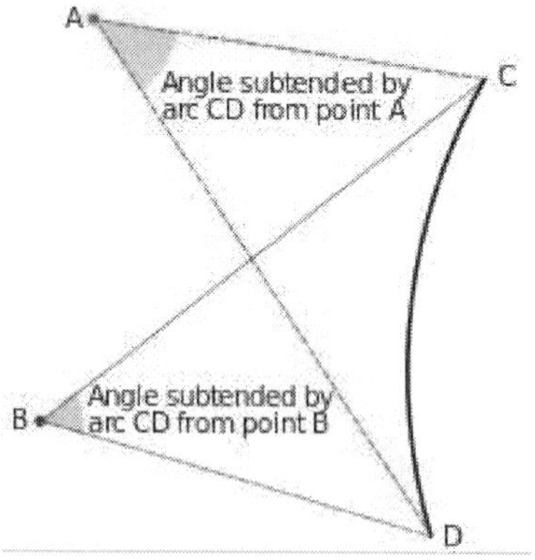

- A polygon is a flat 2D shape made up of straight lines and is fully closed.
- A regular polygon is a polygon, where each side is the same length, and all interior angles are equal.
- Rotational symmetry is when a shape can be rotated and will look the same as it did when it started. For example, a square rotated 90° will look the same. The order of rotation is how many times this would happen in a rotation of 360°. A square would

have rotational symmetry of 4. Every shape has a rotational symmetry of 1, because it will always return to its original shape after $360°$.

- Reflectional symmetry in polygons is when a shape can be split into two by a line, and the two halves will exactly match using the line as a mirror line. You can think of it as folding one half onto the other exactly on the mirror line.

M5.2 Angle rules and interior angles

- The total angle around a point is $360°$ and forms a mini circle around.
- Angles on a straight line will sum to $180°$. This is technically half a circle.
- When two lines intersect, 4 angles are created. The vertically opposite angles are equal.
- When two parallel lines are intersected by another line, the corresponding angles are equal as shown.

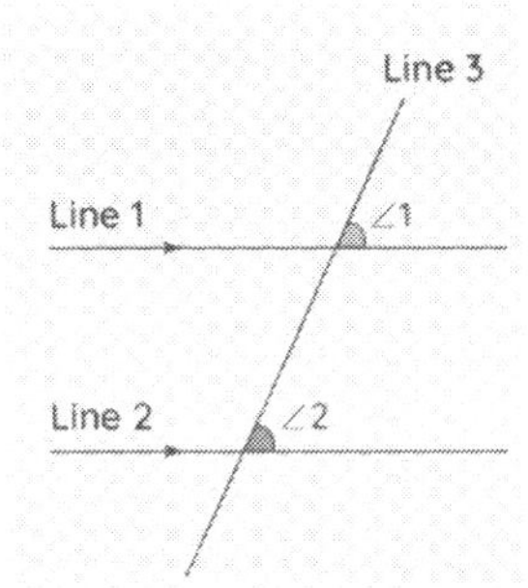

- The angles that are alternate when two parallel lines intersect another line will be equal. This can be thought of being a Z angle, as shown.

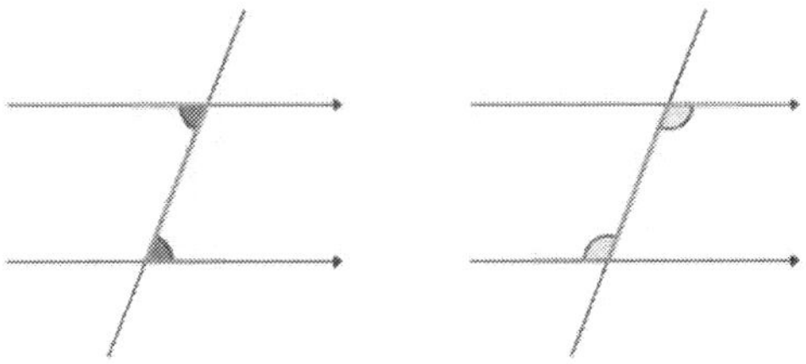

- Two angles are supplementary if they sum to $180°$.
- The sum of angles in a triangle is $180°$.
- A quadrilateral is any 4-sided shape such as a square or trapezium. The sum of all interior angles in a quadrilateral will always be $360°$.
- To find the sum of interior angles in any n-sided shape, use the formula $180(n-2)$. This can be easily tested using a square and triangle.

- For regular polygons where each angle is the same, the interior angle can be calculated using $\frac{180(n-2)}{n}$.
- The exterior angle at a vertex is not the $360 - interior$. It is the angle created when one of the sides is extended. It does not matter which side is extended as vertically opposite angles are equal. The exterior angles of a pentagon are shown below.

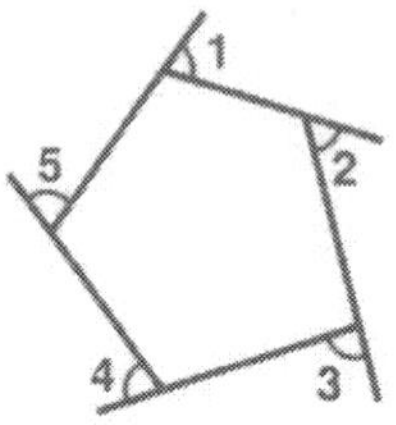

- At a point, the sum of the interior angle and the exterior angle will always be $180°$.
- The sum of exterior angles in any polygon will always be $360°$. Therefore, to find the exterior angle of a regular polygon, do $\frac{360}{n}$.

M5.3 Quadrilaterals and triangles

- A quadrilateral is any 4-sided shape.
- A square is a shape which has 4 equal sides which each meet at right angles. There are two pairs of parallel lines.
- A rectangle is an elongated square. It has two pairs of equal sides, and all the sides meet at right angles. There are two pairs of parallel lines.
- A rhombus is a shape which has 4 equal sides, and the opposite interior angles are equal. A rhombus also has two pairs of parallel lines.
- A parallelogram is like a rhombus but has two pairs of equal sides (like a rectangle). The opposite interior angles are equal, and it has two pairs of parallel sides.
- A trapezium is a shape that has one pair of parallel sides. The diagonals will bisect each other, meaning they will cut the angle in exactly half.
- A kite is a shape with two pairs of equal sides. The two pairs of adjacent sides are equal, and the opposite angles are equal.

Quadrilateral	Shape
Square	
Rectangle	
Parallelogram	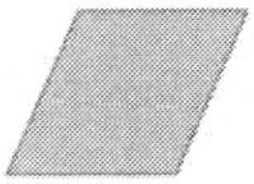
Trapezium	
Rhombus	
Kite	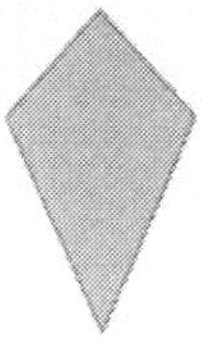

- There are 4 different types of triangles.
- An equilateral triangle is a triangle where all the side lengths are equal, and the interior angles are all $60°$.
- An isosceles triangle is a triangle which has one pair of equal sides. This means that two of the angles where the two equal sides meet with the third will also be equal.
- A right-angled triangle is a triangle which has one $90°$ angle.
- A scalene triangle is a triangle where each side and angle are different.

M5.4 Congruence

- Congruence involves identifying whether two shapes are identical.
- There are 4 ways of identifying if two triangles are congruent.
- SSS = side, side, side. If all three side lengths are the same in both triangles, they are congruent. This is because it would follow that the angles are also the same.
- SAS = side, angle, side. If two of the lengths are equal and the angle between them is the same, then the two triangles are congruent.
- ASA or AAS= angle, side, angle. If two angles are the same and the corresponding side that they share are equal, then the two triangles are congruent.
- RHS = right angle, hypotenuse, side. If the right angle, hypotenuse and corresponding side are equal in length, then the two triangles are congruent.

M5.5 Congruence and similarity

- Congruence is when two shapes are identical, with every angle and side having the same numerical value.
- Similarity is when the angles are all the same and the two shapes have the exact same scale factor. All squares are therefore similar, because the ratio between each side will always be the same.
- Similar triangles will not have the same side lengths, but only equal angles.

M5.6 Transformations to construct congruent or similar shapes

- Rotating a shape will result in the outcome still being congruent to the shape rotated. Rotations have 3 key pieces of information: the angle, the direction and the rotation point. The angle tells you how much the shape is to be rotated by. the direction is clockwise or anticlockwise and the point of rotation is the point at which the shape is rotated around.
- Note that if the angle is $180°$, the direction does not matter as both directions will yield the same outcome.
- To rotate a shape, the easiest way is to use tracing paper, which should be provided by your school during the exam. Draw the shape onto the tracing paper using a pencil. Then place your pencil point on the point of rotation and rotate the tracing paper by the angle required. Then draw the new shape as it is shown on the tracing paper.
- Reflecting a shape will also result in the outcome still being congruent. The easiest way to reflect a shape along a line is to mirror each vertex of the shape first. To do this, find how to get from the mirror line to that point and apply the same process to the other side. Once all the points have been reflected, join them up to give the reflected shape.
- Translating a shape also results in the outcome being congruent. Translating means moving the shape around the grid. Translating a shape requires one piece of information which is the translation vector, represented as $\binom{a}{b}$, where a is the translation in the x axis and b is the translation in the y.
- A positive value of a means moving it to the right a units, whereas a negative value means moving it left.
- A positive value of b means moving it up b units, whereas a negative value means moving the shape down.
  e.g. a translation vector of $\binom{-2}{1}$ means moving the shape 2 units to the left and 1 unit up.
- An enlargement is the only transformation in which the outcome will not be congruent, but similar. This is because it is changing the size of the shape.

- There are 2 key pieces of information for enlargements: the scale factor and the point of enlargement. The scale factor shows how big or small the new shape will be compared to before.
- A scale factor between 0 and 1 will result in the new shape being smaller than the first, whereas a scale factor greater than 1 will result in the new shape being bigger.
- A negative scale factor is also possible, and it is the same concept, but the enlargement occurs in the other direction.
- To enlarge a shape, find the horizontal and vertical distance from each point to the centre of enlargement. Then, apply the scale factor to these distances and draw the new points. Then, draw the new shape.
- Note, a negative scale factor does not always mean the shape will decrease in size, it always means that the resulting shape needs to be enlarged in the opposite direction.

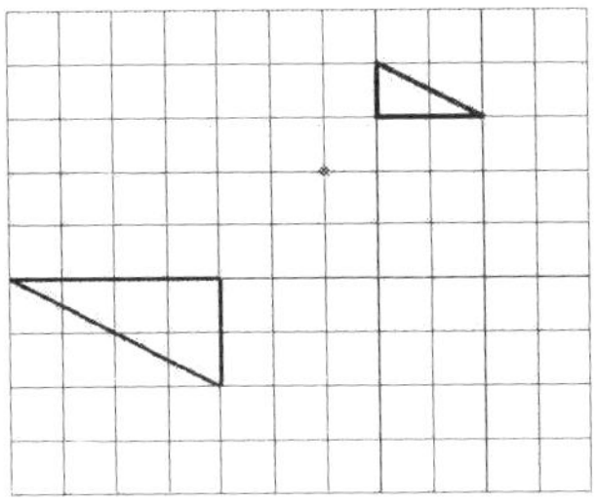

M5.7 Pythagoras' theorem

- Pythagoras's theorem states that for right-angled triangles, $a^2 + b^2 = c^2$, where c is the longest side of the triangle.
- The longest side is called the hypotenuse.
- This can be used to find the distance between two points in 2 and 3 dimensions.

M5.8 Circle terminology

- The centre of a circle is the point in the exact middle. It is the point which is equidistant to every point on the circle.
- The radius of a circle is the length from the centre of the circle to any point on the circumference. It is any straight line drawn from the centre to the circumference.
- The diameter is twice the size of the radius. It is any line drawn from two points on the circumference of the circle that goes through the centre.
- A chord is a line that joins two points on the circumference of the circle. It does not go through the centre, otherwise it would become the diameter.
- The circumference of the circle is its perimeter. It is the total distance around the circle.
- The tangent is a straight line that touches the circle at one point. It does not intersect the circle, but brushes past it with one touch. The tangent makes a right angle with the radius of the circle at the point it touches.

- The arc of a circle is any portion of the circumference of the circle.
- A sector of a circle is an area that is bounded by part of the circumference and two radii. For example, a pizza is split into equal sectors. There are two sectors created when two radii are drawn. The bigger sector is called the major sector whereas the smaller one is the minor.
- A segment is an area of a circle that is "cut off" by a chord, as shown below.
- The equation of a circle is $(x-a)^2+(y-b)^2=r^2$, where (a,b) is the centre of the circle and r is the radius.

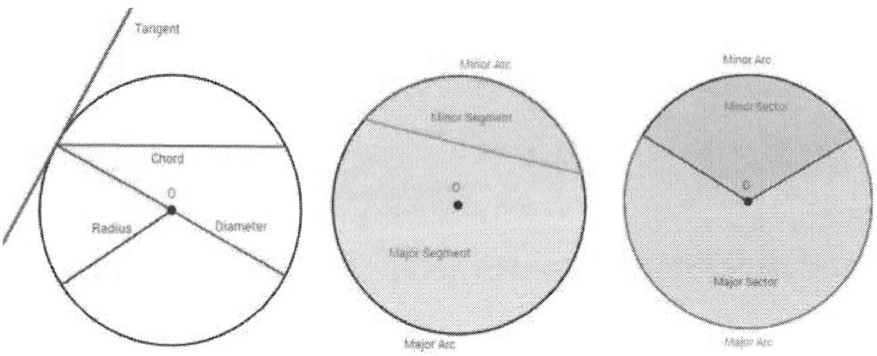

M5.9 Circle theorems

- The angle at the centre is twice the angle at the circumference.
- The angle subtended at the circumference of a semicircle where one side is the diameter will always be a right angle.
- The tangent will always meet the radii at a right angle.
- Angles in the same segment are always going to be equal.
- A cyclic quadrilateral is a quadrilateral in which all 4 vertices are on the circumference of a circle. Opposite angles in a cyclic quadrilateral add up to $180°$.
- The alternate segment states that the angle between a tangent and a chord is equal to the angle in the alternate segment.

M5.10 Solving geometric problems

- Use the information and content so far to be able to solve geometric problems on coordinate axes.

M5.11 3 dimensional shapes definitions

- A face represents one surface of a 3D shape. A cube for example has 6 faces since it has 6 surfaces.
- An edge is a line that joins together two vertices in a shape. For example, a cube has 12 edges.
- A vertex is the point at which two edges meet. It is a corner of a shape. A cube has 8 edges.

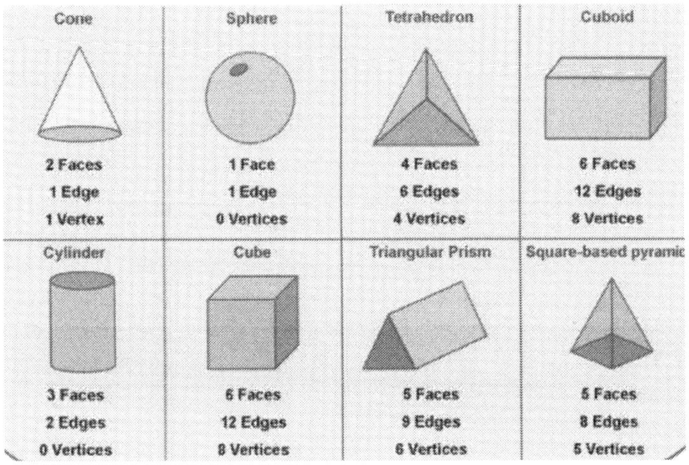

Cone
2 Faces
1 Edge
1 Vertex
Sphere
1 Face
1 Edge
0 Vertices
Tetrahedron
4 Faces
6 Edges
4 Vertices
Cuboid
6 Faces
12 Edges
8 Vertices
Cylinder
3 Faces
2 Edges
0 Vertices
Cube
6 Faces
12 Edges
8 Vertices
Triangular Prism
5 Faces
9 Edges
6 Vertices
Square-based pyramid
5 Faces
8 Edges
5 Vertices

M5.12 Plans and elevations

- The plan of a 3D shape is what a viewer would see if they saw the shape from the top. For example, the plan of a cube would be a square of the same side length.
- The elevation of a 3D shape is the 2D view of the shape when it is viewed from the side or front.

M5.13 Maps, scale factors and bearings

- Scale factors are used in maps to show what a certain distance on the map represents in real life. For example, a 1:750,000 scale factor shows that 1cm on the map is 7.5km in real life.
- Bearings are angles that are used to represent a sense of direction. They are a three-digit number, which represents the angle, clockwise to the North direction that is being moved. For example, moving East would be moving at a bearing of 090°.
- Note that bearings are always 3 digits, so add a 0 to the beginning if the angle is only two digits.
- A common mistake made is to think that the bearing from A to B is the same as the bearing from B to A. However, this is not true, as bearings are always measured from a clockwise direction.
- It is helpful to always draw diagrams out and work out the bearing using the angle rules.

M5.14 Formulae for areas and volumes

- The area of a triangle is $\frac{1}{2}bh$, where b is the base length and h is the perpendicular height. This means that the high is perpendicular to the base.
- The area of a square and rectangle is the length × width. In the case for a square, these two values will be the same.
- The area of a rhombus and parallelogram is the base × vertical height
- The area of a trapezium is $\frac{1}{2}(a+b)h$, where a and b are the lengths of the two parallel sides and h is the vertical height between the two parallel sides.

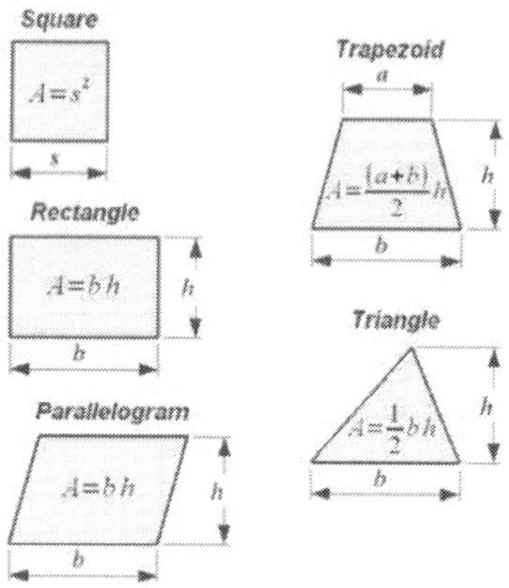

- The volume of a cuboid is the length × width × height. Simply, multiply the three lengths together. To find the volume of a cube, just cube the side length.
- The volume of a prism is the cross-sectional area × length. This is because a prism can be thought of as a 2D shape being extended a certain length.

M5.15 Areas and volumes for circles and spherical shapes

- The area of a circle is πr^2.
- The circumference of a circle is $2\pi r = \pi d$.
- The surface area of a 3D shape is the total sum of all the areas of each "face" or the total area that can be seen.
- The volume of a cylinder is $\pi r^2 h$. This formula can be derived using the volume of a prism formula, since a cylinder is technically a prism. The cross-sectional area is πr^2 and the length is the height, h.
- The surface area of a cylinder is $2\pi r^2 + 2\pi rh$.
- The formulas for the volumes of a sphere, pyramid and cone will be provided in the exam, but it is worth knowing them anyways.

- The volume of a sphere is $\frac{4}{3}\pi r^3$.
- The surface area of as sphere is $4\pi r^2$.
- The volume of a cone is $\frac{1}{3}\pi r^2 h$.
- The surface area of a cone is $\pi r^2 + \pi r l$, where l is the slant height of the cone.

M5.16 Arc lengths and areas of sectors

- To find the arc length and area of a sector involves finding the area/perimeter of a certain proportion of the circle.
- To find the area of a sector, multiply the area by the proportion that the sector takes up of the whole circle. $A = \frac{\theta}{360} \times \pi r^2$, where θ is the angle taken up by the sector.
- To find the arc length of a sector, use the same method as above, resulting in the formula $P = \frac{\theta}{360} \times 2\pi r$.

M5.17 Congruence and similarity involving lengths, areas and volume

- Shapes that are similar means that each corresponding length has the exact same ratio. Shapes that are congruent will have ratio 1.
- The area ratio will be the square of the length ratio.
- The volume ratio will be the cube of the length ratio.

M5.18 Trigonometric functions

- Sine (sin), cosine (cos) and tangent (tan) are three trigonometric functions that are used in relation to right angled triangles.
- $sine = \frac{opposite}{hypotenus}$.
- $cosine = \frac{adjacent}{hypotenus}$.
- $tangent = \frac{opposite}{adjacent}$.
- The ratios are all relative to a certain angle x. The hypotenuse is the longest side of the triangle, opposite is the side that is opposite to x, and adjacent is the third.
- These ratios can be used to find the value of sides/angles in a right-angled triangle.
- The graphs for the trigonometric functions can be found in M4.12.

$\theta \rightarrow$	0	30	45	60	90
$\sin\theta$	0	$\frac{1}{2}$	$\frac{\sqrt{2}}{2}$	$\frac{\sqrt{3}}{2}$	1
$\cos\theta$	1	$\frac{\sqrt{3}}{2}$	$\frac{\sqrt{2}}{2}$	$\frac{1}{2}$	0
$\tan\theta$	0	$\frac{\sqrt{3}}{3}$	1	$\sqrt{3}$	Undefined

M5.19 Vectors

- Vectors are used to represent a sense of movement from one point to another. They are most represented as column vectors in the form $\binom{a}{b}$, where a is the change in the x direction and b is the change in the y direction.
- Adding two column vectors involves adding the top two components and the bottom two components together. This is the same concept used for subtracting two components.
- When multiplying a vector by a scalar, this involves multiplying each component by that scalar. This means $a\begin{pmatrix} x \\ y \end{pmatrix} = \begin{pmatrix} ax \\ ay \end{pmatrix}$.
- A vector $\overrightarrow{OA}$ would represent the direction travelled from point O to get to point A. This can be shown diagrammatically.

M6 Statistics

M6.1 Understanding various representations of data

- A two-way table is used to display information about the frequencies of two different variables.

	Baseball	Basketball	Football	Total
Male	13	15	20	48
Female	23	16	13	52
Total	36	31	33	100

- A frequency table is used to display information about the frequencies of different outcomes in a sample.

Score	Frequency
6	2
7	3
8	7
9	7
10	1

- A bar chart is a graph that displays the frequencies or numerical values of data using rectangles. The numerical values make up the height of the rectangle, whilst the width is any constant value.

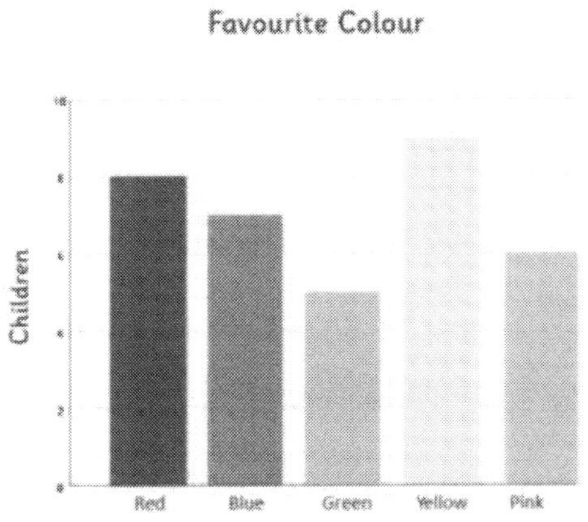

- A pie chart is a circular representation of data where the frequencies of answers are recorded as a proportion of the whole. The proportion of each category is equivalent to the proportion that the corresponding sector will take of the whole circle.

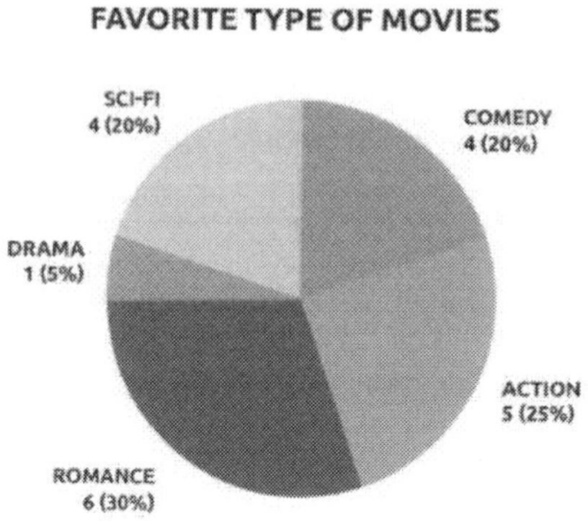

- A pictogram is a table in which the frequency of categories is represented using pictures. Each picture is worth a certain frequency, indicated by a key.

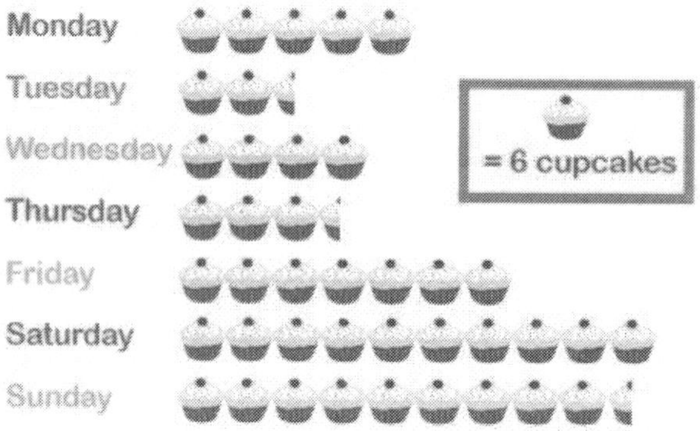

- A vertical line chart is a series of different data points and is used to display ungrouped discrete data. It is like a bar chart, but each line does not have a width.

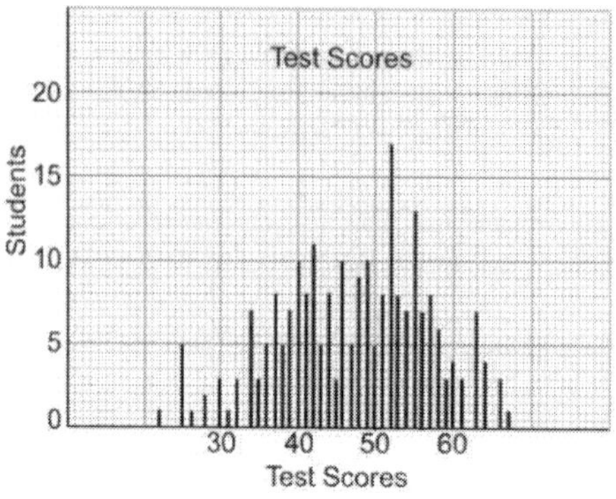

- Time series data is data which changes over time. To represent this, either a table or line graph can be used. The moving average over a period can be plotted over time.

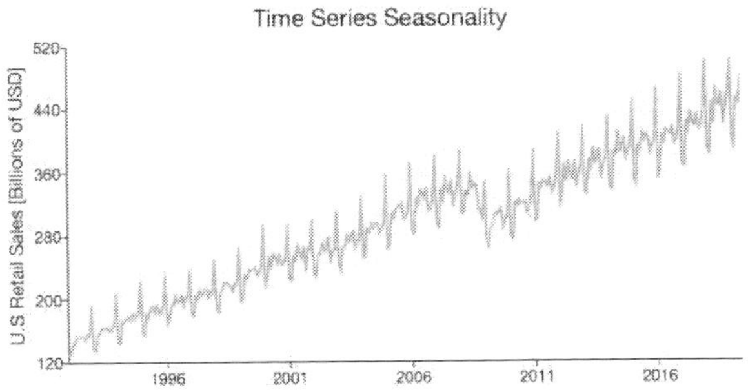

M6.2 Discrete and continuous date, histograms and cumulative frequency

- Discrete data is data that can only take certain values and cannot take values in between. For example, shoe sizes can only come in intervals of $\frac{1}{2}$. It is not possible to have a shoe size of 6.2.
- Continuous data is data that can take any numerical value. For example, height and weight can take any numerical value.
- A histogram is a representation of data used for grouped discrete or continuous data. A cumulative frequency diagram would also be able to show this type of data.
- A histogram looks like a bar chart, but each bar has different widths. Histograms are useful, because they can provide information about both the spread and distribution of data.
- The width of each bar in a histogram shows the range of values that it takes, and the height of the bar shows the frequency density.
- The area of each bar, which is the frequency density × class width, is $k \times frequency$. If $k = 1$, then the area of the bar is the frequency.
- To find k, divide the total area of the bars by the total frequency.
- A frequency polygon is formed by joining up dots from the midpoint of each bar.

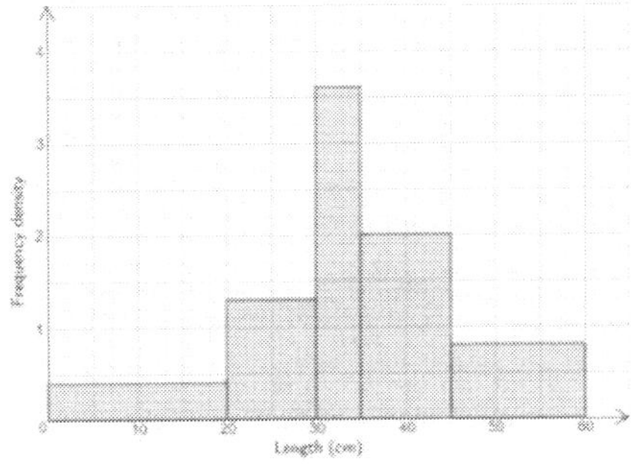

- A cumulative frequency diagram is a diagram that plots the cumulative frequency of a set of data against the upper bound of the data. To plot a cumulative frequency diagrams, it is much easier to find the lower quartile, the median and upper quartile and then plotting the values for each and joining them up.

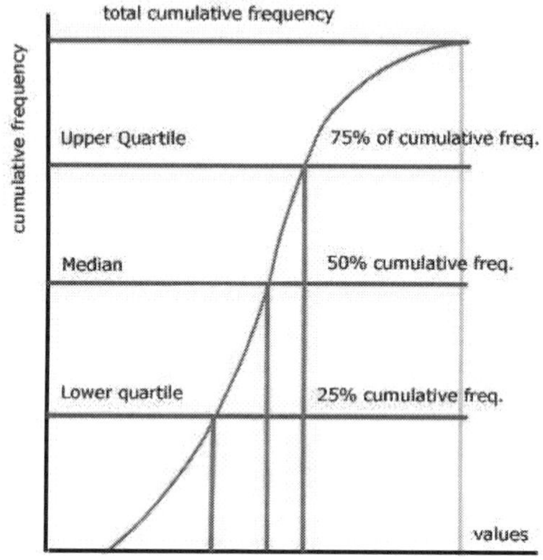

<u>M6.3 Data definitions, averages and calculations</u>

- A population in statistics is all the objects and sets which are of interest in question or experiment. It consists of all the data in a group.
- The mean of a set of data is the "average" value that the data takes. This is calculated by adding all the data points together and dividing by the number of data points.
- The median of a set of values generally means taking the value in the middle. For data with an odd number of values, this is easy. It is the $(n+1)^{th}$ value.
- The mode is the data value that occurs the greatest number of times. This would be the value with the greatest frequency.
- The range of a set of data is the greatest value take away the lowest value.
- The lower quartile is the data value that occurs at the 25% mark. The upper quartile occurs at the 75% mark.
- Although these are the general definitions for the averages, they're calculations vary depending on the type of data
- For list data that is discrete, use $\frac{n}{2}$. If this is a decimal, round up, and if not a decimal, round up by half. For example, if $n = 12$, use the 6.5^{th} value. To calculate the quartiles, do $\frac{n}{4}$ or $\frac{3n}{4}$. If it is an integer, round up by half, and if not an integer, round up to the next integer. The other averages are calculated normally.

- For a frequency table, use the same calculations as above. The mean is calculated by $\frac{\Sigma fx}{\Sigma f}$. This means the sum of the products of the frequency and the data value and diving it by the total frequency.
- For a grouped frequency table, the mean is also calculated using the formula $\frac{\Sigma fx}{\Sigma f}$. However, since the data is grouped, take the midpoint of each group as the x value. This is because we are assuming that the mean of the data is the midpoint, assuming that the data is perfectly spread across the range.
- For grouped frequency, we are taking the data to be continuous, so to find the quartiles and the median, simply use $\frac{n}{4}, \frac{n}{2}$ and $\frac{3n}{4}$, and do not round anything. Then, use interpolation to find the data value at this point.

<u>M6.4 Scatter graphs</u>

- Bivariate data is data that has two variables, where one is usually an independent variable and the other a dependent one.
- Bivariate data can be represented on a scatter graph.

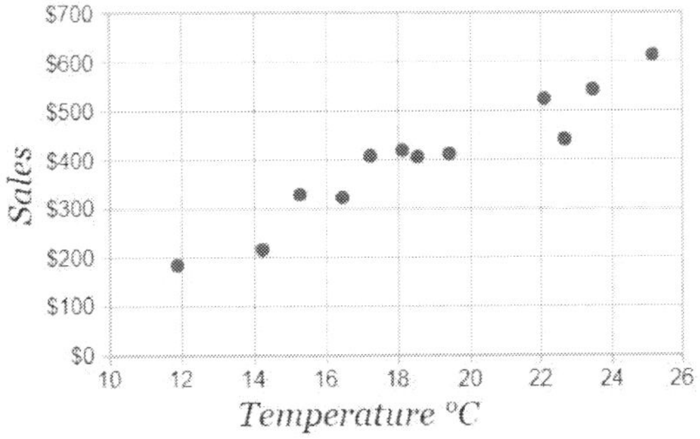

- The correlation of two variables explains how they are related. There are two areas of correlation. Firstly, the type of correlation (positive, negative or nothing) and the strength of the correlation (strong or weak).
- The type of correlation explains how the two variables are related. A positive correlation is when one variable increases, the other variable also increases and vice versa. A negative correlation is when if one variable increases, the other decreases and vice versa. For example, temperature and number of jackets sold. As temperature increases, the demand for jackets would fall.
- The strength of the correlation is how close the points are to a straight line. The closer the points are to a straight line, the stronger the correlation is between the two variables.

- If the dots do not form any kind of line, then the two variables do not have a correlation. For example, the temperature on Mars and the number of hours I spend watching TV.
- It is important to realise that correlation does not always mean that two events are causally related. It could simply be a coincidence. Therefore, always use common sense to check if two variables could be related.
- Normally, scatter graphs contain a line of best fit. This is a line that attempts to show the exact relation between the two variables given the data. This line is used for interpolation, which is estimating certain values of one variable given the other if it is not present in the data. This is only when the desired data point is within the data range given.
- If the desired data point is not within the range, then this is known as extrapolation. This is less reliable, because it is not known if the same relationship will continue.

M7 Probability

M7.1 Tables and frequency trees

- The probabilities of different outcomes can be calculated using frequency trees and tables. The probability of a certain outcome is the frequency of that outcome over the total frequency.

M7.2 Randomness and expected outcomes

- The expected number of outcomes is calculated by multiplying the probability of the outcome happening multiplied by the total number of experiments.
- An experiment is a repeatable process that leads to one or more outcome. For example, rolling a die and noting down the number.
- If each outcome is equally likely to happen, then the probability of each outcome is 1 divided by the total number of possible outcomes. For example, the probability of each outcome is $\frac{1}{6}$.
- Every outcome is random meaning that even with a probability of $\frac{99}{100}$, it is possible that it may never occur.

M7.3 Expected frequencies, theoretical probability and probability scales

- The expected frequency is calculated by multiplying the probability of the outcome happening multiplied by the total number of experiments.
- Theoretical probability is the probability from reasoning and general logic. It is calculated by dividing the number of "successful" outcomes by the total number of different outcomes.
- Experimental probability is the probability based off the results of experimental data.
- All probabilities have a value between 0 and 1.

M7.4 Probabilities of exhaustive sets and mutual exclusivity

- The sum of the probabilities of all the different outcomes in a set will always be 1.
- Mutual exclusivity is when two outcomes cannot happen at the same time. For example, getting a 4 and a 5 at the same time when rolling a die.
- For events that are not mutually exclusive, they may happen at the same time. For example, rolling a multiple of 3 and 6 is possible with a die.
- When there are only two events and they are mutually exclusive, the probabilities of the two will add to 1.

- For events that are not mutually exclusive, $P(A \cup B) = P(A) + P(B) - P(A \cap B)$. We subtract the probability of both occurring at once, because otherwise it is counted twice.

M7.5 Using sets, tables, grids, Venn diagrams and tree diagrams

- A set is a collection of objects or different outcomes.
- A Venn diagram is a diagram that shows the logical relation between different sets, and the commonality between outcomes.
- There are certain notations and rules used in Venn diagrams and probability.
- The universal set, $\in$, is the set that contains all objects and outcomes.
- The null set, $\emptyset$, is the set with no possible outcomes, or an event with a probability of 0.
- The use of set notation and theory is not formally required, but it is helpful to know and understand the general probability rules.
- $P(A') = 1 - P(A)$. This means the probability of A not happening is essentially 1 minus the probability of it happening.
- In a Venn diagram, the total number of regions is equal to $2^{total\ number\ of\ sets}$. For example, where there are two sets, $A\ and\ B$, then there are 4 regions: just A, just B, both A and B, and neither A nor B.
- Tree diagrams are used to show different outcomes consequentially. For example, first rolling a die and then tossing a coin, or tossing one coin and then another. Branches are drawn with each outcome either happening or not happening.

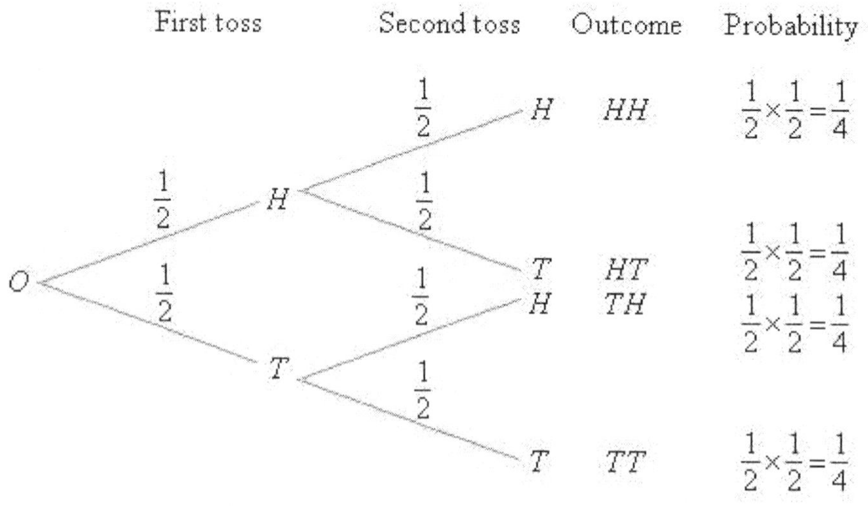

M7.6 Sample space diagrams

- A sample space diagram is a diagram that shows every possible outcome. For example, rolling a die would have a sample space of 1, 2, 3, 4, 5 and 6.
- Sample space diagrams can also be drawn for combined events, such as the product of the two numbers when rolling two dice as shown below.

		Die 1 outcomes					
		1	2	3	4	5	6
Die 2 Outcomes	1	1	2	3	4	5	6
	2	2	4	6	8	10	12
	3	3	6	9	12	15	18
	4	4	8	12	16	20	24
	5	5	10	15	20	25	30
	6	6	12	18	24	30	36

- It is possible to calculate theoretical probabilities from a sample space diagram. Find the total number of outcomes, which in the diagram above is 36. Then, find the number of outcomes required, e.g. for the probability of a multiple of 6, there are 11 outcomes, so the probability is $\frac{11}{36}$.

M7.7 Conditional probability and tree diagrams

- To find the probability from a tree diagram, multiply out the probability of each required branch, giving the probability of a certain outcome happening followed by another.
- Independence means that the second outcome is not reliant on the first outcome. For example, rolling a head on a coin toss is not dependent on the roll of a die before.
- If an outcome is dependent, it means that its probability is affected by the previous outcome. For example, if I wake up late, the probability of me being late to school is greater than if I were to have had woken up on time.
- Dependent events can be used with conditional probability, which looks at the probability of outcomes happening given something else.
- The notation for conditional probability is $P(A|B)$, which is the probability of A, given B happening. $P(A|B) = \frac{P(A \cap B)}{P(B)}$.
- For independent events, this not the case, and the probability of one outcome is not affected by what has happened before.
- For two independent events, A and B, $P(A \cap B) = P(A) \times P(B)$.

1B: Advanced Maths Guide

AM1 Algebra and functions

Laws of Indices

- $x^m \times x^n = x^{m+n}$
- $\frac{x^m}{x^n} = x^{m-n}$
- $(x^m)^n = x^{mn}$
- $x^{-m} = \frac{1}{x^m}$
- $\left(\sqrt[n]{x}\right)^m = x^{\frac{m}{n}}$
- $x^0 = 1$
- $x^1 = x$

Surds

- Surds are used to express irrational expressions involving a root symbol in exact form.
- The following rules apply for the manipulation of surds:
- $\sqrt{a} \times \sqrt{b} = \sqrt{ab}$
- $\frac{\sqrt{a}}{\sqrt{b}} = \sqrt{\frac{a}{b}}$
- To rationalize a surd, you must multiply both the numerator and denominator by the conjugate surd. For Example:
  1. $\frac{1}{\sqrt{a}} \times \frac{\sqrt{a}}{\sqrt{a}} = \frac{\sqrt{a}}{a}$
  2. $\frac{1}{a+\sqrt{b}} \times \frac{a-\sqrt{b}}{a-\sqrt{b}} = \frac{a-\sqrt{b}}{a^2-b}$
  3. $\frac{1}{a-\sqrt{b}} \times \frac{a+\sqrt{b}}{a+\sqrt{b}} = \frac{a+\sqrt{b}}{a^2-b}$
  4. $\frac{1}{\sqrt{a}-\sqrt{b}} \times \frac{\sqrt{a}+\sqrt{b}}{\sqrt{a}+\sqrt{b}} = \frac{\sqrt{a}+\sqrt{b}}{a-b}$
  5. $\frac{1}{\sqrt{a}+\sqrt{b}} \times \frac{\sqrt{a}-\sqrt{b}}{\sqrt{a}-\sqrt{b}} = \frac{\sqrt{a}-\sqrt{b}}{a-b}$

Graphs of quadratic functions

$f(x) = ax^2 + bx + c$ has the following properties:

- y intercept occurs when x=0.
- Roots occur when y=0.
- If the coefficient of x^2 is positive then the parabola is U-shaped, if the coefficient of x^2 is negative then the parabola is ∩-shaped.
- The stationary/turning points can be found through completing the square or through differentiation.

1) To complete the square, use the formula: $ax^2 + bx + c = a\left(x + \frac{b}{2a}\right)^2 - \frac{b^2}{4a^2} + c$. Once you have completed the square and you are left with $f(x) = a(x+b)^2 + c$. Then the turning point is $(-b, c)$.
2) The turning point can also be found using calculus. If $f(x) = ax^2 + bx + c$. You must find the x coordinate where $f'(x) = 0$ and then substitute this value of x into $f(x)$ to find the value of y.

Discriminant of a quadratic function

For $f(x) = ax^2 + bx + c$

- The discriminant is given by: $b^2 - 4ac$ and is useful for determining the number of real roots for $f(x)$.
    1. If $b^2 - 4ac < 0$, then there are no real roots for $f(x)$.
    2. If $b^2 - 4ac = 0$, then there is one repeated real root for $f(x)$.
    3. If $b^2 - 4ac > 0$, then there are two distinct real roots for $f(x)$.

Solutions of Quadratic Equations

When $f(x) = ax^2 + bx + c = 0$. There are 3 ways of finding the solutions to quadratic equations:

1) Factorising- If the function can be factorised then you can set each of the brackets to zero and re-arrange to find the value of x. For Example: if $f(x) = 3x^2 + 7x + 2 = 0$ then $f(x) = (3x+1)(x+2) = 0$. $(3x+1) = 0 \Rightarrow x = -\frac{1}{3}$. $(x+2) = 0 \Rightarrow x = -2$. Then $x = -\frac{1}{3}$ and $x = -2$
2) Completing the Square- To complete the square use the formula: $f(x) = ax^2 + bx + c = a\left(x + \frac{b}{2a}\right)^2 - \frac{b^2}{4a^2} + c$. Once you have completed the square and have the equation in the form $f(x) = a(x+b)^2 + c = 0$ then re-arrange the equation for x.
3) Quadratic Formula- If the function cannot be factorised, then the quadratic formula can also be used to solve the equation. Quadratic Formula is $x = \frac{-b \pm \sqrt{b^2 - 4ac}}{2a}$

Roots of Quadratic Equations

- For a quadratic equation of the form $ax^2 + bx + c = 0$, and has roots α and β. Then:
    1) $\alpha + \beta = -\frac{b}{a}$
    2) $\alpha\beta = \frac{c}{a}$

Simultaneous Equations

For two linear equations involving 2 variables there are 2 methods of solving these equations

- Substitution- Re-arrange one of the equations for one of the variables and substitute this into the other equation, doing so eliminates one of the variables and allows you to re-arrange for the other.
- Elimination-By adding, subtracting and dividing both equations in order to eliminate one of the variables, allowing you to re-arrange and solve for the remaining variable.

For solving one linear and one quadratic simultaneous equation involving 2 variables

- This can be solved using elimination. Re-arrange the linear equation for the variable that you wish to eliminate. Then substitute this into the quadratic equation to eliminate one of the variables, you can now re-arrange to form a single variable quadratic equation of the form of $ax^2 + bx + c = 0$. This can now be solved utilising one of the 3 methods of solving quadratic equations outlined above.

Linear and Quadratic Inequalities

Linear Inequalities

- You must collect like terms and divide by common factors- remembering that when you multiply or divide by a negative number, the direction of the inequality sign is reversed. For Example:

Quadratic Inequalities

1. Rearrange the inequality such that one of the sides is zero.
2. Then, to determine the critical values of the inequality it is useful to treat the inequality as an equation by replacing the inequality sign with an equal sign, and then solving for x (to give the critical values).
3. Using these critical values, you can now draw a sketch of the graph of the corresponding quadratic function and using this whilst considering the direction of the inequality symbol, you can determine the range of values which satisfy the quadratic inequality.
4. You may rarely be asked to approach an inequality with an unfamiliar function, in which case you should attempt to re-arrange the inequality in such a way that the inequality can be sketched (either as one function or two separate functions). Using the sketch, the critical values obtained and the direction of the inequality symbol, you can find the range of values which satisfy the original inequality.

Algebraic Manipulation of Polynomials

Expanding Brackets

- Use FOIL (First Outside Inside Last) to expand brackets. For Example: $(2x+1)(x+3) = 2x^2 + 6x + x + 3 = 2x^2 + 7x + 3$.

Remainder Theorem

- When $f(x)$ is divided by a linear polynomial of the form of $(x-a)$, the remainder is equivalent to $f(a)$.

Factor Theorem

- If $f(x)$ is a polynomial function and $f(a) = 0$, then $(x-a)$ is a factor of $f(x)$.

AM2 Sequences and Series

Arithmetic sequence

- Arithmetic sequences have a common difference between terms.
- They have an nth term formula of $a_n = a + (n-1)d$. Where a_n is the nth term, a is the first term, n is the number of terms and d is the common difference.

Geometric Sequence

- Geometric Sequences have a common ratio between terms.
- They have an nth term formula of $a_n = ar^{n-1}$. Where a_n is the nth term, a is the first term, r is the common ratio and n is the number of terms.

Recurrence Relations

- Recurrence relations give you the formula to calculate the next term, given you know the term before.
- These sequences usually define the first term as x_0 or x_1.
- Recurrence relations have a general formula of: $x_{n+1} = f(x_n)$.
- Occasionally, you may be given the first few terms of a sequence and you may be able to spot that it is a repeating sequence (i.e. the sequence repeats after a fixed number of terms). In this case, if you need to find the nth term of such a sequence, divide n by the period of the repeating sequence (i.e. the number of terms after which the sequence repeats). The remainder of this will correspond to the position in the repeating sequence.
- You may be given an unknown recurrence relation and asked for the nth term. In this scenario, it us useful to list the first few terms of the recurrence relation and this may help to spot a pattern in the terms.
- Sometimes, you may encounter an alternating sequence, in which you must treat each set of alternating terms as a separate sequence.

Arithmetic Series

- The sum of n terms of an arithmetic sequence is given by: $S_n = \frac{n}{2}(a+l)$, where S_n is the sum of n terms, n is the number of terms, a is the first term and l is the last term.
- The sum of n terms of an arithmetic sequence is also given by $S_n = \frac{n}{2}(2a + (n-1)d)$, where S_n is the sum of n terms, n is the number of terms, a is the first term and d is the common difference.

Geometric Series

- The sum of n terms of a finite geometric sequence is $S_n = \frac{a(r^n-1)}{r-1}$ or $S_n = \frac{a(1-r^n)}{1-r}$, where a is the first term, r is the common ratio and n is the number of terms.
- The sum of a convergent infinite geometric series is $S_\infty = \frac{a}{1-r}$, where a is the first term and r is the common ratio. A geometric series can be defined as convergent if $|r| < 1$.

Binomial Expansion

- The general formula of the binomial expansion: $(x+a)^n = \sum_{r=0}^{n} \binom{n}{r} x^r a^{n-r}$.
- The binomial coefficient is given by: $\binom{n}{r} = \frac{n!}{r!(n-r)!}$.
- For example: $(x+a)^n = x^n + \binom{n}{1}(x^{n-1})(a) + \binom{n}{2}(x^{n-2})(a^2) + \cdots + \binom{n}{r}(x^{n-r})(a^r) + a^n$.
- Another way of writing a binomial expansion: $(1+x)^n = 1 + nx + \frac{n(n-1)}{2!}(x^2) + \frac{n(n-1)(n-2)}{3!}(x^3) + \cdots + \frac{n(n-1)\ldots(n-(r+1))}{r!}(x^r)$.
- $n! = n \times (n-1) \times (n-2) \times \ldots \times 2 \times 1$ (Where n is an integer).
- Factorial Notations can be simplified in the following way: $\frac{n!}{(n-1)!} = \frac{n(n-1)!}{(n-1)!} = n$.

AM3 Coordinate Geometry

Straight Lines

- The equation of a straight line has the general form of $y = mx + c$, where m is the gradient of the line, c is the y-intercept of the line.
- You can also give the equation of a line in the form of: $ax + by + c = 0$.
- The midpoint of the line segment joining the two points (x_1, y_1), (x_2, y_2) is $\left(\frac{x_1+x_2}{2}, \frac{y_1+y_2}{2}\right)$.
- The length of a line segment with points (x_1, y_1),(x_2, y_2) is: $d = \sqrt{(y_2 - y_1)^2 + (x_2 - x_1)^2}$.
- The gradient of the line is given by: $m = \frac{y_2-y_1}{x_2-x_1}$.Where m_1 is the gradient.
- If you know the gradient of the line, m and a point (x_1, y_1). The equation of the line can be found by: $y - y_1 = m(x - x_1)$.
- Alternatively, if you are given two points on a curve (x_1, y_1) and (x_2, y_2). Then you can find the equation of the line using: $\frac{y-y_1}{y_2-y_1} = \frac{x-x_1}{x_2-x_1}$.
- If two lines are parallel, then $m_1 = m_2$.
- If two lines are perpendicular, then $m_1 \times m_2 = -1$.

Circles

- The equation of a circle in general form is $(x - a)^2 + (y - b)^2 = r^2$, where (a, b) is the centre of the circle and the radius is r.
- The equation of a circle can also be given in the form of $x^2 + y^2 + ax + by = r^2$.
- To convert from the first form to the second form above, you simply must expand the brackets and re-arrange such that the constants are on the RHS. To convert back to the first form, you can complete the square.
- In some questions you may be asked to work out the number of intersections that a line makes with a circle. In this case you must substitute either of the variables into the equation of the circle to eliminate it. Then use the discriminant to determine the number of real solutions and hence the number of intersections.

Circle Theorems

- The angle between the tangent and the radius is $90°$.
- The angle subtended at the circumference of a semi-circle is always a right angle (The angle in a semi-circle is $90°$).
- The angles subtended by the same arc are always equal (Angles within the same segment are equal).
- Opposite angles in a cyclic quadrilateral are supplementary (i.e, they add up to $180°$).

- The angle between a tangent and a chord is equal to the angle in the alternate segment (Alternate Segment Theorem).
- Two tangents drawn from a point to a circle are equal in length.
- The perpendicular from the centre to a chord bisects the chord.
- The angle subtended by an arc at the centre of a circle is twice the angle subtended by the arc at any point on the circumference.

Properties of a circle

- The chord of a circle is the line segment which joins two points lying on the circle.
- A segment is the region contained between the chord and the circle.
- A sector is the region of the circle contained between the arc and two radii. (i.e. like a pizza slice).
- Minor arc/sector/segment is the smaller of the arcs/lengths/segments, whereas the major arc/sector/segment is the larger one.

AM4 Trigonometry

Trigonometric Formulae

- Sine rule: $\frac{\sin A}{a} = \frac{\sin}{b} = \frac{\sin C}{c}$ or $\frac{a}{\sin A} = \frac{b}{\sin B} = \frac{c}{\sin}$.
- Ambiguous case of the sine rule: This arises when you are given 2 sides and an angle opposite the 2 sides. Under the ambiguous case of the sine rule it is possible to have up to 2 possibilities for the triangle.
- Cosine Rule: $a^2 = b^2 + c^2 - 2bc\cos A$.
- Area of a triangle is: $A = \frac{1}{2}ab\sin C$.
- $\sin(90° - \theta) = \cos\theta$.
- $\cos(90 - \theta) = \sin\theta$.
- $\sin(-x) = -\sin(x)$ (i.e. sine is an odd function).
- $\cos(-x) = \cos x$ (i.e. cosine is an even function).
- $\tan(-x) = -\tan(x)$ (i.e. tangent is an odd function).

Radians

- A radian is the angle subtended from the centre of a circle which forms an arc of length equal to the radius of the circle.
- To convert an angle, θ into radians you can use: $\theta \times \frac{\pi}{180}$.
- Arc length, l, is given by: $l = r\theta$, where r is the radius and θ is the angle in radians.
- Area of a sector, A is given by: $A = \frac{1}{2}r^2\theta$, where r is the radius and θ is the angle in radians.
- Area of a segment, A is given by: $A = \frac{1}{2}r^2(\theta - \sin\theta)$, where r is the radius and θ is the angle in radians.

Common Trigonometric values

$\theta \rightarrow$	0	$\frac{\pi}{6}$	$\frac{\pi}{4}$	$\frac{\pi}{3}$	$\frac{\pi}{2}$
$\sin\theta$	0	$\frac{1}{2}$	$\frac{\sqrt{2}}{2}$	$\frac{\sqrt{3}}{2}$	1
$\cos\theta$	1	$\frac{\sqrt{3}}{2}$	$\frac{\sqrt{2}}{2}$	$\frac{1}{2}$	0
$\tan\theta$	0	$\frac{\sqrt{3}}{3}$	1	$\sqrt{3}$	Undefined

Graphs of Trigonometric Functions

- The graph of $y = \sin\theta$, repeats every 2π radians (360°). It has x intercepts at multiples of π ($n\pi$ or $180n°$ $i.e. -180, 0, 180, 360 \ldots etc$).The function ranges between -1 and 1.
- The graph of $y = \cos\theta$, repeats every 2π radians (360°). It has x intercepts at odd multiples of $\frac{\pi}{2}$.
$\left(\frac{(2n+1)\pi}{2} \text{ or } 90n° \; i.e. -90°, 0°, 90°, 270° \ldots etc, where\ n\ is\ an\ odd\ integer\right)$. The function ranges between -1 and 1.
- The graph of $y = \tan\theta$, repeats every π radians (180°). It has x intercepts at multiples of π ($n\pi$ or $180n°$ $i.e. -180, 0, 180, 360 \ldots etc$). The function's range is all real values of x. The function has vertical asymptotes at odd multiples of $\frac{\pi}{2}$ $\left(\frac{(2n+1)\pi}{2} \text{ or } 90n°\right)$.
$i.e. -90°, 0°, 90°, 270° \ldots etc$, where n is an odd integer

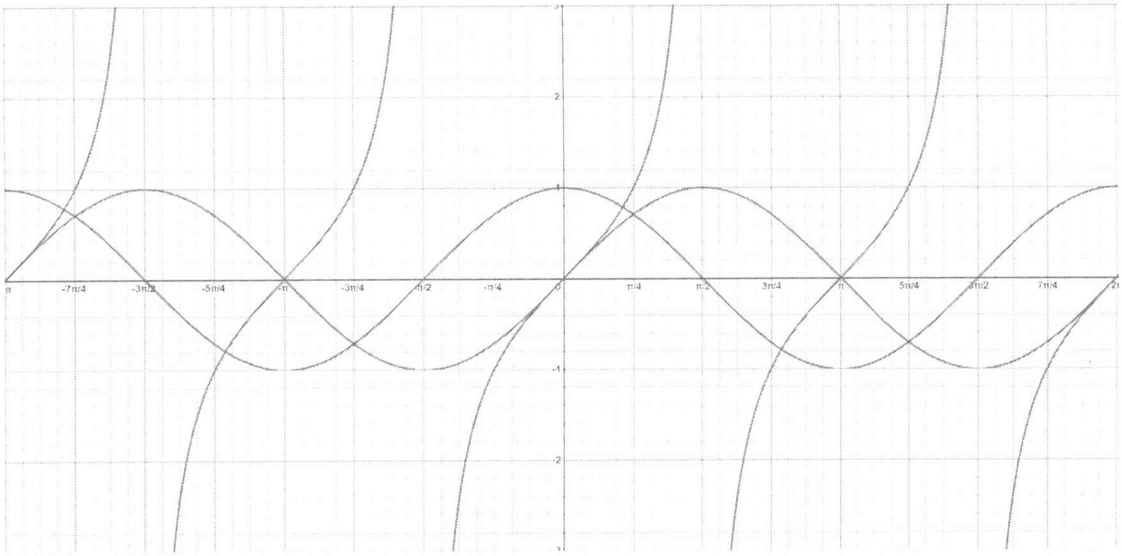

Basic Trigonometric Identities

- $\sin^2\theta + \cos^2\theta = 1$.
- $\tan x = \frac{\sin x}{\cos}$.

Solving Trigonometric Identities

Type 1: e.g. Solve $\tan\theta = \frac{1}{\sqrt{3}}$ for $-\pi < \theta < \pi$.

1) First you need to find the principal value (in this case $\theta = \frac{\pi}{6}$).

2) Then you need to consider all the other values within the domain which produce the same output with the trigonometric function. You can do this by considering periodicity of the function being considered.

Type 2: e.g. Solve $\sin^2\left(2\theta + \frac{\pi}{2}\right) = \frac{1}{4}$ for $-2\pi < \theta < 2\pi$.

1) First, manipulate the equation such that you have isolated a trigonometric function on one side of the equation.
2) Then, you need to find the principal value.
3) Adjust the domain according to what is inside the bracket.
4) Then you need to consider all the other values within the domain which produce the same output with the trigonometric function. You can do this by considering periodicity of the function being considered.
5) Then rearrange for θ.

Type 3: e.g. Solve $12\cos^2\theta + 6\sin\theta - 10 = 2$ for $-2\pi < \theta < 2\pi$.

1) Use the common trigonometric identities to get an equation in terms of one trigonometric function.
2) Solve the trigonometric equation for $\sin\theta$ / $\cos\theta$ / $\tan\theta$.
3) Then you need to find the principal value.
4) Finally, you need to consider all the other values within the domain which produce the same output with the trigonometric function. You can do this by considering periodicity of the function being considered.

AM5 Exponentials and logarithms

The graph of $y = a^x$ (where a is a simple positive value)

- This is an exponential graph and passes through the point $(0,1)$.
- If the value of a is $0 < a < 1$. Then the curve will be a decreasing function and a^x will tend to zero as x tends to infinity.
- For Example: $\left(\frac{1}{4}\right)^x = (4^{-1})^x = 4^{-x}$. Which explains why if $0 < a < 1$, the function is decreasing.
- If the value of $a > 1$. Then the curve will be an increasing function and a^x will tend to infinity as x tends to infinity.
- Whilst x is greater than zero, a greater value of a would produce a greater value of a^x.
- However, when x is less than zero, a greater value of a would produce a smaller value of a^x.

Laws of Logarithms

- $\log_a b = c$, where a is the base, b is the argument and c is the exponent.
- If $b < a$ then the exponent will be fractional.

Standard:

- $a^b = c \Leftrightarrow b = \log_a c$
- $\log_a x + \log_a y = \log_a xy$
- $\log_a x - \log_a y = \log_a \frac{x}{y}$
- $k \log_a x = \log_a x^k$
- $\log_a \frac{1}{x} = \log_a x^{-1} = -\log_a x$
- $\log_a a = 1$
- $\log_a 1 = 0$

Additional ones which may be useful:

- $\log_{a^p} m = \frac{1}{p} \log_a m$
- $x^{\log_b a} = a^{\log_b x}$
- $\log_a b =$ $\log_{a^n} b^n$ $(i.e. \textit{you can raise the base and the argument by the same power})$
- $\log_a b = \frac{1}{\log_b a}$

Solving equations of the form $a^x = b$

- To solve an equation of this form, you can take a log of base a or 10, then manipulate them in order to re-arrange for x. Occasionally, to get to this step, algebraic manipulation will be required and sometimes this may be in the form of a "hidden quadratic" which must be solved through substitution.

Converting logarithmic graphs to linear form

- To convert $y = ax^b$ to linear form you need to take logs of both sides $\log y = \log a + b \log x$, which gives you a straight line when you plot $\log y$ against $\log x$
- To convert $y = ab^x$ to linear you need to take logs of both sides $\log y = \log a + x \log b$, which gives you a straight line if you plot $\log y$ against x.

AM6 Differentiation

The derivative of f(x)

- Is equivalent to the gradient of the tangent to the function at a particular point.
- Can be used to represent the represent the rate of change of a variable.
- The second derivative tells us about the concavity of the function.

	Leibniz's Notation	Lagrange's Notation
First Derivative	$\frac{dy}{dx}$	$f'(x)$
Second Derivative	$\frac{d^2y}{dx^2}$	$f''(x)$

Differentiation Rules

- $\frac{d}{dx}(x^n) = nx^{n-1}$
- $\frac{d}{dx}(e^{kx}) = ke^{kx}$
- $\frac{d}{dx}(\ln x) = \frac{1}{x}$

Some Additional Rules

- $\frac{d}{dx}(\sin x) = \cos x$
- $\frac{d}{dx}(\cos x) = -\sin x$
- $\frac{d}{dx}(e^{f(x)}) = f'(x)e^{f(x)}$
- $\frac{d}{dx}(a^{kx}) = a^{kx}k\ln a$
- $\frac{d}{dx}(\ln|f(x)|) = \frac{f'(x)}{f(x)}$

Application of Derivatives

- A function is increasing when $f(x)$ is increasing when x is increasing, this occurs when $\frac{dy}{dx} > 0$ and the gradient is greater than zero.
- A function is decreasing when $f(x)$ is decreasing when x is increasing, this occurs when $\frac{dy}{dx} < 0$ and the gradient is lesser than zero.
- If $\frac{dy}{dx} = 0$, then there is either a maximum/minimum stationary point or a stationary point of inflection.
- If $\frac{d^2y}{dx^2} > 0$ at the given x coordinate and $\frac{dy}{dx} = 0$, the point is said to be a local minimum.
- If $\frac{d^2y}{dx^2} < 0$ at the given x coordinate and $\frac{dy}{dx} = 0$, the point is said to be a local maximum.

- A point of inflection occurs when $\frac{d^2y}{dx^2} = 0$ and the gradient has the same sign on both sides of the point.
- If $\frac{d^2y}{dx^2} > 0$, it indicates an increasing gradient and hence the function is convex for that value of x.
- If $\frac{d^2y}{dx^2} > 0$, it indicates an increasing gradient and hence the function is convex for that value of x.
- If $\frac{d^2y}{dx^2} > 0$, it indicates decreasing gradient and hence the function is concave for that value of x.

AM7 Integration

The significance of integration

- A definite integral does not always necessarily represent the area between a curve and an axis (for example when the function has a root and hence has a curve the crosses the x axis within the bounds of the integral).

Indefinite Integration of x^n

- If $\frac{dy}{dx} = x^n$. Then $\int \frac{dy}{dx} dx = \int x^n \, dx \Rightarrow y = \frac{x^{n+1}}{n+1} + c$

Fundamental Theorem of Calculus

- $\int_a^b f(x) \, dx = F(b) - F(a)$ where $F'(x) = f(x)$
- $\frac{d}{dx}\left(\int_a^x f(x) \, dx\right) = f(x)$

Combining Integrals with either equal or contiguous bounds

- Contiguous bounds are those which share boundaries.
- Equal bounds are those which have the same boundaries.
- $\int_1^4 f(x) \, dx + \int_1^4 g(x) \, dx = \int_1^4 [f(x) + g(x)] dx$
- $-\int_a^b f(x) \, dx = \int_b^a f(x) \, dx$
- $\int_2^4 f(x) \, dx + \int_4^3 f(x) \, dx = \int_2^4 f(x) \, dx - \int_3^4 f(x) \, dx = \int_2^3 f(x) \, dx$

Trapezium Rule

- The trapezium rule splits the area under a function's graph into trapezia of equal width. (Formula of the trapezium rule is not required).
- If you are asked to determine whether the trapezium rule produces an under or overestimate, then you simply need to find the concavity of the function in the given interval. If a function is concave, then using the trapezium rule will provide an under-estimate. If a function is convex then then using the trapezium rule will provide an over-estimate for the area.

Differential equations

- To solve differential equations of the form $\frac{dy}{dx} = f(x)$, you need to treat $\frac{dy}{dx}$ as a fraction. In doing so you can treat the dy and the dx term as separate terms and re-arrange them like a variable.
- For example: $\frac{dy}{dx} = \frac{2x+2}{y}$ can be re-arranged to $(y) \, dy = (2x + 2) \, dx$. You can then choose to integrate both sides of the differential equation: $\int y \, dy = \int (2x + 2) \, dx$. Which gives: $\frac{y^2}{2} = x^2 + 2x + c$. (Note that when integrating both sides of the

differential equation, you only need to include the constant on one side of the differential equation).

- Following this you can re-arrange for y.

AM8 Graphs of Functions

<u>Graph Sketching Process</u> (This may be useful for Interview Preparation as well)

When you are sketching a curve, try to find out as much of the following information:

1. Where the curve intercepts the coordinate axis. To do this, you need to substitute $x = 0 \; or \; y = 0$ and then solve for $y \; and \; x$ respectively.
2. The location and the nature of any turning points (which can be investigated using differentiation and occur at $\frac{dy}{dx} = 0$).
3. The location of any asymptotes (i.e. vertical asymptotes occur when y approaches $\pm\infty$ as x approaches a certain value and horizontal asymptotes occur when x approaches $\pm\infty$ as y approaches a certain value).
4. The location of the intervals of increase and decrease (which can be investigated using differentiation).
5. The location of any points of inflection occurs (i.e. where the concavity of a function changes and $\frac{d^2y}{dx^2} = 0$).
6. Whether or not there is any reflectional or rotational symmetry (i.e. if the function is odd: $f(-x) = -f(x)$, then there is rotational symmetry of order 2 about the origin. However, if the function is even: $f(-x) = f(x)$, then there is reflectional symmetry in the y axis). Although it is worth noting that graphs may be neither odd or even and the only function which is both odd and even is the constant function $f(x) = 0$.
7. The behaviour of the function as x gets closer to zero.

Graphical transformation

Function notation	Description	Effect on coordinates
$f(x)+a$	Vertical translation upwards by a units with vector $\binom{0}{a}$.	$(x,y)\Rightarrow(x,y+d)$
$f(x)-a$	Vertical translation downwards by a units with vector $\binom{0}{-a}$.	$(x,y)\Rightarrow(x,y-d)$
$f(x+a)$	Horizontal translation by a units leftwards with vector $\binom{-a}{0}$.	$(x,y)\Rightarrow(x-a,y)$
$f(x-a)$	Horizontal translation by a units rightwards with vector $\binom{a}{0}$.	$(x,y)\Rightarrow(x+a,y)$
$-f(x)$	Reflection over x-axis	$(x,y)\Rightarrow(x,-y)$
$f(-x)$	Reflection over y-axis	$(x,y)\Rightarrow(-x,y)$
$af(x)$	Vertical stretch if: $\lvert a\rvert>1$ Vertical compression if: $0<\lvert a\rvert<1$	$(x,y)\Rightarrow(x,ay)$
$f(ax)$	Horizontal compression for $\lvert b\rvert>1$ Horizontal stretch for: $0<\lvert b\rvert<1$	$(x,y)\Rightarrow\left(\frac{x}{b},y\right)$

Order of transformations

- If you have a function being transformed in the following way: $y=Af(Bx+C)+D$. Then you must perform the transformations in the order $CBAD$.

$y=mx+c$

- Increasing the value of m makes the gradient of the line steeper and increasing the value of c shifts the curve vertically upwards and increases the value of the y intercept.

$y=a(x+b)^2+c$

- It is best to think of this as a transformation of the curve $f(x)=x^2$, by $y=af(x+b)+c$. Hence, a represents the vertical stretch, b represents the horizontal translation and c represents the vertical translation.

Use of Differentiation to graph a function

- At the values of x, where $f'(x) = 0$ there is a stationary point for $f(x)$. For values of $f'(x) < 0$, the graph is a strictly decreasing function, when $f'(x) > 0$, the graph is a strictly increasing function.

Finding intercepts with the coordinate axis

- If you want to find where the function intercepts the x and the y axis, then substitute $y = 0$ and $x = 0$ respectively and solve for x and y.

Finding the number of real solutions to polynomials

- For a quadratic you must use the discriminant to work out the number of real solutions (refer to section 1).
- You can choose to sketch the graph of the polynomial function (refer to section 8), by considering the general shape of the polynomial, the turning points and the intervals of increase and decrease etc. Through this you can determine the number of times the graph crosses/touches the x axis and hence the number of real solutions for the polynomial.
- Finally, you can substitute small values of x from -2 to 2 into the polynomial function to determine one of the real solutions. Then using the factor theorem, you can divide by the corresponding linear polynomial (factor) to be able to further factorise the polynomial.
- It is important to remember that if a logarithm is part of a "hidden polynomial", you must check to ensure that the argument of the logarithm is not negative as this doesn't produce a real value of x.

Geometric interpretation of algebraic solutions; relationship between the Intersections of two graphs and the solutions of the corresponding simultaneous equations

- The number of algebraic solutions for two simultaneous equations, geometrically represents the number of times the two functions meet each other.

Maths Practise Questions

1) If $\int_7^b \frac{3}{\sqrt{x}} dx = 27 - 6\sqrt{7}$, then what is the value of b?

$A)\ \frac{81}{2}$ $B)\ \frac{81}{4}$ $C)\ \frac{27}{2}$ $D)\ \frac{9}{2}$ $E)\ 9$ $F)\ 18$

2) If $f(x) = (x+1)(2x+1)(x+3)$, what are the roots of $f\left(-\frac{1}{2}x + \frac{1}{2}\right)$?

$A)\ x = -\frac{3}{2}, -1, -\frac{7}{2}$ $B)\ x = \frac{3}{2}, \frac{1}{2}, \frac{11}{2}$ $C)\ x = 3,2,7$

$D)\ x = 1,0,5$ $E) x = -1,0,-5$

3) A circle of radius 2 cm is contained within an equilateral triangle as shown below:

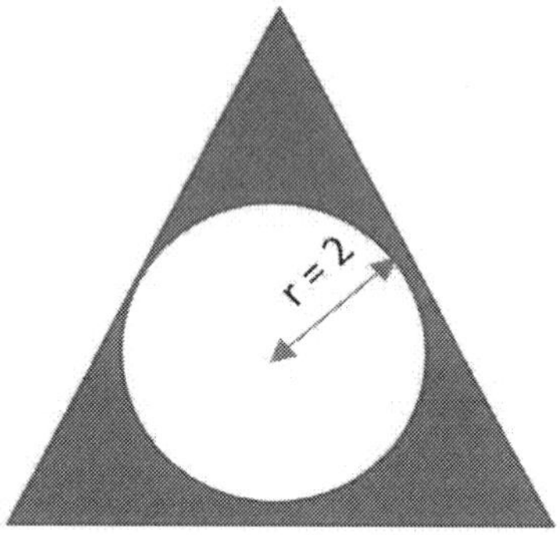

Find the area of the shaded region in terms of π.

$A) 12\sqrt{3} - 4\pi$ $B) 12\sqrt{3} - 16\pi$ $C) 3\sqrt{3} - 4\pi$ $D) 3\sqrt{3} - 16\pi$ $E) \sqrt{3} - 4\pi$

4) Find $\int_1^2 (2x-1)^4 dx$.

$A)\frac{242}{5}$ $B)\frac{243}{5}$ $C)\frac{243}{10}$ $D)\frac{121}{5}$ $E)\frac{121}{10}$

5) What is the y intercept of $y = -\sin\left(\frac{\pi}{6} + 36x\right)$

$A)(0,1)$ B)$(0,-1)$ C)$(0,36)$ D$(0,-36)$ E)$\left(0,-\frac{1}{2}\right)$

6) If $f(x) = x^3 - ax^2 - bx + 18$. C is the negative x intercept. What is the value of a + b + c?

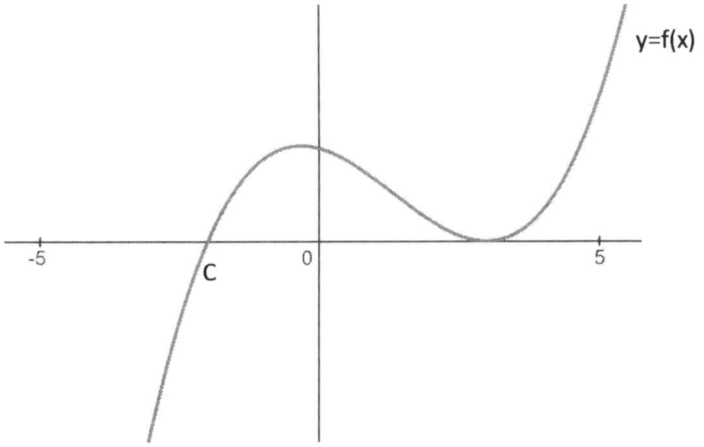

$A)5$ $B)9$ $C)-81$ $D)81$ $E)27$ $F)-27$

7) If $x = 29$, what is the value of $x^5 - 30x^4 + 30x^3 - 30x^2 + 30x$

$A)$ 841 $B)$ 24389 $C)$ 707281 $D)$ 20,511,149 $E)$ 30 $F)$ 29 $G)$ 31

8) **If $(x+1)^2 = 9$ and $(x-1)^2 = 25$. What is the value of x?**

$A)\ 6$ $B)\ 2$ $C)\ 4$ $D)\ -4$ $E)\ 5$ $F)$

9) **There are n counters in a bag, 7 of these counters are red and the rest are green Two counters are taken from the bag, given that the probability that both counters are green is $\frac{3}{10}$. Find the greatest possible number of counters in the bag.**

$A)\ 21$ $B)5$ $C)35$ $D)63$ $E)16$

10) **Evaluate $\lim_{x\to\infty} \frac{x^6+a^2x^3b}{x^6-a^4b^2}$ where a and b are constants**

$A)0$ $B)1$ $C)\infty$ $D)2$ $E)6$

11) **A, B, C, D are points on the same line arranged in the stated order.**
Ratio of AB: BD is 3: 5
Ratio of AC: CD is 4: 1
Find the ratio of AB: BC: CD.

$A)12:20:5$ $B)15:17:8$ $C)15:17:5$ $D)3:5:2$ $E)12:3:5$

12)

Given that the area of the circle is 36π, find the area of the shaded region.

A) $36\pi - 54\sqrt{3}$ B) $6\pi - 9\sqrt{3}$ C) $6\pi - 18\sqrt{3}$ D) $36\pi - 9$ E) $6\pi - 54$

13) Find the sum of $\sqrt{x} + 2, 1, \sqrt{x} - 2, \ldots$

A) $\frac{5\sqrt{5}+11}{9}$ B) $\frac{5\sqrt{5}+11}{4}$ C) $\sqrt{5}+11$ D) $\frac{15\sqrt{5}+11}{4}$ E) $\sqrt{5}$

14) Find the sum of the roots of $9^{x-1} - 30(3^{x-1}) + 81 = 0$.

A) 2   B) 4   C) 6   D) 8   E) 30   F) 81

15) A curve is given by the equation $y = \frac{3-x^2}{x+2}$. Find the value(s) of q for which the line $y = q$ is tangential to the curve.

A) $q = 6$ B) $q = 4$ C) $q = 2,10$ D) $q = 2,6$ E) $q = 4,6$

16) Points $(3, 10)(9, 4)$ and $(-3, 4)$ lie on a circle find the equation of the circle

A) $(x-3)^2 + (y-4)^2 = 36$ B) $(x-3)^2 + (y-2)^2 = 25$
C) $x^2 + (y-4)^2 = 36$ D) $x^2 + y^2 = 36$ E) $x^2 + y^2 = 25$

17) If $f(x) = 5x^3 + 3x^2 - 21x + 77$, find the positive x intercept of $f'(x)$.

$A)1$ $\quad B)\frac{3}{2}$ $\quad C)\frac{7}{5}$ $\quad D)\frac{1}{5}$ $\quad E)\frac{7}{2}$ $\quad F)No\ x\ intercepts$

18) If $\log_a b = \frac{1}{2}$ and $\log_c d = \frac{5}{4}$ and $a - c = 9$, what is the value of $d - b$?

$A) -27$ $\quad B)27$ $\quad C) -9$ $\quad D)37$ $\quad E) -37$

19) Given a, b are integers for what values is $\frac{36^{a-b} \times 12^{a+b}}{27^a \times 4^{2a+b}}$ an integer?

$A)\ a = 0$ $\quad B)\ b = 0$ $\quad C) a + b \leq 0$ $\quad D) a + b \geq 0$
$E)\ b \leq 0$ $\quad F)\ a \leq 0$ $\quad G) a \geq b$ $\quad H) b \geq a$

20) How many real solutions does $27^x + 9 = 9^x + 3^{x+2}$ have?

$A)\ none$ $\quad B) one$ $\quad C) two$ $\quad D) three$ $\quad E)\ four$

21) If $f(x) = (5\cos^2(15x + 23) - 10)^2$, then what is the maximum value of $f(x)$?

$A)25$ $\quad B)125$ $\quad C)100$ $\quad D)225$ $\quad E)4225$

22) How many solutions does $7\cos x + 2\sin^2 x = 5$ have for $0 \leq x \leq 2\pi$?

$A) None$ $\quad B)\ One$ $\quad C) Two$ $\quad D) Three$ $\quad E)\ Four$

23) Which is the largest?

$A)\ln 10$ $\quad B)\ \log_\pi 10$ $\quad C)\ \ln \pi^2$ $\quad D)\frac{1}{\log \pi}$ $\quad E)\frac{e}{\ln 2}$ $\quad F)\sqrt{\log \pi^2}$

24) If $\int_0^2 2f(x)\,dx + \int_2^4 3f(x)\,dx = 10$ & $\int_0^4 6f(x)\,dx - \int_0^2 8f(x)\,dx = 11$.

Find the value of $\int_0^4 f(x)\,dx$

$A)23$ $B)\frac{3}{2}$ $C)35$ $D)\frac{7}{3}$ $E)\frac{10}{3}$ $F)\frac{23}{6}$

25) Determine the point(s) of inflexion of: $f(x) = -2(x+2)^3(x-2)$

$A)(-2,0)$ $B)(2,0)$ $C)\ (0,32)(2,0)$
$D)\ (1,0)$ $E)(1,0)(-2,0)$ $F)(0,32)(-2,0)$

26) $f(x) = 6x^2 + 17x, g(x) = (14x+1)(3x+2), h(x) = g(x) + f(x)$.
What is the minimum point on $h(x)$?

$A)\left(-\frac{1}{2},-10\right)$ $B)\left(-10,-\frac{1}{2}\right)$ $C)\left(\frac{1}{2},-10\right)$ $D)\left(-\frac{1}{2},10\right)$ $E)\left(\frac{1}{2},10\right)$

27) Given that $16(\ln a)^2 + (\ln b)^2 = 1$**, What is the max value of a?**

$A)\frac{1}{16}$ $B)\sqrt[4]{e}$ $C)\frac{1}{\sqrt[4]{e}}$ $D)1$ $E)\frac{1}{2}$ $F)\frac{1}{4}$

28) What is the rational term in $\left(\frac{4+\sqrt{5}}{4-\sqrt{5}}\right)^2$?

$A)\frac{450}{121}$ $B)1$ $C)\frac{900}{121}$ $D)\frac{761}{121}$ $E)\frac{336}{121}$

29) If $\log_4 x + \log_2 x = 9$**, find the value of x**

$A)\ 2$ $B)4$ $C)8$ $D)16$ $E)32$ $F)64$ $G)5$ $H)\ 7$

30) Find the closest point on $\left(x-\frac{11}{2}\right)^2+\left(y-\frac{9}{2}\right)^2=4$ to $\left(x-\frac{3}{2}\right)^2+\left(y-\frac{3}{2}\right)^2=4$.

$A)(4,3)$ $B)(3.9,3.3)$ $C)\left(\frac{15}{2},\frac{13}{2}\right)$ $D)\left(\frac{7}{2},\frac{5}{2}\right)$

31) The sum to infinity of a convergent geometric series is 12. If a second geometric series is formed by squaring each term in the first one and has a sum to infinity of 60. Find the common ratio of the original series.

$A)\frac{7}{24}$ $B)\frac{17}{24}$ $C)1$ $D)\frac{7}{17}$ $E)\frac{3}{4}$ $F)\frac{1}{4}$

32) If $a^{6y}b^{4-y}=b^{y+3}a^{4y}$ then y =

$A)\frac{-\log b}{2[\log a+\log b]}$ $B)\frac{-\log b}{2[\log a-\log b]}$ $C)\frac{\log b}{2[\log a+\log b]}$ $D)\frac{-\log b}{[\log a-\log b]}$

33) In the expansion: $(4m+3n^2x)^4$, the coeficient of x^2 is 3 times that of x^3. Find m in terms of n.

$A)m=\frac{3}{2}n$ $B)m=\frac{3}{2}n^2$ $C)m=\frac{3}{2}n^3$ $D)m=\frac{1}{2}n$ $E)\frac{1}{2}n^2$ $F)\frac{1}{2}n^3$

34) If $x-2y=0$ and $x+ay+5=0$ for what values of a are the lines parallel?

$A)0$ $B)1$ $C)2$ $D)3$ $E)4$ $F)-3$ $G)-2$ $H)-1$

35) A cuboid has side lengths of $x, \sqrt{3x}, 3x$, the ratio of the Surface Area to Volume is 14: 9. What is the product of the possible values of x?

$A)\frac{144}{49}$ $B)0$ $C)3$ $D)\frac{48}{49}$ $E)3\frac{46}{49}$ $F)\frac{46}{49}$

36) If $\ln(a^2 - b^2) = 0$, find the possible values of a and b

$A) a = 1, b = 0$ $B) a = 0, b = 1$ $C) a = 0, b = 0$
$D) a = -1, b = 0$ $E) a = 1, b = 0,$ $F)\ a = -1, b = 0$

37) If $\log_4 x - 1 = \log_2 x - 3$. Then how many real solutions exist?

$A)$no real solutions $B)\ 1$ $C)2$ $D)3$ $E)4$

38) $4x - 3y - 1 = 0$ and $3x - 3y - 1 = 0$. Find the equation of the line through the origin and the point of intersection.

$A)\ y = \frac{2}{3}x$ $B)\ y = \frac{1}{3}x$ $C) y = \frac{1}{6}x$ $D) y = \frac{5}{6}x$ $E) \frac{1}{2}x$

39) The sum of the first 3 terms of a decreasing arithmetic sequence is 27 and the sum of the squares is 293. Find the nth term of the sequence?

A) $u_n = 19 - 5n$ $B) u_n = 5n - 1$ $C) 14 - 5n$ $D) 5n - 3$ $E) 3 - 5n$

40) Rationalise $\frac{3}{\sqrt{6} - 2\sqrt{3}}$:

$A) -\frac{2\sqrt{3}-\sqrt{6}}{2}$ $B) \frac{2\sqrt{3}+\sqrt{6}}{2}$ $C) \frac{2\sqrt{3}-\sqrt{6}}{2}$ $D) -\frac{2\sqrt{3}+\sqrt{6}}{2}$ $E) \frac{-3\sqrt{3}+\sqrt{6}}{2}$

41) If $\frac{1}{6}\log_2(x-2) - \frac{1}{3} = \log_{\frac{1}{8}} \sqrt{3x-5}$ then what is the product of the possible values of x which satisfy the equation?

$A)3$ $B) \frac{2}{3}$ $C) \frac{11}{3}$ $D) \frac{7}{3}$ $E)1$ $F)2$ $G) \frac{4}{3}$

42) How many solutions does $4 - 2\sin^8 x = (3 + \cos x)^2$ have for $0 \leq x \leq 360°$?

$A)$none $B)1$ $C)2$ $D)3$ $E)4$ $F)5$ $G)6$ $H)7$ $I)8$

43) Points A, B, C are (4, 1), (5, −2) and (3, 7) respectively. If ABCD is a parallelogram then find the coordinates of D?

$A)(4,4)$ $B)(4,5)$ $C)(5,5)$ $D)(2,10)$ $E)(1,10)$ $F)(0,10)$ $G)(2,8)$

44) $x+3+\frac{3}{x-1}=\frac{4-x}{x-1}$. **What values of x satisfy the equation?**

$A)x=4$ $B)x=1\ \&\ x=4$ $C)x=1$ $D)x=-4$
$E)x=-1$ $F)x=-4\ \&\ x=-1$

45) If $\log_4(2^x+3)+1=x$, find the value of x

$A)\log 6$ $B)\log 2$ $C)\frac{\log 6}{\log 2}$ $D)\frac{\log 2}{\log 6}$ $E)1$ $F)-1$

46) The curve $y=x^3-3x^2+ax-2$ has 2 distinct turning points for what values of a?

$A)a<3$ $B)a\leq 3$ $C)a>3$ $D)a\geq 3$ $E)a\neq 3$

47) Inspector Sandy is carrying out an investigation, he wants to know which of these events is most likely when flipping a fair coin?
1)Flipping 2 or more heads in 3 trials
2)Flipping 20 or more heads in 30 trials
3)Flipping 200 or more heads in 300 trials

A)1 B)2 C)3 D) They are all equally likely

48) What is the remainder when $P(x)=x^3-ax^2+6x-a$ **is divided by** $(x-a)$

$A)a$ $B)2a$ $C)3a$ $D)\ 4a$ $E)\ 5a$

49) An increasing geometric sequence has a sum of the first and last term of 99 The product of its second and the second last term is 288 and the sum of the series. What is the number of terms in the series?

$A)3$ $B)4$ $C)5$ $D)6$ $E)7$ $F)8$ $G)9$

50) Find $\int_0^2 \frac{1-x^2}{x^{\frac{3}{2}}+\sqrt{x}}dx$.

$A)\sqrt{2}$ $B)\frac{2\sqrt{2}}{3}$ $C)2\sqrt{2}$ $D)\frac{\sqrt{2}}{3}$ $E)\frac{2}{3}$ $F)3\sqrt{2}$

51) $2^{(x-1)(x^2+5x-50)} = 1$. **What is the sum of all the real values of which satisfy the equation?**

A)14 B)16 C) − 5 D) − 1 E) − 4 F)1 G)2

52) A 2 digit number is 7 times the sum of its digits. The number formed by reversing the digits is 18 less than the original number. Find the original number.

A)12 B)16 C)20 D)24 E)32 F)42 G)48

53) $81x^2 + kx + 256 = 0$ **has two real roots where one is a cube of the other, Find the value of k?**

$A) -5$ $B)16)$ $C)14$ $D) -4$ $E)8$ $F)10$

answer : k= -300

54) $e^{2x} + e^x + e^{-2x} + e^{-x} = 3(e^{-2x} + e^x)$. **How many real values of x satisfy the equation?**

$A)none$ $B)1$ $C)2$ $D)3$ $E)4$ $F)5$ $G)6$

55) $\log x - \frac{1}{2}\log\left(x - \frac{1}{2}\right) = \log\left(x + \frac{1}{2}\right) - \frac{1}{2}\log\left(x + \frac{1}{8}\right)$. **Solve for x.**

$A)x = -\frac{1}{3}$ $B)x = \frac{1}{3}$ $C)x = 1, -\frac{1}{3}$ $D)x = -1$ $E)1$

56) Find the area between the curve $1 - x^2$, the x axis and the lines $x = -2$ and $x = 2$

A) $\frac{4}{3}$ B) $\frac{2}{3}$ C)4 D)2 E)6 F)8 $G)10$

57) If $f(x) = \frac{x^4}{4} - x^3 - 5x^2 + 24x + 12$, then under which interval is the function increasing?

$A)\{x: x \geq 4\}$ $B)\ \{x: x \leq 4\}$ $C)\ \{x: -3 \leq x \leq 2\}$
$D)\{x: x \leq -3\}$ $E)\ \{x: 2 \leq x \leq 4\}$ $F)\ \{x: x \leq -3\} \cap \{x: 2 \leq x \leq 4\}$
$G)\ \{x: -3 \leq x \leq 2\} \cap \{x: x \geq 4\}$

58) Mr Lahiri has a box of 10 chocolates, 7 of which are milk chocolate and the rest are dark chocolate. Mr Lahiri picks two chocolates at random from the box, without replacement. Calculate the probability that at least one of Mr Lahiri's chocolates is milk chocolate

$A)\frac{1}{15}$ $B)\frac{14}{15}$ $C)\frac{7}{10}$ $D)\frac{49}{100}$ $E)\frac{17}{20}$ $F)\frac{91}{100}$

59) Which of these equations is a tangent to $x^2 + y^2 = 20$?

$A)x = \sqrt{10}$ $B)x + y = \sqrt{10}$ $C)y = x - \sqrt{10}$
$D)x + y = \sqrt{20}$ $E)y = x + \sqrt{40}$

60) a, b, c are in a geometric sequence and 4a, 5b and 4c are in an arithmetic sequence If a + b + c = 70. Then what is the magnitude of c − a?

$A)5$ $B)10$ $C)20$ $D)30$ $E)\ 40$ $F)50$ $G)100$

61) Malthus has made the following measurements of a material:
Mass: 2.7 (1.d.p)
Volume: 1.23 (2.d.p)
What are the upper and lower bounds of the density?

$A) Upper: \frac{110}{49}, Lower: \frac{530}{247},$ $B) Upper: \frac{550}{247}, Lower: \frac{106}{49},$
$C) Upper: \frac{247}{530}, Lower: \frac{49}{110}$ $D) Upper: \frac{247}{530}, \; Lower: \frac{49}{106}$

62) $\frac{\frac{x}{y}}{z^2} + \frac{\frac{x}{y}}{z^2}$ **is equivalent to:**

A) $\frac{x(1+z^4)}{yz}$ B) $\frac{(1+z^4)}{yz^2}$ C) $\frac{x(1+z^4)}{yz^2}$
D) $\frac{x(1+z^2)}{yz^2}$ E) $\frac{x+z^4}{yz}$ F) $\frac{(1+z^4)}{yz}$

63) Find the reigon for x which satisfies: $\frac{x}{x-8} > \frac{1}{2}$.

$A) x < -8 \; and \; x > 8$ $B) x < -8$ $C) x > 8$
$D) -8 < x < 8$ $E) x < 8$ $F) x > -8$

64) Find the equation of the normal to the curve $y = x + \frac{1}{x}, x > 0$ **perpendicular to** $3x - 4y = 7$

$A) 8x - 6y = 31$ $B) 4x + 3y = 42$ $C) 4x - 3y = 42$

$D) 12x + 9y = 14$ $E) 12x + 9y = 31$ $F) 8x + 6y = 31$

65) Two vertices of an equiltaeral triangle are (11, 7) and (3, 13). Find the area of the triangle?

A) $50\sqrt{3}$ B) $25\sqrt{3}$ C) $5\sqrt{5}$ D) $25\sqrt{5}$
E) $125\sqrt{5}$ F) $5\sqrt{3}$ G) 50

66) **A group of 3 students A, B, C are given a problem. The probabilities of each student solving the problem correctly is $\frac{1}{2}, \frac{1}{3}$ and $\frac{1}{4}$ respectively. What is the probability that the problem will be solved?**

$A)\frac{3}{4}$ $\quad B)\frac{5}{6}$ $\quad C)\frac{7}{8}$ $\quad D)\frac{1}{4}$ $\quad E)\frac{1}{24}$ $\quad F)\frac{23}{24}$

67) **If $(x-2)^{\log^2(x-2)+\log(x-2)^5-12} = 10^{\log(x-2)^2}$ then x=:**

$A)102, 10^{-7}+2, 3$ $\quad B)102, 3$ $\quad C)3$ $\quad D)0, 2, -7$ $\quad E)2$ $\quad F)0, 2$

68) **Convert $0.4\dot{7}\dot{3}$ to a fraction.**

$A)\frac{473}{100}$ $\quad B)\frac{473}{999}$ $\quad C)\frac{47}{99}$ $\quad D)\frac{469}{999}$ $\quad E)\frac{469}{990}$

69) **Find the perpendicular distance from (5, 18) to $5x - 5y + 25 = 0$**

$A)5\sqrt{2}$ $\quad B)2\sqrt{2}$ $\quad C)3\sqrt{2}$ $\quad D)4\sqrt{2}$ $\quad E)\sqrt{2}$ $\quad F)6\sqrt{2}$

70) **What is the equation of the tangent to $y = x^3 - x$ at $x = 2$**

$A)y = 11x - 22$ $\quad B)y = 11x - 16$ $\quad C)y = 11x - 6$
$D)y = -11x - 16$ $\quad E)y = -11x + 16$ $\quad F)y = 11x - 3$

71) **If $\sqrt{x} + \sqrt{y} = 1$. Find the area bound between the curve and the coordinate axis.**

$A)\frac{17}{6}$ $\quad B)3$ $\quad C)4$ $\quad D)6$ $\quad E)\frac{1}{6}$ $\quad F)\frac{1}{3}$

72) **Find the range of values of x which satisfy: $\frac{1}{x^3} < x$.**

$A)\{x: x > 1\}$ $\quad B)\{x: -1 < x < 0\} \cup \{x: x > 1\}$ $\quad C)\{x: x < -1\} \cup \{x: x > 1\}$
$D)\{x: -1 < x < 0\}$ $\quad E)\{x: x < 1\}$ $\quad F)\{x: x < -1\}$ $\quad G)\{x: x > -1\}$

73) The infinite sum of the series: $\frac{7}{17}+\frac{77}{17^2}+\frac{777}{17^3}+\cdots$ is:

$A)=\frac{77}{100}$ $B)\frac{23}{100}$ $C)\frac{23}{16}$ $D)\frac{16}{17}$ $E)\frac{17}{16}$

74) 3 children A, B, C are playing a game, each taking turns to flip a fair coin. Their turns follow alphabetical order. The winner is the child who first lands on heads. Find the probability that A wins given that it takes less than 7 attempts to determine a winner.

$A)\frac{4}{7}$ $B)\frac{3}{7}$ $C)\frac{1}{8}$ $D)\frac{7}{8}$ $E)\frac{127}{128}$ $F)\frac{1}{128}$ $G)\frac{512}{889}$ $H)\frac{377}{889}$

75) $9^{(\log_3 1-2x)}=5x^2-5$**. The value of x is:**

$A)2+\sqrt{10}$ $B)-2+\sqrt{10}$ $C)-2-\sqrt{10}$ $D)72$
$E)-72$ $F)-30$ $G)-40$

76) The normal to $y=x^{\frac{2}{3}}$ **at** $x=8$ **intersects both coordinate axis, find the length of the line segment which joins these two points.**

$A)\sqrt{10}$ $B)\frac{\sqrt{10}}{2}$ $C)\frac{28\sqrt{10}}{3}$ $D)28\sqrt{10}$ $E)\frac{\sqrt{10}}{3}$

77) $x^2+2mx+10-3m>0$ **for** $x\in\mathbb{R}$**. Determine the range of values for m.**

$A)m>5$ $B)2<m<5$ $C)-5<m<2$
$D)m<-5$ $E)m>-5$ $F)m<5$

78) 1st, 2nd and 7th term of an arithmetic sequence form a geometric sequence. The sum of these 3 terms is 93. What is the value of the 4th term?

$A)120$ $B)150$ $C)175$ $D)200$ $E)250$ $F)375$ $G)400$

79) **If $f(x) = (x^2 + 2)^2$. What is the minimum value of $5f(3x - 11) + 4$**

A)(11,20) B)(55,20) C)(11,100) D)$\left(\frac{11}{3}, 84\right)$ E)$\left(\frac{11}{3}, 20\right)$

80) $\frac{x}{x+4} = \frac{3-x}{x-1}$ **. Find the value of x which satisfies the equation.**

A)$x = 1$ B)$x = 2$ C) $x = 3$ D)$x = 4$

E)$x = 5$ F)$x = 6$ G)$x = \pm 6$ H) $\pm\sqrt{6}$

81) $P(E) = 0.8, P(F) = 0.7$ **and** $P(E \cap F) = 0.6$. **What is the value of** $P(E'|F')$?

A)$\frac{1}{2}$ B)$\frac{1}{3}$ C)$\frac{1}{4}$ D)$\frac{1}{5}$ E)$\frac{1}{6}$ F)$\frac{1}{8}$

82) $\log_6(x + 3) = 1 - \log_6(x - 2)$, **What is the value of x?**

A)1 B)2 C)3 D)4 E)5 F)6

83) A shop reduced the price of a bag of sand by 40% on Saturday and then further reduces the price by 10%. What is the overall percentage reduction in the price?

A)50% B)60% C)56% D)75% E)66% F)46% G)44%

84) $y = f(x)$ **has one real solution. Now consider:**

$y = -f(x)$

$y = f(-x)$

$y = f(x + 3)$

$y = f(x) + 3$

$y = 3f(x)$

$y = f(3x)$

$y = 3 - f(x)$

How many of the following still necessarily have one real solution?

A)0 B)1 C)2 D)3 E)4 F)5 G)6 H)7

85) **Evaluate the value of $\int_{-3}^{1} |x|(x-1)dx$.**

$A)\frac{41}{3}$ $B)-\frac{41}{3}$ $C)\frac{41}{6}$ $D)-\frac{41}{6}$ $E)\frac{41}{9}$ $F)-\frac{41}{9}$

86) **If $p:q$ is $5:6$ and $q:r$ is $4:13$. If $p+q+r$ is equal to 244. Then what is the value of $p+r$**

$A)98$ $B)100$ $C)99$ $D)198$ $E)196$ $F)200$

87) **The expansion of $f(x) = \left(3+\frac{x}{k}\right)^8$ has a coefficient of x^2 which is 3 times the coefficient of x^3. Find the value of the constant k.**

$A)0$ $B)1$ $C)2$ $D)3$ $E)4$ $F)5$ $G)6$

88) **What is the area enclosed between $y^2 = 8x$ and $x = 2$.**

$A)\frac{32}{3}$ $B)\frac{16}{3}$ $C)16$ $D)\frac{8}{3}$ $E)\frac{4}{3}$ $F)\frac{64}{3}$

89) **The infinite sum of a geometric series is 3 times the sum of its even terms. If the first term is not equal to zero, find the common ratio**

$A)\frac{1}{8}$ $B)\frac{1}{4}$ $C)\frac{3}{8}$ $D)\frac{1}{2}$ $D)\frac{5}{8}$ $E)\frac{3}{4}$ $F)\frac{7}{8}$

90) **A rectangle fits into a circle as shown. The line $3y = x + 7$ contains the diameter. Two adjacent vertices which lie on the circle are $(-8,5)$ and $(6,5)$. Find the area of the rectangle.**

$A)98$ $B)102$ $C)72$ $D)75$ $E)56$ $F)84$

91) What is the sum of the series: $m(m+n)+m^2(m^2+n^2)+m^3(m^3+n^3)+\ldots$ given $|m|<1$ and $|n|<1$

$A)\frac{n^2}{n^2-1}+\frac{mn}{1-mn}$ $B)\frac{n}{1-n}+\frac{m}{1-m}$

$C)\frac{n}{n-1}+\frac{mn}{mn-1}$ $D)\frac{m^2}{1-m^2}+\frac{mn}{1-mn}$

92) $\int_1^3\left(2x+\frac{3}{x}\right)^2 dx =$

$A)\frac{64}{3}$ $B)\frac{94}{3}$ $C)\frac{134}{3}$ $D)\frac{194}{3}$ $E)\frac{191}{3}$ $F)\frac{197}{3}$ $G)64$

93) The simulatneous equations:

$y+\frac{1}{2}=5x$

$x^2-4ky+3k=0$

Have exactly one pair of solutions where $\neq 0$ and is a constant.
Find the value of $x+y$.

$A)\frac{5}{2}$ $B)\frac{3}{2}$ $C)\frac{1}{2}$ $D)\frac{7}{2}$ $E)\frac{9}{2}$ $F)\frac{11}{2}$ $G)\frac{13}{2}$

94) $f(x)=(3+ax)(1+bx)^5$. If the expansion of $f(x)$ is $3+17x+\frac{70}{3}x^2+kx^3$.
Find the value of k.

$A)\frac{1250}{9}$ $B)\frac{130}{9}$ $C)\frac{40}{3}$ $D)50$

$E)\frac{50}{3}$ $F)\frac{25}{3}$ $G)\frac{20}{3}$ $H)\frac{10}{3}$

95) A straight line has the equation $5y-4x=6$ and has a y intercept of $(0,p)$.
Another staight line is parrallel to the original line and passes through the point $(2,3)$, it also has a y intercept of $(0,q)$, then what is the value of $q-p$?

$A)\frac{1}{5}$ $B)\frac{2}{5}$ $C)\frac{3}{5}$ $D)\frac{4}{5}$ $E)1$ $F)\frac{6}{5}$ $G)\frac{7}{5}$ $H)\frac{8}{5}$

96) Given $x^{1+\log x} = 10x$, the number of solutions is:

$A)10$ $B)none$ $C)1$ $D)2$ $E)3$
$F)4$ $G)5$ $H)6$ $I)7$

97) Rearrange $a = 5\sqrt{\frac{b+3}{2}} - 1$ for b:

$A)b = 2\left(\frac{a+1}{5}\right) - 3$ $B)b = 2\left(\frac{a+1}{5}\right) - 3$ $C)b = 2\left(\frac{a+3}{5}\right)^2 - 1$
$D)b = 2\left(\frac{a-3}{5}\right)^2 + 1$ E)$b = 2\left(\frac{a+3}{5}\right) - 1$ $F)b = 2\left(\frac{a-3}{5}\right) + 1$
$G)b = 2\left(\frac{a+1}{5}\right)^2 - 3$

98) The coefficient of x^4 term in the expansion $\left(4\sqrt{p} + 5x\right)^6$ is 3×10^5. What is the value of p?

A)0 B)1 C)2 D)3 E)4 F)5 G)6 H)7

99) The ratio of dogs to cats at a pet shop is 1: 5. If the number of dogs is x. 2 pets are chosen at random and the probability that they are both dogs is y. What is the expression for the number of dogs (x)in terms of y?

A)$x = \frac{6y-1}{36y-1}$ B)$x = \frac{6y-6}{36y-1}$ C)$x = \frac{36y-1}{6y-1}$
$D)x = \frac{6y-6}{36y-6}$ E)$x = \frac{36y-6}{6y-1}$

100) Vertex A of a rectangle has coordinates (7, 2), it is rotated by 90° ACW about the centre and then reflected along the line of y = x, what are th resulting coordinates from this transformation?

$A)(7,2)$ $B)(-7,2)$ $C)(-7,-2)$
$D)(7,-2)$ $E)(-2,7)$ $F)(2,-7)$

101) Xiang Yufei decides to subtract 2, 7, 9 and 5 from 4 consecutive terms of a geometric sequence and notices that the resulting terms form an arithmetic sequence. What is the smallest of the 4 terms in the geometric sequence?

$A) -100$ $B) -16$ $C) 3$ $D) 6$
$E) -12$ $F) -24$ $G) -3$ $H) -6$

102) Two fair dice are rolled and it is revealed that at least one of the numbers was a 4. What is the probability that the other number is a 6?

$A)\frac{1}{36}$ $B)\frac{1}{18}$ $C)\frac{1}{9}$ $D)\frac{1}{6}$ $E)\frac{2}{11}$ $F)\frac{1}{11}$

103) $\left(a^{\log_b x}\right)^2 - 5x^{\log_b a} + 6 = 0$**. The value of x is:**

$A) 2^{\log_a b}, 3^{\log_a b}$ $B) 3^{\log_a b}$ $C) 2^{\log_a b}$ $D) 2^{\log_b a}$

$E) 2^{\log_b a}, 3^{\log_b a}$ $F) 3^{\log_b a}$ $G)$ *no solutions*

104) Convert $2.1\dot{4}\dot{5}$ **to a mixed number fraction**

$A) 2\frac{4}{55}$ $B) 2\frac{145}{999}$ $C) 2\frac{16}{111}$ $D) 2\frac{29}{198}$ $E) 2\frac{2}{55}$ $F) 2\frac{8}{55}$

105) Find the ~~equation~~ x-intercept of the normal at $y = -2x^2 - 8x + \frac{2}{x}$ **at** $(-1, 4)$

A)(25,0) B)(−25,0) C)(5,0) D)(−5,0) E)(44,0) F)(−44,0)

106) If $k = x^3 + 5x^2 + 3x - 3$ **has 3 roots, what is the range of values for k?**

$A) -\frac{94}{27} < k < 6$ $B) k > 6 \text{ and } k < -\frac{94}{27}$ $C) k > 6$

$D) k < -\frac{94}{27}$ $E) k < 6$

107) How many real solutions does $e^{\sin x} - e^{-\sin x} = 4$ have?

A)none B)1 C)2 D)3 E)4 F)5

108) Rationalize $\frac{1}{\sqrt{2}+\sqrt{3}+\sqrt{5}}$

$A)\frac{2\sqrt{3}+3\sqrt{2}-\sqrt{30}}{6}$ $B)\frac{\sqrt{3}+\sqrt{2}-\sqrt{10}}{12}$ $C)\frac{2\sqrt{3}+\sqrt{2}-\sqrt{30}}{12}$

$D)\frac{2\sqrt{3}+3\sqrt{2}-\sqrt{30}}{2}$ $E)\frac{2\sqrt{3}-\sqrt{30}}{12}$ $F)\frac{2\sqrt{3}+3\sqrt{2}-\sqrt{30}}{12}$

109) A geometric sequence has $u_2 = 2$ and $S_\infty = 8$. Find the value of the first term.

$A)\frac{1}{2}$ $B)1$ $C)4$ $D)8$ $E)16$ $F)32$

110) How many solutions does $4\cos^3 x - 4\cos^2 x - \cos(180 + x) - 1 = 0$ have in the range: $-360 \leq x \leq 360$

$A)none$ $B)1$ $C)2$ $D)3$ $E)4$ $F)5$ $G)6$

111) $(2x-3)^2 - (x+3)^2$ is written in the form of $p(x+q)^2 + r$ ...?

A) − 9 B) − 27 C) − 3 D)0 E)9 F)27 G)3

112) If $\left(\frac{\log x}{2}\right)\log^2 x + \log x^2 - 2 = \log\sqrt{x}$, what is the value of x?

$A)1$ $B)\frac{1}{10}$ $C)\frac{1}{100}$ $D)6$ $E)7$ $F)8$ $G)10$ $H)100$

113) How many solutions does : $(6-x)^4+(8-x)^4=16$ have?

$A)none$ $B)1$ $C)2$ $D)3$ $E)4$ $F)8$

114) Find the area of the reigon bounded by the line $y=\sqrt{3}x$, the curve $x^2+y^2=4$ and the x axis in the 1st quadrant.

A) $\frac{\pi}{3}$ B) $\frac{\pi}{6}$ C) $\frac{4\pi}{3}$ D) $\frac{2\pi}{3}$ E) 4π F) 2π

115) If $4^{\frac{a+1}{b}}=125$ and $5^{\frac{b}{a}}=2$. Then what is the value of $\frac{25^b}{a^2}$?

A) 4^{-3} B) 4^{-2} C) 4^{-1} D) 4^0

E) 4^1 F) 4^2 G) 4^3 H) 4^4

116) What is the minimum vertical distance between the curves $y=x^2+1$ and $y=x-x^2$?

A) $\frac{1}{8}$ B) $\frac{1}{4}$ C) $\frac{3}{8}$ D) $\frac{1}{2}$

E) $\frac{5}{8}$ F) $\frac{3}{4}$ G) $\frac{7}{8}$ H) 1

117) Find the locus of the points equidistant from the lines: $9x+6y-7=0$ and $3x+2y+6=0$.

A) $12y+18x+13=0$ B) $12y+18x+7=0$ C) $12y+18x+5=0$

D) $12y+18x+11=0$ E) $12y+18x+17=0$ F) $12y+18x+19=0$

118) If the circumeference of a circle is reduced by 50%, its area is reduced by:

A)75% B)66.7% C)50% D)25% E)12.5% F)6.25%

119) If $1, \log_{81} 3^x + 48, \log_9 3^x - \frac{8}{3}$ are in an arithmetic progression, then x =

$A)2$ $B)3$ $C)4$ $D)4$ $E)5$ $F)6$ $G)7$ $H)8$

120) $x^{x+y} = y$ and $y^{x+y} = x^2y$. What is the product of all solutions of x and y?

$A) -8$ $B)8$ $C)64$ $D) -64$ $E)6$ $F)4$

121) a, b, c are the 7th, 11th and 13th numbers of an arithmetic sequence. These 3 terms also form a geometric progression. Then what is the value of $\frac{a}{c}$?

$A)\frac{3}{4}$ $B)\frac{5}{4}$ $C)\frac{7}{4}$ $D)\frac{9}{4}$ $E)4$ $F)\frac{1}{4}$

122) In order to make a party hat (an open ended cone), a sector is cut out of a circle with a radius of 20cm. The party hat has a slant height of 20cm and a radius of 10cm. What fraction of the circle is cut out?

A) $\frac{1}{10}$ B) $\frac{1}{8}$ C) $\frac{1}{4}$ D) $\frac{1}{3}$ E) $\frac{1}{2}$ F) $\frac{3}{4}$

123) If $\frac{2^{399} - 2^{394}}{31} = 32^k$. what is the value of k?

A) $k = \frac{294}{5}$ B) $k = \frac{194}{5}$ C) $k = \frac{394}{5}$ D) $k = \frac{494}{5}$ E) $\frac{594}{5}$

124) AC and BD are diagonals of the rhombus, ABCD. If AC = $2x + 5$ and BD = $5 - 2x$. If the area of the rhombus is 10, what is the value of x?

A) $x = \frac{\sqrt{15}}{2}$ B) $x = \pm\frac{\sqrt{15}}{2}$ C) $x = \frac{\sqrt{5}}{2}$

D) $x = \pm\frac{\sqrt{5}}{2}$ E) $x = \frac{\sqrt{3}}{2}$ F) $x = \pm\frac{\sqrt{3}}{2}$

125) How many solutions does $3\sin^2 x - 7\sin x + 2 = 0$ have in the interval $[0, 5\pi]$?

A)none B)1 C)2 D)3 E)4 F)5 G)6 H)7

126) If $f(x) = px^3 + (p-1)x$ and $p > 0$ then for what values of p an increasing function?

A) $-\sqrt{\dfrac{p-1}{3p}} < x < \sqrt{\dfrac{p-1}{3p}}$

B) $x > \sqrt{\dfrac{p-1}{3p}}$ and $x < -\sqrt{\dfrac{p-1}{3p}}$

C) $\dfrac{1-p}{3p} < x < \dfrac{p-1}{3p}$

D) $x > \dfrac{p-1}{3p}$ and $< \dfrac{1-p}{3p}$

E) $-\sqrt{\frac{p-1}{3p}} < x < \sqrt{\frac{p-1}{3p}}$

F) $x > \sqrt{\frac{p-1}{3p}}$ and $x < -\sqrt{\frac{p-1}{3p}}$

127) Find the shortest distance between the line $y = x$ and $y = x^2 + 2$

A) $\frac{3\sqrt{2}}{8}$ B) $\frac{5\sqrt{2}}{8}$ C) $\frac{7\sqrt{2}}{8}$ D) $\frac{9\sqrt{2}}{8}$ E) $\frac{11\sqrt{2}}{8}$ F) $\frac{13\sqrt{2}}{8}$

128) Find the complete range of values of x which satisfy the following inequality:

$$\frac{1}{3}(3x-4) - \frac{1}{2}(x-2) < x.$$

A) $x > -\dfrac{1}{3}$ B) $x > -\dfrac{4}{3}$ C) $x > -\dfrac{5}{3}$ D) $x > -\dfrac{2}{3}$

E) $x < -\frac{2}{3}$ F) $x < -\frac{1}{3}$

129) $3\sqrt{\log_2 x} - \log_2 8x + 1 = 0$. Find the product of the two real roots.

A)1 B)2 C)4 D)8 E)16 F)32 G)64

130) How many real solutions does $x^4 + 8x^2 + 16 = 4x^2 - 12x + 9$ have?

A)none B)1 C)2 D)3 E)4

131) $5732a + 2134b + 2134c = 7866$
$2134a + 5732b + 2134c = 670$
$2134a + 2134b + 5732c = 11464$
Find abc.

A)1 B)2 C)3 D) -1 E) -2 F) -3

132) $1, 1, \frac{1}{2}, 2, \frac{1}{4}, 4, \frac{1}{8}, 8, \frac{1}{16}, 16 \ldots$ **is a sequence.**
Find the sum of the first 16 terms of the sequence.

A)256 B)$256\frac{127}{128}$ C)$255\frac{127}{128}$ D)255

E)251 F)$252\frac{127}{128}$ G)64

133) Find the greatest positive integer for k such that $49^k + 1$ is a factor of the sum of: $49^{125} + 49^{124} + \cdots + 49^2 + 49^1 + 49^0$

A)48 B)49 C)50 D)51 E)52 F)53 G)54 H)63

134) If $\frac{2^{x+2}-2}{2^{2x+1}} = 1$. Find the sum of the solutions.

A)0 B)1 C)2 D)3 E)4 F)5 G)6 H)7

135) Determine the range of values for m such that $y = \frac{3}{4}|x - 4| + 5$ and $y = mx + 3$ have 2 points of intersection.

A) $m > \frac{3}{4}$ B) $m > \frac{1}{2}$ C) $m < -\frac{3}{4}$

D) $m < -\frac{3}{4}, m > \frac{3}{4}$ E) $m < -\frac{3}{4}, m > \frac{1}{2}$ F) $\frac{1}{2} < m < \frac{3}{4}$

136) If $\sqrt{\log_2(2x^2) \times \log_4 16x} = \log_4 x^3$,
Then what is product of the values of x which satisfies the equation.

A) $4^{\frac{9}{5}}$ B) 4 C) 16 D) $4^{\frac{7}{5}}$ E) $4^{\frac{3}{5}}$ F) $4^{\frac{1}{5}}$

137) A bag contains red and blue balls. Gary picks out one ball and then another ball 15 seconds later . The probability that both balls were blue is $\frac{2}{15}$. How many red balls were there in the bag?

A) 1 B) 2 C) 3 D) 4 E) 5 F) 6 G) 7 H) 8

138) If $f(x) = 2x^4 - 6x^3 + 8x^2 + k$, for what range of values of k does f(x) have 2 solutions?

A) $k < 0$ B) $k >$ C) $k > 1$ D) $k < 1$ E) $k = 0$

139) Find the area bound between $y = x^{\frac{1}{3}}$ and $y = \frac{x}{4}$.

A) 1 B) 2 C) 4 D) 8 E) 16 F) 32

140) Find the locus of points which are equidistant from the centre of circles:
$$x^2 - 2x + y^2 - 8y - 8 = 0 \text{ and } x^2 + 4x + y^2 + 6y - 51 = 0$$

A) $y = \frac{3}{7}x - \frac{2}{7}$ B) $y = \frac{3}{7}x + \frac{2}{7}$ C) $y = -\frac{1}{7}x - \frac{2}{7}$
D) $y = -\frac{3}{7}x + \frac{2}{7}$ E) $y = -x - \frac{2}{7}$ F) $y = -\frac{3}{7}x - 1$

141) Given a geometric sequence has $\sum_{r=1}^{9} a_r = 4\lambda, \sum_{r=1}^{2} a_r = 4, \sum_{r=1}^{4} a_r = 20$ and $a_1 < 0$. Find the value of λ.

A) $\frac{511}{3}$ B) -171 C) $-\frac{257}{3}$ D) 171 E) 91 F) -91

142) Find the area bound between the curve $f(x) = x(x - a)(x + 2a)$, the lines $x = a$ and $x = -2a$

A) $\frac{7}{12}a^4$ B) $\frac{1}{4}a^4$ C) $\frac{37}{12}a^4$ D) $\frac{5}{6}a^4$

E) $\frac{11}{6}a^4$ F) $\frac{31}{12}a^4$ G) $\frac{37}{3}a^4$

143) $6 - \left(2 + 4(9)^{4-2\log_{\sqrt{3}} 3}\right) \log_{49} x = \log_7 x$. Find the value of x:

A) $\sqrt{7}$ B) $2\sqrt{7}$ C) $3\sqrt{7}$ D) $4\sqrt{7}$
E) $5\sqrt{7}$ F) $6\sqrt{7}$ G) $7\sqrt{7}$

144) The roots of $3y^2 + 13y - c = 0$ differ by 7. What is the value of c?

A) $\frac{68}{3}$ B) $\frac{209}{16}$ C) $\frac{122}{15}$

D) $\frac{353}{21}$ E) $\frac{123}{45}$ F) $\frac{123}{40}$

145) $\left(2x+\frac{p}{x}\right)^8$ **The constant term in this expansion is** 7×10^5**. What is the value of p?**

A)1 B)2 C)3 D)4

E)5 F)6 G)7 H)8

146) If $a=\sqrt{\frac{b+3}{b-k}}$**, then make b the subject of the formula.**

$A)b=\dfrac{ak+3}{(a^2-1)}$ $\quad$ B)$b=\dfrac{a^2k+3}{(a-1)}$ $\quad$ C)$b=\dfrac{a^2k+3}{(a^2-1)}$

D)$b=\dfrac{a^2k+3}{(1-a^2)}$ $\quad$ E)$b=\dfrac{a^2k+3}{(2a^2-1)}$ $\quad$ F)$b=\dfrac{a^2k+3}{(1-2a^2)}$

147) Find the sum of the solutions of $|\sqrt{x}-2|+\sqrt{x}(\sqrt{x}-4)+2=0$

A)10 B)9 C)4 D)5 E)8 F)12 G)1

148) Find the range of values of values of x which satisfy $\left(\frac{1}{2}\right)^{x^2-2x}<\frac{1}{4}$.

$A)1-\sqrt{3}<x<1+\sqrt{3}$ $\quad$ B)$x>3, x<-3$

C)$-3<x>3$ $\quad$ D)$x<1-\sqrt{3}$ and $x>1+\sqrt{3}$

$E)x<1-\sqrt{2}$ and $x>1+\sqrt{2}$ $\quad$ $F)1-\sqrt{2}<x<1+\sqrt{2}$

$G)1-\sqrt{5}<x<1+\sqrt{5}$ $\quad$ $H)x<1-\sqrt{5}$ and $x>1+\sqrt{5}$

149) $20, 19\frac{1}{3}, 18\frac{2}{3}$ **... is an arithemtic sequence. Find the least number of terms such that the sum of the sequence is 300?**

A)25,36 B)36 C)24 D)56 E)96 F)108 G)25

150) What is the infinite sum of: $\frac{1}{2}+\frac{1}{4}+\frac{2}{8}+\frac{3}{16}+\frac{5}{32}+\frac{8}{64}+\frac{13}{128}+\cdots$

A)1 B)2 C)4 D)8 E)16 F)32

151) The straight-line L passes through ($7\boldsymbol{a}$,5) and ($3\boldsymbol{a}$,3).
An equation of L is $\boldsymbol{x+by-12=0}$. Find the value of $\boldsymbol{a}$ and $\boldsymbol{b}$.

A) $a=-2, b=4$ B) $a=4, b=-8$ C) $a=3, b=7$

D) $a=-4, b=8$ E) $a=6, b=3$

152) Solve for $\boldsymbol{x}$ simultaneous equation:

$$\boldsymbol{y=2-4x}$$

$$\boldsymbol{3x^2+xy+11=0}$$

A) $x=2\pm2\sqrt{3}$, B) $x=2\pm3\sqrt{2}$ C) $1\pm2\sqrt{3}$ D) $x=4\pm6\sqrt{2}$

153) The first three terms of a geometric series are given by $\boldsymbol{8-x}$, $\boldsymbol{2x}$ and $\boldsymbol{x^2}$ respectively where $\boldsymbol{x>0}$. Find the value of the 7th term.

A) 64 B) 88 C) 256 D) 512 E) 1024

154) Let the function, $\boldsymbol{p(x)=\frac{1}{x-2}}$ and let another function, $\boldsymbol{q(x)=3x+4}$ Solve $\boldsymbol{qp(x)=16}$

A) $\frac{1}{2}$ B) $\frac{3}{4}$ C) $\frac{5}{4}$ D) $\frac{5}{2}$ E) $\frac{9}{4}$

155) $f(x) = \frac{12}{p\sqrt{x}} + x$, where p is a real constant and $x > 0$

Given that $f'(2) = 3$, find the value of p

A) $-2\sqrt{2}$ B) $-\frac{3}{4}\sqrt{2}$ C) $2\sqrt{3}$ D) $\frac{1}{2}\sqrt{3}$ E) $\frac{1}{2}$

156) What is the value of $2^{30} + 2^{30} + 2^{30} + 2^{30}$

A) 8^{120} B) 8^{30} C) 2^{32} D) 4^{30} E) 2^{34}

157) Alex is staying at a hotel which charges £75 per night plus tax for a room. A tax rate of 9% is levied to the room rate, and an additional onetime untaxed fee of £7 is charged by the hotel. Which of the following is Alex's total cost, for staying x nights.

A) $(75 + 0.09x) + 7$ B) $1.09(75x) + 7$

C) $1.09(75x + 7)$ D) $1.09(75 + 7)x$

158) A bag contains 4 blue balls and 7 green balls. A ball is selected at random from the bag and its colour is recorded. The ball is not replaced. A second ball is then selected at random, and its colour is also recorded. Find the probability that, both balls are green given that the second ball selected is green.

A) $\frac{3}{5}$ B) $\frac{1}{2}$ C) $\frac{3}{4}$ D) $\frac{3}{8}$ E) $\frac{5}{8}$ F) $\frac{2}{7}$

159) An arithmetic series is given by $(\boldsymbol{k}+\mathbf{1})+(\mathbf{2}\boldsymbol{k}+\mathbf{3})+(\mathbf{3}\boldsymbol{k}+\mathbf{5})+\cdots+\mathbf{303}$
Given that $S_n = 2568$, find the value of $\boldsymbol{k}$.

A) 14 B) 15 C) 16 D) 17 E) 18 F) 20

160) One of the roots of the equation, $\mathbf{2}\boldsymbol{x}^{\mathbf{2}}+\mathbf{9}\boldsymbol{x}-\boldsymbol{k}=\mathbf{0}$, where $\boldsymbol{k}$ is a constant, is 4 more than the other root. Find the value of $\boldsymbol{k}$.

A) $-\frac{77}{8}$ B) $\frac{55}{8}$ C) $\frac{175}{8}$

D) $-\frac{73}{8}$ E) $-\frac{17}{8}$

161) What is the remainder when $\mathbf{1234}\times\mathbf{5678}$ is divided by 5?

A) 0 B) 1 C) 2 D) 3 E) 4

162) There are fewer than 30 students in the Cambridge Economics class. One half of them play the violin, one quarter play cricket and one seventh will perform in the university play. What is the greatest number of students which can play cricket?

A) 3 B) 4 C) 5 D) 6 E) 7

163) Which of the following numbers is the largest?

A) $\frac{487}{121}$ B) $\frac{678}{173}$ C) $\frac{596}{153}$ D) $\frac{397}{101}$ E) $\frac{796}{203}$

164) Jacob cycles to work each day. Given the varying terrains, Jacob averages a speed of 12kmph for the first 5 minutes, followed by 15kmph for the next 10 minutes, then finally cycling for 15 minutes at a speed of 18kmph.
What was Jacob's average speed for the whole journey?

A) 13km/h B) 14km/h C) 15km/h

D) 16km/h E) 17km/h

165) The curve, C, has equation $\boldsymbol{y} = \frac{1}{x}$. C is then reflected in the line $\boldsymbol{y} = \mathbf{1}$, and this resulting image is reflected in the line $\boldsymbol{y} = -\boldsymbol{x}$. What is the equation of the final image?

A) $y = \frac{1}{x-1}$ B) $y = -\frac{1}{x-1}$ C) $y = \frac{1}{x-2}$ D) $y = -\frac{1}{x+2}$

166) In the expansion, $(\mathbf{1} + \boldsymbol{px})^{\mathbf{15}}$, the coefficients of $\boldsymbol{x}$ and $\boldsymbol{x}^{\mathbf{2}}$ are $(-\boldsymbol{q})$ and $(\mathbf{5}\boldsymbol{q})$ respectively.
Find the value of $\boldsymbol{q}$

A) $\frac{-5}{7}$ B) $\frac{17}{7}$ C) $\frac{45}{7}$ D) $\frac{75}{7}$ E) 15

167) Provided that $\boldsymbol{a} > \boldsymbol{b}$, and both are positive constants, solve the following simultaneous equations:

$$\boldsymbol{a} + \boldsymbol{b} = \mathbf{13}$$

$$\log_6 \boldsymbol{a} + \log_6 \boldsymbol{b} = \mathbf{2}$$

A) $a = 4, b = 9$ B) $a = 1, b = 12$ C) $a = 9, b = 4$ D) $a = 3, b = 10$

E) $a = 6, b = 7$ F) $a = 2, b = 11$

168) Simplify the algebraic fraction: $\frac{6x^3+3x^2-84x}{6x^2-33x+42}$

A) $\frac{2x(x-1)}{x+3}$ B) $\frac{x(x-2)}{x+1}$ C) $\frac{x(x+4)}{x-2}$ D) $\frac{2x(x-1)}{x+2}$ E) $\frac{x(x-1)}{x+2}$

169) The line, $\boldsymbol{l}$, has equation $\boldsymbol{y} = \mathbf{6} - \mathbf{2}\boldsymbol{x}$.
A second line, $\boldsymbol{m}$, is perpendicular to $\boldsymbol{l}$ and passes through the point (-6,0).

Find the area of the region enclosed by the two lines and $\boldsymbol{x}$-axis.

A)18 B) 27 C) $\frac{81}{5}$ D) $\frac{81}{2}$ E) $\frac{45}{2}$ F) $\frac{88}{5}$

170) Find the exact value of the area enclosed by the curve $\boldsymbol{y} = \boldsymbol{x}^2(\mathbf{2} - \boldsymbol{x})$ and the positive $\boldsymbol{x}$-axis.

A) $\frac{1}{2}$ B) $\frac{2}{3}$ C) 2 D) $\frac{4}{3}$ E) $\frac{8}{3}$

171) Mr and Mrs Harrison have two children. One of them is called Sarah. What is the probability that Mr and Mrs Harrison have two daughters?

A) $\frac{1}{4}$ B) $\frac{1}{3}$ C) $\frac{1}{2}$ D) $\frac{3}{4}$

172) The diagram shows ABCDEFGH, which is a regular octagon.
The two regular pentagons, KLQFP and MNREQ are equal and inscribed in the octagon. Find the angle $\boldsymbol{x}$.

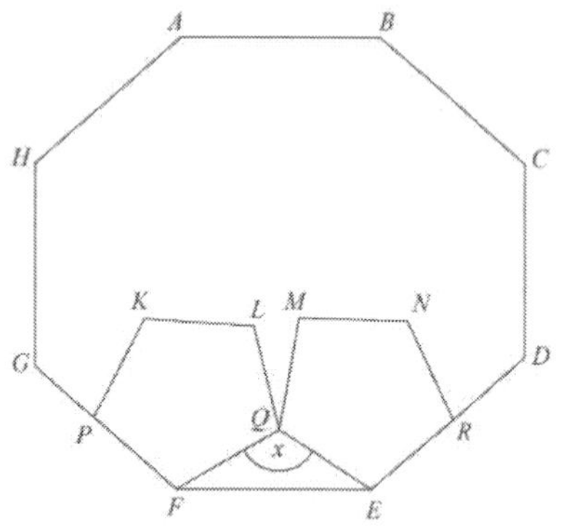

Diagram NOT accurately drawn

A) 108° B) 144° C) 168° D) 120° E) 126°

173) Benjamin goes to the archery range one weekend to practise his shooting. Given that each attempt is independent, and Benjamin has a 0.3 chance of hitting the target, what is the probability he hits the target for the first time on his third attempt.

A) 0.147 B) 0.49 C) 0.063 D) 0.09 E) 0.21

174) Evaluate the integral

$$\int_2^8 |x-5|dx$$

A) -18 B) -9 C) 27 D) 36 E) 45 F) 9

175) The curve, C has equation $\boldsymbol{y = \frac{1}{x} + 27x^3}$. C has stationary points at the values $\boldsymbol{x = \pm a}$.
Find the value of $\boldsymbol{a}$.

A) $\frac{1}{2}$ B) $\frac{1}{3}$ C) $\frac{1}{4}$ D) 2 E) 3

F) 4 G) 6

176) Find the coefficient of $\boldsymbol{x}$ in the expression:
$\boldsymbol{(1+x)^0 + (1+x)^1 + (1+x)^2 + (1+x)^3 + \ldots + (1+x)^{59} + (1+x)^{60}}$

A)60 B) 61 C) 119 D) 1830 E) 3660

177) Find the set of values for $\boldsymbol{x}$ which satisfies the inequality
$\boldsymbol{2x^2 - 5x - 12 < 0}$

A) $-\frac{3}{2} < x < 4$ B) $-3 < x < 8$ C) $-2 < x < 1$ D) $x < -\frac{3}{2}$ or $x > 4$

E) < -3 or $x > 8$ F) < -2 or $x > 1$

178) $\boldsymbol{Y}$ is proportional to the square of $\boldsymbol{x}$
When $\boldsymbol{x = 3, y = 36}$

Given $\boldsymbol{x > 0}$, what is the value of $\boldsymbol{x}$ when $\boldsymbol{y = 9}$

A)324 B) $\frac{9}{2}$ C) $\frac{9}{4}$ D) 2 E) $\frac{3}{2}$

179) The ratio of Q:R is 7:2 and the ratio of R:S is 3:7
Given that the ratio of Q:S can be written in the form of 1:$\boldsymbol{n}$, what is the value of $\boldsymbol{n}$?

A) $\frac{1}{2}$ B) $\frac{2}{3}$ C) $\frac{7}{2}$ D) 2 E) 3 F) 14

180) A new television is bought on sale for £12,000
Given that the sale benefitted consumers by giving a 20% discount, what was the original price of the television?

A)£10,800 B) £12,800 C) £15,000 D) £13,500

181) How can the following trigonometric equation be written in a form using only the cosine trigonometric function?
$\boldsymbol{2sinx} = \frac{\boldsymbol{4cosx-1}}{\boldsymbol{tanx}}$

A) $cos^2x + cosx - 4 = 0$ B) $3cos^2x - 2cosx + 6 = 0$ C) $x - cosx + 1 = 0$ D) $6cos^2x - cosx - 2 = 0$ E) $4cos^2x - 2cosx - 1 = 0$

182) Simplify $\frac{\boldsymbol{16^{\frac{1}{2}}}}{\boldsymbol{81^{\frac{3}{4}}}}$

A) $\frac{2}{3}$ B) 2 C) $\frac{4}{27}$ D) $\frac{1}{2}$ E) $\frac{1}{3}$

183) The figure below shows a circle with centre C at (4,2).

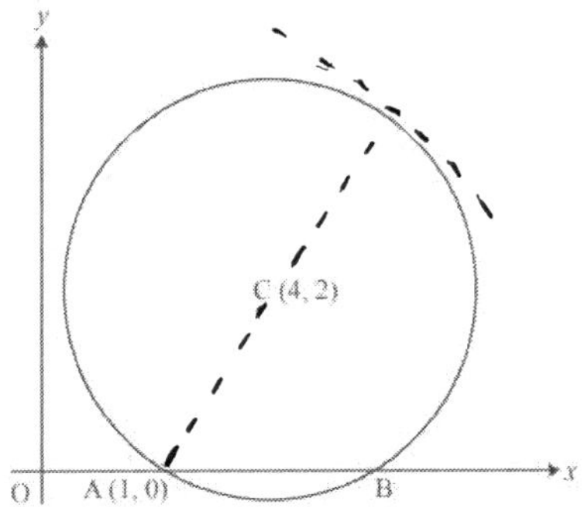

Given AD is the diameter, find the value of $\boldsymbol{b}$, where the tangent of the circle at D has equation $\boldsymbol{y} = \boldsymbol{ax} + \boldsymbol{b}$.

A) $\frac{3}{2}$ B) $\frac{9}{4}$ C) 2 D) $\frac{29}{2}$ E) 4

184) Given that $\boldsymbol{x^y} = \frac{1}{8}$, what is the value of $\boldsymbol{x^{-3y}}$.

A) 729 B) $\frac{1}{9}$ C) 128 D) $\frac{1}{64}$ E) 256 F) 512 G) 81

185) Sam's age is a two-digit number, which is also a power of 5. Nick's age is also a 2-digit number, but a power of 2. Given that the sum of the digits of the two ages is an odd number, what is the product of Sam's and Nick's age?

A) 1600 B) 80 C) 2000 D) 625

E) 5000

186) The right-angle triangle below has side lengths of $\boldsymbol{x\ cm}$ and $\boldsymbol{(12-x)cm}$

Find the greatest possible area of the triangle.

A) 9 B) 18 C) 36 D) 45 E) 72

187) Find the value of $\int_1^4 \frac{3-2x}{x\sqrt{x}}$

A) -1 B) -3 C) $-\frac{7}{2}$ D) $-\frac{13}{2}$ E) 2 F) $\frac{17}{2}$

188) Rathore states that if $\boldsymbol{f'(x) > 0}$ for all real values of $\boldsymbol{x}$, then $\boldsymbol{f(x) > 0}$ for all real values of x.

Which of the following would disprove the statement of Rathore?

A) $f(x) = x^2 - 1$ B) $f(x) = x^2 + 1$ C) $f(x) = 1 - x$

D) $f(x) = x^3 + x + 1$ E) $f(x) = 2^x$

189) Make $\boldsymbol{x}$ the subject of the formula: $\boldsymbol{y} = \frac{1-2x}{x+3}$.

A) $x = \frac{2-3y}{y+2}$ B) $x = \frac{2y-6}{y-2}$ C) $x = \frac{1-3y}{y+2}$ D) $x = \frac{1-2y}{y-2}$

E) $x = \frac{3-3y}{y+2}$

190) Given that $\boldsymbol{f(x) = 2x^2 + kx + 18 = 0}$, find the range of values for $\boldsymbol{k}$ for which $\boldsymbol{f(x)}$ has no real roots.

A) $k < -12, k > 12$ B) $k < -4, k > 4$ C) $k < -16, k > 16$

D) $-16 < k < 16$ E) $-4 < k < 4$ F) $-12 < k < 12$

191) The expression $\boldsymbol{1 + \frac{1}{1+\frac{1}{1+\frac{1}{5}}} = \frac{x}{y}}$, where $\boldsymbol{x}$ and $\boldsymbol{y}$ do not share any common factors except from 1. What is the value of $\boldsymbol{x + y}$?

A) 14 B) 28 C) 17 D) 25 E) 42 F)19

192) Find the value of $\boldsymbol{y}$ in the hexagon below.

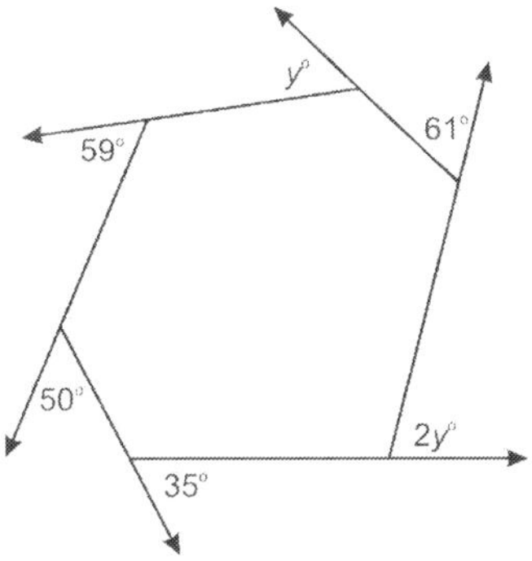

A)20° B) 40° C) $\frac{155}{3}°$ D) 48° E) 54°

193) Let $\boldsymbol{f(x) = x^3 - 7x^2 + 13x - 4}$.
Given that $\boldsymbol{f(4) = 0}$, find the sum of all the roots of $\boldsymbol{f(x)}$

A)7 B) $7 + \sqrt{5}$ C) $7 - 2\sqrt{5}$

D) $\frac{-1+\sqrt{3}}{2}$ E) 0 F) 4

194) The expression $\frac{2x^2-x^{\frac{3}{2}}}{\sqrt{x}}$ can be written in the form $\boldsymbol{cx^a - x^b}$.
Find the value of $\boldsymbol{a - b + c}$

A)2 B) 6 C) $\frac{3}{2}$ D) $\frac{5}{2}$ E) 3 F) 4

195) On Friday, the value of a cricket bat reduces by 30%. The next day, the price reduces even further by 20% of its most recent price. What is the overall reduction in price of the cricket bat?

A)6% B) 15% C) 25%

D) 40% E) 44% F) 56%

196) The diagram below shows a $\mathbf{4 \times 4}$ grid. It also shows that $\mathbf{1 + 3 + 5 + 7 = 16}$

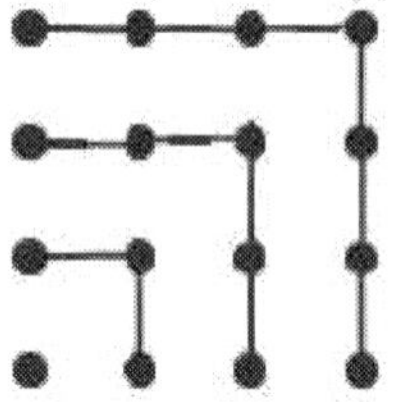

What is the value of $\mathbf{1 + 3 + 5 + 7 + 9 + 11 + \cdots + 41}$?

A)256 B) 361 C) 400 D) 441 F) 484

197) In shape below, the side length of one square is equal to 18cm and the inner hexagon is regular. What is the perimeter of the whole shape?

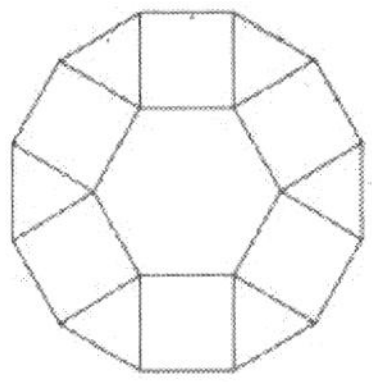

A) 180cm B) 216cm C) 256cm D) 324cm E) 400cm

198) Solve the equation $\log_3(x+11) - \log_3(x-5) = 2$

A) 1 B) 2 C) $\frac{5}{2}$ D) $\frac{9}{2}$ E) 7

199) Given that $y = \frac{x^3}{8}$, what is the value of $k+n$, where $\frac{1}{2}y^{-2} = kx^n$

A) 26 B) 32 C) 44 D) 15 E) 12 F) 9

200) By simplifying the expression $\frac{3-2\sqrt{5}}{\sqrt{5}-1}$ into the form $p + q\sqrt{5}$, find the value of $q - p$.

A) 0 B) $\frac{3}{2}$ C) 2 D) 4 E) $\frac{7}{2}$

201) x, y, and z are consecutive terms of a geometric sequence. If $x + y + z = \frac{7}{3}$ and $x^2 + y^2 + z^2 = \frac{91}{9}$, what is xyz?

A) $-\frac{1}{3}$ B) -1 C) 1 D) $\frac{2}{3}$ E) 3

202) $\boldsymbol{x}$ satisfies the equation $\mathbf{2\log_3 x - 3\log_3 \frac{1}{x} = 10}$. What is the value of $\boldsymbol{x}$?

A) $\frac{1}{3}$ B) 3 C) 9 D) 27 E) 81

203) When dropped, a ball takes 1 second to hit the ground. It then takes 90% of this time to rebound to its new height, and this continues until the ball comes to rest. How long does it take for the ball to come to rest?

A)19 B)20 C)21 D)22 E)23

204) The tangent to $\boldsymbol{y = x^2\sqrt{1-x}}$ at $\boldsymbol{x = -3}$ cuts the axes at points A and B. What is the area of triangle OAB?

A) $\frac{2854}{149}$ B) $\frac{3586}{149}$ C) $\frac{2584}{152}$ D) $\frac{3267}{152}$ E) $\frac{4572}{165}$

205) Find the equation of the normal to $\boldsymbol{y = \frac{x+1}{x^2-2}}$ at the point where $\boldsymbol{x = 1}$

A) $y = -\frac{1}{5}x + \frac{11}{5}$ B) $y = -\frac{1}{5}x - \frac{11}{5}$ C) $y = -5x - 3$ D) $y = -5x + 3$

E) $y = \frac{1}{5}x - \frac{11}{5}$ F) $y = \frac{1}{5}x + \frac{11}{5}$ G) $y = \frac{1}{6}x - \frac{14}{5}$

206) A manufacturer of open steel boxes must make one with a square base and a capacity of $\mathbf{1}\mathrm{m}^3$. The steel costs £2 per square metre. What are the dimensions of the box which would cost the least in steel to make?

A) 1m by 1m by 1m B) $\sqrt{3}$ m by $\sqrt{3}$ m by $\frac{1}{\sqrt{3}}$ m C) $\sqrt{3}$ m by $\sqrt{3}$ m by $\frac{1}{3}$ m

D) $\sqrt{2}$ m by $\sqrt{2}$ m by $\frac{1}{2}$ m E) $\sqrt[3]{2}$ m by $\sqrt[3]{2}$ m by $\frac{1}{\sqrt[3]{2}}$ m F) $\sqrt[3]{2}$ m by $\sqrt[3]{2}$ m by $\frac{1}{\sqrt[3]{4}}$

207) If $\sin x = -\frac{3}{4}, \pi \le x \le \frac{3\pi}{2}$, what is the value of $\cos x \tan 2x$?

A) $2\sqrt{6}$ B) $2\sqrt{7}$ C) $3\sqrt{5}$ D) $-3\sqrt{6}$ E) $-3\sqrt{7}$ F) -4 G) 9

208) $x + 3$ and $x - 2$ are the first two terms of a geometric series. What are the values of x for which the series converges?

A) $x > -1$ B) $x > -\frac{1}{2}$ C) $x > 0$ D) $x < -1$

E) $x < -\frac{1}{2}$ F) $x > \frac{1}{2}$ G) $x > 1$

209) Suppose that x and y satisfy the equations:

$\mathbf{3 \sin x + 4 \cos y = 5}$

$\mathbf{4 \sin y + 3 \cos x = 2}$

Using the fact that $\sin(x + y) = \sin x \cos y + \cos x \sin y$.

What is the value of $\sin(x + y)$?

A) $-\frac{1}{2}$ B) $-\frac{1}{4}$ C) $-\frac{1}{6}$ D) $-\frac{1}{8}$

E) $\frac{1}{8}$ F) $\frac{1}{6}$ G) $\frac{1}{4}$ H) $\frac{1}{2}$

210) ABCDEF is a regular hexagon with sides length of 9. A circular arc with radius 9 is drawn from centre D. What is the area of the shaded region?

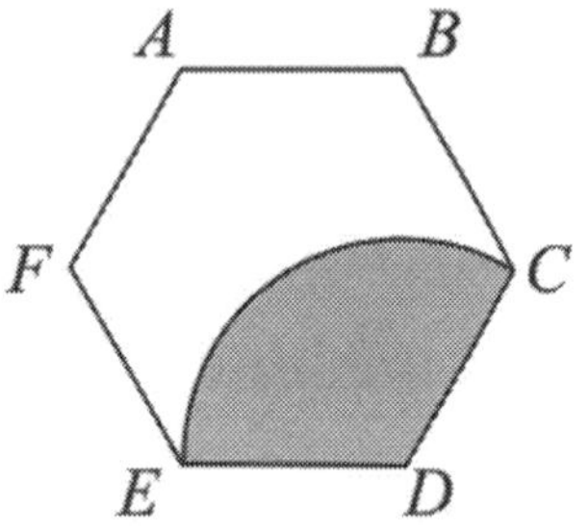

A) 15π B) 18π C) 21π D) 24π

E) 27π F) 30π G) 33π

211) Alice runs around a circular track with a radius of 60m at a constant speed of 6m/s. Dylan runs around a track with a shape of an equilateral triangle with side length $\boldsymbol{x}$ m, at a constant speed of 5m/s. Alice and Dylan each run one lap in the same amount of time. What is $\boldsymbol{x}$?

A) $\frac{50\pi}{3}$ B) 20π C) 25π D) $\frac{10}{3}$

E) 50π

212) Given that $\boldsymbol{f'(x) = x^2 - 3x + 2}$ and $\boldsymbol{f(1) = 3}$, find $\boldsymbol{f(3)}$.

A) $\frac{14}{9}$ B) $\frac{11}{7}$ C) $\frac{13}{6}$ D) $\frac{17}{5}$ E) $\frac{19}{5}$ F) $\frac{23}{3}$

213) If $\boldsymbol{2^{200} \times 2^{203} + 2^{163} \times 2^{241} + 2^{126} \times 2^{277} = 32^n}$, what is the value of $\boldsymbol{n}$?

A)78 B) 79 C) 80 D) 81 E) 82

214) For the equation $\log_a b = \frac{\log_b c}{2} = \frac{\log_c a}{4}$, a, b, and c are real numbers greater than 1. What is the value of $\log_a b + \log_b c + \log_c a$?

A) $\frac{5}{2}$ B) $\frac{7}{2}$ C) $\frac{9}{2}$ D) $\frac{11}{2}$ E) 4

215) **ABC** is an equilateral triangle with side length 1. Point D and **E** are set on extensions of segment **AB** and segment AC respectively, so that **AD** = **CE**. Given that DE = $\sqrt{13}$, what is the area of triangle BDE?

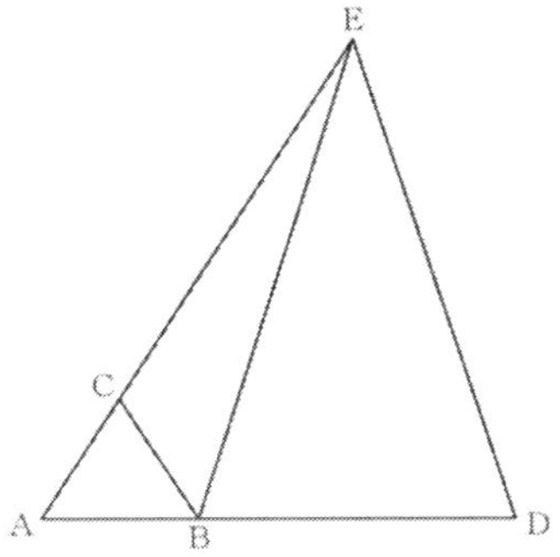

A) $\sqrt{2}$ B) $2\sqrt{2}$ C) $3\sqrt{2}$ D) $\sqrt{3}$ E) $2\sqrt{3}$ F) $3\sqrt{3}$

216) Given $f(x) = a(x-2)(x-b)$, where a and b are natural numbers,
$f(0) = 6$ ... (1) and

$f(x) > 0$ when $x > 2$ ... (2)

What is the value of $f(4)$?

A) 10 B) 12 C) 14 D) 16 E) 18

217) When $y = 5^x$ is translated by the vector $\binom{a}{b}$, it becomes $y = \frac{1}{9} \times 5^{x-1} + 2$. ($a$ and b are constants)
What is the value of $5^a + b$?

A) 45 B) 46 C) 47 D) 48 E) 49

218) What is the coefficient of x^3 in the expansion of $\left(x + \frac{4}{x^2}\right)^6$?

A) 21 B) 24 C) 27 D) 30
E) 33 F) 36

219) What is the value of $f'(1)$ when $f(x) = x\ln(2x - 1)$?

A) $\frac{1}{3}$ B) $\frac{1}{2}$ C) 1 D) $\frac{3}{2}$ E) 2 F) $\frac{7}{2}$

220) a is a number randomly chosen from $1, 3, 5$ and 7. b is a number randomly chosen from $4, 6, 8$ and 10. What is the probability that $1 < \frac{b}{a} < 4$?

A) $\frac{5}{16}$ B) $\frac{3}{8}$ C) $\frac{7}{16}$ D) $\frac{8}{16}$ E) $\frac{9}{16}$ F) $\frac{5}{8}$

221) Rearrange the following equation for x in terms of y.

$$y = 6\sqrt[3]{\frac{3x+1}{4}} + 5$$

A) $x = \frac{4}{3}\left(\frac{y-5}{6}\right)^3 - \frac{1}{3}$ B) $x = \frac{4}{3}\left(\frac{y-5}{6}\right)^3 + \frac{1}{3}$ C) $x = \frac{4}{3}\left(\frac{y-5}{6}\right)^2 - \frac{1}{3}$

D) $x = \frac{4}{3}\left(\frac{y-5}{6}\right)^2 + \frac{1}{3}$ E) $x = \frac{2}{3}\left(\frac{y-5}{3}\right)^3 - \frac{1}{3}$ F) $x = \frac{2}{3}\left(\frac{y-5}{3}\right)^3 + \frac{1}{3}$

G) $x = \frac{4}{3}\left(\frac{y-5}{6}\right)^3 - \frac{2}{3}$

222) The equation $\boldsymbol{x^3 - x^2 - 8x + k = 0}$ has two real roots. What is the value of $\boldsymbol{k}$? $(\boldsymbol{k > 0})$

A) 6 B) 7 C) 8 D) 9 E) 10 F) 11

G) 12 H) 13

223) Solve $\boldsymbol{\sqrt[3]{2} \times 2^{\frac{2}{3}}}$

A) 1 B) 2 C) 4 D) 8 E) 16

224) Given $\boldsymbol{f(x) = x^3 - 2x - 7}$, what is $\boldsymbol{f'(1)}$?

A) 1 B) 2 C) 3 D) 4 E) 5

225) Solve $\boldsymbol{\int_0^2 (3x^2 + 6x)\,dx}$

A) 18 B) 19 C) 20 D) 21 E) 22 F) 23

226) It is given that $\boldsymbol{f(x) = x^2 - 2x}$. What is the area enclosed by $\boldsymbol{y = f(x)}$ and $\boldsymbol{y = -f(x-1) - 1}$?

A) $\frac{1}{6}$ B) $\frac{1}{4}$ C) $\frac{1}{3}$ D) $\frac{7}{12}$ E) $\frac{1}{2}$ F) $\frac{5}{6}$

227) The function $\boldsymbol{f(x) = x^3 - 3ax^2 + 3(a^2 - 1)x}$ ($\boldsymbol{a}$ is a constant) has maximum of 4 and $\boldsymbol{f(-2) > 0}$. What is $\boldsymbol{f(-1)}$?

A) 0 B) 1 C) 2 D) 3 E) 4

228) Sequence $\{a_n\}$ satisfies $a_{n+1} + a_n = 3n - 1$, where n is all the natural numbers. When $a_3 = 4$, what is the value of $a_1 \times a_5$?

A) 1 B) 2 C) 3 D) 4 E) 5 F) 6

G) 7 H) 8

229) In how many different orders can you pick three red balls, two blue balls, and a yellow ball?

A) 52 B) 56 C) 60 D) 64 E) 68

230) There are two points $(2, \log_4 a)$ and $(3, \log_2 b)$, where $a, b > 0$. A straight line passing both points passes $(0, 0)$, what is the value of $\log_a b$? $(a \neq 1)$

A) $\frac{5}{4}$ B) 1 C) $\frac{3}{4}$ D) $\frac{1}{2}$ E) $\frac{1}{4}$

231) When two different cards were chosen randomly from card 1 to 9 inclusive, the sum of the numbers on the picked card was even. What is the probability that both cards had odd numbers?

A) $\frac{1}{2}$ B) $\frac{5}{8}$ C) $\frac{3}{4}$ D) $\frac{7}{8}$ E) $\frac{1}{4}$ F) $\frac{3}{4}$ G) $\frac{5}{12}$

232) A die is thrown twice, and the numbers are recorded. The first number is a and the second number is b, what is the probability that $|a - 3| + |b - 3| = 2$ or $a = b$?

A) $\frac{1}{4}$ B) $\frac{1}{3}$ C) $\frac{5}{12}$ D) $\frac{1}{2}$ E) $\frac{1}{5}$ F) $\frac{7}{12}$

233) Triangle ABC is inscribed in a circle with radius 15. Given that $\boldsymbol{\sin B} - \frac{\mathbf{7}}{\mathbf{10}}$, what is the length of AC?

A) 18 B) 19 C) 20 D) 21 E) 22

234) Find $\frac{dy}{dx}$ when $y(x) = xe^{3x}$

A) $e^{3x} + xe^{3x}$ B) $e^{x}(1 + 3x)$ C) $e^{\frac{1}{3}x}(1 + 3x)$

D) $e^{3x}(1 + 3x)$ E) $e^{3x}(1 - 3x)$ F) $e^{3x}(1 + x)$

235) What is the value of $\boldsymbol{k}$ for which the two roots of the equation $\mathbf{3}x^2 + \mathbf{4}kx + k - \mathbf{1} = \mathbf{0}$ are closest together?

A) $\frac{3}{8}$ B) $\frac{1}{2}$ C) $\frac{5}{8}$ D) $\frac{1}{3}$ E) $\frac{4}{9}$

236) In the given diagram, **OA** = **3** cm, **AB** = **2** cm, **BC** = **4** cm, ∠**COD** = **30°**. What is the area of the shaded area?

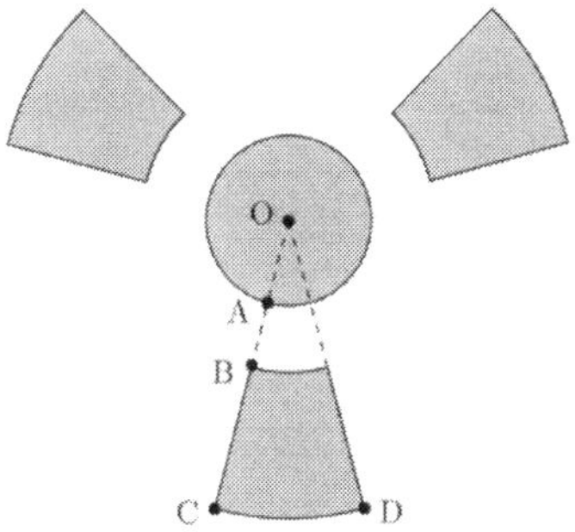

A) 17π B) 18π C) 19π D) 20π E) 21π F) 22π

G) 23π

237) What is the minimum value of the function $\boldsymbol{f(x) = \log_2(x^2 - 4x + 20)}$ when $\boldsymbol{-3 \leq x \leq 3}$?

A) 2 B) 3 C) 4 D) 5 E) 6 F) 7 G)8

238) $\boldsymbol{0 < \theta < \frac{\pi}{2}}$ and $\boldsymbol{\tan\theta = \frac{3}{4}}$, what is the value of $\boldsymbol{\cos\left(\frac{\pi}{2} - \theta\right) + 2\sin(\pi - \theta)}$?

A)1 B) $\frac{6}{5}$ C) $\frac{7}{5}$ D) $\frac{8}{5}$ E) $\frac{9}{5}$ F) 2

239) $\{\boldsymbol{a_n}\}$ is an arithmetic sequence where $\boldsymbol{a_1}$ and difference are not 0. Its terms $\boldsymbol{a_2}$, $\boldsymbol{a_5}$, and $\boldsymbol{a_{14}}$ form a geometric sequence in the given order. What is $\frac{a_{23}}{a_3}$?

A) 5 B) 6 C) 7 D) 8 E) 9

240) 6 dots equally divide circumference of a circle with radius 3. Out of the 6, 3 dots that are continuous to each other are**A B** and **C**. Arc AC does not include dot B and has point P, where **AP + CP = 8**. What is the area of rectangle **ABCP**?

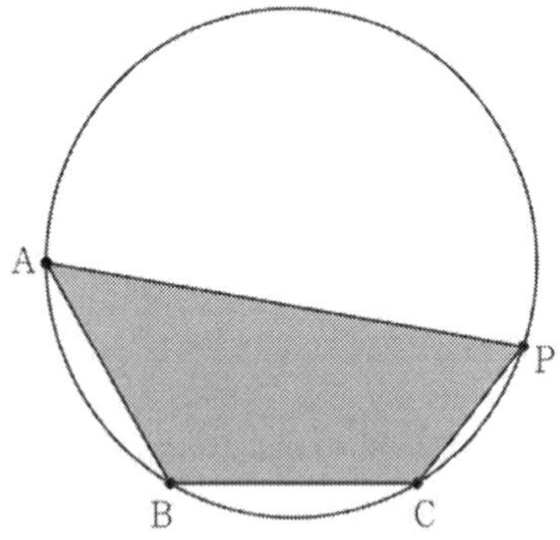

A) $\frac{13\sqrt{3}}{3}$ B) $\frac{16\sqrt{3}}{3}$ C) $\frac{19\sqrt{3}}{3}$ D) $\frac{22\sqrt{3}}{3}$ E) $\frac{25\sqrt{3}}{3}$

241) Find the value of $\mathbf{8\sin\frac{\pi}{6}+\tan\frac{\pi}{4}}$

A) 1 B) 2 C) 3 D) 4 E) 5

F) 6 G) 7

242) Find the value of $\mathbf{\log 20+\log 5}$

A) 2 B) 4 C) 6 D) 8 E) e^2 F) e^4 G) $\frac{1}{2}$

243) When the sum of all real roots of the equation $\mathbf{\frac{2}{\sqrt{3}}\sin(x+\frac{\pi}{3})-\frac{7}{8}=0}$ is expressed as $\mathbf{\frac{q}{p}\pi}$, find the value of $\mathbf{p+q}$. (Given that $\mathbf{0\le x\le 2\pi}$ and $\mathbf{p}$ and $\mathbf{q}$ are coprime natural numbers)

A) 6 B) 7 C) 8 D) 9 E) 10 F) 11

G) 12 H) 13

244) For a sequence $\{a_n\}$, $\mathbf{a_1=6, a_{n+1}=a_n+3^n\ \ (n=1,2,3,\dots)}$. What is $\mathbf{a_4}$?

A) 36 B) 39 C) 42 D) 45 E) 48 F) 51

245) Two lines $\mathbf{y=\left(\frac{1}{3}\right)^x, y=\left(\frac{1}{9}\right)^x}$ meet $\mathbf{y=9}$ at point A and B respectively. What is the area of triangle OAB, where O is the origin?

A) $\frac{9}{2}$ B) 5 C) $\frac{11}{2}$ D) 6 E) $\frac{13}{2}$ F) 7

246) Find real number x that satisfies the equation $3^x - 3^{4-x} = 24$

A) 1 B) $\frac{3}{2}$ C) 2 D) $\frac{5}{2}$ E) 3

247) Find the sum of all possible values of natural number a, so that $\sqrt[3]{-x^2 + 2ax - 6a} < 0$ for all x

A) 3 B) 6 C) 10 D) 15 E) 21

F) 28 G) 36

248) ***W*hat** is the sum of all possible values of n for $\log_n 4 \times \log_2 9$, where n is a natural number greater than 2?

A) 93 B) 94 C) 95 D) 96 E) 97 F) 98

249) A quadratic equation $x^2 - 24x + 10 = 0$ has two roots α ***and*** β, where the three numbers α, k, β form a geometric sequence in the given order. What is the value of k?

A) 0 B) 1 C) 3 D) 6 E) 9 F)12 G) 15

250) The probability that a salesman forgets his wallet behind in any store is $\frac{1}{5}$. Suppose this salesman visits two stores in succession and leaves his wallet behind in one of them. What is the probability that he left his wallet in the first store?

A) $\frac{2}{9}$ B) $\frac{3}{9}$ C) $\frac{4}{9}$ D) $\frac{5}{9}$ E) $\frac{6}{9}$

251) The following box-and-whisker plot represents the commute time, in minutes, for a group of workers. The range is 23 minutes, and the interquartile range is 10 minutes. What is the value of $\boldsymbol{p-q}$?

A) -10 B) -11 C) -12 D) -13 E) -14 F) -15

252) A particle is moving in a straight line, and has velocity of $\boldsymbol{v}$ kms^{-1} $\boldsymbol{and}$ displacement $\boldsymbol{s}$ km. The velocity $\boldsymbol{v}$ is $\boldsymbol{v(t) = 3e^{2t} + 2t}$. When $\boldsymbol{t = 0, s = 8}$.
What is the expression for the displacement of the particle in terms of $\boldsymbol{t}$

A) $s(t) = \frac{3e^{2t}}{2} + t^2$ B) $s(t) = \frac{3e^{t}}{2} + t^2 + 6.5$ C) $s(t) = \frac{3e^{2t}}{2} + t^2 + 6.5$

D) $s(t) = \frac{3e^{2t}}{4} + t^2 + 9$ E) $s(t) = \frac{3e^{2t}}{4} + t^3 + 9$ F) $s(t) = e^{2t} + t^2 + 5$

G) $s(t) = e^{2t} + t^2$

253) An integer$\boldsymbol{n}$, is chosen at random where n is positive and between 10 and 99 inclusive If every integer has equal chances of getting chosen, what is the probability that the sum of the digits of $\boldsymbol{n}$ is a multiple of 7?

A) $\frac{1}{10}$ B) $\frac{11}{90}$ C) $\frac{2}{15}$ D) $\frac{13}{90}$ E) $\frac{7}{45}$ F) $\frac{1}{6}$

254) The following box-and-whisker plot shows the number of tweets sent by students during school lunch on a particular day. One person sent $\boldsymbol{k}$ tweets, where $\boldsymbol{k} > \mathbf{7}$. Given that $\boldsymbol{k}$ is an outlier, find the least value of $\boldsymbol{k}$.

A) 12.5 B) 13 C) 13.5 D) 14 E) 14.5

F) 15 G) 15.5 H) 16

255) Suppose that $\boldsymbol{a}, \boldsymbol{b}, \boldsymbol{c}, \boldsymbol{d}$ and $\boldsymbol{e}$ are consecutive positive integers with $\boldsymbol{a} < \boldsymbol{b} < \boldsymbol{c} < \boldsymbol{d} < \boldsymbol{e}$. If $\boldsymbol{a}^2 + \boldsymbol{b}^2 + \boldsymbol{c}^2 = \boldsymbol{d}^2 + \boldsymbol{e}^2$, what is the value of $\boldsymbol{a}$?

A) 10 B) 11 C) 12 D) 13 E) 14 F) 15

256) $\boldsymbol{g}(\boldsymbol{x}) = \mathbf{3}\boldsymbol{f}(\boldsymbol{x} - \mathbf{2}) + \mathbf{1}$ for all real numbers of $\boldsymbol{x}$. The graph of $\boldsymbol{g}(\boldsymbol{x})$ is obtained from $\boldsymbol{f}(\boldsymbol{x})$ after a vertical stretch by a factor of $\boldsymbol{k}$ followed by a translation by the vector $\binom{\boldsymbol{a}}{\boldsymbol{b}}$. What is the value of $\boldsymbol{k} \times \boldsymbol{a} \times \boldsymbol{b}$?

A) 6 B) 7 C) 8 D) 9 E) 10

257) Two graphs $\boldsymbol{y} = -\frac{\mathbf{1}}{\mathbf{2}}|\boldsymbol{x}|$ and $\boldsymbol{y} = \mathbf{2}|\boldsymbol{x}| - \boldsymbol{a}$, ($\boldsymbol{a}$ is a positive integer) enclose a region of area 40 square units. What is the value of $\boldsymbol{a}$?

A) 8 B) 9 C) 10 D) 11 E) 12

258) A car and a van drive from London to Cambridge. The car travels at a constant speed of 40km/h and the van travels at a constant speed of 50km/h. The van passes the car 10 minutes before the car arrives at Cambridge. How many minutes pass between the time at which the van arrives at Cambridge and the time at which the car arrives at Cambridge?

A) 2 minutes B) 4 minutes C) 6 minutes D) 8 minutes E) 10 minutes

259) The average height of Isaac, James and Karl is 4% larger than the average height of Isaac and James. If Isaac and James are each 175cm tall, how tall is Karl?

A) 183 cm	B) 184 cm	C) 185 cm	D) 190 cm
E) 193 cm	F) 196 cm	G) 196.5 cm	

260) Solve the inequality $\boldsymbol{f(|x|) < \frac{8}{3}}$, where $\boldsymbol{f(x) = \frac{4x}{5-x}}$, for $\boldsymbol{x \neq 5}$.

A) $\{x < -5 \cup x > 5\}$

B) $\{-2 < x < 2 \cup x > 5\}$

C) $\{x < -5 \cup -2 < x < 2 \cup x > 5\}$

D) $\{x < 2\}$

E) $\{x < -5 \cup -2 < x < 2\}$

F) $\{x < -5 \cup -2 < x < 5\}$

261) Max graphs six possible lines of the form $\boldsymbol{y = mx + b}$ where $\boldsymbol{m}$ is either 1 or -2, and $\boldsymbol{b}$ is either 0, 1 or 2. For example one of the lines is $\boldsymbol{y = x + 2}$. The lines are all graphed on the same axes. There are exactly $\boldsymbol{n}$ distinct points, each of which lies on two or more of these lines. What is the value of $\boldsymbol{n}$?

A)6 B) 7 C) 8 D) 9 E) 10

262) Given that $\log_{x^2} y = 9\log_y(x^2)$ find all the possible expressions of y as a function of x.

A) $y = \frac{1}{x^6}$ or x^6 B) $y = \frac{1}{x^5}$ or x^5 C) $y = \frac{1}{x}$ or x

D) $y = -\frac{1}{x^6}$ or $-x^6$ E) $y = -\frac{1}{x^5}$ or $-x^5$ F) $y = -\frac{1}{x}$ or -x

263) If $3k = 10$ what is the value of $\frac{6k}{5} - 2$?

A) 1 B) 2 C) 3 D) 4 E) 5 F) 6 G) 7

264) At 7:00 am yesterday, Sean correctly determined what time it had been 100 hours before. What was his answer?

A) 1:00 am B) 2:00 pm C) 3:00 am D) 1:00 pm E) 2:00 am F) 3:00 pm

265) When the line with equation $y = -2x + 7$ is reflected across the line with equation $x = 3$, the equation of the resulting line is $y = ax + b$. What is the value of $2a + b$?

A) -1 B) $-\frac{3}{8}$ C) $-\frac{1}{7}$ D) 0 E) $\frac{1}{5}$ F) $\frac{2}{3}$

266) Solve the inequality $f(|x|) < 2$, where $f(x) = 1 + \frac{4x}{x+3}$ $for\ x \neq -3$

A) $-2 < x < 1$ B) $-1 < x < 0$ C) $-1 < x < 1$

D) $0 < x < 1$ E) $1 < x < 2$

267) $\boldsymbol{f(x) = \log_k(8x - 2x^2)}$ $\boldsymbol{for\ 0 < x < 4}$, where $\boldsymbol{k > 0}$. The equation $\boldsymbol{f(x) = 3}$ has exactly one solution. What is the value of $\boldsymbol{k}$?

A) 7 B) 6 C) 5 D) 4 E) 3 F) 2

268) A six faced die is tossed, and its total number of dots on the five faces that are not lying on the table is counted. What is the probability that the total is at least 19?

A) $\frac{1}{12}$ B) $\frac{1}{4}$ C) $\frac{1}{6}$ D) $\frac{1}{3}$ E) $\frac{3}{8}$ F) $\frac{5}{6}$

269) $\boldsymbol{f'(x) = x^3 - 9x^2 + 24x + 3}$ There are two points of inflection on the graph of $\boldsymbol{f}$. What are the $\boldsymbol{x}$-coordinates of these points?

A) 1, 3 B) 1, 4 C) $2, \frac{1}{2}$ D) $2, \frac{1}{3}$ E) 2, 4 F) $3, \frac{1}{3}$

270) Alex makes his own chocolate beverage by mixing volumes of milk and syrup in the ratio $\boldsymbol{5:2}$. Milk come in $\boldsymbol{2}$L bottles and syrup comes in $\boldsymbol{1.4}$L bottles. Alex has a limitless supply of full bottles of milk and syrup. What is the smallest volume of chocolate beverage that Alex can make that uses only whole bottles of both milk and syrup?

A) 16 L B) 17.8 L C) 18 L D) 19.3 L E) 19.6 L

271) What is the value of $\boldsymbol{a}$ for which $\boldsymbol{5^a + 5^{a+1} = \sqrt{4500}}$?

A) $\frac{1}{4}$ B) $\frac{1}{2}$ C) 1 D) $\frac{3}{2}$ E) 2

272) A point $(\boldsymbol{a}, \mathbf{0})$ is on the line $\boldsymbol{y} = \boldsymbol{x} + \mathbf{8}$. What is the value of $\boldsymbol{a}$?

A) -4 B) -5 C) -6 D) -7 E) -8 F) -9 G) -10

273) Let $\boldsymbol{f}(\boldsymbol{x}) = \boldsymbol{e}^{3x}$. The line $\boldsymbol{L}$ is the tangent to the curve of $\boldsymbol{f}$ at $(\mathbf{0}, \mathbf{1})$. What is the equation of $\boldsymbol{L}$ in the form of $\boldsymbol{y} = \boldsymbol{mx} + \boldsymbol{c}$?

A) $y = x + 1$ B) $y = -x + 1$ C) $y = 2x + 1$

D) $y = -2x + 1$ E) $y = 3x + 1$ F) $y = -3x + 1$

274) It takes 18 people to make 5 product A. It takes 5 product A to make 4 product B. How many people does it take to make 80 product B?

A) 773 people B) 780 people C) 786 people

D) 792 people E) 803 people

275) Jack travelled at 30 km/h for 20 minutes and then at 20 km/h for 40 minutes. What is the distance he travelled?

A) $\frac{55}{3}$ km B) 20 km C) $\frac{65}{3}$ km D) $\frac{70}{3}$km E) $\frac{75}{3}$km

276) What is the inverse function of $\boldsymbol{f}(\boldsymbol{x}) = \sqrt{\frac{6+2x}{6-2x}}$, for $-\mathbf{3} \leq \boldsymbol{x} < \mathbf{3}$?

A) $f^{-1}(x) = \frac{3x-3}{x+1}$ B) $f^{-1}(x) = \frac{3x^2-4}{x^2-1}$ C) $f^{-1}(x) = \frac{3x^2-3}{x^2+1}$

D) $f^{-1}(x) = \frac{3x^3-3}{x^2-1}$ E) $f^{-1}(x) = \frac{x^2+3}{x^2+1}$ F) $f^{-1}(x) = \frac{3x^3-3}{x+1}$

277) Two fair six-sided dice are tossed, and the numbers shown on the top face of each are $\boldsymbol{A}$ and $\boldsymbol{B}$ each. What is the probability that $\boldsymbol{A+B<10}$?

A) $\frac{13}{18}$ B) $\frac{27}{36}$ C) $\frac{7}{9}$ D) $\frac{29}{36}$ E) $\frac{5}{6}$ F) $\frac{31}{36}$

278) $\boldsymbol{y=ax^2+bx+c}$ passes through points $(\boldsymbol{-3,50})$, $(\boldsymbol{-1,20})$ and $(\boldsymbol{1,2})$. What is the value of $\boldsymbol{a+b+c}$?

A) -4 B) -3 C) -2 D) -1 E) 0 F) 1 G) 2

279) For some positive integers $\boldsymbol{m}$ and $\boldsymbol{n}$, $\boldsymbol{2^m-2^n=1792}$. What is the value of $\boldsymbol{m^2+n^2}$?

A) 164 B) 181 C) 185 D) 202 E) 221 F) 242

280) Let $\boldsymbol{f(x)=2x^2+4x+p}$ ($\boldsymbol{x}$ is a real number and $\boldsymbol{p}$ is an integer), and $\boldsymbol{f(x)=0}$ has two equal roots. What is the value of $\boldsymbol{p}$?

A)0 B) 1 C) 2 D) 3 E) 4 F) 5

281) Carl takes 2 hours to ride his bike from town A to town B. It takes him 2 hours and 15 minutes to travel from town B to town A. If he travels downhill at 24 km/h, on level road at 16 km/h, and uphill at 12 km/h, what is the distance between the two towns?

A)30 km B)31 km C)32 km D)33 km

E)34 km F)35 km G)36 km

282) $\boldsymbol{f(x) = 2(x-1)^2 - 8}$, $\boldsymbol{g(x) = 6x^2}$. $\boldsymbol{f(x)}$ is obtained from $\boldsymbol{g(x)}$ by a compression of scale factor $\boldsymbol{a}$ in the $\boldsymbol{y}$-direction, followed by a translation of $\boldsymbol{\binom{h}{k}}$. What is the value of $\boldsymbol{3a \times h \times k}$?

A) -5 B) -6 C) -7 D) -8 E) 5

F) 6 G) 7 H) 8

283) Given a sequence $\boldsymbol{\{a_n\}}$, $\boldsymbol{a_1}$ and $\boldsymbol{a_2}$ are 4 and 5 respectively. Each term after the second is determined by adding 1 to the previous term and dividing the result by the term before that. (For example, $\boldsymbol{a_3 = \frac{5+1}{4}}$.) What is the 1000th term of the sequence?

A) $\frac{1}{2}$ B) 1 C) $\frac{3}{2}$ D) 2 E) 4 F) 5

284) Expand $\boldsymbol{(2x+1)^4}$

A) $16x^4 + 16x^3 + 24x^2 + 16x + 1$

B) $16x^4 + 32x^3 + 12x^2 + 8x + 1$

C) $16x^4 + 32x^3 + 24x^2 + 8x - 1$

D) $16x^4 + 32x^3 + 24x^2 + 8x + 1$

E) $8x^4 + 16x^3 + 12x^2 + 4x + 1$

285) What is the term in $\boldsymbol{x^3}$ for the expansion of $\boldsymbol{(x+2)^5}$?

A) $32x^3$ B) $36x^3$ C) $40x^3$ D) 32 E) 36 F) 40

286) What is the value of the following sum of 10 terms?

$\log_3\left(1-\frac{1}{15}\right)+\log_3\left(1-\frac{1}{14}\right)+\log_3\left(1-\frac{1}{13}\right)+\cdots+\log_3\left(1-\frac{1}{8}\right)+\log_3\left(1-\frac{1}{7}\right)+\log_3\left(1-\frac{1}{6}\right)$

A) -4 B) -3 C) -2 D) -1

E) 0 F) 1 G) 2

287) When $(2x+1)^n$ is expanded the coefficient of the term in x^2 is $40n$, where n is a positive integer. What is n?

A)18 B)20 C)21 D)24 E)36

288) Clare leaves home at 13:00 for a meeting with Lucy. If Clare travels at an average of **20**km/h, she would arrive 30 minutes before their meeting time. If Clare travels at an average of **12**km/h, she would arrive 30 minutes after the meeting time. At what average speed should Clare travel to meet Lucy at the scheduled meeting time?

A) 5 km/h B)10 km/h C)15 km/h D)20 km/h E)25 km/h F)30 km.h

289) What is $P(B|A)$ when $P(A)=\frac{2}{3}$ and $P(A\cap B)=\frac{2}{5}$?

A) $\frac{2}{5}$ B) $\frac{7}{15}$ C) $\frac{8}{15}$ D) $\frac{3}{5}$ E) $\frac{2}{3}$

290) A cube has an edge length of 10 which increased by 10% for all edges. What is the volume of the cube after the edge increase?

A) 1100 B) 1210 C) 1331 D) 1452

E) 1584 F) 1728

291) A cylinder has height of 4 and its circular faces have $\mathbf{10\pi}$ as a circumference. What is the volume of the cylinder?

A) $25\,\pi$ B) $75\,\pi$ C) $100\,\pi$ D) $125\,\pi$ E) $144\,\pi$ F) $200\,\pi$

292) What is the x-coordinate of the point where $\boldsymbol{y = \log_3 x + 3}$ and the asymptote of $\boldsymbol{y = 2^x + 5}$ meet?

A) 3 B) 6 C) 9 D) 12 E) 15

293) Three points $\boldsymbol{A(5,-8)}$, $\boldsymbol{B(9,-30)}$, $\boldsymbol{C(n,n)}$ are on the same straight line. What is the value of $\boldsymbol{n}$?

A) $\frac{4}{3}$ B) $\frac{5}{3}$ C) 2 D) $\frac{7}{3}$ E) $\frac{8}{3}$ F) 3

294) What is the sum of all roots for the equation $\boldsymbol{1 + \sqrt{2}\sin 2x = 0, 0 \le x \le \pi}$?

A) π B) $\frac{5}{4}\pi$ C) $\frac{3}{2}\pi$ D) $\frac{7}{4}\pi$ E) 2π

295) There is a moving sidewalk from point A to B. When the sidewalk is off, it takes Lucy 1 minute 30 seconds to walk from point A to B. It takes her 45 seconds to stand on a movind sidewalk to reach point B from A. If her walking speed and the moving sidewalk speed are constant, how long does it take her to walk from point A to B when the sidewalk is moving?

A) 20 seconds B) 25 seconds C) 30 seconds D) 35 seconds

E) 40 seconds F) 45 seconds G) 50 seconds

296) A square has side length $\boldsymbol{s}$ and a diagonal length of $\boldsymbol{s+1}$. What is the area of the square?

A) $1+2\sqrt{2}$ B) $2+\sqrt{2}$ C) $2+2\sqrt{3}$

D) $3+2\sqrt{2}$ E) $3+\sqrt{5}$

297) $\boldsymbol{f(x)=a^x\ (0<a<1)}$ has minimum $\boldsymbol{\frac{5}{6}}$ and maximum $\boldsymbol{M}$ within the domain $\boldsymbol{\{x|-2<x<1\}}$. What is $\boldsymbol{a\times M}$?

A) $\frac{2}{5}$ B) $\frac{3}{5}$ C) $\frac{4}{5}$ D) 1 E) $\frac{6}{5}$

298) What is the smallest positive angle $\boldsymbol{x}$ that satisfies $\boldsymbol{4^{\sin^2 x}\times 2^{\cos^2 x}=2\sqrt[4]{8}}$?

A) $\frac{1}{6}\pi$ B) $\frac{1}{4}\pi$ C) $\frac{1}{3}\pi$ D) $\frac{1}{2}\pi$ E) π F) $\frac{5}{4}\pi$

299) There are 6 cards written A, A, A, B, B, C each. If the cards are lined up, what is the probability that there are A cards on both ends?

A) $\frac{3}{20}$ B) $\frac{1}{5}$ C) $\frac{1}{4}$ D) $\frac{3}{10}$ E) $\frac{7}{20}$

300) The following box-and-whisker plot represents the commute time, in minutes, for a group of workers. The range is 23 minutes, and the interquartile range is 10 minutes. What is the value of $\boldsymbol{p-q}$?

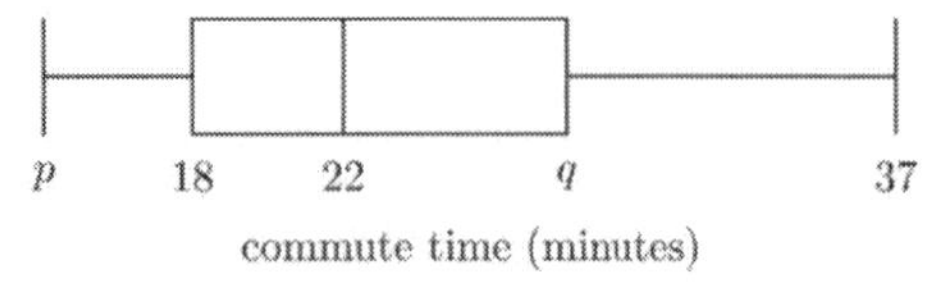

A) -10 B) -11 C) -12 D) -13 E) -14 F) -15

301) What is the value $\boldsymbol{n^5}$ if $\boldsymbol{\log_{3n} 675\sqrt{3} = \log_n 75}$?

A) 5329 B) 5476 C) 5625 D) 5776

E) 5929 F) 6084

302) If $\boldsymbol{g(x)}$ is an inverse function of $\boldsymbol{f(x) = x^3 + 5x + 3}$, what is the value of $\boldsymbol{g'(x)}$?

A) $\frac{1}{7}$ B) $\frac{1}{6}$ C) $\frac{1}{5}$ D) $\frac{1}{4}$ E) $\frac{1}{3}$

303) Squares of the roots of $\boldsymbol{x^2 - 4x - 5 = 0}$ are the roots of $\boldsymbol{x^2 + bx + c = 0}$. What is the value of $\boldsymbol{\frac{c}{b}}$?

A) $\frac{12}{13}$ B) $\frac{25}{26}$ C) 1 D) -1 E) $\frac{-25}{26}$ F) $\frac{-1}{13}$

304) What is the shaded region of the following diagram?

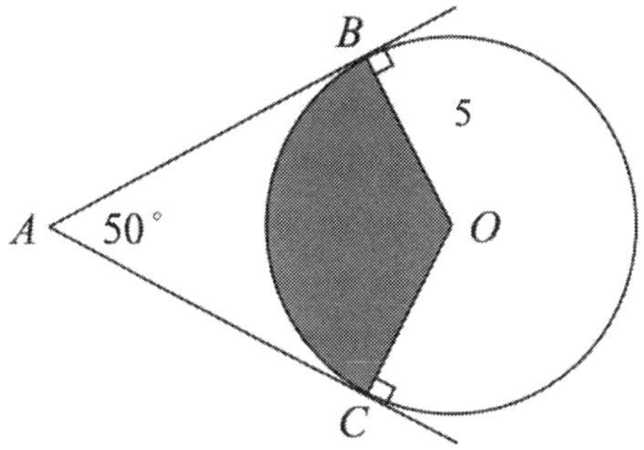

A) 10π B) 11π C) 12π D) 13π E) 14π

305) What is the maximum of $y = \frac{1}{x-1} + 3$, given the domain $\{x|2 \leq x \leq 4\}$?

A) 3 B) 4 C) 5 D) 6 E) 7

306) If AB and BC are each increased by 6, what is the length of AC?

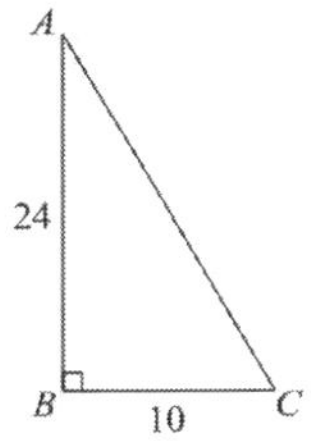

A) 26 B) 27 C) 28 D) 29 E) 30 F) 31

307) Lucy was born in the year n^2. On her birthday in the year $(n+1)^2$ she will be 89 years old. In what year was she born?

A) 1901 B) 1908 C) 1912 D) 1924

E) 1936 F) 1948

308) What is the value of $f'(4)$ for $f(x) = \int_1^x (t-2)(t-3)dt$?

A) 1 B) 2 C) 3 D) 4 E) 5

309) Point $R(a, b)$ lies on the line segment PQ which connects point $P(6, -2)$ and $Q(-3, 10)$. The distance from P to R is $\frac{1}{3}$ of the distance from P to Q. Solve $b - a$.

A) -4 B) -3 C) -2 D) -1 E) 0

310) What is $\frac{1}{a} - \frac{1}{b}$ when $ab = \log_3 5$ and $b - a = \log_2 5$?

A) $\log_5 2$ B) $\log_3 2$ C) $\log_3 5$ D) $\log_2 3$

E) $\log_2 5$ F) $\log_2 6$ G) $\log_6 2$

311) For an arithmetic sequence $\{a_n\}$ $(1 \leq n \leq 20)$, the sum of the last three terms is 12 and the sum of the first three terms is 15. What is the sum of all terms in the sequence?

A) 86 B) 87 C) 88 D) 89 E) 90 F) 91

312) What is $f'(1)$ for $f(x) = 3x^2 - 2x$?

A) 5 B) 4 C) 3 D) 2 E) 1

313) The parabola in the following graph is expressed as $\boldsymbol{y} = \boldsymbol{k}^2 - \boldsymbol{x}^2$, where $\boldsymbol{k}$ is a positive real number. Point $\boldsymbol{A}$ and $\boldsymbol{D}$ are where the parabola crosses the $\boldsymbol{x}$-axis and point $\boldsymbol{B}$ and $\boldsymbol{C}$ are placed so that $\boldsymbol{AB}$ and $\boldsymbol{DC}$ are parallel to the $\boldsymbol{y}$-axis and $\boldsymbol{BC}$ crosses the vertex $\boldsymbol{V}$. Rectangle $\boldsymbol{ABCD}$ has perimeter 48. What is the perimeter of $\boldsymbol{k}$?

A) 2 B) 3 C) 4 D) 5 E) 6 F) 7

314) Max, Jake and Anne joined a sprinting competition. The mean time of their sprints is 10.5 seconds. Kate sprints after Anne and the mean time of the first four sprinters is 12.0 seconds. What is Kate's sprint time(seconds)?

A) 14 B) 14.5 C) 15 D) 15.5 E) 16 F) 16.5 G) 17

315) A can of orange paint has a mass of 12 pounds. The orange paint is made by mixing red paint and yellow paint, where the ratio of red to yellow is 1:4. Then, more yellow paint is added to make the yellow paint 90% of the resulting orange paint. What is the mass of the resulting orange paint?

A) 23.6 pounds B) 24 pounds C) 24.5 pounds D) 25.2 pounds

E) 26 pounds F) 26.6 pounds G) 27.3 pounds

316) When $\boldsymbol{y} = \boldsymbol{2}\sqrt{\boldsymbol{x}}$ is moved by $\boldsymbol{k}$ along the $\boldsymbol{y}$-axis, the graph passes point $(\boldsymbol{1}, \boldsymbol{5})$. What is the value of $\boldsymbol{k}$?

A) 1 B) 2 C) 3 D) 4 E) 5 F) 6

317) Clare is leaving home to visit her relatives in city A or B – either by car or by plane. When travelling to city A, the probability that Clare drives is $\frac{3}{4}$, and when travelling to city B, the probability she flies is $\frac{7}{8}$. Given that the probability of Clare driving is $\frac{5}{12}$, what is the probability that she travels to city A?

A) $\frac{1}{5}$ B) $\frac{4}{15}$ C) $\frac{1}{3}$ D) $\frac{2}{5}$ E) $\frac{7}{15}$ F) $\frac{8}{15}$ G) $\frac{3}{5}$

318) How many sides does a regular polygon have if it has 90 diagonals?

A) 10 sides B) 11 sides C) 12 sides D) 13 sides

E) 14 sides F) 15 sides G) 16 sides H) 17 sides

319) First term $\boldsymbol{a_n}$ and difference $\boldsymbol{d}$ are the same in an arithmetic sequence $\{\boldsymbol{a_n}\}$. When $\boldsymbol{a_2 + a_4 = 24}$, what is the value of $\boldsymbol{a_5}$?

A) 8 B) 11 C) 14 D) 17 E) 20

320) A cylinder has radius $\boldsymbol{r}$ cm and height $\boldsymbol{h}$ cm, with volume of $\boldsymbol{24\pi}$ cm^3. Express $\boldsymbol{h}$ in terms of $\boldsymbol{r}$.

A) $\frac{12}{r^2}$ B) $\frac{16}{r^2}$ C) $\frac{24}{r}$ D) $\frac{24}{r^2}$ E) $\frac{48}{r^3}$ F) $\frac{48}{r^2}$

321) When $\boldsymbol{(a,b)\phi(c,d) = (ac - bd, ad + bd)}$, what is the pair $\boldsymbol{(x,y)}$ for which $\boldsymbol{(x,3)\phi(x,y) = (6,0)}$?

A) (1,0) B) (0, 1) C) (0, -1) D) (-3,-1)

E) (0,-3) F) (0, -2) G) (2, 0)

322) A function $\boldsymbol{f(x)}$ has derivative $\boldsymbol{f'(x) = 7x^2 - 32x}$. The graph of $\boldsymbol{f}$ has an $\boldsymbol{x}$-intercept at $\boldsymbol{x = 2}$. What is $\boldsymbol{f(x)}$?

A) $f(x) = \frac{7}{3}x^3 - 16x^2 + \frac{136}{3}$

B) $f(x) = \frac{7}{3}x^3 - 16x^2 + \frac{117}{3}$

C) $f(x) = \frac{7}{3}x^3 - 16x + \frac{136}{3}$

D) $f(x) = \frac{5}{3}x^3 - 16x^2 + \frac{117}{3}$

E) $f(x) = \frac{5}{3}x^3 - 16x^2 - \frac{136}{3}$

F) $f(x) = \frac{5}{3}x^3 - 16x + \frac{136}{3}$

323) Standard dice A, B and C are rolled at the same time and the number shown on the top is $\boldsymbol{a, b, c}$ respectively. What is the probability that $\boldsymbol{a < b < c}$?

A) $\frac{6}{55}$ B) $\frac{5}{61}$ C) $\frac{5}{54}$ D) $\frac{7}{54}$ E) $\frac{1}{6}$

324) What is the area enclosed by $\boldsymbol{y = 6x^2 - 12x}$ and $\boldsymbol{x}$-axis?

A) 2 B) 4 C) 6 D) 8 E) 10 F) 12

325) Let $\boldsymbol{f(x) = \sqrt{x-3},\ x \geq 3}$. What is $\boldsymbol{f^{-1}(x)}$?

A) $y = x^2 - 3$ B) $y = x^2 + 2$ C) $y = x^2 + 3$ D) $y = x^4 + 2$

E) $y = x^4 + 3$ F) not possible

326) A maths test is given to 24 students, where two students scored 10 and other students scored 12. What is the mean score for the class?

A) $\frac{82}{25}$ B) $\frac{293}{24}$ C) $\frac{83}{6}$ D) $\frac{71}{6}$ E) $\frac{65}{6}$ F) $\frac{245}{24}$

327) What is the largest possible value of $\boldsymbol{r}$, when it is a radius of a circle that is tangent to both the $\boldsymbol{x}$-axis and $\boldsymbol{y}$-axis, passing through $(\mathbf{9}, \mathbf{2})$?

A) 5 B) 7 C) 9 D) 12 E) 17 F) 21

328) Find $\boldsymbol{f^{-1}(3)}$ when $\boldsymbol{f(x) = \sqrt{x+7},\ x \geq -7}$

A) $y = x + 7$ B) $y = x^2 - 7$ C) $y = x^2 + 5$ D) $y = x^2 - 5$ E) $y = -x^2 + 5$

329) Let $\boldsymbol{f(x) = px^3 - qx}$. When $\boldsymbol{x = 0}$, the gradient of the curve is 2. What is $\boldsymbol{p \times q}$ when $\boldsymbol{f^{-1}(12) = 2}$?

A) -2 B) -1 C) 0 D) 1 E) 2 F) 3

330) Peter has a circular cookie with radius 4 cm. The cookie has $\boldsymbol{k}$ circular chocolate chips with radius 0.4 cm. Given that no chocolate chips overlap, for what value of $\boldsymbol{k}$ is exactly $\boldsymbol{\frac{1}{4}}$ of the area of the cookie is covered with chocolate chips? (Do not consider the height of the cookie)

A) 20 B) 21 C) 22 D) 23 E) 24 F) 25

331) $\boldsymbol{f(x) = \frac{x-2}{3}}$ and $\boldsymbol{g(x) = 12x + 4}$, given that $\boldsymbol{(g \circ f)^{-1}(a) = 10}$, what is the value of $\boldsymbol{a}$?

A) 32 B) 34 C) 36 D) 38 E) 40 F) 42

332) A bag has 8 red and 4 blue marbles. When two marbles are randomlly selected without replacement, what is the probability that the selected marbles are of different colours?

A) $\frac{13}{33}$ B) $\frac{11}{18}$ C) $\frac{16}{33}$ D) $\frac{7}{18}$ E) $\frac{17}{33}$ F) $\frac{5}{18}$

333) The normal to the curve $\boldsymbol{f(x) = kx^3 at\ x = 2}$ is parallel to $\boldsymbol{y = \frac{x}{6}}$. What is the value of $\boldsymbol{k}$?

A) $-\frac{1}{2}$ B) $\frac{1}{2}$ C) $-\frac{1}{3}$ D) $\frac{1}{3}$ E) 1

334) How many integer $\boldsymbol{x}$ satisfies $\boldsymbol{2\log_2|x-1| \le 1 - \log_2\frac{1}{2}}$?

A) 0 B) 1 C) 2 D) 3 E) 4 F) 5

335) What is $\boldsymbol{f(1)}$ given $\boldsymbol{\int_1^x f(t)dt = x^2 - a\sqrt{x}\ \ (x > 0)}$?

A) 1 B) $\frac{3}{2}$ C) 2 D) $\frac{5}{2}$ E) 3

336) Two different regular dice are thrown, and if the numbers are the same Jack throws one coin 4 times and if the numbers are different, he throws one coin 2 times. In this game, if the number of heads and tails are the same, what is the probability that the coin in thrown 4 times?

A) $\frac{3}{23}$ B) $\frac{5}{23}$ C) $\frac{7}{23}$ D) $\frac{9}{23}$ E) $\frac{11}{23}$

337) A battery has full capacity Q_0 ($Q_0 > 0$). After the battery is completely depleted and when it is charged for t hours, the battery capacity $Q(t)$ can be modelled as the following: $Q(t) = Q_0\left(1 - 2^{-\frac{t}{a}}\right)$ $(a > 0)$. When $\frac{Q(4)}{Q(2)} = \frac{3}{2}$, what is the value of a?

A) $\frac{3}{2}$ B) 2 C) $\frac{5}{2}$ D) 3 E) $\frac{7}{2}$

338) Given that $f(x) = 2^x + 1$, $g(x) = -2^{x-1} + 7$, what is the shaded area?

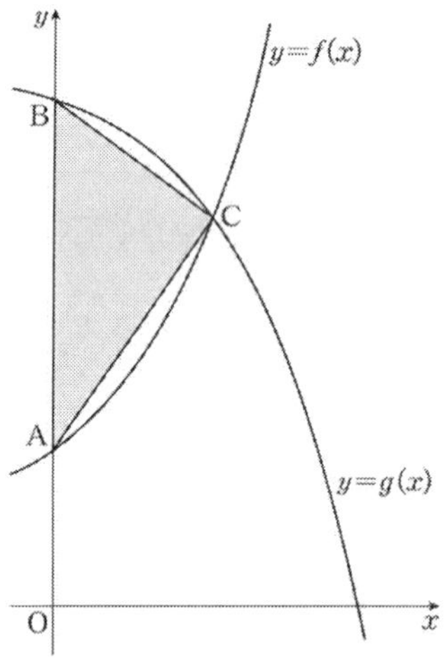

A) $\frac{5}{2}$ B) 3 C) $\frac{7}{2}$ D) 4 E) $\frac{9}{2}$

339) What is the sum of all roots for the equation $2\sin^2 x + 3\cos x = 3$ between $0 \leq x < 2\pi$?

A) $\frac{\pi}{2}$ B) π C) $\frac{3\pi}{2}$ D) 2π E) $\frac{5\pi}{2}$

340) A bag has 2 white balls and 4 red balls. The probability of picking 2 white balls at once is $\frac{p}{q}$. What is $p + q$, given that p and q are coprime?

A) 16 B) 17 C) 18 D) 19 E) 20

341) The semicircle of the following has diameter of $\boldsymbol{AB}$, which has length 12. Arc $\boldsymbol{BC}$ is $\boldsymbol{4\pi}$ and $\boldsymbol{H}$ is drawn from C so that segment $\boldsymbol{CH}$ is perpendicular to AB. What is $\boldsymbol{CH^2}$?

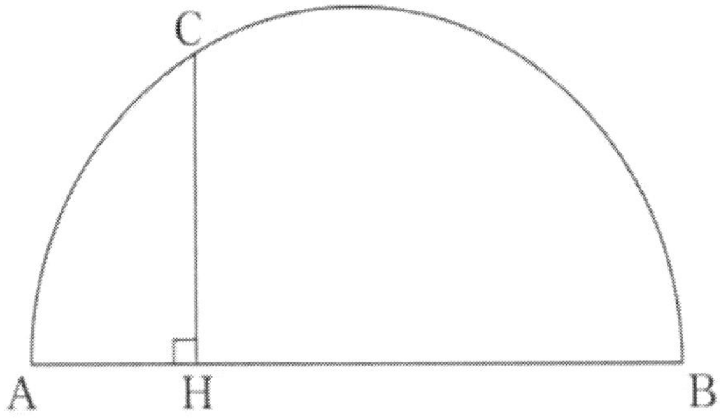

A) 13 B) 15 C) 16 D) 17

E) 21 F) 25 G) 27

342) **If** $\frac{\sqrt{32}+\sqrt{18}}{3+\sqrt{2}} = a\sqrt{2} + b$. **What is the value of** $a + b$?

$A) -2$ $B) -1$ $C)0$ $D)1$ $E)2$

343) **If a curve has equation** $y = 9 - 4x - \frac{8}{x}$, **what is the y intercept of the tangent at** $x = 2$?

$A)(-2,0)$ $B)(-1,0)$ $C)(0,0)$ $D)(1,0)$ $E)(2,0)$

344) **If** $3x^2 + y^2 = 21$ **and** $5x + y = 7$. **Then what are the possible values of** $x + y$?

$A)10, -5$ $B)10, -1$ $C)5, -1$ $D)5, -5$ $E) -5, -1$

345) A curve has equation $\boldsymbol{y} = (\boldsymbol{x} - \boldsymbol{k})^2$, where $\boldsymbol{k}$ is a constant. Given that $\frac{dy}{dx} = 2x - 6$. What is the value of k?

A)1 B)2 C)3 D)4 E)5 F)6 G)7

346) Find the shortest distance between the line (passing through $(-1,3)$ and $(3,4)$) and the line $x - 4y - 21 = 0$.

A) $\frac{17}{2}$ B) $2\sqrt{17}$ C) $3\sqrt{17}$ D) $4\sqrt{17}$ E) $5\sqrt{17}$ F) $\frac{17}{4}$

347) Evaluate $\lim_{x \to 2} \left[\frac{1}{x(x-2)^2} - \frac{1}{x^2-3x+2}\right]$.

A)0 B)1 C)2 D)4 E)8 F)16 G)∞

348) If $y = p$ (where p is a constant) and $y = x^2 - x - 12$ intersect at 2 points, the line segment joining the 2 points has a length of 9, what is the value of a?

A)16 B)8 C)4 D)2 E)1 F)0

349) If $\frac{\sqrt{a}}{\sqrt{a+2b}} = \frac{2\sqrt{a}-b}{3a+b}$ **in its simplest form where $a, b > 0$. What is the value of ab?**

A) $\frac{8}{27}$ B) $\frac{2}{3}$ C) $\frac{4}{9}$ D) $\frac{1}{3}$ E) $\frac{2}{9}$ F) $\frac{7}{27}$ G) $\frac{1}{9}$

350) If $y = \frac{x^4-3}{2x^2}$, Find $\frac{d^2y}{dx^2}$.

A) $\frac{x^4-9}{x^4}$ B) $x + \frac{3}{x^3}$ C) $x + \frac{3}{x^4}$ D) $x^2 + \frac{3}{x^2}$ E) $x - \frac{9}{x^4}$

351) Find the area of the finite region bounded by the curve and the $\boldsymbol{x}$ axis bounded by the curve, $\boldsymbol{y = x(x-1)(x+3)}$.

A) $\frac{7}{2}$ B) $\frac{23}{6}$ C) $\frac{41}{6}$ D) $\frac{71}{6}$ E) $\frac{107}{3}$

352) What is the value of $\boldsymbol{ab - cd}$, where the fraction $\frac{\boldsymbol{2x^2+11x+12}}{\boldsymbol{(x+3)(x+4)}}$ is written in the form $\frac{\boldsymbol{ax+b}}{\boldsymbol{cx+d}}$, where $\boldsymbol{a, b, c}$ and $\boldsymbol{d}$ are integers.

A) -2 B) 3 C) 5 D) -7 E) 1 F) 4

353) The diagram below shows the arrangements of two tiles, ***A*** and ***B***. Given that the two tiles are regular polygons, calculate the number of sides polygon A has.

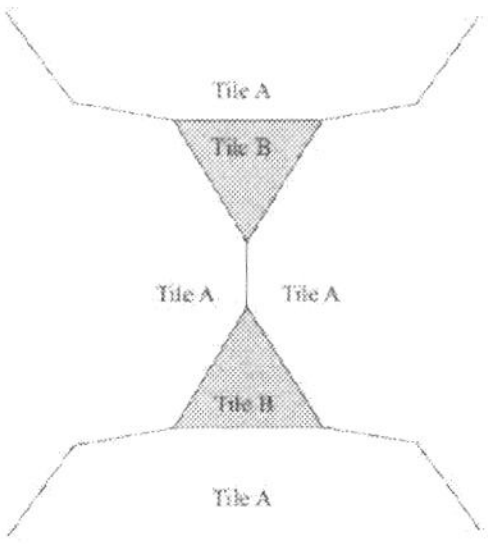

A) 9 B) 10 C) 11 D) 12 E) 13 F) 15

354) What is the value of $\boldsymbol{2015^2 - 2016 \times 2014}$?

A) -2015 B) -1 C) 0 D) 1 E) 2015

355) The set, A, contains three numbers which are 17, 23 and $\boldsymbol{2n}$. Given that the mean of the set is equal to $\boldsymbol{n}$, what is the sum of the digits of $\boldsymbol{n}$?

A) 4 B) 5 C) 6 D) 7 E) 8

356) Let $f(x) = \frac{4x-20}{2}$ and a second function $g(x) = (x+3)(x-3)$. For what input would the output of both functions be the same?

A) -2 B) -4 C) 1 D) 3 E) 6 F)

357) In the diagram below, $ABCD$ is a square, and ABE is a right-angled triangle. Given that the length of BC is 3 and the length of BE is 4, what is the area of the shaded region?

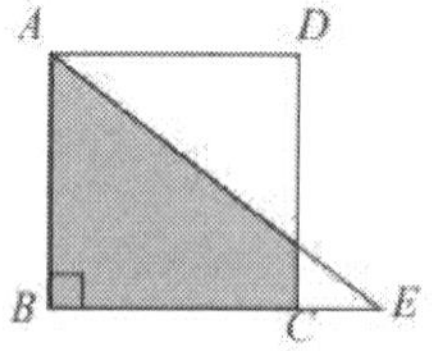

A) $\frac{21}{4}$ B) $\frac{43}{8}$ C) $\frac{11}{2}$ D) $\frac{45}{8}$ E) $\frac{23}{4}$

358) Find the value of $pq - r$, when $f(x) = 3x^2 + 6x + 1$ is written in the form $p(x+q)^2 + r$

A) -2 B) -1 C) 2 D) 3 E) 4 F) 5

359) On Friday, all the prices in Harry's shop are increased by 10% from their normal prices. On Saturday, all the prices are reduced by 10% from their normal prices. Given that James bought a book on Friday for £5.50. What would be the price of another copy of this book on the Saturday?

A) £5.50 B) £5.00 C) £4.95

D) £4.50 E) £4.40

360) There are x number of bananas in a box. Unfortunately, 4 of these bananas have become rotten.
Greg chooses two of these bananas from the crate, without replacement. Given that the probability that he chooses two rotten bananas is $\frac{1}{11}$, find the total number of bananas that were in the crate.

A) 8 B) 9 C)10 D) 11 E)12 F)14

361) Find the sum of the x and y coordinate of the stationary point on the curve, which has equation $y = x^4 - 32x$

A)-46 B) -28 C) 12 D) 16 E) 42 F) 64

362) Which of the following is equal to the expression $2017 - \frac{1}{2017}$?

A) $\frac{2017^2}{2016}$ B) $\frac{2016}{2017}$ C) $\frac{2018}{2017}$

D) $\frac{4045}{2018}$ E) $\frac{2018 \times 2016}{2017}$

363) Find the sum of the first 50 terms of the sequence: 32, 27, 22, 17, 12 ...

A) -4525 B) -1620 C) -240

D) -1248 E) 2512

364) In the following expression, each of the positive real numbers $\boldsymbol{a}, \boldsymbol{b}, \boldsymbol{c}, \textbf{and } \boldsymbol{d}$ is increased by 20%.

$$\frac{\boldsymbol{abc}}{\boldsymbol{2d}}+\frac{\boldsymbol{3bcd}}{\boldsymbol{a+b+c}}$$

What will the overall percentage change of the value of the expression be?

A)20% B) 40% C)44% D) 88% E) 92%

F) 116% G) Depends on a, b, c or d

365) Freddie rolls two fair dice in succession. What is the probability that the sum of the two die is equal to 5, 6 or 7?

A)$\frac{1}{4}$ B) $\frac{1}{3}$ C) $\frac{5}{12}$ D) $\frac{4}{9}$ E) $\frac{1}{6}$

366) An equilateral triangle has side length, $\boldsymbol{x}$. Which of the following expressions give the correct formula for the area of this triangle?

A)$\frac{x\sqrt{3}}{2}$ B) $\frac{x^2\sqrt{3}}{4}$ C) $\frac{2x^2}{3}$ D) $\frac{x\sqrt{3}}{4}$ E) $\frac{x^2}{2}$

367) If Benjamin flips a coin 4 times, what is the probability that he gets 2 heads and 2 tails?

A)$\frac{1}{2}$ B) $\frac{2}{3}$ C) $\frac{3}{16}$ D) $\frac{3}{8}$ E) $\frac{1}{4}$

368) The variable, $\boldsymbol{X}$ is inversely proportional to the square root of another variable, $\boldsymbol{Y}$. When $\boldsymbol{X}=\mathbf{4}, \boldsymbol{Y}=\mathbf{25}$.

What is the value of $\boldsymbol{X}$, when $\boldsymbol{Y}=\mathbf{16}$.

A)2 B) 3 C) 4 D) 5 E) 12 F) 15

369) If one 9cm cube is cut into multiple identical 3cm cubes, what is the scale factor change for the total surface area?

A) $\frac{1}{9}$ B) $\frac{1}{3}$ C) 1 D) 3 E) 9 F) 27

370) Which of the following expressions will be the greatest for $\boldsymbol{x}$ in the range

$\mathbf{0 < x < 1}$?

A) $sinx$ B) $cosx$ C) $\log_8 x$ D) e^x E) x^2

371) Everyday, Bob drives his car on the motorway, travelling at a speed of 70mph. Given his speedometer is in the shape of a hemisphere and has a maximum speed of 200mph, what angle does the arrow show daily when Bob is driving on the motorway?

A) 28° B) 35° C) 63° D) 72° E) 90°

372) In the function, $\boldsymbol{f(x) = (2 - x)^5}$, what is the coefficient of $\boldsymbol{x^2}$?

A) -80 B) -36 C) 40 D) 64 E) 80

373) Given that the volume of a sphere is equal to its surface area, calculate the value of its radius.

A) 1 B) $\frac{1}{2}$ C) $\frac{3}{4}$ D) 2 E) 2 E) $\frac{4}{3}$ F) 3

374) What is the largest prime factor of $\mathbf{106^2 - 15^2}$?

A)3 B) 5 C) 7 D) 11 E) 13 F) 15

375) Alex is double the age of his younger sister, Alexie, and she is triple the age of their youngest sibling, Alexis. If the combined ages of all three siblings is 50 years, how old was the oldest sibling, Alex, when his youngest brother, Alexis was born?

A)12 B) 15 C) 20 D) 25 E) 30

376) Solve the logarithmic equation $\mathbf{\log(3x+1) = 5}$.

A)$\frac{4}{3}$ B) 8 C) 300 D) $\frac{10}{3}$ E) 33,333

377) Given that $\mathbf{\log 27 = 1.431}$, calculate the value of $\mathbf{\log 9}$.

A)0.934 B) 0.945 C)0.954 D)0.958 E) 0.962

378) The price of a television, $\boldsymbol{P}$ has increased by 125%. However, following a fall in demand, the increased price then fell by 40% to price $\boldsymbol{Q}$. What is the value of $\boldsymbol{K}$, where $\boldsymbol{KP} = \boldsymbol{Q}$?

A)$\frac{7}{20}$ B) $\frac{17}{20}$ C) $\frac{27}{20}$ D)$\frac{33}{20}$ E) $\frac{41}{20}$

379) Let S_n denote a geometric series. The first three terms of S_n are $(\boldsymbol{p} - \mathbf{2})$, $(\mathbf{2}\boldsymbol{p} + \mathbf{2})$ and $(\mathbf{5}\boldsymbol{p} + \mathbf{14})$. Given that S_n is universally greater than 0, what is the 5th term in the geometric progression?

A)288

B) 486

C) 1256

D) 2480

E) 4800

380) From the diagram below, find the value of $\boldsymbol{x} + \boldsymbol{y}$.

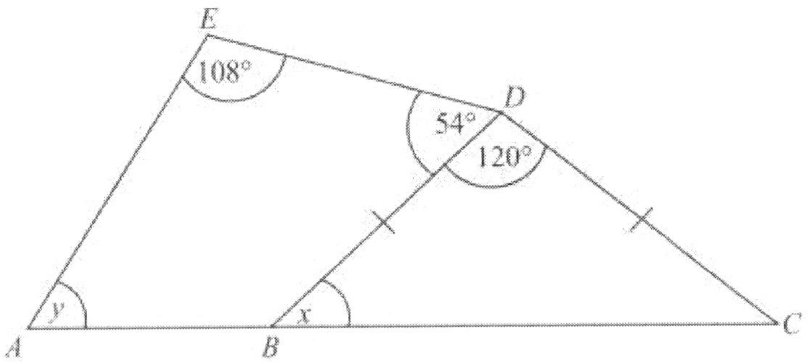

A)78

B) 108

C) 124

D) 72

E) 90

381) Make $\boldsymbol{x}$ the subject of the formula $\frac{x}{x+c} = \frac{p}{q}$.

A) $\frac{p+c}{qp}$

B) $\frac{pc}{q-p}$

C) $\frac{p-c}{p-q}$

D) $\frac{p-c}{q}$

E) $\frac{cp}{q-c}$

382) The following (custom ordered) set contains 6 numbers. For what value of $\boldsymbol{x}$ will the mean of the first three numbers in the set be equal to the mean of the last 4.

$$15, 5, x, 7, 9, 17$$

A)12　　B) 13　　C) 14　　D) 17

E) 19　　F) 21　　G) 22

383) Solve the pair of simultaneous equations:

1) $\boldsymbol{x^2 + 2y = 12}$
2) $\boldsymbol{x + y = 2}$

$A)(4,-2)$ and $(-2,4)$　　B) $(2,-4)$ and $(-2,-4)$

C) $(3,-1)$ and $(-1,3)$　　D) $(-4,6)$ and $(6,-4)$

E) $(-1,2)$ and $(1,2)$

384) Let the function $\boldsymbol{f(x) = 4x^2 + \frac{5-x}{x}, where\ x \neq 0}$. The point, $\boldsymbol{P}$ on the curve has $\boldsymbol{x}$ coordinate of 1. Find the gradient of $\boldsymbol{f(x)}$ at P.

A)-1　　B) 0　　C) 1　　D) 2

E) 3　　F) 5　　G) $\frac{7}{2}$

385) Simplify the expression $\boldsymbol{x^3\sqrt{2} \div \sqrt{\frac{32}{x^2}}}$

A)$\frac{x^3}{2}$　　B) $\frac{x^2}{4}$　　C) $\frac{x^4}{4}$　　D) $\frac{2}{x}$　　E) $\frac{x}{4}$

386) The curve, $\boldsymbol{y} = \boldsymbol{x}^2$ is translated by the vector $\binom{7}{2}$. It is then reflected on the line $\boldsymbol{y} = -\mathbf{1}$. What is the resulting equation of the new curve?

A) $y = (x-7)^2 - 4$ B) $y = -(x-7)^2 - 2$ C) $y = (x+7)^2 - 2$

D) $y = -(x-7)^2 - 4$ E) $y = (x+7)^2 - 4$ F) $y = -(x+7)^2 - 2$

387) Find $\boldsymbol{f}'(\mathbf{4})$ when $\boldsymbol{f}(\boldsymbol{x}) = \frac{2x^2-2}{\sqrt{x}}$

A) $6 + \frac{1}{\sqrt{2}}$ B) $6 - \frac{1}{\sqrt{2}}$ C) 5

D) $\frac{25}{4}$ E) $\frac{49}{8}$ F) $\frac{51}{8}$

388) The equation $\boldsymbol{x}^2 + \boldsymbol{mx} + \mathbf{1} = \mathbf{0}$ has two roots, $\boldsymbol{\alpha}$ ***and*** $\boldsymbol{\beta}$. Given that $\boldsymbol{\alpha\beta} = \frac{1}{\alpha} + \frac{1}{\beta}$, find the value of $\boldsymbol{m}$.

A) -2 B) -1 C) 0 D) 1 E) 2 F) 3

389) The diagram below shows triangle ABH, with side AB extended to C and line DG passing through it. Given that AC and DG are parallel, find the value of $\boldsymbol{x}$.

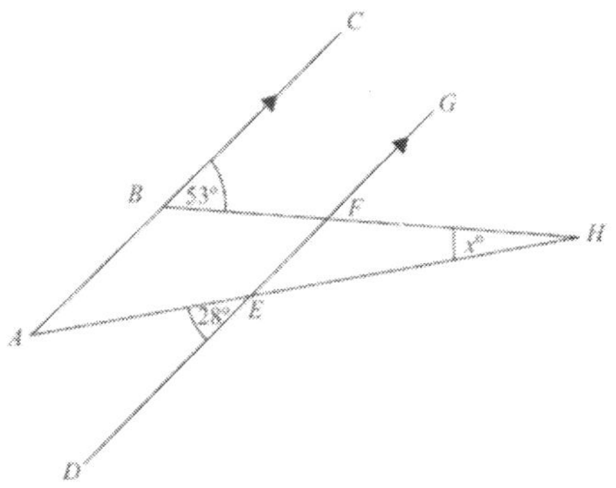

A) 21 B) 25 C) 36 D) 45 E) 48 F) 24

390) A circle has an area of $\frac{25}{9}\pi$ touches the x axis at $(4, 0)$. The point P lies on the circle such that the distance between it and the origin, O is maximised. Find the length of the line segment OP.

A)$\frac{13}{3}$ B)$\frac{14}{3}$ C)5 D)$\frac{16}{3}$ E)$\frac{17}{3}$ F)6 G)$\frac{19}{3}$

391) Find the area enclosed between the line $x = 7$ and the quadratic curve

$$x = 3(y - 1)^2 + 4.$$

A)$\frac{9}{2}$ B) $\frac{17}{2}$ C) 3 D) -2 E) 4 F) -4

392) There are 4 friends, Martin, Andy, Nick and Rathore. Out of the four there is one guilty person who is lying. Who is the liar?

Isabelle, Gina, John and Max = M, A, N, R

Andy: "Rathore is guilty."

Rathore: "Martin is innocent."

Nick: "Andy is guilty."

Martin: "John is innocent."

A) Martin B) Nick C) Andy

D) Rathore E) Not enough information to determine

393) $\boldsymbol{PQRS}$ is a trapezium where sides $\boldsymbol{PQ}$ and $\boldsymbol{RS}$ are parallel. What is the length of $\boldsymbol{RS}$ when the area of the trapezium is $\mathbf{120}\boldsymbol{cm^2}$?

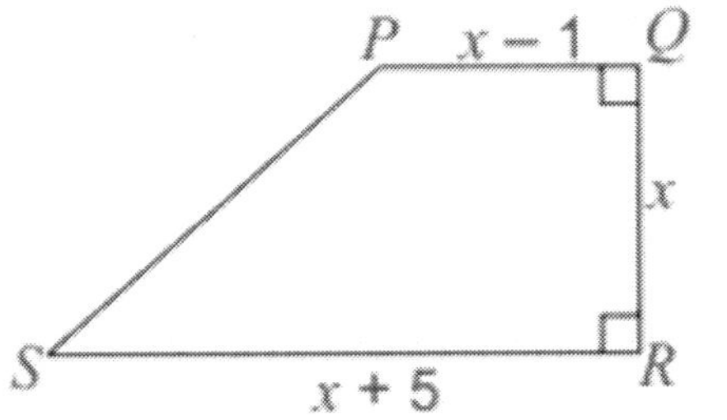

A)10 B) 11cm C) 12cm D) 13cm

E) 14cm F) 15cm G) 16cm

394) Simplify the following logarithmic expression

$$\log\left(\frac{9}{14}\right) - \log\left(\frac{15}{16}\right) + \log\left(\frac{35}{24}\right)$$

A) -1 B) $\log\frac{2}{3}$ C) $\log\frac{3}{4}$ D) 0 E) $\log\frac{3}{2}$ F) $\log\frac{4}{3}$

G) $\log 2$ H) $\log\frac{5}{2}$

395) The function $\boldsymbol{f(x) = kx^2 + 12x + k, (k > 0)}$ has equal roots. What is the value of $\boldsymbol{k}$?

A) Undetermined B) 2 C) 3 D) 4 E) 5 F) 6

396) Solve the logarithmic equation, $\log_6(x+3) = 1 - \log_6(x-2)$

A) -4 B) 3 C) 5 D) 6 E) 8

397) Given that $\boldsymbol{sinx} = \mathbf{2sin}\ (\boldsymbol{x} + \frac{\pi}{6})$, find the exact value of $\boldsymbol{tanx}$. Use the fact that $\mathbf{Sin}(\boldsymbol{A} + \boldsymbol{B}) = \mathbf{sin}\,\boldsymbol{A}\,\boldsymbol{cosB} + \boldsymbol{cosA}\ \boldsymbol{sinB}$

A) $1 + \sqrt{3}$ B) $\frac{2+\sqrt{5}}{2}$ C) $\frac{-1+\sqrt{2}}{2}$

D) $-\frac{1}{2}(1 + \sqrt{3})$ E) $2 - \sqrt{3}$

398) There are 3 numbers which form three consecutive terms of an arithmetic sequence. The mean of the three numbers is 6, and the mean of the squares of the 3 numbers is 132.
Find the product of the three numbers.

A) 720 B) 848 C) -648

D) -1024 E) -729

399) Sally and Yangh are playing a game, where they roll 2 dice. The score of each roll is the number that is smaller. For example, if Sally rolls a 1 and a 6, then her score is 1. If the two dice have the same number, then that number is counted as the score. What is the probability that Yangh and Sally both get a score of 4 on their first go?

A) $\frac{5}{36}$ B) $\frac{64}{1225}$ C) $\frac{1}{12}$ D) $\frac{1}{16}$ E) $\frac{25}{1296}$

400) In the triangle, $\boldsymbol{ABC}$,
side $\boldsymbol{AB} = \boldsymbol{4x}$ cm

side $\boldsymbol{BC} = (\boldsymbol{8} - \boldsymbol{3x})$cm

and the angle $\boldsymbol{ABC} = \boldsymbol{60°}$.

What is the maximum area (cm^2) of triangle ABC?

A) $\frac{16\sqrt{3}}{3}$ B) $\frac{32\sqrt{3}}{3}$ C) $4\sqrt{3}$ D) $\frac{8\sqrt{3}}{3}$ E) $6\sqrt{2}$

Table of Answers

Q	*Ans*	*Q*	*Ans*	*Q*	*Ans*	*Q*	*Ans*	*Q*	*Ans*
1.	A	2.	C	3.	A	4.	D	5.	E
6.	A	7.	F	8.	D	9.	E	10.	B
11.	B	12.	A	13.	B	14.	C	15.	D
16.	A	17.	A	18.	B	19.	E	20.	C
21.	C	22.	C	23.	E	24.	F	25.	F
26.	A	27.	B	28.	D	29.	F	30.	B
31.	D	32.	B	33.	B	34.	G	35.	A
36.	E	37.	C	38.	A	39.	A	40.	D
41.	F	42.	B	43.	D	44.	D	45.	C
46.	A	47.	A	48.	E	49.	D	50.	B
51.	D	52.	F	53.	D	54.	B	55.	E
56.	C	57.	G	58.	B	59.	E	60.	D

61.	A	62.	C	63.	A	64.	F	65.	B
66.	A	67.	B	68.	E	69.	A	70.	C
71.	E	72.	B	73.	E	74.	G	75.	C
76.	C	77.	C	78.	F	79.	D	80.	H
81.	B	82.	C	83.	F	84.	F	85.	B
86.	E	87.	C	88.	A	89.	D	90.	F
91.	D	92.	D	93.	A	94.	B	95.	A
96.	D	97.	G	98.	C	99.	A	100.	D
101.	F	102.	E	103.	A	104.	F	105.	B
106.	A	107.	A	108.	F	109.	C	110.	D
111.	B	112.	G	113.	C	114.	D	115.	E
116.	G	117.	D	118.	A	119.	A	120.	A
121.	E	122.	E	123.	C	124.	D	125.	G
126.	B	127.	C	128.	D	129.	F	130.	B
131.	E	132.	B	133.	H	134.	A	135.	F

136.	A	137.	F	138.	A	139.	D	140.	D
141.	B	142.	C	143.	G	144.	A	145.	E
146.	C	147.	A	148.	D	149.	G	150.	B
151.	D	152.	C	153.	C	154.	E	155.	B
156.	C	157.	B	158.	A	159.	D	160.	E
161.	C	162.	E	163.	A	164.	D	165.	D
166.	D	167.	C	168.	C	169.	C	170.	D
171.	B	172.	E	173.	A	174.	F	175.	B
176.	D	177.	A	178.	E	179.	B	180.	C
181.	D	182.	C	183.	D	184.	F	185.	A
186.	B	187.	A	188.	D	189.	C	190.	F
191.	B	192.	C	193.	A	194.	D	195.	E
196.	D	197.	B	198.	E	199.	A	200.	C
201.	B	202.	C	203.	A	204.	D	205.	E
206.	F	207.	E	208.	B	209.	F	210.	E

211.	D	212.	C	213.	D	214.	B	215.	E
216.	E	217.	C	218.	B	219.	E	220.	E
221.	A	222.	G	223.	B	224.	A	225.	C
226.	C	227.	C	228.	G	229.	C	230.	C
231.	B	232.	B	233.	D	234.	D	235.	A
236.	G	237.	C	238.	E	239.	E	240.	B
241.	E	242.	A	243.	E	244.	D	245.	A
246.	E	247.	D	248.	A	249.	F	250.	D
251.	E	252.	C	253.	C	254.	E	255.	A
256.	A	257.	C	258.	A	259.	F	260.	C
261.	D	262.	A	263.	B	264.	C	265.	A
266.	C	267.	F	268.	D	269.	E	270.	E
271.	D	272.	E	273.	E	274.	D	275.	D
276.	C	277.	E	278.	G	279.	C	280.	C
281.	E	282.	D	283.	B	284.	D	285.	C

286.	D	287.	C	288.	C	289.	D	290.	C
291.	C	292.	C	293.	F	294.	C	295.	C
296.	D	297.	E	298.	C	299.	B	300.	E
301.	C	302.	C	303.	E	304.	D	305.	B
306.	A	307.	E	308.	B	309.	D	310.	D
311.	E	312.	B	313.	C	314.	F	315.	B
316.	C	317.	E	318.	F	319.	E	320.	D
321.	F	322.	A	323.	C	324.	D	325.	C
326.	D	327.	E	328.	B	329.	A	330.	F
331.	C	332.	C	333.	A	334.	E	335.	B
336.	A	337.	B	338.	E	339.	D	340.	A
341.	G	342.	D	343.	D	344.	C	345.	C
346.	B	347.	G	348.	B	349.	A	350.	A
351.	D	352.	B	353.	D	354.	D	355.	A
356.	C	357.	D	358.	F	359.	D	360.	E

361.	A	362.	E	363.	A	364.	C	365.	C
366.	B	367.	D	368.	D	369.	D	370.	D
371.	C	372.	E	373.	F	374.	E	375.	D
376.	E	377.	C	378.	C	379.	B	380.	A
381.	B	382.	E	383.	A	384.	E	385.	C
386.	D	387.	E	388.	B	389.	B	390.	F
391.	D	392.	C	393.	F	394.	D	395.	F
396.	B	397.	D	398.	C	399.	E	400.	A

Solutions

1. ANSWER: B

$$\int_7^b \frac{3}{\sqrt{x}}dx = 27 - 6\sqrt{7}$$

$$= \int_7^b 3x^{-\frac{1}{2}}dx = 27 - 6\sqrt{7}$$

$$= \left[\frac{3x^{\frac{1}{2}}}{\frac{1}{2}}\right]_7^b = 27 - 6\sqrt{7}$$

$$= \left[6x^{\frac{1}{2}}\right]_7^b = 27 - 6\sqrt{7}$$

$$= 6\sqrt{b} - 6\sqrt{7} = 27 - 6\sqrt{7}$$

$$\therefore 6\sqrt{b} = 27$$

$$\therefore \sqrt{b} = \frac{9}{2}$$

$$\therefore b = \frac{81}{4}$$

2. ANSWER: C

Recall that if $f(x)$ is transformed by $Af(Bx + C) + D$, then the transformations are performed in the order CBAD

$f(x)$ has roots $x = -1, -\frac{1}{2}, -3$

$\therefore f\left(x + \frac{1}{2}\right)$ has roots of $x = -\frac{3}{2}, -1, -\frac{7}{2}$

$\therefore f\left(-\frac{1}{2}x + \frac{1}{2}\right)$ has roots of $x = 3,2,7$

3. ANSWER: A

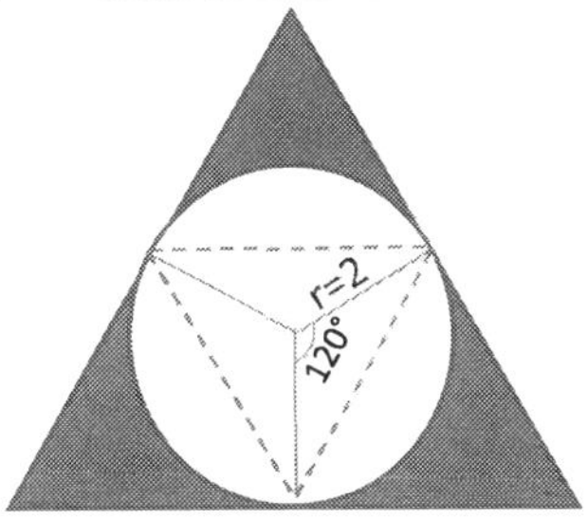

We know that an equilateral triangle can be split into 4 equilateral triangles of the size of the dashed triangle. Therefore, we must first work out the area of the dashed triangle by splitting it into 3.

$$A = \frac{1}{2}\text{ab}\sin C$$

$$A = \frac{1}{2}(2)(2)\sin(120°)$$

$$A = \frac{1}{2}(2)(2)\left(\frac{\sqrt{3}}{2}\right) = \sqrt{3}$$

$3A = 3\sqrt{3}$ (Giving us the area of the dashed triangle)

$4 \times 3\sqrt{3} = 12\sqrt{3}$ (Giving us the area of the whole triangle)

$$A = \pi r^2 = \pi(2)^2 = 4\pi$$

$\therefore$ Shaded area $= 12\sqrt{3} - 4\pi$

4. ANSWER: D

$$\int_1^2 (2x-1)^4 dx$$

$$= \int_1^2 (16x^4 - 32x^3 + 24x^2 - 8x + 1)dx$$

$$= \left[\frac{16x^5}{5} - \frac{32x^4}{4} + \frac{24x^3}{3} - \frac{8x^2}{2} + x\right]_1^2$$

$$= \left[\frac{16x^5}{5} - 8x^4 + 8x^3 - 4x^2 + x\right]_1^2$$

$$= \frac{121}{5}$$

5. ANSWER: E

Recall that if f(x) is transformed by Af(Bx + C) + D, then the transformations are performed in the order CBAD

If we let $f(x) = \sin(x)$ with a y intercept of (0,0),

$-f\left(36x + \frac{\pi}{6}\right)$ is a horizontal shift by $\frac{\pi}{6}$ in the negative x direction followed by a horizontal compression by scale factor $\frac{1}{36}$ and then a reflection in the x axis

$f\left(x + \frac{\pi}{6}\right)$ has a y intercept of $\left(\frac{1}{2}, 0\right)$

$\therefore f\left(36x + \frac{\pi}{6}\right)$ still has a y intercept of $\left(\frac{1}{2}, 0\right)$

$\therefore -f\left(36x + \frac{\pi}{6}\right)$ has a y intercept of $\left(-\frac{1}{2}, 0\right)$

6. ANSWER: A

$y = x^3 - ax^2 - bx + 18$

$x = 3, y = 0$

$\therefore 0 = 27 - 9a - 3b + 18$

$\therefore 15 = 3a + b (1)$

$\frac{dy}{dx} = 3x^2 - 2ax - b$

$\left.\frac{dy}{dx}\right|_{x=3} = 27 - 6a - b = 0$

$\therefore 27 = 6a + b \quad (2)$

$(2) - (1) = 3a = 12$

$\therefore a = 4$

sub in (1)

$15 = 12 + b$

$\therefore b = 3$

$\therefore f(x) = x^3 - 4x^2 - 3x + 18$

$\therefore f(x) = (x - 3)^2(x - c)$

$\therefore f(x) = (x^2 - 6x + 9)(x - c)$

$\therefore -4 = -6 - c$ (*comparing coefficients*)

$\therefore c = -2$

$\therefore f(x) = (x - 3)^2(x + 2)$

$\therefore a + b + c = 4 + 3 + (-2)$

$\therefore a + b + c = 5$

7. ANSWER: F

$x^5 - 30x^4 + 30x^3 - 30x^2 + 30x$

$= x^5 - 29x^4 - x^4 + 29x^3 + x^3 - 29x^2 - x^2 + 29x + x$

We know that $x = 29$

$= x^5 - (x)x^4 - x^4 + (x)x^3 + x^3 - (x)x^2 - x^2 + (x)x + x$
$= x^5 - x^5 - x^4 + x^4 + x^3 - x^3 - x^2 + x^2 + x$
$= x$
$= 29$

8. ANSWER: D

We must find the value of x which satisfies both $(x + 1)^2 = 9$ & $(x - 1)^2 = 25$
$(x + 1)^2 = 9$
$\therefore x + 1 = \pm 3$
$\therefore x = -4,2$
$(x - 1)^2 = 25$
$\therefore x - 1 = \pm 5$
$\therefore x = -4,6$
$\therefore x = -4$ satisfies both solutions

9. ANSWER: E

Let n be the number of counters in the bag
There are 7 red counters in the bag
There are n-7 green counters in the bag

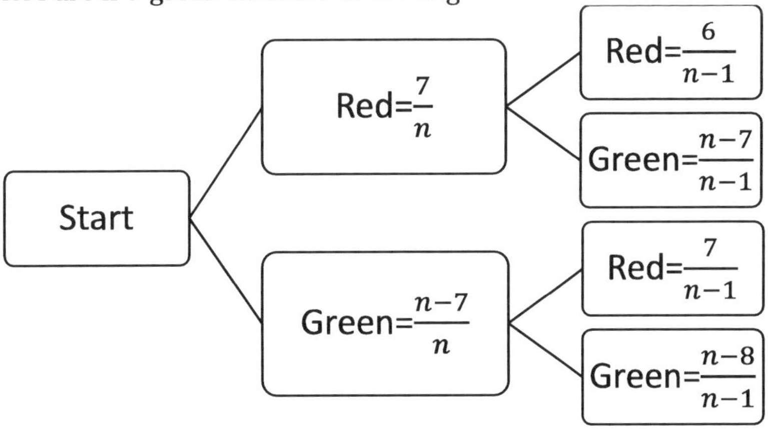

$$P(G,G) = \left(\frac{n-7}{n}\right) * \left(\frac{n-8}{n-1}\right) = \frac{3}{10}$$
$$\frac{n^2 - 15n + 56}{n^2 - n} = \frac{3}{10}$$
$10n^2 - 150n + 560 = 3n^2 - 3n$
$7n^2 - 147n + 560 = 0$
$(n - 16)(n - 5) = 0$
$n = 16 \text{ or } n = 5$
$n = 16$ (*as we want the greatest possible number of counters*)

10. ANSWER: B

$$\lim_{x\to\infty}\frac{x^6+a^2x^3b}{x^6-a^4b^2}$$
$$=\lim_{x\to\infty}\frac{x^3(x^3+a^2b)}{(x^3-a^2b)(x^3+a^2b)}$$
$$=\lim_{x\to\infty}\frac{x^3}{x^3-a^2b}$$
$$=1\ (\textit{as a and b are constants})$$

11. ANSWER: B

Let A, B, C, D be points on a straight line as shown below:

$AB:BD = 3:5$ (8 Parts) $\times 5$

$AC:CD = 4:1$ (5 Parts) $\times 8$

$\therefore$ AB: BD is 15: 25 and AC: CD is 32: 8

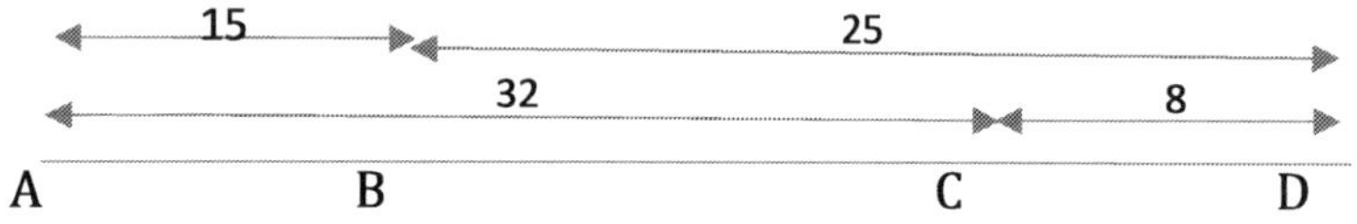

$\therefore$ ratio AB: BC: CD is 15: 17: 8

12. ANSWER: A

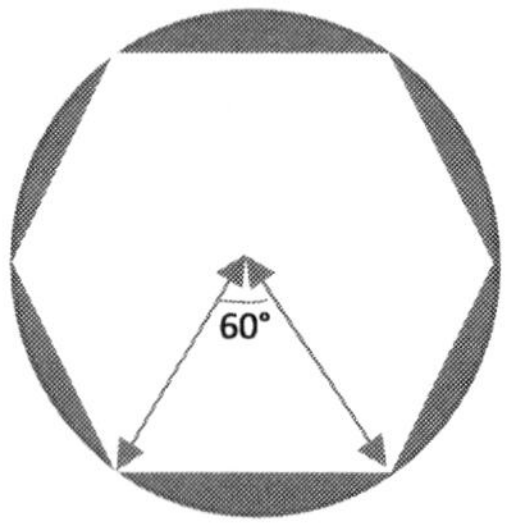

Area of circle is 36π $A = \pi r^2$ $\therefore r = 6$

Area of Segment $= \frac{1}{2}r^2\theta - \frac{1}{2}r^2\sin\theta$

$= \frac{1}{2}6^2\left(\frac{\pi}{3}\right) - \frac{1}{2}6^2\sin\frac{\pi}{3}$

$= 6\pi - 9\sqrt{3}$

Area of 6 segments $= 6\times\left(6\pi - 9\sqrt{3}\right) = 36\pi - 54\sqrt{3}$

13. ANSWER: B

We know that $S_\infty = (\sqrt{x} + 2) + (1) + (\sqrt{x} - 2) + \cdots$

$$S_\infty = \frac{a}{1 - r} \text{ where } |r| < 1$$

$$r = \frac{1}{\sqrt{x} + 2} = \frac{\sqrt{x} - 2}{1}$$

$$\therefore 1 = x - 4$$

$$\therefore x = 5$$

$$\therefore r = \sqrt{5} - 2$$

$$S_\infty = \frac{\sqrt{5} + 2}{1 - (\sqrt{5} - 2)}$$

$$S_\infty = \frac{\sqrt{5} + 2}{3 - \sqrt{5}} \times \frac{3 + \sqrt{5}}{3 + \sqrt{5}} = \frac{3\sqrt{5} + 6 + 5 + 2\sqrt{5}}{9 - 5}$$

$$S_\infty = \frac{5\sqrt{5} + 11}{4}$$

14. ANSWER: C

$$9^{x-1} - 30(3^{x-1}) + 81 = 0$$

$$= 3^{2(x-1)} - 30(3^{x-1}) + 81 = 0$$

Let $y = 3^{x-1}$

$$\therefore y^2 - 30y + 81 = 0$$

$$(y - 27)(y - 3) = 0$$

$$y = 27, y = 3$$

$$3^{x-1} = 27 \Rightarrow x - 1 = 3$$

$$\therefore x = 4$$

$$3^{x-1} = 3 \Rightarrow x - 1 = 1$$

$$\therefore x = 2$$

Sum of Roots: $2 + 4 = 6$

15. ANSWER: D

$$y = \frac{3 - x^2}{x + 2} \text{ and } y = q$$

$$\therefore q = \frac{3 - x^2}{x + 2}$$

$$\therefore q(x + 2) = 3 - x^2$$

$$\therefore x^2 + qx + (2q - 3) = 0$$

$$\therefore q^2 - 4(1)(2q - 3) = 0$$

$\therefore q^2 - 8q + 12 = 0$
$\therefore (q-6)(q-2) = 0$
$\therefore q = 2,6$

16. ANSWER: A

We are told Points (3,10), (9,4) and (−3,4) lie on a circle

$m = \dfrac{y_2 - y_1}{x_2 - x_1}$

Gradient of line through (3,10) and (9,4) $= \dfrac{-6}{6} = -1$, perp gradient $= 1$

Midpoint $= (6,7)$

$\therefore$ Perpendicular bisector: $y - 7 = 1(x - 6) \Rightarrow y = x + 1 \quad (1)$

Gradient of line through (3,10) and (−3,4) $= \dfrac{-6}{-6} = 1$, perp gradient $= -1$

Midpoint (0,7)

$\therefore$ Perpendicular Bisector: $y - 7 = -1(x - 0) \Rightarrow y = 7 - x \quad (2)$

The point of intersection of these perpendicular bisectors is the centre of the circle

Equate (1) and (2)

$x + 1 = 7 - x$

$\therefore 2x = 6$

$\therefore x = 3$

Sub value of x into (1)

$\therefore y = 4$

$\therefore$ circle is centred at (3,4)

$r = \sqrt{(3-3)^2 + (4-10)^2} = \sqrt{36} = 6$

$\therefore$ equation of circle is $(x-3)^2 + (y-4)^2 = 36$

17. ANSWER: A

$f(x) = 5x^3 + 3x^2 - 21x + 77$

$f'(x) = 15x^2 + 6x - 21$

Intersects x axis at $y = 0$

$15x^2 + 6x - 21 = 0$

$3(5x+7)(x-1) = 0$

$\therefore x = 1 \text{ or } x = -\dfrac{7}{5}$

$\therefore$ positive x intercept occurs at (1,0)

18. ANSWER: B

$\log_a b = \frac{1}{2}$ and $\log_c d = \frac{5}{4}$ and $a - c = 9$

$\therefore a^{\frac{1}{2}} = b$ and $c^{\frac{5}{4}} = d$

Let us assume $c = 16$ (as we know it has a fourth root)

$\therefore d = 32$

$a - 16 = 9 \Rightarrow a = 25$

$\therefore b = 5$

$d - b = 32 - 5$

$= 27$

19. ANSWER: E

$\frac{36^{a-b} \times 12^{a+b}}{27^a \times 4^{2a+b}}$

$= \frac{(6^2)^{a-b} \times (3 \times 2^2)^{a+b}}{(3^3)^a \times (2^2)^{2a+b}}$

$= \frac{(3 \times 2)^{2a-2b} \times (3 \times 2^2)^{a+b}}{(3^3)^a \times (2^2)^{2a+b}}$

$= \frac{3^{2a-2} \times 2^{2a} \times 3^{a+b} \times 2^{2a+2b}}{3^{3a} \times 2^{4a+2}}$

$= \left(2^{2a-2b+2a+2b-4a-2}\right)\left(3^{2a-2b+a+b-3a}\right)$

$= \left(2^{-2b}\right)\left(3^{-b}\right)$

$= (4^{-b})(3^{-b})$

$= 12^{-b}$

$\therefore$ Expression is only an integer for $b \leq 0$

20. ANSWER: C

$27^x + 9 = 9^x + 3^{x+2}$

$3^{3x} + 9 = 3^{2x} + 9(3^x)$

$3^{3x} - 3^{2x} - 9(3^x) + 9 = 0$

let $y = 3^x$

$y^3 - y^2 - 9y + 9 = 0$

try $y = 1$

$LHS = 1^3 - 1^2 - 9(1) + 9 = 0$

$\therefore (y - 1)$ is a factor (factor theorem)

$= (y - 1)(y^2 - 9)$

$= (y-1)(y-3)(y+3)$
$\therefore y = 1, y = 3, y = -3$
As $y = 3^x > 0$, only positive values of y satisfy this condition
$\therefore 3^x = 1 \Rightarrow x = 0$
$\therefore 3^x = 3 \Rightarrow x = 1$
$\therefore$ only 2 real solutions exist

21. ANSWER: C

$f(x) = (5\cos^2(15x+23) - 10)^2$
$\cos(15x + 23$ ranges from -1 to 1
$\cos^2(15x+23)$ ranges from 0 to 1
$5\cos^2(15x+23)$ ranges from 0 to 5
$5\cos^2(15x+23) - 10$ ranges from -10 to -5
$(5\cos^2(15x+23) - 10)^2$ ranges from 25 to 100
$\therefore$maximum value is 100

22. ANSWER: C

$7\cos x + 2\sin^2 x = 5$ for $0 \le x \le 2\pi$
$= 7\cos x + 2(1 - \cos^2 x) = 5$
$= 7\cos x + 2 - 2\cos^2 x = 5$
$\therefore 0 = 2\cos^2 x - 7\cos x + 3$
$\therefore (2\cos x - 1)(\cos x - 3) = 0$ or use $b^2-4ac>0$
$\cos x = \frac{1}{2}, \cos x \neq 3($ as $-1 \le \cos x \le 1)$
$\therefore$ 2 solutions exist in the range

23. ANSWER: E

In a question like this we must consider the options:
A)$\ln 10$ B) $\log_\pi 10$ C) $\ln \pi^2$ D)$\frac{1}{\log \pi}$ E)$\frac{e}{\ln 2}$ F)$\sqrt{\log \pi^2}$
Firstly $\ln 10 > \log_\pi 10$ and $\ln \pi^2$ $\therefore$ ANSWER can't be B or C
Now consider option D: $\log \pi \approx 0.5 \therefore \frac{1}{\log \pi} \approx 2$
Now consider option E: $\ln 2 < 1 \therefore \frac{e}{\ln 2} > e$
Now consider option F: $\log \pi^2 \approx 1 \therefore \sqrt{\log \pi^2} \approx 1$
Now we can estimate $\ln 10 < e$, as we roughly know $e^e > 10$

24. ANSWER: F

$$\int_0^2 2f(x)\,dx + \int_2^4 3f(x)\,dx = 10 \;\;\&\;\; \int_0^4 6f(x)\,dx - \int_0^2 8f(x)\,dx = 11.$$

If we let $\int_0^2 f(x)\,dx = a$ and $\int_2^4 f(x)\,dx = b$

$\therefore \int_0^4 f(x)\,dx = a + b$

These integrals can be thought of as simultaneous equations and transformed to:

$2a + 3b = 10 \quad (1)$

$6(a + b) - 8a = 11$

$\therefore 6b - 2a = 11 \quad (2)$

Adding (1)and (2) together we get $9b = 21$

$\therefore b = \frac{7}{3}$

sub this is (1) to get $2a + 7 = 10$

$\therefore a = \frac{3}{2}$

$\int_0^4 f(x) = a + b = \frac{7}{3} + \frac{3}{2} = \frac{23}{6}$

25. ANSWER: F

$f(x) = -2(x + 2)^3(x - 2)$

$\therefore f(x) = -2x^4 - 8x^3 + 32x + 32$

$\therefore f'(x) = -8x^3 - 24x^2 + 32$

$\therefore f''(x) = -24x^2 - 48x$

$f''(x) = 0$ at point of inflexion

$-24x^2 - 48x = 0$

$-24x(x + 2) = 0$

$\therefore$ points of inflexion occur at $x = -2$ or $x = 0$

26. ANSWER: A

$f(x) = 6x^2 + 17x, g(x) = (14x + 1)(3x + 2)$

$h(x) = g(x) + f(x).$

$h(x) = 6x^2 + 17x + (14x + 1)(3x + 2)$

$h(x) = 6x^2 + 17x + 42x^2 + 31x + 2$

$h(x) = 48x^2 + 48x + 2$

$h'(x) = 96x + 48$
$h'(x) = 0$ at minimum point
$96x = -48$

Minimum point occurs at $x = -\dfrac{1}{2}$

$h\left(-\dfrac{1}{2}\right) = 48\left(-\dfrac{1}{2}\right)^2 + 48\left(-\dfrac{1}{2}\right) + 2$

$= 48\left(\dfrac{1}{4}\right) + 48\left(-\dfrac{1}{2}\right) + 2$

$= 12 - 24 + 2$

$= -10$

$\therefore$ Minimum point is $\left(-\dfrac{1}{2}, -10\right)$

27. ANSWER: B

$16(\ln a)^2 + (\ln b)^2 = 1$
To maximise a, $\ln b = 0$

$\therefore (\ln a)^2 = \dfrac{1}{16}$

$\therefore \ln a = \pm\dfrac{1}{4}$

$\therefore$ max value of a is $\sqrt[4]{e}$

28. ANSWER: D

$\dfrac{4+\sqrt{5}}{4-\sqrt{5}} = \dfrac{4+\sqrt{5}}{4-\sqrt{5}} \times \dfrac{4+\sqrt{5}}{4+\sqrt{5}}$

$\therefore \dfrac{4+\sqrt{5}}{4-\sqrt{5}} = \dfrac{21+8\sqrt{5}}{11}$

$\therefore \left(\dfrac{4+\sqrt{5}}{4-\sqrt{5}}\right)^2 = \left(\dfrac{21+8\sqrt{5}}{11}\right)^2$

$= \dfrac{21^2 + 320 + 336\sqrt{5}}{121}$

$= \dfrac{761 + 336\sqrt{5}}{121}$

$\therefore$ Rational Term $= \dfrac{761}{121}$

29. ANSWER: F

$\log_4 x + \log_2 x = 9$
$a = \log_4 x \Rightarrow 4^a = x$

$\therefore 2^{2a} = x$
$b = \log_2 x \Rightarrow 2^b = x$
$2^{2a} = 2^b$
$\therefore b = 2a$
$a + b = 9$
$a = 3$
$3 = \log_4 x$
$x = 64$

30. ANSWER: B

$\left(x - \frac{11}{2}\right)^2 + \left(y - \frac{9}{2}\right)^2 = 4$ has centre $\left(\frac{11}{2}, \frac{9}{2}\right)$
$\left(x - \frac{3}{2}\right)^2 + \left(y - \frac{3}{2}\right)^2 = 4$ has centre $\left(\frac{3}{2}, \frac{3}{2}\right)$

Distance between centres $= \sqrt{\left(\frac{11}{2} - \frac{3}{2}\right)^2 + \left(\frac{9}{2} - \frac{3}{2}\right)^2} = 5$

As radius of both circles is 2 the shortest distance between the circles: 5-2-2=1

Vector from $\left(\frac{11}{2}, \frac{9}{2}\right)$ to $\left(\frac{3}{2}, \frac{3}{2}\right)$ is $\begin{pmatrix} -4 \\ -3 \end{pmatrix}$

$\therefore$ position vector of point at which shortest distance occurs is $\frac{2}{5}\begin{pmatrix} -4 \\ -3 \end{pmatrix} + \begin{pmatrix} \frac{11}{2} \\ \frac{9}{2} \end{pmatrix}$

$= \begin{pmatrix} 3.9 \\ 3.3 \end{pmatrix}$

$\therefore$ point(3.9,3.3)

31. ANSWER: D

$\frac{a}{1 - r} = 12$
$\therefore a = 12 - 12r$
$\frac{a^2}{1 - r^2} = 60$

$\therefore a^2 = 60 - 60r^2$
$(12 - 12r)^2 = 60 - 60r^2$
$17r^2 - 24r + 7 = 0$
$(17r - 7)(r - 1) = 0$
$r = \frac{7}{17}$ or $r = 1$

However as the series is convergent we know r must be $\frac{7}{17}$

32. ANSWER: B

$a^{6y}b^{4-y} = b^{y+3}a^{4y}$
$a^{2y}b^{1-2y} = 1$
$a^{2y}b^{1} = b^{2y}$
$2y\log a + \log b = 2y\log b$
$2y(\log a - \log b) = -\log b$
$y = -\frac{\log b}{2(\log a - \log b)}$

33. ANSWER: B

$x^2\text{coeff} = \frac{4!}{2!\,(4-2)!}(4m)^2(3n^2x)^2 = 864m^2n^4$
$x^3\text{coeff} = \frac{4!}{3!\,(4-3)!}(4m)^1(3n^2x)^3 = 432mn^6$
x^2coeff is 3 times greater than coeff of x^3
$\therefore 864m^2n^4 = 3(432mn^6)$
$864m^2n^4 = (1296mn^6)$
$m = \frac{3}{2}n^2$

34. ANSWER: G

$x - 2y = 0 \Rightarrow y = \frac{1}{2}x$
$x + ay + 5 = 0$
$ay = -5 - x$
$y = -\frac{5}{a} - \frac{x}{a}$

$$-\frac{1}{a} = \frac{1}{2}x$$
$$a = -2$$

35. ANSWER: A

Surface Area: $(2x)\sqrt{3x} + (6x)(\sqrt{3x}) + 6x(x) = 8\sqrt{3}x^{\frac{3}{2}} + 6x^2$

Volume: $x(\sqrt{3x})(3x) = 3\sqrt{3}x^{\frac{5}{2}}$

The ratio of the Surface Area to Volume is 14: 9.

$$\therefore 14\left(3\sqrt{3}x^{\frac{5}{2}}\right) = 9\left(8\sqrt{3}x^{\frac{3}{2}} + 6x^2\right)$$
$$42\sqrt{3}x^{\frac{5}{2}} = 72\sqrt{3}x^{\frac{3}{2}} + 54x^2$$
$$42\sqrt{3}x^{\frac{5}{2}} - 54x^2 - 72\sqrt{3}x^{\frac{3}{2}} = 0$$
$$7\sqrt{3}x^{\frac{5}{2}} - 9x^2 - 12\sqrt{3}x^{\frac{3}{2}} = 0$$
$$x^{\frac{3}{2}}\left(7\sqrt{3}x - 9x^{\frac{1}{2}} - 12\sqrt{3}\right) = 0$$
$$x^{\frac{3}{2}}\left(7\sqrt{3}x - 21x^{\frac{1}{2}} + 12x^{\frac{1}{2}} - 12\sqrt{3}\right) = 0$$
$$x^{\frac{3}{2}}\left(7x^{\frac{1}{2}}(\sqrt{3x} - 3) + 4\sqrt{3}(\sqrt{3x} - 3)\right) = 0$$
$$x^{\frac{3}{2}}\left(\left(7x^{\frac{1}{2}} + 4\sqrt{3}\right)(\sqrt{3x} - 3)\right) = 0$$
$$x^{\frac{3}{2}}\left(7x^{\frac{1}{2}} + 4\sqrt{3}\right)(\sqrt{3x} - 3) = 0$$
$$x = 0,$$
$$7x^{\frac{1}{2}} + 4\sqrt{3} = 0$$
$$x^{\frac{1}{2}} = -\frac{4\sqrt{3}}{7}$$
$$x = \frac{48}{49}$$
$$\sqrt{3x} - 3 = 0$$
$$\sqrt{3x} = 3$$
$$3x = 9$$
$$x = 3$$

The only possible values of x are $x = \frac{48}{49}$, and $x = 3$ (as $x > 0$)

$\therefore$ The product of the possible values of x are: $\frac{48}{49} \times 3 = \frac{144}{49}$

36. ANSWER: E

$\ln(a^2 - b^2) = 0$
$a^2 - b^2 = 1$
$(a+b)(a-b) = \cancel{\pm}1$
~~Case 1~~
~~$a+b=-1$ & $a-b=-1$~~
~~$a=-1, b=0$~~
~~Case 2~~
$a+b=1$ & $a-b=1$
$a=1, b=0$

37. ANSWER: C

$\log_4 x - 1 = \log_2 x - 3$
$\log_4 x - 1 = \log_{2^2}(x-3)^2$ (With logs you can square both the base and the argument)
$\therefore x - 1 = (x-3)^2$
$x - 1 = x^2 - 6x + 9$
$x^2 - 7x + 10 = 0$
$(x-5)(x-2) = 0$
$\therefore x = 5$ and $x = 2$
$\therefore$ 2 real solutions exist

38. ANSWER: A

$4x - 3y - 2 = 0 \ \ (1)$
$3x - 3y - 1 = 0 \ \ (2)$
$(1) - (2) = x - 1 = 0$
$\therefore x = 1$
sub in (2)
$3(1) - 3y - 1 = 0$
$2 - 3y = 0$
$$y = \frac{2}{3}$$
$\therefore \left(1, \frac{2}{3}\right)$ is the point of intersection

Line passes through origin and $\left(1, \frac{2}{3}\right)$
$$\therefore \frac{y - y_1}{y_2 - y_1} = \frac{x - x_1}{x_2 - x_1}$$

$$\frac{y-\frac{2}{3}}{0-\frac{2}{3}}=\frac{x-1}{0-1}$$

$$y=\frac{2}{3}$$

39. ANSWER: ~~A~~ C

$a, a+d, a+2d$

$\therefore 3a+3d=27$

$\therefore a+d=9\ \ (1)$

$a^2+(a+d)^2+(a+2d)^2=293$

$3a^2+6ad+5d^2=293$

$a=9-d$

$d^2=25$

$d=\pm 5$

However we know it is a decreasing sequence $\therefore d=-5$

$a=14$

$\therefore u_n = ~~19~~ - 5n$

14

40. ANSWER: D

$$\frac{3}{\sqrt{6}-2\sqrt{3}}\times\frac{\sqrt{6}+2\sqrt{3}}{\sqrt{6}+2\sqrt{3}}$$

$$=\frac{3\sqrt{6}+6\sqrt{3}}{6-12}$$

$$=\frac{3\sqrt{6}+6\sqrt{3}}{-6}$$

$$=-\frac{\sqrt{6}+2\sqrt{3}}{2}$$

41. ANSWER: F

$$\frac{1}{6}\log_2(x-2)-\frac{1}{3}=\log_{\frac{1}{8}}\sqrt{3x-5}$$

$$\log_2(x-2)-2=6\log_{\frac{1}{8}}\sqrt{3x-5}$$

$$\log_2(x-2)-2=\log_{\frac{1}{8}}(3x-5)^3$$

$$\log_2(x-2)-2=\log_{2^{-3}}(3x-5)^3$$

Remember that we can raise the base and the argument to the same power.

$\log_2(x-2) - 2 = \log_2(3x-5)^{-1}$

$\log_2(x-2) - 2 = -\log_2(3x-5)$

$\log_2(x-2) + \log_2(3x-5) = 2$

$\log_2(x-2)(3x-5) = 2$

$(x-2)(3x-5) = 2^2$

$3x^2 - 11x + 10 = 4$

$3x^2 - 11x + 6 = 0$

$(3x-2)(x-3) = 0$

$x = \frac{2}{3}, x = 3$

∴ Product of the 2 values of x which satisfy the equation are: $\frac{2}{3} \times 3 = 2$

42. ANSWER: B

$4 - 2\sin^8 x = (3 + \cos x)^2$ for $0 \le x < 360°$

Trying to solve this conventionally would be difficult so alternatively we can consider the ranges of LHS and RHS of the equation.

LHS $= 4 - 2\sin^8 x$ has a range from 2 to 4 (inclusive)

RHS $= (3 + \cos x)^2$ has a range from 4 to 16 (inclusive)

As you can see the ranges of both sides of the equation only coincide at one value.

∴The only condition under which LHS=RHS is when they both equal 4

Let us now consider RHS = 4 (as this looks easier to deal with than LHS=4)

$4 = (3 + \cos x)^2 \Rightarrow 2 = 3 + \cos x$

$\therefore \cos x = -1 \Rightarrow x = 180°$ (principle value)

$\therefore x = 180°$ is the only solution in the range

check with LHS:

$4 - 2\sin^8 x = 4 - 2(0) = 4$

∴ only one solution exists

43. ANSWER: D

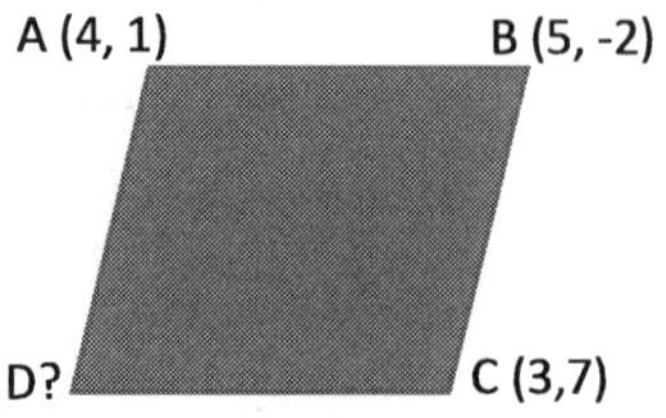

$\overrightarrow{BC} = \overrightarrow{OC} - \overrightarrow{OB}$

$\overrightarrow{BC} = \begin{pmatrix}3\\7\end{pmatrix} - \begin{pmatrix}5\\-2\end{pmatrix}$

$\overrightarrow{BC} = \begin{pmatrix}-2\\9\end{pmatrix}$

$\overrightarrow{OA} + \overrightarrow{BC} = \overrightarrow{OD}$

$\begin{pmatrix}4\\1\end{pmatrix} + \begin{pmatrix}-2\\9\end{pmatrix} = \begin{pmatrix}2\\10\end{pmatrix}$

$\overrightarrow{OD} = \begin{pmatrix}2\\10\end{pmatrix}$

$\therefore$ Coords of D (2,10)

44. ANSWER: D

$x + 3 + \frac{3}{x - 1} = \frac{4 - x}{x - 1}$

$x + 3 = \frac{1 - x}{x - 1}$ $*$

$x + 3 = \frac{-1(x - 1)}{x - 1}$

$x + 3 = -1$

$x = -4$

$*$ You may chose this method instead:

$(x + 3)(x - 1) = 1 - x$

$x^2 + 2x - 3 = 1 - x$

$x^2 + 3x - 4 = 0$

$(x + 4)(x - 1) = 0$

$x = -4$ or $x = 1$

$x = -4$ (as $x = 1$ is not a valid solution as $(x - 1)$ is in the denominator)

45. ANSWER: C

$\log_4(2^x + 3) + 1 = x$

$\log_4(2^x + 3) = x - 1$

$2^x + 3 = 4^{x-1}$

$2^x + 3 = (2^2)^{x-1}$

$2^x + 3 = 2^{2x-2}$

$\frac{1}{4}2^{2x} - 2^x - 3 = 0$

$2^{2x} - 4(2^x) - 12 = 0$

$(2^x - 6)(2^x + 2) = 0$

$\therefore 2^x = 6, 2^x \neq -2$ (as this is impossible for all real values of x)

$\log 2^x = \log 6$

$x \log 2 = \log 6$

$$x = \frac{\log 6}{\log 2}$$

46. ANSWER: A

$y = x^3 - 3x^2 + ax - 2$

$$\frac{dy}{dx} = 3x^2 - 6x + a$$

At stationary points $\frac{dy}{dx} = 0$

$\therefore$ To have 2 stationary points $3x^2 - 6x + a = 0$ must have 2 real distinct solutions

$\therefore b^2 - 4ac > 0$

$36 - 12a > 0$

$a < 3$

47. ANSWER: A

It is not worth making a calculation, rather thinking about it intuitively:
In a sample of trials you should expect that as the number of trials increases, the proportion of heads tends closer to 50% for a fair coin
I.e. anomalous results may happen a few times, but are unlikely to occur 100s of times

48. ANSWER: E

$P(x) = x^3 - ax^2 + 6x - a$ is divided by $(x - a)$

Rather than using long division we can use the remainder theorem

$P(a) = a^3 - a(a^2) + 6a - a = 5a$

$\therefore$ Remainder is 5a

49. ANSWER: D

The geometric series is increasing $\therefore r > 1$

$a + ar^{n-1} = 99$ and $ar \times ar^{n-2} = 288$

$$\frac{a(1 - r^n)}{1 - r} = 189$$

$a(1 + r^{n-1}) = 99$
$a^2 r^{n-1} = 288$
$\therefore r^{n-1} = \dfrac{288}{a^2}$
$\therefore a\left(1 + \dfrac{288}{a^2}\right) = 99$
$\therefore a^2 + 288 = 99a$
$\therefore a^2 - 99a + 288 = 0$
$(a - 3)(a - 96) = 0$
$\therefore a = 3 \text{ or } a = 96$
$\text{As } r^{n-1} = \dfrac{288}{a^2} \Rightarrow r^{n-1} = 32, \dfrac{1}{32}$
$\text{However as } r > 1 \Rightarrow r^{n-1} = 32 \text{ and } a = 3$
$\dfrac{a(1 - r^n)}{1 - r} = 189 \Rightarrow \dfrac{a(1 - r \cdot r^{n-1})}{1 - r} = 189$
$\therefore \dfrac{3(1 - r \cdot 32)}{1 - r} = 189$
$\dfrac{(1 - r \cdot 32)}{1 - r} = 63$
$\therefore 1 - 32r = 63 - 63r$
$\therefore 31r = 62$
$\therefore r = 2$
$\therefore 2^{n-1} = 32$
$\therefore n$
$= 6$

50. ANSWER: B

$$\int_0^2 \frac{1 - x^2}{x^{\frac{3}{2}} + \sqrt{x}} dx$$
$$= \int_0^2 \frac{(1 - x)(1 + x)}{\sqrt{x}(x + 1)} dx$$
$$= \int_0^2 \frac{(1 - x)}{\sqrt{x}} dx$$
$$= \int_0^2 \left(x^{-\frac{1}{2}} - \sqrt{x}\right) dx$$
$$= \left[2x^{\frac{1}{2}} - \frac{2}{3}x^{\frac{3}{2}}\right]_0^2$$
$$= \left(2\sqrt{2} - \frac{2}{3}(2\sqrt{2})\right)$$

$$= \frac{2\sqrt{2}}{3}$$

51. ANSWER: ~~D~~ E

$2^{(x-1)(x^2+5x-50)} = 1.$
$\therefore (x-1)(x^2+5x-50) = 0$
$x = 1$
$(x^2+5x-50) = 0$
$(x+10)(x-5) = 0$
$x = 5, x = -10$
$\therefore$ sum of all real values of x satisfying the equation:
$1 + 5 - 10 = -4$

52. ANSWER: F

Let the original number be $x + 10y$ and hence the reversed number be $10x + y$
$x + 10y = 7(x + y)$ (As the 2 digit number is 7 times the sum of its digits)
$x + 10y = 7x + 7y$
$3y = 6x$
$y = 2x$ (1)
$(x + 10y) - (10x + y) = 18$ (as number formed by reversing digits is 18 less than the original number)
$9y - 9x = 18$ (2)
$y - x = 2$
sub $y = 2x$ in (2)
$\therefore x = 2$
$\therefore y = 4$
$\therefore$ original number is $x + 10y = 2 + 10(4) = 42$

53. ANSWER:D

$81x^2 + kx + 256 = 0$
Using roots of polynomials:
$\alpha^3 = \beta$ (as one root is a cube of the other)

$\alpha\beta = a^4 = \frac{256}{81}$

$\therefore \alpha = \frac{4}{3}$

$\alpha^3 = \left(\frac{4}{3}\right)^3 = \frac{64}{27} = \beta$

$\alpha + \beta = -\frac{k}{81} = \frac{64}{27} + \frac{4}{3} = \frac{100}{27}$

$k = -\frac{8100}{27}$

$\therefore k = -300$

54. ANSWER: B

$e^{2x} + e^{x} + e^{-2x} + e^{-x} = 3(e^{-2} \ + e^{x})$

$e^{2x} + e^{x} + e^{-2} \ + e^{-x} = 3e^{-2x} + 3e^{x}$

$e^{2x} - 2e^{x} - 2e^{-2x} + e^{-x} = 0$

$e^{4x} - 2e^{3x} + e^{x} - 2 = 0$

This can be transformed with the substitution $y = e^x$

$y^4 - 2y^3 + y - 2 = 0$

By trying small values of y we can see that $y = 2$ is a solution

$\therefore$ Using the factor theorem $(y - 2)$ is a factor

Through comparison of coefficients or polynomial long division:

$(y - 2)(y^3 + 1) = 0$

$\therefore y = 2$ and $y^3 = -1 \therefore y = -1$

$e^x = 2 \Rightarrow x = \ln 2\,, e^x = -1 \Rightarrow$ no real solution

$\therefore$ Only one real solution exists

55. ANSWER: E

$\log x - \frac{1}{2}\log\left(x - \frac{1}{2}\right) = \log\left(x + \frac{1}{2}\right) - \frac{1}{2}\log\left(x + \frac{1}{8}\right)$

$2\log x - \log\left(x - \frac{1}{2}\right) = 2\log\left(x + \frac{1}{2}\right) - \log\left(x + \frac{1}{8}\right)$

$2\log x + \log\left(x + \frac{1}{8}\right) \cancel{-\log\left(x - \frac{1}{2}\right)} = 2\log\left(x + \frac{1}{2}\right) + \log\left(x - \frac{1}{2}\right)$

$x^2\left(x + \frac{1}{8}\right) = \left(x + \frac{1}{2}\right)^2\left(x - \frac{1}{2}\right)$

$x^3 + \frac{1}{8}x^2 = \left(x^2 + \frac{1}{4}\right)\left(x - \frac{1}{2}\right)$

$$x^3 + \frac{1}{8}x^2 = x^3 + \frac{1}{2}x^2 - \frac{1}{4}x - \frac{1}{8}$$
$$0 = \frac{3}{8}x^2 - \frac{1}{4}x - \frac{1}{8}$$
$$0 = 3x^2 - 2x - 1$$
$$0 = (3x + 1)(x - 1)$$
$$x = 1 \text{ or } x = -\frac{1}{3}$$
$$x = 1 \text{ (as } x = -\frac{1}{3} \text{ yields a negative argument)}$$

56. ANSWER:C

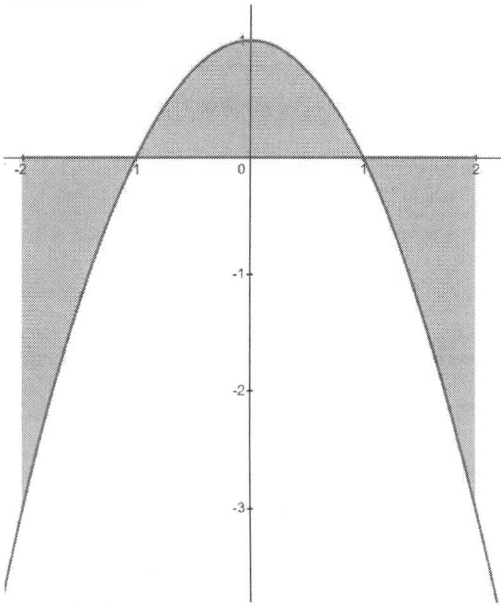

$1 - x^2$, the x axis and the lines $x = -2$ and $x = 2$

As some of the shaded area is above the graph and some is below we can't do:

$$\int_{-2}^{2} 1 - x^2 \, dx$$

Therefore in order to avoid the area below being subtracted from the area above:

$$\text{Area above the curve} = \int_{-1}^{1} 1 - x^2 \, dx$$

$$= \left[x - \frac{x^3}{3}\right]_{-1}^{1}$$

$$= \left(\frac{2}{3}\right) - \left(-\frac{2}{3}\right) = \frac{4}{3}$$

Area below the curve $= 2\int_1^2 1 - x^2\, dx$

$= 2\left[x - \frac{x^3}{3}\right]_1^2$

$= 2\left[2 - \frac{8}{3}\right] - 2\left[1 - \frac{1}{3}\right]$

$= -\frac{8}{3}$

Area below the curve $= \frac{8}{3}$

Total shaded area $= \frac{4}{3} + \frac{8}{3} = \frac{12}{3}$

$= 4$

57. ANSWER: G

$f(x) = \frac{x^4}{4} - x^3 - 5x^2 + 24x + 12$

$f'(x) = x^3 - 3x^2 - 10x + 24$

$f'(x) = x^3 - 3x^2 - 10x + 24$

In order to find out where the gradient is positive(i.e. the function is increasing) we must find the intervals over which the gradient function is greater than 0.

Therefore $f'(x)$must be factorised

Trying small values of x indicates that x=2 is a solution as

$f'(2) = (2)^3 - 3(2)^2 - 10(2) + 24 = 0$

Using polynomial division or comparing coefficients gives :

$f'(x) = (x - 2)(x^2 - x - 12) = 0$

$f'(x) = (x - 2)(x - 4)(x + 3) = 0$

$x = 2, x = 4$ and $x = -3$ are roots of the gradient function (stationary points for f(x))

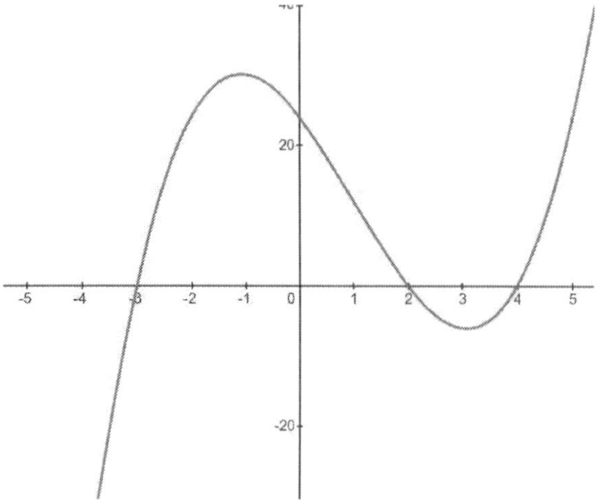

From the graph of the gradient function we know that the function is increasing for values of $f'(x)$above the x axis. As we can see this occurs over when:
$\{x: -3 \leq x \leq 2\} \cap \{x: x \geq 4\}$

58. ANSWER: B

$\text{P(0 milk chocolates out of 2)} = \frac{3}{10} \times \frac{2}{9} = \frac{6}{90} = \frac{1}{15}$
$\text{P(at least one out of 2)} = 1 - \text{P(0 milk chocolates out of 2)}$
$= 1 - \frac{1}{15} = \frac{14}{15}$

59. ANSWER: E

$x^2 + y^2 = 20$
You know the radius is centred at origin and hence the intercepts must be $\geq 2\sqrt{5}$
This eliminates the first three options.
Option D has an intercept of $2\sqrt{5}$ but its gradient is-1, hence it cannot be the tangent.
This is because in order to have an intercept= $2\sqrt{5}$(radius), the gradient must equal 0 (i.e. parallel to x axis)

60. ANSWER: D

$a + b + c = 70 \quad (1)$
$\therefore a + ar + ar^2 = 70 \quad (2)$
arithmetic series: 4a, 5b,4c
$5b - 4a = 4c - 5b$

$10b = 4a + 4c$

$\therefore 10ar = 4a + 4ar^2$

$\therefore 5r = 2 + 2r^2$

$\therefore 2r^2 - 5r + 2 = 0$

$\therefore (2r - 1)(r - 2) = 0$

$\therefore r = \frac{1}{2}$ and $r = 2$

For $r = 2$

Sub in (2): $a + 2a + 4a = 70$

$\therefore 7a = 70$

$\therefore a = 10, b = 20, c = 40$

$\therefore |c - a| = 30$

For $r = \frac{1}{2}$

Sub in (2): $a + \frac{1}{2}a + \frac{1}{4}a = \frac{7}{4}a = 70$

$\therefore a = 40, b = 20, c = 10$

$\therefore |c - a| = 30$

$\therefore |c - a| = 30$ for both values of r

61. ANSWER: A

We know that density $= \frac{\text{mass}}{\text{volume}}$

To work out upper bound of density: $\frac{\text{UB of mass}}{\text{LB of volume}}$

Upper Bound of Density: $\frac{2.75}{1.225} = \frac{110}{49}$

To work out lower bound of density: $\frac{\text{LB of mass}}{\text{UB of volume}}$

Lower Bound of Density: $\frac{2.65}{1.235} = \frac{530}{247}$

62. ANSWER: C

$$\frac{x}{\frac{y}{z^2}} + \frac{\frac{x}{y}}{z^2}$$

$$= \frac{xz^2}{y} + \frac{x}{yz^2}$$

$$= \frac{xz^4 + x}{yz^2}$$
$$= \frac{x(1 + z^4)}{yz^2}$$

63. ANSWER: A

$$\frac{x}{x - 8} > \frac{1}{2}$$
$$\frac{x}{x - 8} - \frac{1}{2} > 0$$
$$\frac{2x - (x - 8)}{2(x - 8)} > 0$$
$$\frac{x + 8}{2(x - 8)} > 0$$
$$\frac{x + 8}{(x - 8)} > 0$$

This can only be satisfied if $x < -8$ or $x > 8$

64. ANSWER: F

We want to find the equation of the normal to the curve $y = x + \frac{1}{x}, x > 0$ which is perpendicular to $3x - 4y = 7$

$$4y = 3x - 7$$
$$y = \frac{3}{4}x - \frac{7}{4}$$
$$\therefore m = \frac{3}{4}$$

$$\therefore m_{perp} = -\frac{4}{3}$$

Now we must find the value of x for which the tangent to the curve is parrallel to the line

$$y = x + \frac{1}{x}$$
$$\frac{dy}{dx} = 1 - \frac{1}{x^2}$$
$$1 - \frac{1}{x^2} = \frac{3}{4}$$

$$\frac{1}{4} = \frac{1}{x^2}$$
$$x^2 = 4$$
$$x = 2 \text{ (as } x > 0)$$
$$y = 2 + \frac{1}{2} = \frac{5}{2}$$
$\therefore$ point at which tangent is parallel to the line: $\left(2, \frac{5}{2}\right)$

To find the equation of the normal to the curve perpendicular to the line $3x - 4y = 7$ we must find the equation of the line through $\left(2, \frac{5}{2}\right)$ with a gradient of $-\frac{4}{3}$

$$y - y_1 = m(x - x_1)$$
$$y - \frac{5}{2} = -\frac{4}{3}(x - 2)$$
$$y - \frac{5}{2} = -\frac{4}{3}x + \frac{8}{3}$$
$$y = -\frac{4}{3}x + \frac{31}{6}$$
$$6y = -8x + 31$$
$$8x + 6y = 31$$

65. ANSWER: B

Two vertices of an equilateral triangle are (11,7) and (3,13)

$$d = \sqrt{(11 - 3)^2 + (7 - 13)^2}$$
$$= \sqrt{100}$$
$$= 10$$
$\therefore$ side length of the equilateral triangle is 10

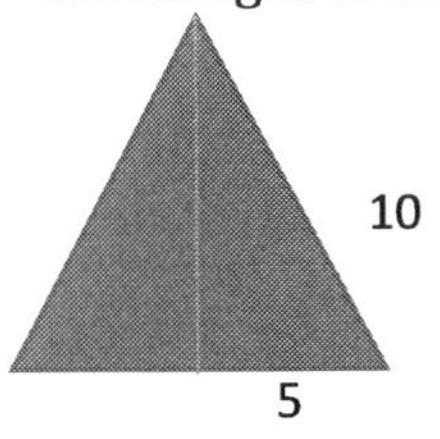

$$h = \sqrt{10^2 - 5^2}$$
$$h = \sqrt{75}$$
$$h = 5\sqrt{3}$$
$$A = \frac{1}{2}bh$$

$$A = \frac{1}{2} \times 10 \times 5\sqrt{3}$$
$$A = 25\sqrt{3}$$

66. ANSWER: A

$$P(\text{A correct}) = \frac{1}{2}, P(\text{B correct}) = \frac{1}{3}, P(\text{C correct}) = \frac{1}{4}$$
$$\therefore P(\text{A incorrect}) = \frac{1}{2}, P(\text{B incorrect}) = \frac{2}{3}, P(\text{C incorrect}) = \frac{3}{4}$$
$$\therefore P(\text{All incorrect}) = \frac{1}{2} \times \frac{2}{3} \times \frac{3}{4} = \frac{6}{24} = \frac{1}{4}$$
$$\therefore P(\text{ At least one gets correct}) = 1 - P(\text{All incorrect}) = 1 = \frac{1}{4} = \frac{3}{4}$$

67. ANSWER: B

$$(x-2)^{\log^2(x-2)+\log(x-2)^5-12} = 10^{\log(x-2)^2}$$
$$\log(x-2)^{\log^2(x-2)+\log(x-2)^5-12} = \log(x-2)^2$$
$$(\log^2(x-2) + \log(x-2)^5 - 12)\log x - 2 = 2\log x - 2$$
If we let $\alpha = \log x - 2$
$$(\alpha^2 + 5\alpha - 12)\alpha = 2\alpha$$
$$\alpha^3 + 5\alpha^2 - 14\alpha = 0$$
$$\alpha(\alpha + 7)(\alpha - 2) = 0$$
$$\alpha = 0, 2, -7$$
$$x = 3, 102, 10^{-7} + 2$$
However $x = 10^{-7}$ yields a negative argument
$$\therefore x = 3, 102$$

68. ANSWER: E

Let $x = 0.4\dot{7}\dot{3}$
$$10x = 4.\dot{7}\dot{3}$$
$$1000x = 473.\dot{7}\dot{3}$$
$$1000x - 10x = 990x = 469$$
$$x = \frac{469}{990}$$

69. ANSWER: ~~A~~ C

We want to find the shortest distance from (7,18) to $5x - 5y + 25 = 0$
A quicker way of working this out is through utilising the shortest distance (between a point and a plane) formula from the vectors chapter in AS Further Maths and adapting it for use in 2d:

$$d = \frac{|Ax_0 + By_0 + C\,|}{\sqrt{A^2 + B^2}}$$

For a point (x_0, y_0) at a shortest distance, d from $Ax + By + C = 0$

$$\therefore d = \frac{|5(7) - 5(18) + 25\,|}{\sqrt{5^2 + 5^2}}$$

$$d = \frac{|-30|}{\sqrt{50}}$$

$$d = \frac{30}{\sqrt{50}}$$

$$d = 3\sqrt{2}$$

70. ANSWER: C

$y = x^3 - x$ at $x = 2$

$$\frac{dy}{dx} = 3x^2 - 1$$

$$\left.\frac{dy}{dx}\right|_{x=2} = 3(2)^2 - 1$$

$$= 11$$

To find the co-ordinates at which tangent occurs:

$$y = (2)^3 - 2$$

$$y = 6$$

$\therefore$ (2,6) is the co-ordinate at which tangent occurs
We must now find the equation of the line with gradient 11 passing through (2,6)

$$y - 6 = 11(x - 2)$$

$$y - 6 = 11x - 22$$

$y = 11x - 16$ is the equation of the tangent

71. ANSWER: E

$$\sqrt{x} + \sqrt{y} = 1.$$

Intersects the x axis at $y = 0$:

$\sqrt{x} + \sqrt{0} = 1.$

$\therefore x = 1$

$\therefore$ x intercept is $(1,0)$

Intersects the y axis at $x = 0$

$\sqrt{0} + \sqrt{y} = 1.$

$\therefore y = 1$

$\therefore$ y intercept is $(0,1)$

$\sqrt{x} + \sqrt{y} = 1$

$\sqrt{y} = 1 - \sqrt{x}$

$y = (1 - \sqrt{x})^2$

$y = 1 + x - 2\sqrt{x}$

To find the area contained between the coordinate axis and curve:

$$\int_0^1 1 + x - 2\sqrt{x}\, dx$$

$$= \left[x + \frac{x^2}{2} - \frac{4x^{\frac{3}{2}}}{3}\right]_0^1$$

$$\left[1 + \frac{1}{2} - \frac{4}{3}\right] - [0]$$

$$= \frac{1}{6}$$

72. ANSWER: B

In order to work through this we can draw the graphs of $y = x$ and $y = \dfrac{1}{x^3}$

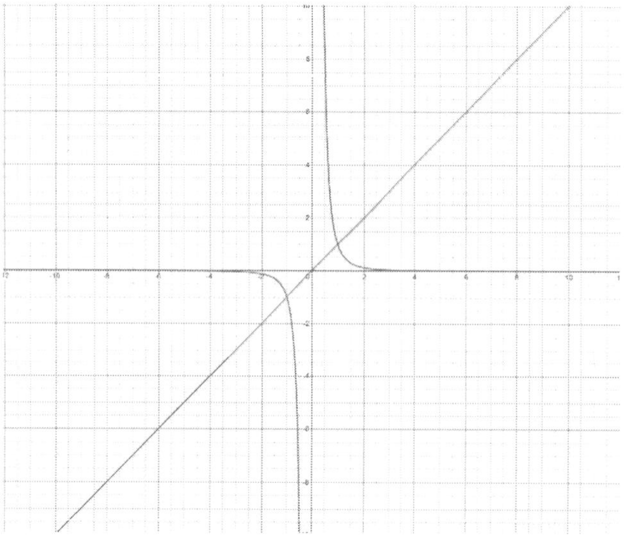

We can determine the points of intersection through the following:

$$\frac{1}{x^3} = x$$

$$1 = x^4$$

$$x^4 - 1 = 0$$

$$(x^2 + 1)(x^2 - 1) = 0$$

$$(x^2 + 1)(x + 1)(x - 1) = 0$$

$\therefore$ $x = 1$ and $x = -1$ at the points of intersection

$\therefore$ The points of intersection are: $(1,1)$ and $(-1,-1)$

If we want to satisfy the condition: $\frac{1}{x^3} < x$, we must find the reigon where the $y = x$ line is greater than the $y = \frac{1}{x^3}$ curve.

As we can see from above graph this occurs when: $-1 < x < 0$ and $x > 1$

$\{x: -1 < x < 0\} \cup \{x: x > 1\}$

73. ANSWER: E

$$S = \frac{7}{17} + \frac{77}{17^2} + \frac{777}{17^3} + \cdots \ (1)$$

$$\frac{S}{17} = \frac{7}{17^2} + \frac{77}{17^3} + \frac{777}{17^4} + \cdots (2)$$

$$(2) - (1) = \frac{16}{17} S = \frac{7}{17} + \frac{70}{17^2} + \frac{700}{17^3} + \cdots (2)$$

This is a geometric series with $r = \frac{10}{17}$ and $a = \frac{7}{17}$

$$\therefore \frac{16}{17} S = \frac{\frac{7}{17}}{1 - \frac{10}{17}} = \frac{\frac{7}{17}}{\frac{7}{17}} = 1$$

$$\therefore S = \frac{17}{16}$$

74. ANSWER: ~~C~~ ~~E~~ G

$$P(\text{less than 7 trials to determine winner}) = 1 - P(\text{no winner after 7 trials})$$

$$= 1 - \left(\frac{1}{2}\right)^7 = \frac{127}{128}$$

$$P(\text{A wins}) = \frac{1}{2} + \left(\frac{1}{2}\right)^3\left(\frac{1}{2}\right) + \left(\frac{1}{2}\right)^6\left(\frac{1}{2}\right) + \cdots$$

(P(A wins on 1st attempt)+P(A wins on 2nd attempt)+P(A wins on 3rd attempt)+...)
The sum of probabilities of A winning is the sum of an infinite geometric series.

$$a = \frac{1}{2}, r = \left(\frac{1}{2}\right)^3 = \frac{1}{8}$$

$$\therefore P(\text{A wins}) = S_\infty = \frac{\frac{1}{2}}{1-\frac{1}{8}} = \frac{\frac{1}{2}}{\frac{7}{8}} = \frac{1}{2} \times \frac{8}{7} = \frac{4}{7}$$

$$P(\text{A wins}|\text{less than 7 trials to determine winner}) = \frac{\frac{4}{7}}{\frac{127}{128}} = \frac{512}{889}$$

75. ANSWER: C

$$9^{(\log_3 1-2x)} = 5x^2 - 5$$
$$3^{2\,(\log_3 1-2x)} = 5x^2 - 5$$
$$(1-2x)^2 = 5x^2 - 5$$
$$0 = x^2 + 4x - 6$$
$$x = -2 \pm \sqrt{10}$$
$x = -2 - \sqrt{10}$ (as $-2 + \sqrt{10}$ yields a negative argument in the original log)

76. ANSWER: C

First we want to find out the equation of normal to the curve

$$y = x^{\frac{2}{3}}$$
$$\frac{dy}{dx} = \frac{2}{3}x^{-\frac{1}{3}}$$
$$\left.\frac{dy}{dx}\right|_{x=8} = \frac{2}{3}(8)^{-\frac{1}{3}}$$
$$\left.\frac{dy}{dx}\right|_{x=8} = \frac{2}{3}\left(\frac{1}{8}\right)^{\frac{1}{3}}$$
$$\left.\frac{dy}{dx}\right|_{x=8} = \frac{2}{3}\left(\frac{1}{2}\right)$$
$$\left.\frac{dy}{dx}\right|_{x=8} = \frac{1}{3}$$

If $m_{tangent} = \frac{1}{3}$

Then $m_{normal} = -3$

We must know find out what coordinate the normal passes through:

$x = 8$

$y = x^{\frac{2}{3}}$

$y = 8^{\frac{2}{3}}$

$y = 4$

$\therefore$ normal passes through (8,4) and has gradient of -3

We can substitute these values into: $y - y_1 = m(x - x_1)$

$y - 4 = -3(x - 8)$

$y - 4 = -3x + 24$

$\therefore$ equation of the normal is: $y = 28 - 3x$

$\therefore$ the y intercept is (0,28) and the x intercept is $\left(\frac{28}{3}, 0\right)$

$\therefore$ The distance between these 2 points is: $\sqrt{\left(\frac{28}{3}\right)^2 + 28^2}$

$= \sqrt{\frac{784}{9} + 784}$

$= \sqrt{784\left(\frac{1}{9} + 1\right)}$

$= \sqrt{784\left(\frac{10}{9}\right)}$

$= \frac{28\sqrt{10}}{3}$

77. ANSWER:C

$x^2 + 2mx + 10 - 3m > 0$

As the expression remains positive, the curve doesn't intersect the x axis. Therefore the discriminant is less than zero

$\therefore b^2 - 4ac < 0$

$(2m)^2 - 4(1)(10 - 3m) < 0$

$4m^2 - 4(10 - 3m) < 0$

$4m^2 + 12m - 40 < 0$

$(4m - 8)(m + 5) < 0$

$m = 2$ and $m = -5$ are the critical values
The range is: $-5 < m < 2$

78. ANSWER: F

Geometric sequence: $a, a + d, a + 6d$

$$\frac{a + d}{a} = \frac{a + 6d}{a + d}$$
$$(a + d)^2 = a(a + 6d)$$
$$d^2 = 4ad$$
$$d^2 - 4ad = 0$$
$$d(d - 4a) = 0$$
$d = 0$ or $d = 4a$
$$(a) + (a + d) + (a + 6d) = 3a + 7d = 93$$
$$3a + 7(4a) = 93$$
$$a = 3$$
$$d = 12$$
$$r = \frac{a + d}{a} = \frac{3 + 12}{3} = 5$$
$3\text{rd term} = a + 6d = 3 + 6(12) = 75$
$4\text{th term} = 75 \times 5 = 375$

79. ANSWER:D

$f(x) = (x^2 + 4)^2$.What is the minimum value of $5f(3x - 11) + 4$
$f(x) = x^4 + 8x^2 + 16$

$f'(x) = 0$ at minimum value
$f'(x) = 4x^3 + 16x$
$f'(x) = 4x(x^2 + 4)$
$\therefore$ minimum value occurs at $x = 0$ (we know this is a minimum as we we can think of the general shape of a quartic)
$\therefore$ $(0,16)$ is the minimum point
Min point of $f(x - 11) \Rightarrow (11,16)$
Min point of $f(3x - 11) \Rightarrow \left(\frac{11}{3}, 16\right)$
Min point of $5f(3x - 11) \Rightarrow \left(\frac{11}{3}, 80\right)$
Min point of $5f(3x - 11) + 4 \Rightarrow \left(\frac{11}{3}, 84\right)$

80. ANSWER: H

$$\frac{x}{x+4} = \frac{3-x}{x-1}$$

$x(x-1) = (3-x)(x+4)$

$x^2 - x = -x^2 - x + 12$

$2x^2 - 12 = 0$

$x^2 - 6 = 0$

$x^2 = 6$

$\therefore x = \pm\sqrt{6}$

81. ANSWER: B

We know that $P(E \cap F) + P(F' \cap E) = P(E)$

$\therefore 0.6 + P(F' \cap E) = 0.8$

$\therefore P(F' \cap E) = 0.2$

We also know that $P(E \cap F) + P(E' \cap F) = P(F)$

$\therefore 0.6 + P(E' \cap F) = 0.7$

$P(E' \cap F) = 0.1$

Finally:

$P(E' \cap F') = 1 - [P(E \cap F) + P(E' \cap F) + P(F' \cap E)]$

$P(E' \cap F') = 1 - [0.6 + 0.1 + 0.2]$

$P(E' \cap F') = 1 - [0.9] = 0.1$

The following information can be represented on a Venn Diagram:

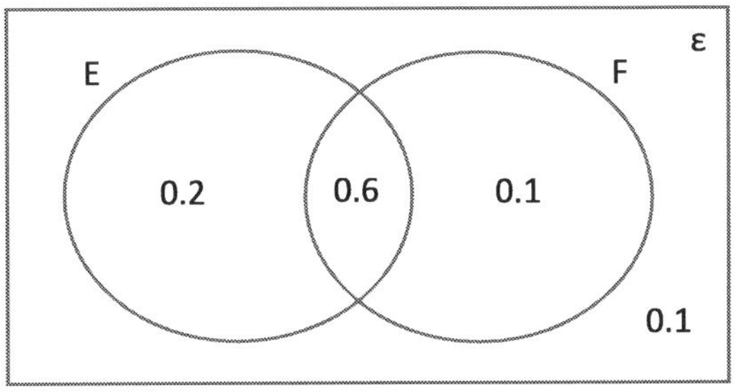

$$P(E'|F') = \frac{P(E' \cap F')}{P(F')}$$

$$P(E'|F') = \frac{0.1}{0.3} = \frac{1}{3}$$

82. ANSWER: C

$\log_6(x+3) = 1 - \log_6(x-2)$
$\log_6(x+3) + \log_6(x-2) = 1$
$\log_6(x-2)(x+3) = 1$
$(x-2)(x+3) = 6$
$x^2 + x - 6 = 6$
$x^2 + x - 12 = 0$
$(x+4)(x-3) = 0$
$x = 3 \text{ or } x = -4$
$x = 3$ $(as\ x = -4\ provides\ a\ negative\ argument)$

83. ANSWER: F

Let the price of the bag of sand be P
Following a reduction of price by 40% the price is: $P - (0.4 \times P) = 0.6P$

Following a further reduction by 10%, the price is: $0.6P - (0.1 \times 0.6P) = 0.54P$
$\therefore$ Total Reduction: 46% reduction in price

84. ANSWER: F

There are two scenarios for a function with one real root;
1)A polynomial or a straight line which passes through the x axis once
2)A polynomial which touches the x axis once (i. e. at stationary point)
Hence any transformation which affects the y coordinate of 0 will alter the number of roots
Let the x intercept of a curve be (x, 0)
$y = -f(x)$ will not have an effect on the intercept as it maps (x,y) to (x,-y)
y=f(-x) will not have an effect on the intercept as it maps (x,y) to (-x,y)
y=f(x+3) will not have an effect on the intercept as it maps (x,y) to (x-3,y)
y=f(x)+3 will have an effect on the intercept as it maps (x,y) to (x,y+3)

y=3f(x) will not have an effect on the intercept as it maps (x, y) to $(x, 3y)$

y=f(3x)will have an effect on the intercept as it maps (x,y) to $(\frac{x}{3}, y)$

y=3-f(x) will not have an effect on the intercept as it maps (x, y) to $(x, 3-y)$

85. ANSWER: B

There is no rule for the ~~intergal~~ integral: $\int_{-3}^{1} |x|(x-1)dx$.

In such a case it is best to sketch the graph and then evaluate the integral accordingly:

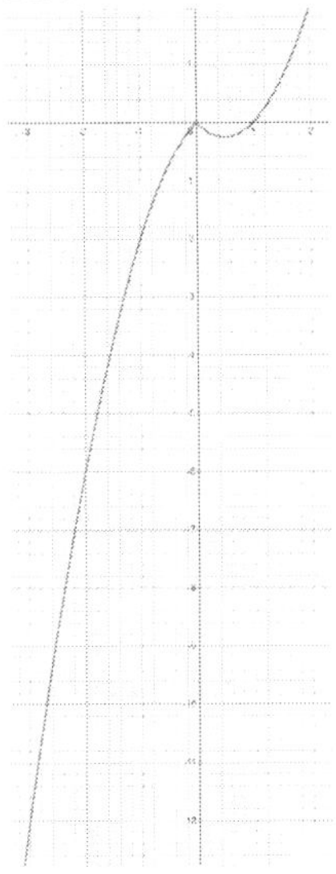

$$I = \int_{-3}^{1} |x|(x-1)dx.$$

$$I = \int_{-3}^{0} x - x^2\, dx + \int_{0}^{1} x^2 - x\, dx$$

$$I = -\frac{41}{3}$$

86. ANSWER: E

p: q is 5: 6

q: r is 4: 13

∴ p: q is 20: 24

$\therefore$ q: r is 24: 78

$\therefore$ p: q: r is 20: 24: 78

$20 + 24 + 78 = 122$

$\frac{244}{122} = 2$ $\therefore$ Multiply the ratio of p: q: r by 2 to get p, q and r

$\therefore p = 40, q = 48, r = 156$

$\therefore p + r = 196$

87. ANSWER:C

We know that the expansion of $f(x) = \left(3 + \frac{x}{k}\right)^8$ has a coefficient of x^2 which is 3 times the coefficient of x^3

Coefficient of x^2: $\binom{8}{2} \times 3^6 \times \left(\frac{1}{k}\right)^2 = 28 \times 729 \times \frac{1}{k^2} = \frac{20{,}412}{k^2}$

Coefficient of x^3: $\binom{8}{3} \times 3^5 \times \left(\frac{1}{k}\right)^3 = 56 \times 243 \times \frac{1}{k^3} = \frac{13608}{k^3}$

$\therefore \frac{20{,}412}{k^2} = 3\left(\frac{13608}{k^3}\right)$

$\frac{20{,}412}{k^2} = \frac{40824}{k^3}$

$20412k^3 = 40824k^2$

$20412k^3 - 40824k^2 = 0$

$20412k^2(k - 2) = 0$

$k = 2$

88. ANSWER: A

What is the area enclosed between $y^2 = 8x$ and $x = 2$.

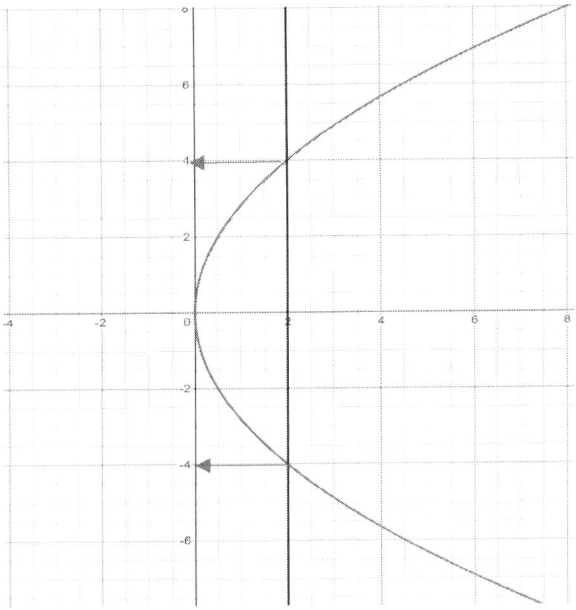

We can integrate with respect to y:

First we must re – arrange to get x in terms of y:

$$y^2 = 8x$$

$$x = \frac{y^2}{8}$$

Area of a rectangle: $8 \times 2 = 16$

Area between curve and y axis:

$$= \int_{-4}^{4} \frac{y^2}{8} dy$$

$$= \left[\frac{y^3}{24}\right]_{-4}^{4}$$

$$= \left[\frac{64}{24}\right] - \left[-\frac{64}{24}\right]$$

$$= \frac{128}{24}$$

$$= \frac{16}{3}$$

Area bound between $y^2 = 8x$ and $x = 2$:

$$16 - \frac{16}{3} = \frac{32}{3}$$

89. ANSWER:D

$$\text{let } S_1 = a + ar + ar^2 + \cdots + ar^{n-1} + \cdots \infty$$
$$\text{let } S_2 = ar + ar^3 + ar^5 + \cdots \infty$$
$$\text{Infinite Sum of } S_1 = \frac{a}{1-r}$$
$$\text{Infinite Sum of } S_2 = \frac{ar}{1-r^2}$$
$$S_1 = 3S_2$$
$$\frac{a}{1-r} = 3\left(\frac{ar}{1-r^2}\right)$$
$$a(1-r^2) = 3ar(1-r)$$
$$a(1-r)(1+r) = 3ar(1-r)$$
$$a(1+r) = 3ar$$
$$1 + r = 3r \text{ (as a is non-zero)}$$
$$\therefore r = \frac{1}{2}$$

90. ANSWER: F

First we can start of by calculating the distance between the two adjacent vertices, this will give us one side length of the rectangle.

$d = \sqrt{14^2 + 0^2} = 14$

We can also work out the centre of the circle:

The midpoint of the top side is $(-1,5)$, Hence we know that the centre has an x coordinate of -1.

We also know that the line $3y = x + 7$ contains the diameter and hence contains the centre.

Substituting the value $x = -1$:

$3y = -1 + 7$

$3y = 6$

$y = 2$

$\therefore$ The centre of the circle is $(-1,2)$

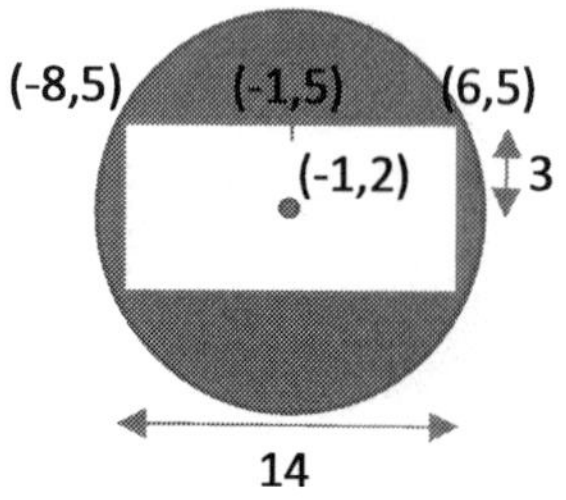

We know that half of the height of the rectangle is 3 due to the difference in y coordinates of the centre and the midpoint of the top side.
Hence the area of the rectangle is: $6 \times 14 = 84$

91. ANSWER: D

What is the sum of the series: $m(m+n) + m^2(m^2+n^2) + m^3(m^3+n^3)+\ldots$
given $|m| < 1$ and $|n| < 1$
We know that $|m| < 1$ and $|n| < 1$
$\therefore |mn| < 1$
$m(m+n) + m^2(m^2+n^2) + m^3(m^3+n^3)+\ldots$
$= (m^2 + m^4 + m^6 + \cdots) + [mn + (mn)^2 + (mn)^3 + \cdots]$
$= \dfrac{m^2}{1-m^2} + \dfrac{mn}{1-mn}$

92. ANSWER:D

$$\int_1^3 \left(2x + \frac{3}{x}\right)^2 dx$$
$$\left(2x + \frac{3}{x}\right)^2 = \left(4x^2 + 12 + \frac{9}{x^2}\right)$$
$$\therefore \int_1^3 (4x^2 + 12 + 9x^{-2})\, dx$$
$$= \left[\frac{4x^3}{3} + 12x - 9x^{-1}\right]_1^3$$
$$= \left[\frac{4(3)^3}{3} + 12(3) - 9(3)^{-1}\right] - \left[\frac{4}{3} + 12 - 9\right]$$
$$= \left[\frac{4(27)}{3} + 12(3) - 9(3)^{-1}\right] - \left[\frac{4}{3} + 12 - 9\right]$$
$$= [36 + 36 - 3] - \left[\frac{4}{3} + 3\right]$$
$$= 66 - \frac{4}{3}$$
$$= \frac{194}{3}$$

93. ANSWER: A

$y + \frac{1}{2} = 5x \quad (1)$
$x^2 - 4ky + 3k = 0 \quad (2)$
$(1) \Rightarrow y = 5x - \frac{1}{2}$
Sub the value of y into (1)
$x^2 - 4k\left(5x - \frac{1}{2}\right) + 3k = 0$
$x^2 - 20kx + 2k + 3k = 0$
$x^2 - 20kx + 5k = 0 \quad (3)$
As there are only one pair of solutions – the discriminant is equal to zero.
$(-20k)^2 - 4(1)(5k) = 0$
$400k^2 - 20k = 0$
$20k(20k - 1) = 0$
$k = \frac{1}{20}$ (as $k \neq 0$ is defined in the question)
Substitute the value of k into equation (3)
$x^2 - 20\left(\frac{1}{20}\right)x + 5\left(\frac{1}{20}\right) = 0$
$= x^2 - x + \frac{1}{4} = 0$
$= 4x^2 - 4x + 1 = 0$
$= (2x - 1)^2 = 0$
$\therefore x = \frac{1}{2}$
Sub the value of x into (1)
$y + \frac{1}{2} = \frac{5}{2}$
$y = \frac{5}{2} - \frac{1}{2}$
$y = 2$

$x + y = 2 + \frac{1}{2} = \frac{5}{2}$

94. ANSWER: B

$f(x) = (3 + ax)(1 + bx)^5$. and the expansion of f(x) is $3 + 17x + \frac{70}{3}x^2 + kx^3$
$f(x) = (3 + ax)(1 + 5bx + 10b^2x^2 + 10b^3x^3 + 5b^4x^4 + b^5x^5)$
$f(x) = 3 + 15bx + 30b^2x^2 + 30b^3x^3 + ax + 5abx^2 + 10ab^2x^3$
$f(x) = 3 + (15b + a)x + (30b^2 + 5ab)x^2 + (30b^3 + 10ab^2)x^3$

$17 = 15b + a \quad (1)$

$\frac{70}{3} = 30b^2 + 5ab \quad (2)$

$(1) \Rightarrow a = 17 - 15b$

Substitute the value of a into (2)

$\frac{70}{3} = 30b^2 + 5(17 - 15b)b$

$\frac{70}{3} = 30b^2 + (85 - 75b)b$

$\frac{70}{3} = 30b^2 + 85b - 75b^2$

$\frac{70}{3} = -45b^2 + 85b$

$45b^2 - 85b + \frac{70}{3} = 0$

$135b^2 - 255b + 70 = 0$

$27b^2 - 51b + 14 = 0$

$(9b - 14)(3b - 1) = 0$

$b = \frac{1}{3}, b = \frac{14}{9}$

$a = 12, a = -\frac{19}{3}$

However as both constants are given to be positive:

$\therefore a = 12, b = \frac{1}{3}$

We know from the expansion that $k = 30b^3 + 10ab^2$

$k = 30\left(\frac{1}{3}\right)^3 + 10(12)\left(\frac{1}{3}\right)^2$

$k = \frac{30}{27} + \frac{40}{3}$

$k = \frac{10}{9} + \frac{40}{3}$

$k = \frac{130}{9}$

95. ANSWER: A

$5y - 4x = 6$

$5y = 4x + 6$

$y = \frac{4}{5}x + \frac{6}{5}$

$\therefore p = \frac{6}{5}$

We know that the other straight line is parallel and hence the gradient must be the same and that it passes through (2,3)
Hence substitute the values into: $y - y_1 = m(x - x_1)$.

$$y - 3 = \frac{4}{5}(x - 2)$$
$$y - 3 = \frac{4}{5}x - \frac{8}{5}$$
$$y = \frac{4}{5}x + \frac{7}{5}$$
$$\therefore q = \frac{7}{5}$$
$$\therefore q - p = \frac{7}{5} - \frac{6}{5} = \frac{1}{5}$$

96. ANSWER: D

$$x^{1+\log x} = 10x$$
$$= \log x^{1+\log} = \log 10x$$
$$= 1 + \log x\,(\log x) = \log 10 + \log x$$
$$\text{let } \alpha = \log x$$
$$= (1 + \alpha)\alpha = 1 + \alpha$$
$$= \alpha^2 - 1 = 0$$
$$\alpha = \pm 1$$
$$\therefore x = 10, \frac{1}{10}$$

97. ANSWER: G

$$a = 5\sqrt{\frac{b+3}{2}} - 1$$
$$b = 2\left(\frac{a+1}{5}\right)^2 - 3$$

98. ANSWER:C

We want the x^4 term in the expansion $(4\sqrt{p} + 5x)^6$

As per the binomial theorem the x^4 term is:

$= \binom{6}{4}\left(4\sqrt{p}\right)^2(5x)^4$

$= 15(16p)(625x^4)$

$= 150{,}000px^4$

We know that the coefficient of the x^4 term is 300,000

$150{,}000p = 300{,}000$

$\therefore p = 2$

99. ANSWER: A

If the number of dogs is x, then the number of cats is 5x.

Total $= 5x + x = 6x$

$P(\text{Dog on 1st Attempt}) = \frac{x}{6x} = \frac{1}{6}$

$P(\text{Dog on 2nd Attempt}) = \frac{(x-1)}{6x-1}$

$y = P(\text{Dog, Dog}) = \frac{1}{6} \times \frac{(x-1)}{6x-1} = \frac{(x-1)}{6(6x-1)} = \frac{x-1}{36x-6}$

$y = \frac{x-1}{36x-6}$

$(36x-6)y = x-1$

$36xy - 6y = x - 1$

$36xy - x = 6y - 1$

$x(36y-1) = 6y - 1$

$\therefore x = \frac{6y-1}{36y-1}$

100. ANSWER:D

Whilst you can obviously solve this by drawing out a coordinate grid, it may be quicker to consider this problem through matrix transformations: (although pay close attention to the order of the transformation)

$90°$ ACW matrix $\Rightarrow \begin{pmatrix} 0 & -1 \\ 1 & 0 \end{pmatrix}$

Reflection across line $y = x \Rightarrow \begin{pmatrix} 0 & 1 \\ 1 & 0 \end{pmatrix}$

$\therefore \begin{pmatrix} 0 & 1 \\ 1 & 0 \end{pmatrix}\begin{pmatrix} 0 & -1 \\ 1 & 0 \end{pmatrix}\begin{pmatrix} 7 \\ 2 \end{pmatrix} = \begin{pmatrix} 7 \\ -2 \end{pmatrix}$

$\therefore (7, -2)$ is the resulting coordinate.

101. ANSWER: F

Original sequence: a, ar, ar^2, ar^3
Altered sequence: $a-2, ar-7, ar^2-9, ar^3-5$ (is an arithmetic sequence)

$ar-7-(a-2)=ar^2-9-(ar-7)$

$\therefore a+ar^2=2ar-3 \Rightarrow 1+r^2=2r-\frac{3}{a} \quad (1)$

$ar^3-5-(ar^2-9)=ar^2-9-(ar-7)$

$\therefore ar+ar^3=2ar^2-6 \Rightarrow\ 1+r^2=2r-\frac{6}{ar} \quad (2)$

$\therefore 2r-\frac{6}{ar}=2r-\frac{3}{a}$

$\frac{6}{ar}=\frac{3}{a}$

$\therefore r=2$

Sub value of r in (1)

$1+4=4-\frac{3}{a}$

$\therefore a=-3$

$\therefore$ original sequence is: $-3,-6,-12,-24$

$\therefore$ smallest number is -24

102. ANSWER: E

Two fair dice are rolled and it is revealed that at least one of the numbers was a 4. What is the probability that the other number is a 6?

Let A be the event of rolling a 6 on the other dice

Let B be the event of either dice rolling a 4

Using a sample space:

(First roll, Second Roll)

(1,1)	(1,2)	(1,3)	(1,4)	(1,5)	(1,6)
(2,1)	(2,2)	(2,3)	(2,4)	(2,5)	(2,6)
(3,1)	(3,2)	(3,3)	(3,4)	(3,5)	(3,6)
(4,1)	(4,2)	(4,3)	(4,4)	(4,5)	(4,6)
(5,1)	(5,2)	(5,3)	(5,4)	(5,5)	(5,6)
(6,1)	(6,2)	(6,3)	(6,4)	(6,5)	(6,6)

$P(A\cap B)=\frac{2}{36}=\frac{1}{18}$

$P(B)=\frac{11}{36}$

$$P(A|B) = \frac{P(A \cap B)}{P(B)}$$

$$= \frac{\frac{1}{18}}{\frac{11}{36}}$$

$$= \frac{2}{11}$$

103. ANSWER: A

$\left(a^{\log_b x}\right)^2 - 5x^{\log_b a} + 6 = 0$

$= \left(x^{\log_b a}\right)^2 - 5x^{\log_b a} + 6 = 0$

let $\alpha = x^{\log_b a}$

$\alpha^2 - 5\alpha + 6 = 0$

$(\alpha - 3)(\alpha - 2) = 0$

$\alpha = 3$ or $\alpha = 2$

$x^{\log_b a} = 3$ or $x^{\log_b a} = 2$

$x = 2^{\log_a b}, 3^{\log_a b}$

104. ANSWER: F

Convert $2.1\dot{4}\dot{5}$ to a mixed number fraction

let $x = 0.1\dot{4}\dot{5}$

$1000x = 145.\dot{4}\dot{5}$

$10x = 1.\dot{4}\dot{5}$

$1000x - 10x = 990x = 144$

$x = \frac{144}{990} = \frac{8}{55}$

$\therefore 2.1\dot{4}\dot{5} = 2\frac{8}{55}$

105. ANSWER: B

equation of the normal at $y = -2x^2 - 8x + \frac{2}{x}$ at $(-1,4)$

$\frac{dy}{dx} = -4x - 8 - 2x^{-2}$

$\left.\frac{dy}{dx}\right|_{x=-1} = -4(-1) - 8 - 2(-1)^{-2}$

$= -6$

$\therefore$ gradient of normal is $\frac{1}{6}$

We want to find the equation of the line through (-1,4) with gradient $\frac{1}{6}$

$y - 4 = \frac{1}{6}(x + 1)$

$y - 4 = \frac{1}{6}x + \frac{1}{6}$

$y = \frac{1}{6}x + \frac{25}{6}$

The x intercepts the axis when $y = 0$

$0 = \frac{1}{6}x + \frac{25}{6}$

$-\frac{1}{6}x = \frac{25}{6}$

$x = -25$

$(-25,0)$ is the x intercept of the normal to the line at $(-1,4)$

106. ANSWER: A

$k = x^3 + 5x^2 + 3x - 3$ has 3 roots

In order to find the range of values for k we must consider the range between the intersection of the two stationary points with the coodinate axis.

$y = x^3 + 5x^2 + 3x - 3 - k$

$\frac{dy}{dx} = 3x^2 + 10x + 3$

$\frac{dy}{dx} = 0$ at the stationary points

$0 = 3x^2 + 10x + 3$

$0 = (3x + 1)(x + 3)$

$x = -\frac{1}{3}, x = -3$ are the coordinates at which the stationary points occur.

Now we must find the coordinates of these stationary points in terms of k.

For $x = -3$

$y = (-3)^3 + 5(-3)^2 + 3(-3) - 3 - k$

$y = -27 + 5(9) - 9 - 3 - k$

$y = 6 - k$

For $x = -\frac{1}{3}$

$y = \left(-\frac{1}{3}\right)^3 + 5\left(-\frac{1}{3}\right)^2 + 3\left(-\frac{1}{3}\right) - 3 - k$

$y = -\frac{94}{27} - k$

$\therefore$ Coordinates are: $(-3, 6 - k)$ and $\left(-\frac{1}{3}, -\frac{94}{27} - k\right)$

Considering the shape of a general positive cubic we know that:

$\Rightarrow (-3, 6 - k)$ is a local maxima

$\Rightarrow \left(-\frac{1}{3}, -\frac{94}{27} - k\right)$ is a local minima

$\therefore$ We want $6 - k > 0$ (above the x axis)

and $-\frac{94}{27} - k < 0$ (below the x axis)

$\therefore k < 6$ and $k > -\frac{94}{27}$

$\therefore$ range is: $-\frac{94}{27} < k < 6$

107. ANSWER: A

$e^{\sin x} - e^{-si} \quad = 4$

$-1 \leq \sin x \leq 1$

$\therefore \frac{1}{e} \leq e^{\sin x} \leq e$

$\therefore \frac{1}{e} \leq e^{-\sin} \quad \leq e$

$\therefore$ The maximum value of the LHS is: $e - \frac{1}{e}$

$\therefore$ There are no real solutions

108. ANSWER: F

$$\frac{1}{\sqrt{2} + \sqrt{3} + \sqrt{5}}$$

In order to solve this question we will utilise the usual method but we will group terms

$$= \frac{1}{(\sqrt{2} + \sqrt{3}) + \sqrt{5}}$$

$$= \frac{1}{(\sqrt{2} + \sqrt{3}) + \sqrt{5}} \times \frac{(\sqrt{2} + \sqrt{3}) - \sqrt{5}}{(\sqrt{2} + \sqrt{3}) - \sqrt{5}}$$

$$= \frac{(\sqrt{2}+\sqrt{3})-\sqrt{5}}{(\sqrt{2}+\sqrt{3})^2-5}$$

$$= \frac{(\sqrt{2}+\sqrt{3})-\sqrt{5}}{(2+3+2\sqrt{6})-5}$$

$$= \frac{\sqrt{2}+\sqrt{3}-\sqrt{5}}{2\sqrt{6}}$$

$$= \frac{\sqrt{2}+\sqrt{3}-\sqrt{5}}{2\sqrt{6}} \times \frac{\sqrt{6}}{\sqrt{6}}$$

$$= \frac{\sqrt{12}+\sqrt{18}-\sqrt{30}}{2(6)}$$

$$= \frac{2\sqrt{3}+3\sqrt{2}-\sqrt{30}}{12}$$

109. ANSWER: C

$u_2 = 2$ and $S_\infty = 8$

$ar = 2$ and $\frac{a}{1-r} = 8$

$a = \frac{2}{r}$

$\therefore \frac{\frac{2}{r}}{1-r} = 8$

$\therefore \frac{2}{1-r^2} = 8$

$8r^2 - 8r + 2 = 0$

$4r^2 - 4r + 1 = 0$

$(2r-1)^2 = 0$

$r = \frac{1}{2}$

$a\left(\frac{1}{2}\right) = 2$

$a = 4$

110. ANSWER: D

$4\cos^3 x - 4\cos^2 x - \cos(180 + x) - 1 = 0$, range: $-360 \leq x \leq 360$
$= 4\cos^3 x - 4\cos^2 x + \cos x - 1$
let $t = \cos\theta$
$\therefore 4t^3 - 4t^2 + t - 1 = 0$
$(t - 1)(4t^2 + 1) = 0$
$t = 1$
$\cos\theta = 1$
$\therefore$ there are 3 solutions in the range

111. ANSWER: B

$(2x - 3)^2 - (x + 3)^2$
$= (4x^2 - 12x + 9) - (x^2 + 6x + 9)$
$= (3x^2 - 18x)$
$= 3(x^2 - 6x)$
$= 3(x - 3)^2 - 27$
$\therefore r = -27$

112. ANSWER: G

$\left(\frac{\log x}{2}\right)\log^2 x + \log x^2 - 2 = \log\sqrt{x}$
$= \left(\frac{\log x}{2}\right)\log^2 x + 2\log x - 2 = \frac{1}{2}\log x$
let $\alpha = \log x$
$\therefore \left(\frac{\alpha}{2}\right)(\alpha^2) + 2\alpha - 2 = \frac{1}{2}\alpha$
$= \frac{\alpha^3}{2} + \frac{3}{2}\alpha - 2 = 0$
$\alpha^3 + 3\alpha - 4 = 0$
$\alpha = 1$ is a solution and hence $(\alpha - 1)$ is a factor (factor theorem)
$(\alpha - 1)(\alpha^2 + \alpha + 4) = 0$
$\alpha^2 + \alpha + 4$ has $b^2 - 4ac < 0$ hence no real solutions
$1 = \log x$
$\therefore x = 10$

113. ANSWER: C

$(6-x)^4 + (8-x)^4 = 16$

You can obviously expand this to get a hidden quadratic and solve. However a quicker way is to look at different cases:

If $x < 6$ or $x > 8$. Then $f(x) > 16$

If $6 < x < 8$, Then $f(x) < 16$

If $x = 6$ and $x = 8$. Then $f(x) = 16$

$\therefore$ 2 solutions exist

114. ANSWER:D

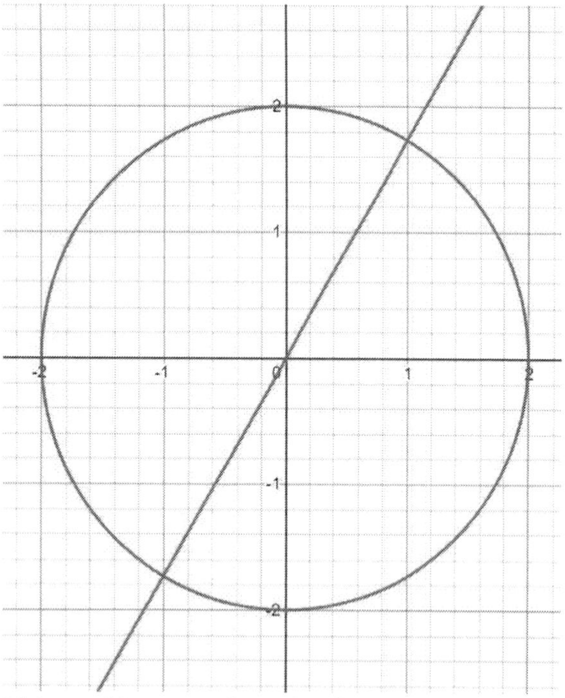

This problem may be solved using integration, however a quicker method is:

We can find the angle between the line and the positive x axis:

$$\tan\theta = \frac{y}{x} = \frac{\sqrt{3}}{1}$$

$$\tan\theta = \sqrt{3}$$

$\therefore \theta = \frac{\pi}{3}$

$\therefore$ The area bounded between the x axis, the curve and the line can be calculated as a fraction of a circle.

As $\theta = \frac{\pi}{3}$, we know that the area is $\frac{1}{6}$th of a circle.

Equation of the circle is: $x^2 + y^2 = 4 \Rightarrow \therefore r^2 = 4$

Area bound by curve, line and positive x axis $= \frac{1}{6} \times$ Area of circle

Area bound by curve, line and positive x axis $= \frac{1}{6} \times \pi r^2$

Area bound by curve, line and positive x axis $= \frac{1}{6} \times \pi(4)$

Area bound by curve, line and positive x axis $= \frac{2}{3}\pi$

115. ANSWER: E

If $4^{\frac{a+1}{b}} = 125$ and $5^{\frac{b}{a}} = 2$. Then what is the value of $\frac{25^b}{a^2}$

$= \left(5^{\frac{b}{a}}\right)^2 = 2^2$

$= 5^{\frac{2b}{a}} = 4$

$\therefore \left(5^{\frac{2b}{a}}\right)^{\frac{a+1}{b}} = 4^{\frac{a+1}{b}} = 125$

$5^{\frac{2b(a+1)}{ab}} = 125 = 5^3$

$\therefore 3 = \frac{2(a+1)}{a}$

$3a = 2a + 2$

$a = 2$

$5^{\frac{b}{2}} = 2$

$\therefore 5^b = 4$

$\frac{25^b}{a^2} = \frac{(5^2)^b}{4} = \frac{5^{2b}}{4} = \frac{16}{4} = 4 = 4^1$

116. ANSWER: G

We want to find the minimum vertical distance between the curves $C_1 = y = x^2 + 1$ and $C_2 = y = x - x^2$.

First consider the general points on C_1 and C_2.

$C_1: (x, x^2 + 1)$ $C_2: (x, x - x^2)$

As the general x coordinate is the same we can use :

$D = \sqrt{(x_2 - x_1)^2 + (y_2 - y_1)^2}$ in order to minimise vertical distance between curves

$D = \sqrt{(x - x)^2 + \left((x - x^2) - (x^2 + 1)\right)^2}$

$D = \sqrt{(-2x^2 + x - 1)^2}$

$D = \sqrt{\left(-1(2x^2 - x + 1)\right)^2}$

$D = \sqrt{(2x^2 - x + 1)^2}$

$D = 2x^2 - x + 1$

$\frac{dD}{dx} = 4x - 1$

$\frac{dD}{dx} = 0$ at the minimum point

$0 = 4x - 1$

$x = \frac{1}{4}$ at the minimum point

at $x = \frac{1}{4}$:

$D = 2\left(\frac{1}{4}\right)^2 - \left(\frac{1}{4}\right) + 1$

$D = 2\left(\frac{1}{16}\right) - \frac{1}{4} + 1$

$D = \frac{1}{8} - \frac{1}{4} + 1$

$D = \frac{7}{8}$

117. ANSWER: D

Let $l_1: 9x + 6y - 7 = 0$ and $l_2: 3x + 2y + 6 = 0$.

You should notice that these 2 lines are parallel to each other as they have the same gradient.

$l_1: y = -\frac{3}{2}x + \frac{7}{6}$

$l_2: y = -\frac{3}{2}x - 3$

In order to find the locus of points equidistant from 2 lines, we must find the line that is half way between l_1 and l_2

y intercepts of the respective curves are the following: $\left(0. \frac{7}{6}\right)$ and $(0, -3)$

Mid point of y intercepts is: $\left(0, -\frac{11}{12}\right)$

$\therefore$ the equation of the locus is: $y = -\frac{3}{2}x - \frac{11}{12}$

$12y = -18x - 11$

$12y + 18x + 11 = 0$

118. ANSWER: A

circumeference of a circle is reduced by 50%, We want to know what its area is reduced by

$2\pi r = C$

$\frac{1}{2}C$ means r must halve as well because 2π is a constant

$A = \pi r^2$

$A = \pi\left(\frac{1}{2}r\right)^2$

$A = \frac{\pi r^2}{4}$

$$\%change = \frac{\pi r^2 - \frac{\pi r^2}{4}}{\pi r^2} \times 100 = 75\%$$

119. ANSWER: A

$1, \log_{81}(3^x + 48), \log_9\left(3^x - \frac{8}{3}\right)$

$= \log_9 9, \log_9(3^x + 48)^{\frac{1}{2}}, \log_9\left(3^x - \frac{8}{3}\right)$ (You can root the base and the argument)

$\log_9(3^x + 48)^{\frac{1}{2}} - \log_9 9 = \log_9\left(3^x - \frac{8}{3}\right) - \log_9(3^x + 48)^{\frac{1}{2}}$

$$\therefore \frac{\sqrt{3^x + 48}}{9} = \frac{3^x - \frac{8}{3}}{\sqrt{3^x + 48}}$$

This is because in general, if logs of the same base are in an arithmetic sequence, their arguments are said to be in a geometric sequence.

$3^x + 48 = 9\left(3^x - \frac{8}{3}\right)$

$3^x + 48 = 9(3^x) - 24$

$72 = 8(3^x)$

$3^x = 9$

$\therefore x = 2$

120. ANSWER: A

$x^{x+y} = y \qquad (1)$
$y^{x+y} = x^2y \qquad (2)$
$(1) \Rightarrow \log x^{x+y} = \log y$
$= (x + y)\log x = \log y$
$x\log x + y\log x = \log y$
$(2) \Rightarrow \log y^{x+y} = \log x^2y$
$= (x + y)\log y = \log x^2 + \log y$
$= x\log y + y\log y = 2\log x + \log y$
Sub in value for $\log y$ from (1)
$= x\log y + y\log y = 2\log x + x\log x + y\log x$
$= x(\log y - \log x) + y(\log y - \log x) = 2\log x$
$(x + y)(\log y - \log x) = 2\log x$
$(2) \times (1) = (xy)^{x+y} = x^2y^2$
$= (xy)^{x+y} = (xy)^2$
$\therefore x + y = 2 \quad (3)$
$\therefore 2(\log y - \log x) = 2\log x$
$= (\log y - \log x) = \log x$
$\log y = 2\log x$
$\log y = \log x^2$
$y = x^2 \ (4)$
Sub value of y from (4)
$x^2 + x = 2$
$x^2 + x - 2 = 0$
$(x + 2)(x - 1) = 0$
$x = -2$ or $x = 1$
so $y = 4$ or 1
$\therefore$ Product of all solutions $= (-2)(1)(4)(1) = -8$

121. ANSWER: E

$a = a + 6d$
$b = a + 10d$
$c = a + 12d$
$\therefore \frac{a}{c} = \frac{a + 6d}{a + 12d}$
As a, b, c are in a geometric progression we know:
$r = \frac{a + 10d}{a + 6d} = \frac{a + 12d}{a + 10d}$

$\therefore (a + 10d)^2 = (a + 12d)(a + 6d)$

$28d^2 + 2ad = 0$

$a = -14d$

$\therefore \frac{a}{c} = \frac{-14d + 6d}{-14d + 12d} = 4$

122. ANSWER: E

Circumference of base of party hat $= \pi D = 20\pi$

Circumference of original circle $= \pi D = 40\pi$

Circumference required to be cut off $= 40\pi - 20\pi = 20\pi$

$\frac{20\pi}{40\pi} = \frac{1}{2}$

123. ANSWER:C

$\frac{2^{399} - 2^{394}}{31} = 32^k$

$\frac{2^{394}(2^5 - 1)}{31} = 32^k$

$\frac{2^{394}(31)}{31} = 32^k$

$2^{394} = 32^k$

$2^{394} = 2^{5k}$

$\therefore 5k = 394$

$k = \frac{394}{5}$

124. ANSWER:D

The area of a rhombus is half the product of its 2 diagonals.

$\frac{(2x + 5)(5 - 2x)}{2} = 10$

$(5 + 2x)(5 - 2x) = 20$

$25 - 4x^2 = 20$

$5 = 4x^2$

$x^2 = \frac{5}{4}$

$$x = \pm\frac{\sqrt{5}}{2}$$

125. ANSWER: G

$$3\sin^2 x - 7\sin x + 2 = 0$$
$$(3\sin x - 1)(\sin x - 2) = 0$$
$$\sin x = \frac{1}{3} \text{ and } \sin x = 2$$

We can observe the graph of $y = \sin x$ from 0 to 5π:

$\sin x = 2$ has no solutions between 0 and 5π

$\sin x = \frac{1}{3}$ has 6 solutions between 0 and 5π

126. ANSWER: B

$$f(x) = px^3 + (p-1)x$$

We want to find the range of values for which the gradient is positive

$$\therefore f'(x) > 0$$
$$f'(x) = 3px^2 + p - 1$$
$$3px^2 + p - 1 > 0$$
$$x^2 > \frac{p-1}{3p}$$
$$x^2 - \frac{p-1}{3p} > 0$$
$$\left(x + \sqrt{\frac{p-1}{3p}}\right)\left(x - \sqrt{\frac{p-1}{3p}}\right) > 0$$
$$\therefore \text{ either } x > \sqrt{\frac{p-1}{3p}} \text{ or } x < -\sqrt{\frac{p-1}{3p}}$$

127. ANSWER: C

Shortest distance between the line $l_1 : y = x$ and $C_1 : y = x^2 + 2$

Shortest distances occur when the gradient of the 2 curves is the same and occurs along a normal

The gradient of the line is 1

Let the general point, P on C_1 *be* $(t, t^2 + 2)$

To find the point at which the curve has a gradient of 1:

$$C_1: \frac{dy}{dx} = 2x$$

$$\left.\frac{dy}{dx}\right|_{x=t} = 2t$$

$$1 = 2t$$

$$t = \frac{1}{2} \text{ (at the point of shortest distance)}$$

$$\therefore P\left(\frac{1}{2}, \frac{9}{4}\right)$$

We must now find the distance between P and where its normal intersects C_1

$$m_{l_1} = 1$$

$$m_{normal} = -1$$

$$y - y_1 = m(x - x_1)$$

$$y - \frac{9}{4} = -1\left(x - \frac{1}{2}\right)$$

$$y - \frac{9}{4} = -x + \frac{1}{2}$$

$$y = \frac{11}{4} - x$$

To find the intersection of the normal with l_1:

$$\frac{11}{4} - x = x$$

$$\frac{11}{4} = 2x$$

$$x = \frac{11}{8}$$

$$y = x$$

$\therefore$ point of intersection with l_1 *is* $\left(\frac{11}{8}, \frac{11}{8}\right)$

$\therefore$ shortest distance is distance between $\left(\frac{11}{8}, \frac{11}{8}\right)$ and $\left(\frac{1}{2}, \frac{9}{4}\right)$

$$d = \sqrt{\left(\frac{11}{8} - \frac{1}{2}\right)^2 + \left(\frac{11}{8} - \frac{9}{4}\right)^2}$$

$$d = \frac{7\sqrt{2}}{8}$$

128. ANSWER:D

$$\frac{1}{3}(3x-4)-\frac{1}{2}(x-2)<x.$$
$$\therefore x-\frac{4}{3}-\frac{1}{2}x+1<x$$
$$\therefore \frac{1}{2}x-\frac{1}{3}<x$$
$$\therefore -\frac{1}{3}<\frac{1}{2}x$$
$$\therefore x>-\frac{2}{3}$$

129. ANSWER: F

$$3\sqrt{\log_2 x}-\log_2 8x+1=0$$
$$3\sqrt{\log_2 x}-(\log_2 8+\log_2 x)+1=0$$
Let $\alpha^2=\log_2 x$
$$3\alpha-(3+\alpha^2)+1=0$$
$$3\alpha-\alpha^2-2=0$$
$$\alpha^2-3a+2=0$$
$$(\alpha-2)(\alpha-1)=0$$
$\alpha=2$ or $\alpha=1$
$4=\log_2 x$ or $1=\log_2 x$
$x=16$ or $x=2$

130. ANSWER: B

$$x^4+8x^2+16=4x^2-12x+9$$
$$(x^2+4)^2=(2x-3)^2$$
$$x^2+4=\pm(2x-3)$$
$x^2+2x+1=0$ or $x^2-2x+7=0$
$\therefore x=-1$ or no solution
Hence equation only has one real solution

131. ANSWER: E

$$5732a + 2134b + 2134c = 7866 \quad (1)$$
$$2134a + 5732b + 2134c = 670 \quad (2)$$
$$2134a + 2134b + 5732c = 11464 \quad (3)$$
$$(1) + (2) + (3) = 10000a + 10000b + 10000c = 20{,}000$$
$$a + b + c = 2$$
$$\therefore 2134a + 2134b + 2134c = 4268 \quad (4)$$
$$(1) - (4) = 3598a = 3598 \Rightarrow a = 1$$
$$(2) - (4) = 3598b = -3598 \Rightarrow b = -1$$
$$(3) - (4) = 3598c = 7196 \Rightarrow c = 2$$
$$\therefore abc = (1)(-1)(2) = -2$$

132. ANSWER: B

We can see that this is an alternating sequence, therefore we must work out the sum to 8 terms of each individual sequence.

Sequence 1

$$S_8 = \frac{1\left(\left(\frac{1}{2}^8\right) - 1\right)}{\frac{1}{2} - 1}$$
$$= \frac{\frac{1}{256} - 1}{-\frac{1}{2}}$$
$$= \frac{-\frac{255}{256}}{-\frac{1}{2}}$$
$$= \frac{255}{128}$$

Sequence 2

$$S_8 = \frac{1(2^8 - 1)}{2 - 1} = 255$$

Adding together the sums of the individual sequences: $255 + \frac{255}{128} = 256\frac{127}{128}$

133. ANSWER: H

$$49^{125} + 49^{124} + \cdots + 49^2 + 49^1 + 49^0$$

$$S_n = \frac{1(49^{126} - 1)}{48}$$

$$S_n = \frac{(49^{63} - 1)(49^{63} + 1)}{48}$$

$\therefore$ 63 is the largest value of k

This is because we know that $(49^{63} - 1)$ can be divided by 48 as $x - 1$ is a factor of $x^n - 1$ (using the factor theorem)

134. ANSWER: A

We know $\frac{2^{x+2} - 2}{2^{2x+1}} = 1$, and want to work out the sum of the solutions

$$\frac{2^{x+2} - 2}{2^{2x+1}} = 1$$

$$2^{x+2} - 2 = 2^{2x+1}$$

$$2(2^{2x}) - 4(2^x) + 2 = 0$$

let $y = 2^x$

$$2y^2 - 4y + 2 = 0$$

$$y^2 - 2y + 1 = 0$$

$$(y - 1)^2 = 0$$

$$y = 1$$

$$2^x = 1$$

$$\therefore x = 0$$

135. ANSWER: F

$y = \frac{3}{4}|x - 4| + 5$ and $y = mx + 3$ have 2 points of intersection.

First we need to find the vertex of $y = \frac{3}{4}|x - 4| + 5$

Consider $y = \frac{3}{4}|x - 4|$ when $y = 0$

$$0 = \frac{3}{4}(x - 4)$$

$$0 = \frac{3}{4}x - 3$$

$$\frac{3}{4}x = 3$$

$$x = 4$$

$\therefore$ The vertex of $y = \frac{3}{4}|x - 4|$ is (4,0)

$\therefore$ The vertex of $y = \frac{3}{4}|x - 4| + 5$ is (4,5)

The critical values for which $y = mx + 3$ has 2 intersections with $y = \frac{3}{4}|x - 4| + 5$ are:

1)When m is $\frac{3}{4}$

2)Where $y = mx + 3$ intersects the vertex

$\therefore$ Sub in $(x, y) = (4,5)$ in $y = mx + 3$

$5 = 4m + 3$

$2 = 4m$

$m = \frac{1}{2}$

$\therefore \frac{1}{2} < m < \frac{3}{4}$ is the range of values of m for which there are 2 points of intersection.

136. ANSWER: ***A***

$\sqrt{\log_2(2x^2) \times \log_4 16x}$
$= 3\log_4 x$

$\log_2(2x^2) \times \log_4 16x = (3\log_4 x)^2$

$(\log_2(2) + \log_2(x^2)) \times (\log_4 16 + \log_4 x) = 9(\log_4 x)^2$

Remember that you can square the base and the argument.

$(\log_2(2) + \log_4(x^4)) \times (\log_4 16 + \log_4 x) = 9(\log_4 x)^2$

$(1 + 4\log_4(x)) \times (2 + \log_4 x) = 9(\log_4 x)^2$

let $\alpha = \log_4 x$

$(1 + 4\alpha)(2 + \alpha)$
$= 9\alpha^2$

$4\alpha^2 + 9\alpha + 2 = 9\alpha^2$

$5\alpha^2 - 9\alpha - 2 = 0$

$(5\alpha + 1)(\alpha - 2) = 0$

$\alpha = -\frac{1}{5}, \alpha = 2$

$\therefore -\frac{1}{5} = \log_4 x \Rightarrow x = 4^{-\frac{1}{5}}$

$\therefore 2 = \log_4 x \Rightarrow x = 4^2$

$\therefore$ Product of all possible values of x satisfying the equation: $4^2 \times 4^{-\frac{1}{5}} = 4^{\frac{9}{5}}$

137. ANSWER: F

The bag contains red and blue balls. Gary picks out one ball and then another ball 15 minutes later. The probability that both balls were blue is $\frac{2}{15}$. We need to find out the number of red balls in the bag.

Let the number of blue balls be: b

Which means that the number of red balls is: $10 - b$

$$\frac{b}{10} \times \frac{b-1}{9} = \frac{b(b-1)}{90} = \frac{2}{15}$$

$$\therefore b(b-1) = \frac{180}{15}$$

$$b(b-1) = 12$$

$$b^2 - b - 12 = 0$$

$$(b-4)(b+3) = 0$$

$b = 4$ or $b = -3$

$\therefore b = 4$ (as b cannot be negative)

$\therefore$ Number of red balls is $= 10 - 4 = 6$

138. ANSWER: A

$$f(x) = 2x^4 - 6x^3 + 8x^2 + k$$

$$f'(x) = 8x^3 - 18x^2 + 16x$$

$$f''(x) = 24x^2 - 36x + 16$$

$f'(x) = 0$ at stationary points

$$8x^3 - 18x^2 + 16x = 0$$

$$x(4x^2 - 9x + 8) = 0$$

$x = 0$ is the only solution as $4x^2 - 9x + 8$ has discriminant < 0

$\therefore$ only one stationary point at $x = 0$

$f''(0) = 16 > 0 \Rightarrow$ (global minimum)

Now we must find the coordinates of this stationary point in terms of k:

For $x = 0$

$y = k$

$(0, k)$ is the coordinate of the minimum point of $f(x)$

$\therefore$ we want $k < 0$

139. ANSWER: D

Find the area bound between $y = x^{\frac{1}{3}}$ and $y = \frac{x}{4}$.

$x^{\frac{1}{3}} = \frac{x}{4}$

$\therefore x = \frac{x^3}{64}$

$\therefore 0 = x^3 - 64x$

$\therefore 0 = x(x^2 - 64)$

$\therefore 0 = x(x+8)(x-8)$

$x = -8, x = 0$ and $x = 8$

A quick sketch shows:

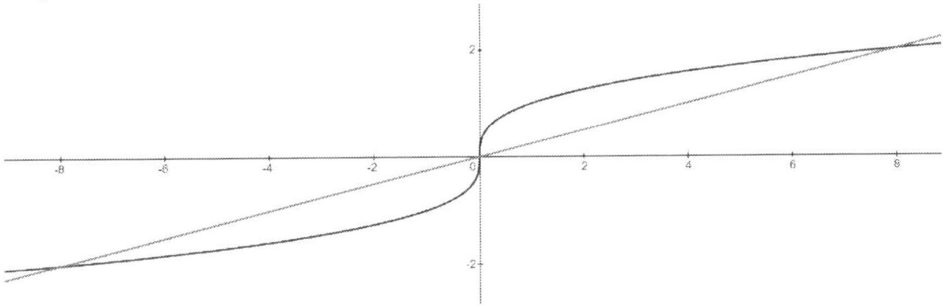

We know that the areas bounded between the intersection of the two curves are the same in the 1st and 3rd quadrants.

Using the fundamental theorem of calclus we can say that the area bounded between the two curves is:

$$= \int_0^8 x^{\frac{1}{3}} - \frac{x}{4}\,dx$$

$$= \left[\frac{3x^{\frac{4}{3}}}{4} - \frac{x^2}{8}\right]_0^8$$

$$= \left[\frac{3(8)^{\frac{4}{3}}}{4} - \frac{(8)^2}{8}\right] - [0]$$

$= 12 - 8 = 4$

4×2

$= 8$ (as the area in the 1st quadrant must be doubled to find the total area bound by by the curve)

140. ANSWER: D

$x^2 - 2x + y^2 - 8y - 8 = 0$ and $x^2 + 4x + y^2 + 6y - 51 = 0$

$(x-1)^2 - 1 + (y-4)^2 - 16 - 8 = 0$

$(x-1)^2 + (y-4)^2 = 25$

$\therefore$ Circle is centred at: (1,4) with radius 5

$(x+2)^2 - 4 + (y+3)^2 - 9 - 51 = 0$

$(x+2)^2 + (y+3)^2 = 64$

$\therefore$ Circle is centred at: $(-2,-3)$ with radius 8

In order to find the locus of points equidistant from the centres of these 2 circles we must find the perpendicular bisector of the line joining the 2 centres.

The midpoint of the points (1,4) and (−2, −3) is $\left(-\frac{1}{2},\frac{1}{2}\right)$

Gradient of line joining centres: $\frac{7}{3}$

$\therefore$ perpedndicular gradient: $-\frac{3}{7}$

To find the equation of the perpendicular bisector use:

$y - y_1 = m(x - x_1)$

$y - \frac{1}{2} = -\frac{3}{7}\left(x + \frac{1}{2}\right)$

$y - \frac{1}{2} = -\frac{3}{7}x - \frac{3}{14}$

$y = -\frac{3}{7}x - \frac{2}{7}$

141. ANSWER: B

We know that $\sum_{r=1}^{9} a_r = 4\lambda, \sum_{r=1}^{2} a_r = 4, \sum_{r=1}^{4} a_r = 20$

$\sum_{r=1}^{4} a_r - \sum_{r=1}^{2} a_r = \sum_{r=3}^{4} a_r$

$\sum_{r=3}^{4} a_r = 20 - 4 = 16$

$a + ar = 4 \quad (1)$

$ar^2 + ar^3 = 16 \quad (2)$

$\sum_{r=1}^{9} a_r = \frac{a(r^9 - 1)}{r - 1} = 4\lambda \quad (3)$

$(1) \Rightarrow 1 + r = \frac{4}{a}$

$(2) \Rightarrow 1 + r = \frac{16}{ar^2}$

$\frac{4}{a} = \frac{16}{ar^2}$

$16 = 4r^2$(we can multiply both sides by a as it is<0)

$r^2 = 4$
$r = \pm 2$
For $r = 2$
Sub in (1): $a(1 + 2) = 4$
$\therefore a = \frac{4}{3}$ (however this doesn't satisfy the original condition)
$\therefore$ try $r = -2$ instead
Sub in (1): $a(1 - 2) = 4$
$\therefore a = -4$
Sub $a = -4$ and $r = -2$ into the (3)
$$(3) \Rightarrow 4\lambda = \frac{-4((-2)^9 - 1)}{-2 - 1}$$
$$\lambda = \frac{(-2)^9 - 1}{3}$$
$$\lambda = -\frac{513}{3}$$
$$\therefore \lambda = -171$$

142. ANSWER:C

Area bound between the curve $f(x) = x(x - a)(x + 2a)$, the lines

$x = a$ and $x = -2a$
$f(x) = x(x - a)(x + 2a)$
$f(x) = (x^2 - ax)(x + 2a)$
$f(x) = x^3 - ax^2 + 2ax^2 - 2a^2x$ $\quad f(x) = x^3 + ax^2 - 2a^2x$
$$A = \int_0^a x^3 - ax^2 + 2ax^2 - 2a^2x\,dx$$
$$A = \left[\frac{x^4}{4} - \frac{ax^3}{3} + \frac{2ax^3}{3} - a^2x^2\right]_0^a +$$
$$A = \left[\frac{a^4}{4} - \frac{a(a)^3}{3} + \frac{2a(a)^3}{3} - a^2(a)^2\right] - [0]$$

$$= -\frac{5}{12}a^4 \Rightarrow \frac{5}{12}a^4$$
$$\int_{-2a}^0 x^3 - ax^2 + 2ax^2 - 2a^2x\,dx$$
$$= \left[\frac{x^4}{4} - \frac{ax^3}{3} + \frac{2ax^3}{3} - a^2x^2\right]_{-2a}^0$$

$$= [0] - \left[\frac{(-2a)^4}{4} - \frac{a(-2a)^3}{3} + \frac{2a(-2a)^3}{3} - a^2(-2a)^2\right]$$
$$= \left[\frac{(16a)^4}{4} + \frac{8a^4}{3} - \frac{16a^4}{3} - 4a^4\right]$$
$$= \left[-\frac{8a^4}{3}\right] \Rightarrow \frac{8a^4}{3}$$
$$\text{Total Area} = \frac{8}{3}a^4 + \frac{5}{12}a^4 = \frac{37}{12}a^4$$

143. ANSWER: G

$$6 - \left(2 + 4(9)^{4-2\log_{\sqrt{3}}3}\right)\log_{49} x = \log_7 x$$
$$= 6 - \left(2 + 4(9)^{4-2(2)}\right)\log_{49} x = \log_7 x$$
$$= 6 - (2+4)\log_{49} x = \log_7 x$$
$$= 6 - 6\log_{49} x = \log_7 x$$
$$= 6 - \log_{49} x^6 = \log_{49} x^2$$
$$= 6 = \log_{49} x^8$$
$$= 6 = \log_7 x^4$$
$$= 7^6 = x^4$$
$$x = 7\sqrt{7}$$

144. ANSWER: A

The roots of $3y^2 + 13y - c = 0$ differ by 7

Let the roots be α and $\alpha - 7$

Sum of roots $= a + (a - 7) = 2a - 7 = -\frac{b}{a} = -\frac{13}{3}$ (1)

Product of roots $= \alpha(\alpha - 7) = \alpha^2 - 7\alpha = -\frac{c}{3}$ (2)

$(1) \Rightarrow 6\alpha - 21 = -13$

$6a = 21 - 13$

$6a = 8$

$a = \frac{4}{3}$

$(2) \Rightarrow 3\alpha^2 - 21\alpha = -c$

$c = 21\alpha - 3\alpha^2$

$c = 21\left(\frac{4}{3}\right) - 3\left(\frac{4}{3}\right)^2$

$c = \frac{84}{3} - 3\left(\frac{16}{9}\right)$

$$c = \frac{84}{3} - \frac{16}{3}$$
$$c = \frac{68}{3}$$

145. ANSWER: E

The expansion of $\left(2x + \frac{p}{x}\right)^8$ has a constant term of 7×10^5.

The expansion is given by: $\binom{8}{n} \times (2x)^{8-n} \times \left(\frac{p}{x}\right)^n$

In order for the terms to be independent of x it requires:

$$x^{8-n}\left(\frac{1}{x}\right)^n = x^0$$
$$x^{8-n}(x^{-1})^n = x^0$$
$$x^{8-n}(x^{-n}) = x^0$$
$$x^{8-2n} = x^0$$
$$8 - 2n = 0$$
$$2n = 8$$
$$n = 4$$

The constant in the expansion:

$$\binom{8}{4} \times (2x)^4 \times \left(\frac{p}{x}\right)^4 = \frac{8!}{4!\,(4!)} \times 2^4 \times p^4 = 7 \times 10^5$$
$$= 70 \times 16 \times p^4 = 7 \times 10^5$$
$$= p^4 = \frac{7 \times 10^5}{70 \times 16}$$
$$p^4 = 625$$
$$p = 5$$

146. ANSWER: C

We want to make b the subject of the formula:

$$a = \sqrt{\frac{b+3}{b-k}}$$
$$= a^2 = \frac{b+3}{b-k}$$
$$a^2(b-k) = b+3$$
$$a^2b - a^2k = b+3$$
$$a^2b - b = a^2k + 3$$
$$b(a^2 - 1) = a^2k + 3$$

$$b = \frac{a^2k + 3}{(a^2 - 1)}$$

147. ANSWER: A

$$|\sqrt{x} - 2| + \sqrt{x}(\sqrt{x} - 4) + 2 = 0$$
$$|\sqrt{x} - 2| + x - 4\sqrt{x} + 2 = 0$$
$$|\sqrt{x} - 2|^2 + |\sqrt{x} - 2| - 2 = 0$$
$$\therefore |\sqrt{x} - 2| = -2 \text{ } (\therefore \text{ no solution}), |\sqrt{x} - 2| = 1$$
$$\sqrt{x} - 2 = 1, -1$$
$$\sqrt{x} = 3,1$$
$$\therefore x = 9,1$$
$$\therefore \text{Sum} = 9 + 1 = 10$$

148. ANSWER:D

$$\left(\frac{1}{2}\right)^{x^2-2x} < \frac{1}{4}.$$

Take logs of both sides:

$$\log\left(\frac{1}{2}\right)^{x^2-2x} < \log\frac{1}{4}$$
$$\log\left(\frac{1}{2}\right)^{x^2-2x} < \log\frac{1}{4}$$
$$(x^2 - 2x)\left(\log\left(\frac{1}{2}\right)\right) < \log\frac{1}{4}$$

$$(x^2 - 2x)\left(\log\left(\frac{1}{2}\right)\right) < \log\left(\frac{1}{2}\right)^2$$
$$(x^2 - 2x)\left(\log\left(\frac{1}{2}\right)\right) < 2\log\left(\frac{1}{2}\right)$$

Divide both sides by $\log\left(\frac{1}{2}\right)$

$$x^2 - 2x > 2 \left(\text{however as } \log\left(\frac{1}{2}\right) < 0 \text{ the inequality sign changes direction}\right)$$
$$x^2 - 2x - 2 > 0$$

In order to determine the critical value:

$x^2 - 2x - 2 = 0$

$$x = \frac{2 \pm \sqrt{(-2)^2 - 4(1)(-2)}}{2(1)}$$

$$x = \frac{2 \pm \sqrt{4 - (-8)}}{2}$$

$$x = \frac{2 \pm \sqrt{12}}{2}$$

$$x = \frac{2 \pm 2\sqrt{3}}{2}$$

$x = 1 \pm \sqrt{3}$ are the critical values

Considering the shape of the quadratic graph, the inequalities are:

$\therefore x > 1 + \sqrt{3}$ and $x < 1 - \sqrt{3}$

149. ANSWER: G

$$20, 19\frac{1}{3}, 18\frac{2}{3} \ldots$$

$$d = -\frac{2}{3}, a = 20$$

$S_n = 300$

$$300 = \frac{n}{2}\left(40 - \frac{2}{3}(n-1)\right)$$

$$600 = n\left(40 - \frac{2}{3}n + \frac{2}{3}\right)$$

$$600 = n\left(\frac{122}{3} - \frac{2}{3}n\right)$$

$1800 = 122n - 2n^2$

$n^2 - 61n + 900 = 0$

$n = 36$ or $n = 25$

$n = 25$ as this is the first time the sum is 300 (as specified by the question)

150. ANSWER: B

$$S_\infty = \frac{1}{2} + \frac{1}{4} + \frac{2}{8} + \frac{3}{16} + \frac{5}{32} + \frac{8}{64} + \frac{13}{128} + \cdots$$

$$\therefore \frac{S_\infty}{2} = \frac{1}{4} + \frac{1}{8} + \frac{2}{16} + \frac{3}{32} + \frac{5}{64} + \frac{8}{128} + \frac{13}{256} + \cdots$$

$$\therefore S_\infty - \frac{S_\infty}{2} = \frac{S_\infty}{2} = \frac{1}{2} + 0 + \frac{1}{8} + \frac{1}{16} + \frac{2}{32} + \frac{3}{64} + \cdots$$
$$\therefore \frac{S_\infty}{2} = \frac{1}{2} + 0 + \frac{1}{8} + \frac{1}{16} + \frac{2}{32} + \frac{3}{64} + \cdots$$
$$\therefore \frac{S_\infty}{2} = \frac{1}{2} + \frac{1}{4}\left(\frac{1}{2} + \frac{1}{4} + \frac{2}{8} + \frac{3}{16} + \cdots\right)$$
$$\therefore \frac{S_\infty}{2} = \frac{1}{2} + \frac{1}{4}(S_\infty)$$
$$\therefore \frac{S_\infty}{2} - \frac{S_\infty}{4} = \frac{1}{2}$$
$$\therefore \frac{S_\infty}{4} = \frac{1}{2}$$
$$\therefore S_\infty = 2$$

151. ANSWER: D

Line through (7a,5) and (3a,3)

Gradient $= \frac{5-3}{7a-3a}$

$= \frac{2}{4a} = \frac{1}{2a}$

$y - y_1 = m(x - x_1)$

$y - 5 = \frac{1}{2a}(x - 7a)$

$2ay - 10a = x - 7a$

$x - 2ay + 3a = 0$

Using the fact that L has the form $x + by - 12 = 0$, we can equate coefficients, giving

$a = -4$ and $b = 8$

152. ANSWER: C

Let $y = 2 - 4x$ be equation 1

$3x^2 + xy + 11 = 0$ be equation 2

Substitute 1 in 2, giving

$3x^2 + x(2 - 4x) + 11 = 0$

Expanding and rearranging this gives

$x^2 - 2x - 11 = 0$

Solving for x using the quadratic formular gives

$x = 1 + 2\sqrt{3}$ and $x = 1 - 2\sqrt{3}$

153. ANSWER: C

Since it is a geometric series: $r = \frac{2x}{8-x} = \frac{x^2}{2x}$

Rearranging this equation gives $x^3 - 4x^2 = 0$

Solving this gives $x = 0$ or $x = 4$

Since $x > 0, x = 4$

Using this value, the starting term is 4, and the common ratio is 2.

7th term $= ar^6 = 256$

154. ANSWER: E

Using the definitions of composite functions,

$3\left(\frac{1}{x-2}\right) + 4 = 16$

Rearranging this equation gives

$\frac{1}{x-2} = 4$

$x = \frac{9}{4}$

155. ANSWER: B

Firstly, f(x) can be rewritten as $\frac{12}{p}x^{-\frac{1}{2}} + x$

Differentiating this using basic rules gives

$$f'(x) = -\frac{6}{p}x^{-\frac{3}{2}} + 1$$

Substituting $x = 2$ into $f'(x)$ gives

$$f'(2) = -\frac{6}{p}(2)^{-\frac{3}{2}} + 1$$

Rewriting this gives

$$-\frac{6}{2p\sqrt{2}} + 1 = 3$$

Solving this equation,

$$p = -\frac{3}{2\sqrt{2}}$$

$$p = -\frac{3}{4}\sqrt{2}$$

156. ANSWER: C

Firstly, it is possible to factorise 2^{30} from each term giving this expression

$= 2^{30}(1 + 1 + 1 + 1)$

$= 2^{30} \times 4$

$= 2^{30} \times 2^2$

$= 2^{32}$

157. ANSWER: B

It is important to understand each component that Alex must pay.

Firstly, each night, he pays £75 for the room which is taxed at 9%. As a result his total cost just for the nightly room charge is given by 1.09(75x).

However, on top of this, he is subject to a £7 onetime fee which is untaxed.

As a result, the total cost is given by 1.09(75x) + 7.

158. ANSWER: A

To solve this question, it is appropriate to draw a probability tree diagram

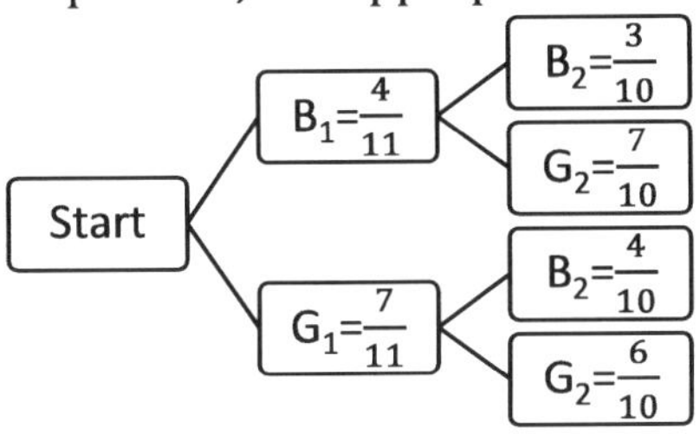

Since the ball is not replaced, there are only 10 balls in the bag after the first ball has been selected. Since it is known that the second ball is green, the second and fourth branches need to be used.

The probability of B_1, G_2 is $\frac{4}{11} \times \frac{7}{10} = \frac{14}{55}$.

The probability of G_1, G_2 is $\frac{7}{11} \times \frac{6}{10} = \frac{21}{55}$

Therefore, using conditional probability, $P(G_1, G_2) = \frac{\frac{21}{55}}{\frac{21}{55}+\frac{14}{55}} = \frac{3}{5}$

159. ANSWER: D

The first step to solving this problem is to find the number of terms.

Let the final term of this sequence, 303, be given by Un

The nth term of an arithmetic sequence will be $a + (n - 1)d$

Substituting $(k + 1)$as a and $(k + 2)$ as d, an expression for the nth term can be given as $(k + 1) + (n - 1)(k + 2)$

Equate this to 303,

$$(k + 1) + (n - 1)(k + 2) = 303$$

Solving for n in terms of k,

$$n = \frac{304}{k+2}$$

Then, substitute this in the sum of series formula for an arithmetic series.

$\text{Sn} = \frac{n}{2}(a + l)$

$2568 = \frac{\frac{304}{k+2}}{2}(k + 1 + 303)$

Solving this equation, $k = 17$

160. ANSWER: E

Firstly, it is wise to find the roots of the quadratic equation in terms of k using the quadratic formula. This will give the following two solutions for x

$$x = \frac{-9+\sqrt{81+8k}}{4} \text{ and } x = \frac{-9-\sqrt{81+8}}{4}$$

From this, it is intuitive that the second root will be lower than the first due.

Therefore, given that one root is 4 more than the other, the following equation can be set up.

$$\frac{-9+\sqrt{81+8}}{4} = \frac{-9-\sqrt{81+8}}{4} + 4$$

$$-9 + \sqrt{81 + 8k} = -9 - \sqrt{81 + 8k} + 16$$

$$2\sqrt{81 + 8k} = 16$$

$$81 + 8k = 64$$

$$k = -\frac{17}{8}$$

161. ANSWER: C

Rather than actually multiply out the numbers, it is much easier to simply multiply the last digit of each.

$4 \times 8 = 32$, meaning the last digit of the product will be 2.

Therefore, when divided by 5, the remainder will be 2.

162. ANSWER: E

Since the class is split into fractions of $\frac{1}{2}, \frac{1}{4}$ and $\frac{1}{7}$, it follows that the total number of people must be a multiple of 2, 4 and 7. This will be multiples of 28, and since the number of students is lower than 30, there must be 28 students at maximum.

Therefore, the number of people who play cricket must be $\frac{1}{4}$ of 28, 7.

163. ANSWER: A

The key to checking each solution is to check how many times the denominator can go into the numerator.

After this is done, it follows that A is the only fraction which is greater than 4.

164. ANSWER: D

The average speed of a journey is the total distance travelled divided by the total time taken. Jacob's journey can be split into three separate parts to calculate the total distance travelled.

The total distance travelled is $\left(12 \times \frac{5}{60}\right) + \left(15 \times \frac{10}{60}\right) + \left(18 \times \frac{15}{60}\right) = 8\text{km}$

The total time taken is $5 + 10 + 15 = 30$

Average speed $8 \div \frac{30}{60} = 16\text{kmph}$

165. ANSWER: D

First, let any general point on C have coordinates (x, y). After being reflected in the line $y = 1$, the x coordinate will be unchanged.
However, the y coordinate will be reflected onto $2 - y$. This is because the vertical distance between (x, y) and the line $y = 1$ is $y - 1$.
Therefore, to find the reflected point, $y - 1$ should be subtracted from 1,

$1 - (y - 1) = 2 - y$. After the reflection, the image of (x, y) will be $(x, 2 - y)$.

Therefore, the image of C is $2 - y = \frac{1}{x}$. (Replace with new y coordinate)

The second transformation is a reflection in the line $y = -x$. From a sketch, this transformation will replace x with $-y$ and y with $-x$. Subbing these into the equation above gives

$2 - (-x) = \frac{1}{-y}$. Rearranging this gives

$y = -\frac{1}{x+2}$

166. ANSWER: D

Using binomial expansion rules, firstly find the coefficients of x and x^2 in terms of p.

$\therefore (1 + px)^{15} = 1^{15} + 15 \cdot px + 105 \cdot (px)^2 + \cdots$

$= 15px + 105p^2x^2 + \cdots$

Now, the coefficients in terms of p can be equated to the coefficients in terms of q, giving a pair of simultaneous equations.

$15p = -q$

$105p^2 = 5q$

Substituting the first equation into the second gives

$105p^2 = -75p$

$21p^2 + 15p = 0$

$p(21p + 15) = 0$

$p = -\frac{5}{7}$, as it cannot be 0.

Substitute this in equation 1 to get $q = \frac{75}{7}$

167. ANSWER: C

Using the law of logarithms, the second equation can be rewritten as

$\log_6 ab = 2$

$ab = 36$

$a = \frac{36}{b}$

Substituting this into the first equation gives

$\frac{36}{b} + b = 13$

$36 + b^2 = 13b$

Solving this quadratic gives $b = 4$ or $b = 9$

Substituting these values into the first equation, two pair of solutions are obtained.

$a = 9, b = 4$

$a = 4, b = 9$

Since $a > b$, $a = 9$ and $b = 4$

168. ANSWER C

This question can easily be solved by factorising the numerator and denominator and thereby, simplifying the expression.

$$\frac{6x^3+3x^2-84x}{6x^2-33x+42} = \frac{3x(2x^2+x-28)}{3(2x^2-11x+14)}$$

$$= \frac{x(2x-7)(x+4)}{(2x-7)((x-2)}$$

$$= \frac{x(x+4)}{x-2}$$

169. ANSWER: C

Firstly, find the equation of line, m.

Since it is perpendicular, the gradient of m must be $\frac{1}{2}$.

Using $y - y_1 = m(x - x_1)$,

The equation of m can be written as $y - 0 = \frac{1}{2}(x + 6)$

$y = \frac{x}{2} + 3$

It is now helpful to sketch the two lines to identify the region required.

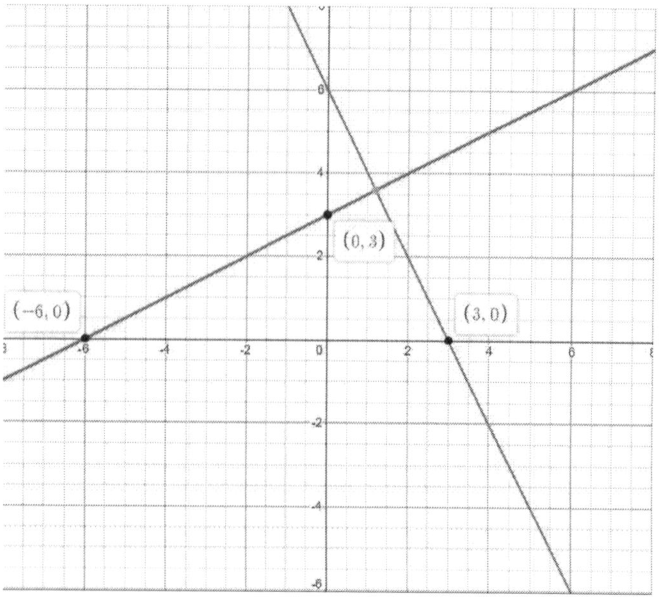

Evidently, the region is a triangle. To find the height of the triangle, find the y-coordinate of the intersection of l and m.

$6 - 2x = \frac{x}{2} + 3$

$x = \frac{6}{5}$. Substitute into either l or m to get $y = \frac{18}{5}$

The area of the region is therefore $\frac{1}{2} \times 9 \times \frac{18}{5} = \frac{81}{5}$

170. ANSWER: D

Firstly, the solution to $y = x^2(2 - x)$ is $x = 0$ and $x = 2$, which will be the limits of the integral.

$\text{Area} = \int_0^2 x^2(2 - x)dx$

$Area = \int_0^2 2x^2 - x^3dx = \left[\frac{2x^3}{3} - \frac{x^4}{4}\right]_0^2$

$= \frac{16}{3} - 4 - 0$

$= \frac{4}{3}$

171. ANSWER: B

Intuitively, most candidates would be quick to state the ANSWER as $\frac{1}{2}$. However, delving deeper, this is not the case.

With two children, there are 4 different possible combinations:

BB, BG, GB, GG. Knowing that there is one girl, Sarah, there are 3 different combinations that can be true (excluding BB).

Consequently, the probability of there being two girls is $\frac{1}{3}$.

172. ANSWER: E

Since both polygons are regular, it is possible to find the interior angle of each using the formula $\frac{180(n-2)}{n}$, where n is the number of sides.

Substituting 5 and 8 into this, the interior angle of a pentagon is 108° and 135°.

The mini triangle FQE is an isosceles triangle as sides FQ and QE are equal.

Angle QFE = Angle QEF = $135° - 108° = 27°$

Since the angles in a triangle sum to 180, $x = 180° - 27° - 27° = 126°$

173. ANSWER: A

If Benjamin hits the target for the first time on his third attempt, in other words, it means that his first two attempts failed, and his third attempt was a success.

Since 0.3 is the probability of success, it follows that 0.7 is the probability of failing.

Therefore, if he fails twice and succeeds on the third, the probability of this happening is $0.7 \times 0.7 \times 0.3 = 0.147$

174. ANSWER: F

Although this problem seems very simple at first, many students make the mistake of disregarding the modulus around the $x - 5$.

When the modulus graph is drawn, it is important to appreciate the different regions.

The first step is to find where the line $y = x - 5$ crosses the x-axis.

$0 = x - 5$

$x = 5$

Due to 5 falling in the range of the two limits, the integral needs to be split up as

$\int_2^5 |x - 5| dx + \int_5^8 |x - 5| dx$

However, between 2 and 5, the graph for $y = x - 5$ will be in the negative, even though $y = |x - 5|$ will be in the positive.

Therefore, a negative sign must be added to account for this.

The integral is therefore

$-\int_2^5 |x - 5| dx + \int_5^8 |x - 5| dx$

Since the modulus signs have been accounted for, it is now possible to integrate and evaluate normally.

$= -\left[\frac{x^2}{2} - 5x\right]_2^5 + \left[\frac{x^2}{2} - 5x\right]_5^8$

$= -\left(-\frac{9}{2}\right) + \frac{9}{2}$

$= 9$

175. ANSWER: B

The equation of C can be rewritten as

$y = x^{-1} + 27x^3$

To find the stationary points, first differentiate to get

$\frac{dy}{dx} = -x^{-2} + 81x^2$

At stationary points, $\frac{dy}{dx} = 0$

$-\frac{1}{x^2} + 81x^2 = 0$

Since x is evidently not 0 at the stationary points, we can multiply through by x^2.

$-1 + 81x^4 = 0$

$81x^4 = 1$

$x^4 = \frac{1}{81}$

$x = \pm\frac{1}{3}, \rightarrow a = \frac{1}{3}$

176. ANSWER: D

$(1+x)^0 + (1+x)^1 + (1+x)^2 + (1+x)^3 + \ldots + (1+x)^{59} + (1+x)^{60}$

Using Pascals triangle and binomial expansion, we can calculate that the coefficient of each bracket will be the value of the power. This can be shown below:

$(1+x)^0 = 1$

$(1+x)^1 = 1 + x$

$(1+x)^2 = 1 + 2x + x^2$

Therefore, the sum of the coefficients will be $1 + 2 + 3 + \cdots + 59 + 60$

Using the sum of an arithmetic series, we get $\frac{1}{2} \times 60 \times 61 = 1830$

177. ANSWER: A

$2x^2 - 5x - 12 < 0$

Firstly, treat the inequality sign as an equal sign, and solve the quadratic.

$2x^2 - 5x - 12 = 0$

Factorising this gives

$(2x+3)(x-4) = 0$, which when solved, gives $x = -\frac{3}{2}$ *and* $x = 4$

A quick sketch of this quadratic below shows the region required

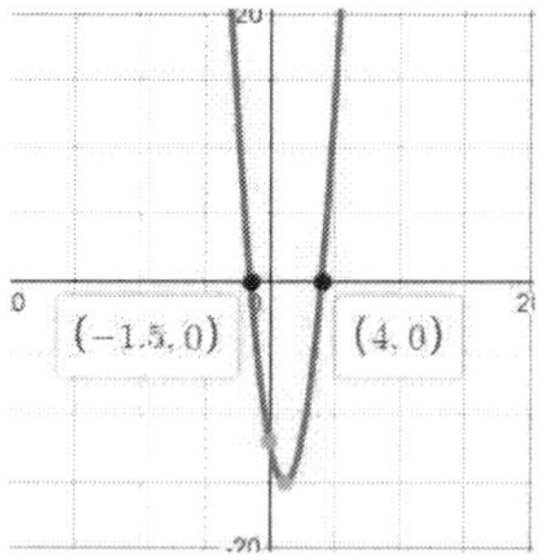

Since we need the graph to be less than 0, the required region is $-\frac{3}{2} < x < 4$

178. ANSWER: E

Given direct proportion, we can form an equation from the question given.

$y \propto x^2$

Let equation 1 be $y = kx^2$

Substituting the values given,

$36 = 9k$

$k = 4$

Now, we can substitute this and $y = 9$ in equation 1

$9 = 4x^2$

Since x is positive, solving this gives $x = \frac{3}{2}$

179. ANSWER: B

Given that Q: R is 7:2 and R:S is 3:7, we can equate the R terms, allowing us to then calculate ratio for Q:S.

Multiplying out the first ratio by 3 gives 21:6 and multiplying the second by 2 gives 6:14.

This shows that the ratio of Q:S is 21:14.

Since we need it in the form 1:n, dividing both sides by 21 gives $n = \frac{2}{3}$

180. ANSWER: C

Given that the discount is 20%, it means that the new price is $100 - 20 = 80\%$ of the old price.

To find the old price, firstly find 1% by dividing by 80.

$80\% = £12{,}000$

$1\% = £150$

$100\% = £15{,}000$, which is the original price of the television.

181. ANSWER: D

Solving this question requires the use of trigonometric identities.

$$2sinx = \frac{4cosx - 1}{tanx}$$

Firstly, we can multiply both sides by $tanx$ to give

$$2sinxtanx = 4cosx - 1$$

Then rewriting $tanx$ into $\frac{sinx}{cosx}$ gives

$$\frac{2sin^2x}{cosx} = 4cosx - 1$$

Multiplying through by $cosx$, as well as rewriting sin^2x as $1 - cos^2x$ gives

$$2(1 - cos^2x) = cosx(4cosx - 1)$$

Expanding and simplifying this gives

$$6cos^2x - cosx - 2 = 0$$

182. ANSWER: C

$$\frac{16^{\frac{1}{2}}}{81^{\frac{3}{4}}}$$

The numerator has a power of $\frac{1}{2}$, which represents a square root, giving $\frac{4}{81^{\frac{3}{4}}}$.

Using the law of fractional powers, the denominator can be rewritten as $(\sqrt[4]{81})^3$, which is 27.

Putting these two together gives $\frac{4}{27}$.

183. ANSWER: D

First, it would be appropriate to find the value of D. Since AD is the diameter, we can form a vector such that $\overrightarrow{AC} = \overrightarrow{CD}$.

This means the coordinates of D are (7,4).

We are required now to find the equation of the tangent, so first we will need to find the gradient of the diameter. The gradient, using points C and D, is

$$\frac{4-2}{7-4} = \frac{2}{3}$$

Since the tangent is perpendicular to the diameter, the gradient will be the negative reciprocal, which is $-\frac{3}{2}$.

Since we know that point D lies on the tangent, we can substitute it into the equation $y = ax + b$,

$$4 = -\frac{3}{2} \times 7 + b$$

Solving for this will obtain $b = \frac{29}{2}$

184. ANSWER: F

It is important that there are two unknowns and only one equation. This means you cannot assume the values of x and y purely because it could be numbers you are familiar with.

Instead, the given equation must be manipulated to obtain the final form.

Firstly, taking the reciprocal of both sides allows the power to become negative, giving

$$x^{-y} = 8$$

Then, both sides should be cubed allowing the left-hand side to be in the form required.

This means that $x^{-3y} = 512$.

185. ANSWER: A

We are given information about both ages, and from this we can make a list of the possible ages of the two boys.

Since Sam's age is 2 digits and a power of 5, the only possibility is 25.

Nick's age is also 2 digits which is a power of 2 giving the possibilities of 16, 32 and 64.

The 4 possibilities are (25,16), (25,32) and 25,64)

The only pairing in which the sum of the digits is an odd number is (25, 64)

The ANSWER is therefore $25 \times 64 = 1600$

186. ANSWER: B

Given the two side lengths, we can formulate an expression for the area of the triangle as

$$A = \frac{x(12-x)}{2}$$

Expanding this gives $A = 6x - \frac{x^2}{2}$

Since we need to find the maximum possible area, we need to find the value of x at which the expression for A is at its maximum. To do this, we must differentiate

$$\frac{dA}{dx} = 6 - x$$

It will be at its maximum when $\frac{dA}{dx} = 0$, so $x = 6$

Substituting $x = 6$ into the area of the triangle equation gives 18cm^2

187. ANSWER: A

$$\int_1^4 \frac{3-2x}{x\sqrt{x}}$$

The fraction can be rewritten as two separate fractions, each over the denominator.

$$\frac{3-2x}{x\sqrt{x}} = \frac{3}{x\sqrt{x}} - \frac{2x}{x\sqrt{x}} = 3x^{-\frac{3}{2}} - 2x^{-\frac{1}{2}}$$

This expression is much easier to integrate giving

$$\int_1^4 3x^{-\frac{3}{2}} - 2x^{-\frac{1}{2}} = \left[-6x^{-\frac{1}{2}} - 4x^{\frac{1}{2}}\right]_1^4$$

Expanding out the definite integral gives

$$\left(-6 \cdot 4^{-\frac{1}{2}} - 4 \cdot 4^{\frac{1}{2}}\right) - (-6 - 4) = -11 - -10 = -1$$

188. ANSWER: D

The wording of this question is very important. For "if" and "then" statements, for the statement to be disproved, the equation must satisfy the "if" clause but not satisfy the "then" clause.

Let us first check if each option satisfies the "if" clause.

Option A will have $f'(x) = 2x$, which will not always be positive so this option can automatically be ruled out.

Option B will be the same case, so it is also not correct as a disproof.

Option C has $f'(x) = -1$, which does satisfy the first clause, hence can be eliminated.

Option D has $f'(x) = 3x^2 + 1$, which will always be positive because all squares are positive. Since it satisfies the first clause, let us check the second. $f(x)$ includes x^3, which can take negative values, and hence for some negative values of x, $f(x)$ will be negative.

Hence, option D serves as a counterexample.

189. ANSWER: C

$$y = \frac{1-2x}{x+3}$$

First, multiply both sides by $(x+3)$, giving

$y(x+3) = 1-2x$, then expanding the brackets gives

$xy + 3y = 1-2x$, then bringing all the x terms to one side gives

$xy + 2x = 1-3y$, then factorising x gives

$x(y+2) = 1-3y$, then $x = \frac{1-3y}{y+2}$

190. ANSWER: F

$$f(x) = 2x^2 + kx + 18 = 0$$

For a quadratic to have no solutions, the discriminant must be less than 0.

The discriminant is $b^2 - 4acm$ which for $f(x)$ is

$k^2 - 4 \cdot 2 \cdot 18 = k^2 - 144$. We can now set up an inequality

$$k^2 - 144 < 0$$

Solving this inequality gives $-12 < k < 12$

191. ANSWER: B

$1 + \frac{1}{1+\frac{1}{1+\frac{1}{5}}}$. The key to this question is simplifying the expression from the inside and working outwards one step at a time as follows.

$$1 + \frac{1}{1+\frac{1}{1+\frac{1}{5}}} = 1 + \frac{1}{1+\frac{1}{\frac{6}{5}}} = 1 + \frac{1}{1+\frac{5}{6}} = 1 + \frac{1}{\frac{11}{6}} = 1 + \frac{6}{11} = \frac{17}{11}.$$

Therefore, $x = 17$ and $y = 11$, so $x + y = 28$.

192. ANSWER: C

You should realise that all the angles shown represent the exterior angles of the hexagon.

The sum of the exterior angles in every shape is always 360°, which allows us to form an equation to find y.

$$59 + y + 61 + 2y + 35 + 50 = 360$$

$$3y = 155$$

$$y = \frac{155}{3}°$$

193. ANSWER: A

Firstly, since $f(4) = 0$, we know that $(x - 4)$ must be a factor of $f(x)$, because of the factortheorem.

$f(x) = x^3 - 7x^2 + 13x - 4$. By dividing through polynomials, we get that

$$f(x) = x^3 - 7x^2 + 13x - 4 = (x - 4)(x^2 - 3x + 1)$$

Now, to find the other potential roots, we must solve the quadratic factor using the quadratic formula. This gives

$$x = \frac{3 \pm \sqrt{5}}{2}$$

Since the question asks for the sum of all factors, we do

$$4 + \frac{3+\sqrt{5}}{2} + \frac{3-\sqrt{5}}{2} = 4 + 3 = 7$$

194. ANSWER:D

$\frac{2x^2 - x^{\frac{3}{2}}}{\sqrt{x}}$ can be rewritten as $\frac{2x^2 - x^{\frac{3}{2}}}{x^{\frac{1}{2}}}$. The fraction can be split into two separate fractions as such

$\frac{2x^2 - x^{\frac{3}{2}}}{x^{\frac{1}{2}}} = \frac{2x^2}{x^{\frac{1}{2}}} - \frac{x^{\frac{3}{2}}}{x^{\frac{1}{2}}}$. Then simplifying each fraction using the laws of indices gets

$$\frac{2x^2}{x^{\frac{1}{2}}} - \frac{x^{\frac{3}{2}}}{x^{\frac{1}{2}}} = 2x^{\frac{3}{2}} - x$$

This gives $a = \frac{3}{2}, b = 1, c = 2$

Therefore, $a - b + c = \frac{5}{2}$

195. ANSWER: E

Let the original price of the cricket bat be 100%.

After the first day, its price reduces by 30%, so it goes down to 70%.

After the second day, its price reduces by 20% of the most recent price. This means that the new price is 80% of the 70%. This is 56%

Therefore, the overall price reduction is 44%.

196. ANSWER: D

Using the grid, it can be observed that $1 + 3 + 5 + 7 = 16$.

The sum of 4 odd digits is equal to the square of 4.

If another layer were to be drawn, we would obtain that $1 + 3 + 5 + 7 + 25$, showing that the sum of the first 5 odd digits is equal to the sum of 5.

Since the $1 + 3 + 5 + 7 + 9 + 11 + \cdots + 41$ contains the first 21 odd digits, it follows that the sum would be the square of 21, which is 441.

197. ANSWER: B

The perimeter consists of 6 squares and 6 triangles. Since we already know the side length of the square, it follows that the perimeter covered by only the squares is 108cm.

However, we do not know the outer side length of the triangle yet, because we do not know if it is equilateral.

However, since the two-inner side lengths of each triangle are covered by the square, we know for sure that it is isosceles at minimum.

Since the inner hexagon is regular, we know that the angle must be 120. We can work out the inner angle of the triangle by doing $360 - (120 + 90 + 90) = 60$. Since the inner angle is 60 and it is isosceles it follows that the triangle is equilateral.

Therefore, the outer side length of the triangle is also going to be 18cm

Therefore, the total perimeter is going to be $18 \times 12 = 216$cm

198. ANSWER: E

This question involves using the laws of logarithms.

$\log_3(x + 11) - \log_3(x - 5) = 2$. First combine the left-hand side to obtain

$\log_3\left(\frac{x+11}{x-5}\right) = 2$, then using the definition of a logarithm, we get

$\frac{x+11}{x-5} = 9$, solving this linearly gets

$x = 7$

199. ANSWER: A

$y = \frac{x^3}{8}$. This question requires algebraic manipulation of the fractions.

Firstly, obtain the reciprocal to get $y^{-1} = \frac{8}{x^3}$. Then squaring both sides gets

$y^{-2} = \frac{64}{x^6}$. Then, halving both sides gets $\frac{1}{2}y^{-2} = \frac{32}{x^6}$.

The RHS can be written as $32x^{-6}$, such that $k = 32$ and $n = -6$

Therefore, $k + n = 26$

200. ANSWER: C

$$\frac{3 - 2\sqrt{5}}{\sqrt{5} - 1}.$$

To simplify this fraction, first we must rationalise the denominator by multiply the both the numerator and the denominator by the conjugate.

The fraction can be manipulated to make it easier by factoring out a minus sign.

$$\frac{2\sqrt{5}-3}{1-\sqrt{5}} = \frac{2\sqrt{5}-3}{1-\sqrt{5}} \times \frac{1+\sqrt{5}}{1+\sqrt{5}} = \frac{(2\sqrt{5}-3)(1+\sqrt{5})}{-4} = \frac{2\sqrt{5}-3-3\sqrt{5}+10}{-4} = \frac{7-\sqrt{5}}{-4} = \frac{\sqrt{5}}{4} - \frac{7}{4}$$

This means that $p = -\frac{7}{4}$ and $q = \frac{1}{4}$, and $q - p = 2$

201. ANSWER: B

If x, y, and z are consecutive terms of a geometric sequence, then

$\frac{y}{x} = \frac{z}{y}$ (equating constant ratios)

$\therefore y^2 = xz$ .... (1)

Now $x + y + z = \frac{7}{3}$ .... (2)

$$\therefore (x + y + z)^2 = \frac{49}{9}$$

$$\therefore x^2 + y^2 + z^2 + 2xy + 2xz + 2yz = \frac{49}{9}$$

$$\therefore \frac{91}{9} + 2(xy + xz + yz) = \frac{49}{9}$$

$$\therefore 2(xy + xz + yz) = -\frac{42}{9}$$

$$\therefore xy + xz + yz = -\frac{7}{3}$$

$\therefore xy + y^2 + yz = -\frac{7}{3}$ (using (1))

$\therefore y(x + y + z) = -(x + y + z)$ $\left(x + y + z = \frac{7}{3}\right)$

$\therefore y = -1$

Substituting $y = -1$ into (1) and (2) gives $xz = 1$ and $x + z = \frac{10}{3}$ .... (4)

$\therefore z = \frac{1}{x}$ .... (3)

Substituting (3) into (4) gives $x + \frac{1}{x} = \frac{10}{3}$

$\therefore 3x^2 - 10x + 3 = 0$

$\therefore (3x - 1)(x - 3) = 0$

$\therefore x = \frac{1}{3}$ or 3

Using (3), if $x = \frac{1}{3}$, $z = 3$ and if $x = 3$, $z = \frac{1}{3}$

$\therefore x = \frac{1}{3}, y = -1, z = 3$ or $x = 3, y = -1, z = \frac{1}{3}$

$\therefore xyz = -1$

202. ANSWER: C

$$2\log_3 x - 3\log_3 \frac{1}{x} = 10$$

$$\therefore \log_3 x^2 + (\log_3 \frac{1}{x^3})^{-1} = 10$$

$$\therefore \log_3(x^2 \times x^3) = 10$$

$$\therefore \log_3 x^5 = 10$$

$$\therefore x^5 = 3^{10}$$

$$\therefore x = \sqrt[5]{3^{10}}$$

$$\therefore x = 9$$

203. ANSWER: A

Total time of motion can be written as

$$1 + (90\% \times 1) + (90\% \times 1) + (90\% \times 90\% \times 1) + (90\% \times 90\% \times 1) + (90\% \times 90\% \times 90\% \times 1) + \cdots$$

$= 1 + 0.9 + 0.9 + (0.9)^2 + (0.9)^2 + (0.9)^3 + \cdots$

$= 1 + 2(0.9) + 2(0.9)^2 + 2(0.9)^3 + \cdots$

$= [2 + 2(0.9) + 2(0.9)^2 + 2(0.9)^3 + \cdots] - 1$

So, $S_n = \frac{u_1(1-r^n)}{1-r} - 1$, where $u_1 = 2$ and $r = 0.9$

$\therefore S_n = \dfrac{2(1-0.9^n)}{1-0.9} - 1$

$\therefore S_n = 20(1 - 0.9^n) - 1$

$\therefore S_n = 19 - 20 \times 0.9^n$

For the ball to come to rest, n must approach infinity. ∞

As $n \longrightarrow \infty$, $0.9^n \longrightarrow 0$ and so $20 \times 0.9^n \longrightarrow 0$ also.

$\therefore S_n \longrightarrow 19$

Hence it takes 19 seconds for the ball to come to rest.

204. ANSWER: D

When $x = -3, y = (-3)^2\sqrt{1-(-3)} = 9\sqrt{4} = 18 \ \{y \geq 0\}$

$\therefore$ the point of contact is $(-3, 18)$

When, $y = x^2\sqrt{1-x}$,

$\dfrac{dy}{dx} = 2x(1-x)^{\frac{1}{2}} - x^2(\dfrac{1}{2})(1-x)^{-\frac{1}{2}}$

$\therefore$at $x = -3$, $\frac{dy}{dx} = 2(-3)\left(1-(-3)\right)^{\frac{1}{2}} - (-3)^2\left(\frac{1}{2}\right)\left(1-(-3)\right)^{-\frac{1}{2}} = -\frac{57}{4}$

$\therefore$ the tangent at (-3, 18) has equation $y = -\frac{57}{4}x - \frac{99}{4}$

Now when $x = 0, y = -\frac{99}{4}$ and when $y = 0, x = -\frac{99}{57}$

$\therefore$ the area of OAB is $\frac{1}{2} \times \left(\frac{99}{4}\right) \times \left(\frac{99}{57}\right) = \frac{3267}{152}$

205. ANSWER: E

When $x = 1, y = \frac{1+1}{1^2-2} = -2$

$\therefore$ the point of contact is (1, -2).

$\frac{dy}{dx} = \frac{1(x^2-2)-(x+1)(2x)}{(x^2-2)^2}$ (using quotient rule)

At $x = 1, \frac{dy}{dx} = \frac{(1-2)-2(1+1)}{(1-2)^2}$

$= \frac{-1-4}{1} = -5$

$\therefore$ the normal at (1,-2) has gradient $\frac{1}{5}$

$\therefore y = \frac{1}{5}x - \frac{11}{5}$

206. ANSWER: F

If the base measures x m by x m and the height is y m, area is $x^2 + 4xy$.

$\therefore$ cost$= 2x^2 + 8xy$

$C = 2x^2 + 8xy$

$= 2x^2 + \frac{8}{x}$ pounds

$\frac{dC}{dx} = \frac{4(x^3-2)}{x^2}$

So, $\frac{dC}{dx} = 0$ when $x = \sqrt[3]{2}$ m. Using sign diagrams, we determine that the minimum cost is when $x = \sqrt[3]{2}$, $y = \frac{1}{\sqrt[3]{4}}$.

Hence the box is $\sqrt[3]{2}$ m by $\sqrt[3]{2}$ m by $\frac{1}{\sqrt[3]{4}}$ m.

207. ANSWER: E

1) $\sin^2 x + \cos^2 x = 1$

$\therefore \frac{9}{16} + \cos^2 x = 1$

$\therefore \cos^2 x = \frac{7}{16}$

$\therefore \cos x = -\frac{\sqrt{7}}{4}$ $(\cos x < 0)$

2) $\sin 2x = 2 \sin x \cos x$

$= 2(-\frac{3}{4})(-\frac{\sqrt{7}}{4})$

$= \frac{3\sqrt{7}}{8}$

3) $\cos 2x = \cos^2 x - \sin^2 x$

$= \left(-\frac{\sqrt{7}}{4}\right)^2 - \left(-\frac{3}{4}\right)^2$

$= -\frac{1}{8}$

4) $\tan 2x = \frac{\sin 2x}{\cos 2x}$

$= \frac{\frac{3\sqrt{7}}{8}}{-\frac{1}{8}} = -3\sqrt{7}$

208. ANSWER: B

ratio$= r = \frac{x-2}{x+3}$

The series will converge if $|r| < 1$

$\therefore |\frac{x-2}{x+3}| < 1$

$\therefore |x-2| < |x+3|$

$\therefore (x-2)^2 < (x+3)^2$

$\therefore x^2 - 4x + 4 < x^2 + 6x + 9$

$\therefore x > -\frac{1}{2}$

209. ANSWER: F

Squaring both sides of the equation gives

$9\sin^2 x + 24\sin x\cos y + 16\cos^2 y = 25$

$16\sin^2 y + 24\sin y\cos x + 9\cos^2 x = 4$

Adding these equations and re-arranging them, we get

$9\sin^2 x + 9\cos^2 x + 16\sin^2 y + 16\cos^2 y + 24\sin x\cos y + 24\sin y\cos x = 29$

Since $\sin^2 x + \cos^2 x = 1$,

$9 + 16 + 24(\sin x\cos y + \sin y\cos x) = 29$

from which we obtain

$\sin x\cos y + \sin y\cos x = \frac{4}{24}$

$\therefore \sin(x+y) = \frac{1}{6}$

210. ANSWER: E

Each interior angle is 120°. ($\frac{(n-2)\times 180°}{n}$, n is 6)

The area of the shaded sector is a third of the area of a complete circle of radius 6 that passes C and E. Hence the area is $\frac{1}{3} \times 81\pi = 27\pi$

211. ANSWER: D

The time it takes Alice to run one lap of the circular track is $\frac{2\times60\times\pi\text{ m}}{6\text{m/s}} = 20\pi$ seconds. Since they both run one lap in the same amount of time, Dylan also runs 20π seconds to complete one lap. The length of Dylan's track is $\frac{5\text{m}}{s} \times 20\pi$ seconds $= 100\pi$ m.

$$\therefore x = \frac{100\pi}{3}$$

212. ANSWER: C

$$f'(x) = x^2 - 3x + 2$$

$$f(x) = \frac{x^3}{3} - \frac{3x^2}{2} + 2x + c$$

$$f(1) = 3 \text{ so } \frac{1}{3} - \frac{3}{2} + 2 + c = 3$$

$$\therefore c = \frac{13}{6}$$

$$\therefore f(x) = \frac{x^3}{3} - \frac{3x^2}{2} + 2x + \frac{13}{6}$$

$$f(3) = \frac{3^3}{3} - \frac{3\times3^2}{2} + 2\times3 + \frac{13}{6} = \frac{11}{3}$$

213. ANSWER: D

$$2^{403} + 2^{404} + 2^{403} = 2^{5n}$$

$$2^{403}(1+1+2) = 2^{5n}$$

$$2^{403} \times 2^2 = 2^{5n}$$

$$405 = 5n$$

$n = 81$

214. ANSWER: B

$a > 0,\ b > 0,\ c > 0$

$\therefore \log_a b > 0,\ \log_b c > 0,\ \log_c a > 0$

Assuming

$\log_a b = \frac{\log_b c}{2} = \frac{\log_c a}{4} = t$, where t is a positive number,

$\log_a b = t, \log_b c = 2t, \log_c a = 4t$

Since $\log_a b \times \log_b c \times \log_c a = 1$

$t \times 2t \times 4t = 1$

$\therefore t = \frac{1}{2}$

Therefore $\log_a b + \log_b c + \log_c a = t + 2t + 4t$

$= 7t$

$= \frac{7}{2}$

215. ANSWER: E

Assuming that

$\mathrm{AD} = \mathrm{CE} = a\ (a > 0)$

Using cosine rule for triangle ADE

$(\sqrt{13})^2 = a^2 + (a+1)^2 - 2a(a+1)\cos\frac{\pi}{3}$

$\therefore\ a^2 + a - 12 = 0$

$\therefore (a+4)(a-3) = 0$

$\therefore a = 3$

Area of triangle ADE $= \frac{1}{2} \times 4 \times 3 \times \sin\frac{\pi}{3} = 3\sqrt{3}$

Area of triangle ABE$= \frac{1}{2} \times 4 \times 1 \times \sin\frac{\pi}{3} = \sqrt{3}$

Area of triangle BDE$=$ Area of triangle ADE $-$ Area of triangle ABE

$= 2\sqrt{3}$

216. ANSWER: E

$f(0) = 2ab = 6$

$\therefore ab = 3$

Since a and b are natural numbers, it is either

$a = 1, b = 3$ or $a = 3, b = 1$

When $a = 1, b = 3, f(x) = (x - 2)(x - 3)$

$f(x) \leq 0$ when $2 < x \leq 3$, hence the condition does not satisfy (2)

When $a = 3, b = 1, f(x) = 3(x - 2)(x - 1)$

$f(x) > 0$ when $x > 2$, hence the condition satisfies (2)

Hence $f(x) = 3(x - 2)(x - 1)$

$\therefore f(4) = 18$

217. ANSWER: C

The translated equation is

$y = 5^{x-a} + b$

$5^{-a} = \frac{1}{9} \times 5^{-1}, b = 2$

$\therefore\ 5^a = 45$ and $b = 2$

$\therefore\ 5^a + b = 47$

218. ANSWER: B

Using binomial expansion, the general term is

$$\binom{6}{r} \times x^{6-r} \times \left(\frac{4}{x^2}\right)^r$$

$$= \binom{6}{r} \times 4^r \times x^{6-3r}$$

Coefficient of x^3 is

When $6 - 3r = 3, \therefore r = 1$

Hence,

$$\binom{6}{1} \times 4^1 = 24$$

219. ANSWER: E

$$f'(x) = \ln(2x - 1) + x \times \frac{2}{2x - 1}$$

Hence $f'(1) = 0 + 1 \times 2 = 2$

220. ANSWER: E

There are $4 \times 4 = 16$ total ways to choose both numbers a and b.

i) when $a = 1$,

$1 < \frac{b}{1} < 4$, hence $1 < b < 4$

$\therefore b$ does not exist

ii) when $a = 3$,

$1 < \frac{b}{3} < 4$, hence $3 < b < 12$

$\therefore b = 4, 6, 8, 10$

ii) when $a = 5$,

$1 < \frac{b}{5} < 4$, hence $5 < b < 20$

$\therefore b = 6, 8, 10$

iii) when $a = 7$,

$1 < \frac{b}{7} < 4$, hence $7 < b < 28$

$\therefore b = 8, 10$

From i)~iii) the number of ways to choose a and b is $0 + 4 + 3 + 2 = 9$

$\therefore$ the probability is $\frac{9}{16}$

221. ANSWER: A

$$y - 5 = 6\sqrt[3]{\frac{3x+1}{4}}$$

$$\frac{y-5}{6} = \sqrt[3]{\frac{3x+1}{4}}$$

$$\left(\frac{y-5}{6}\right)^3 = \frac{3x+1}{4}$$

$$4\left(\frac{y-5}{6}\right)^3 - 1 = 3x$$

$$x = \frac{4}{3}\left(\frac{y-5}{6}\right)^3 - \frac{1}{3}$$

222. ANSWER: G

$$x^3 - x^2 - 8x = -k$$

Assume $f(x) = x^3 - x^2 - 8x$,

$$f'(x) = 3x^2 - 2x - 8$$
$$= (3x + 4)(x - 2)$$

When $f'(x) = 0, x = -\frac{4}{3}$ or $x = 2$

$$f\left(-\frac{4}{3}\right) = \frac{176}{27}, f(2) = -12$$

Using sign diagram, we notice that $f\left(-\frac{4}{3}\right)$ is the local maximum and $f(2)$ is the local minimum. Hence, the graph of $f(x)$ looks like the following:

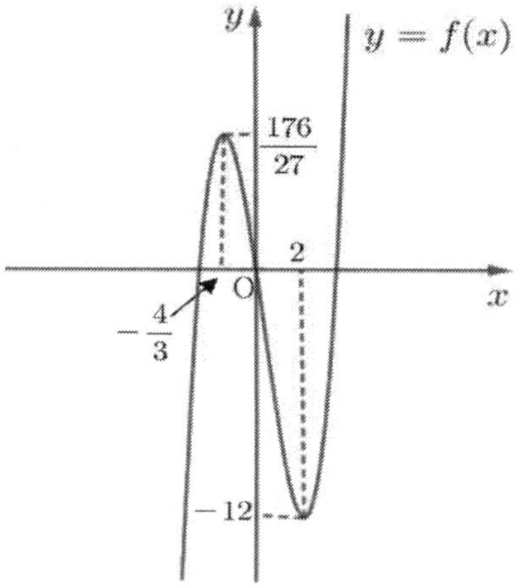

For $f(x) = -k$ to have two real roots $y = f(x)$ should meet $y = -k$ at two distinctive points.

$-k = \frac{176}{27}$ or $-k = -12$

$\therefore k = -\frac{176}{27}$ or $k = 12$

$\therefore k = 12\ (k > 0)$

223. ANSWER: B

$2^{\frac{1}{3}} \times 2^{\frac{2}{3}} = 2^1 = 2$

224. ANSWER: A

$f'(x) = 3x^2 - 2$

$f'(1) = 1$

225. ANSWER: C

$\int_0^2 (3x^2 + 6x)\, dx$

$= [x^3 + 3x^2]_0^2$

$= 8 + 12 = 20$

226. ANSWER: C

$-f(x-1) - 1$

$= -\{(x-1)^2 - 2(x-1)\} - 1$

$= -(x^2 - 4x + 3) - 1$

$= -x^2 + 4x - 4$

Hence the two lines meet when

$x^2 - 2x = -x^2 + 4x - 4$

$x^2 - 3x + 2 = 0$

$(x-1)(x-2) = 0$

$\therefore x = 1 \text{ or } x = 2$

The area enclosed by the two lines is

$\int_1^2 \{(-x^2 + 4x - 4) - (x^2 - 2x)\}\, dx$

$= \frac{1}{3}$

227. ANSWER: C

$f'^{(x)} = 3x^2 - 6ax + 3(a^2 - 1) = 0$

$3x^2 - 6ax + 3(a^2 - 1) = 0$

$3(x - a + 1)(x - a - 1) = 0$

$\therefore x = a - 1, a + 1$

Drawing sign diagram shows that $f(x)$ has maximum at $x = a - 1$.

Hence $f(a - 1) = 4$

$\therefore (a - 1)^3 - 3a(a - 1)^2 + 3(a^2 - 1)(a - 1) = 4$

Rearranging and solving gives $a = -1, 2$

i) $a = -1$

$f(x) = x^3 + 3x^2$

Here, $f(-2) = 4 > 0$, hence i) satisfies the condition.

ii) $a = 2$

$f(x) = x^3 - 6x^2 + 9x$

Here, $f(-2) = -50 < 0$, hence ii) does not satisfy the condition.

Considering results from i) and ii),

$f(x) = x^3 + 3x^2$

$\therefore f(-1) = (-1)^3 + 3(-1)^2 = 2$

228. ANSWER: G

$a_{n+1} + a_n = 3n - 1,$

When $n = 1, a_2 + a_1 = 2$

When $n = 2, a_3 + a_2 = 5$

When $n = 3, a_4 + a_3 = 8$

When $n = 4, a_5 + a_4 = 11$

Since $a_3 = 4$, from $a_4 + a_3 = 8$ we find that $a_4 = 4$

Similarly, substitute $a_4 = 4$ into $a_5 + a_4 = 11$ and we get $a_5 = 7$.

With similar steps, we find $a_2 = 1$ and $a_1 = 1$

$\therefore a_1 \times a_5 = 1 \times 7 = 7$

229. ANSWER: C

$$\frac{6!}{3!2!} = \frac{6\times5\times4}{2} = 60$$

230. ANSWER: C

The gradient of lines passing the origin and two points should be the same (the line passes both points and the origin).

Hence

$$\frac{\log_4 a}{2} = \frac{\log_2 b}{3}$$

$$\therefore \frac{1}{4}\log_2 a = \frac{1}{3}\log_2 b$$

$$\therefore \log_2 a = \frac{4}{3}\log_2 b$$

Therefore $\log_a b = \frac{\log_2 b}{\log_2 a} = \frac{\log_2 b}{\frac{4}{3}\log_2 b} = \frac{3}{4}$

231. ANSWER: B

P(both cards have odd numbers | sum of the numbers is even)

$= \frac{\text{P(both cards have odd numbers} \cap \text{sum of the numbers is even)}}{\text{P(sum of the numbers is even)}}$

$= \frac{\frac{5}{9} \times \frac{4}{8}}{\frac{5}{9} \times \frac{4}{8} + \frac{4}{9} \times \frac{3}{8}}$

$= \frac{5}{8}$

232. ANSWER: B

$P(|a-3| + |b-3| = 2) = \frac{8}{36}$ (ways that (a, b) is possible are (1,3), (2,2), (2,4), (3,1), (3,5), (4,2), (4,4), (5,3), hence 8)

$P(a = b) = \frac{6}{36}$ (ways that (a,b) is possible are (1,1), (2,2), (3,3), (4,4), (5,5), (6,6), hence 6)

$P(|a-3| + |b-3| = 2 \cap a = b) = \frac{2}{36} =$ ((2,2) and (4,4))

$P(|a-3| + |b-3| = 2 \cup a = b)$

$= P(|a-3| + |b-3| = 2) + P(a = b) - P((|a-3| + |b-3| = 2 \cap a = b))$

$= \frac{8}{36} + \frac{6}{36} - \frac{2}{36}$

$= \frac{1}{3}$

233. ANSWER: D

According to sine rule,

$\frac{AC}{\sin B} = 2 \times 15$

$\therefore AC = 30 \times \sin B = 30 \times \frac{7}{10} = 21$

234. ANSWER: D

$$\frac{dy}{dx} = 1 \times e^{3x} + x \times 3e^{3x} = e^{3x} + 3xe^{3x} = e^{3x}(1 + 3x)$$

235. ANSWER: A

$$\Delta = b^2 - 4ac = 16k^2 - 4 \times 3 \times (k - 1) = 16k^2 - 12k + 12$$

$$= 16\left(k - \frac{3}{8}\right)^2 + \frac{39}{4}$$

The two roots are closest together when Δ is least. The minimum value occurs when $k = \frac{3}{8}$.

236. ANSWER: G

$$Area = 3\left\{\frac{1}{2}[OC^2 - OB^2] \times \frac{\pi}{6}\right\} + \pi[OA^2] \text{ (using the area of a sector formula)}$$

$$= 3\left\{\frac{1}{2}[9^2 - 5^2] \times \frac{\pi}{6}\right\} + \pi[3^2]$$

$$= 23\pi$$

237. ANSWER: C

$f(x)$ has a minimum value when $x^2 - 4x + 20$ is at its minimum.

$$x^2 - 4x + 20 = (x - 2)^2 + 16$$

$\therefore$ when $-3 \le x \le 3, x^2 - 4x + 20$ has a minimum value of 16 when $x = 2$

Hence, minimum value of $f(x) = \log_2 16 = 4$

238. ANSWER: E

$\tan\theta = \frac{3}{4}$ $(0 < \theta < \frac{\pi}{2})$ hence $\sin\theta = \frac{3}{5}$

$\cos\left(\frac{\pi}{2} - \theta\right) + 2\sin(\pi - \theta) = \sin\theta + 2\sin\theta$

$= 3\sin\theta = \frac{9}{5}$

239. ANSWER: E

$(a_5)^2 = a_2 \times a_{14}$

$(a + 4d)^2 = (a + d)(a + 13d)$

$3d^2 = 6ad$

Since $d \neq 0$, $d = 2a$

$\frac{a_{23}}{a_3} = \frac{a+22d}{a+2d} = \frac{45a}{5a} = 9$

240. ANSWER: B

Assume that the centre of the circle is O.

Two triangles OAB and OBC are equilateral triangles hence AB=BC $= 3$

In triangle ABC, $\angle ABC = \frac{2\pi}{3}$

According to the cosine rule in triangle ABC,

$AC^2 = 3^2 + 3^2 - 2 \times 3 \times 3 \times \cos\frac{2\pi}{3} = 27$

$AC = 3\sqrt{3}$

Since rectangle ABCP is inscribed in the circle,

$\angle\text{ABC}+\angle\text{APC} = \pi$, hence $\angle\text{APC} = \frac{\pi}{3}$

Let $\text{AP} = x$, and $\text{CP} = y$.

According to the cosine rule in triangle ACP,

$(3\sqrt{3})^2 = x^2 + y^2 - 2xy\cos\frac{\pi}{3}$

$27 = (x+y)^2 - 3xy$

$x + y = 8$ hence $xy = \frac{37}{3}$

Area of triangle ABC is

$\frac{1}{2} \times 3 \times 3 \times \sin\frac{2\pi}{3} = \frac{9\sqrt{3}}{4}$

Area of triangle ACP is

$\frac{1}{2} \times x \times y \times \sin\frac{\pi}{3} = \frac{37\sqrt{3}}{12}$

Hence area of rectangle ABCP is

$\frac{9\sqrt{3}}{4} + \frac{37\sqrt{3}}{12} = \frac{16\sqrt{3}}{3}$

241. ANSWER: E

$8\sin\frac{\pi}{6} + \tan\frac{\pi}{4} = 8 \times \frac{1}{2} + 1 = 5$

242. ANSWER: A

$\log 20 + \log 5$

$= \log 100$

$= 2$

243. ANSWER: E

$\frac{2}{\sqrt{3}}\sin(x + \frac{\pi}{3}) - \frac{7}{8} = 0$

$\sin(x + \frac{\pi}{3}) = \frac{7\sqrt{3}}{16}$

Let $t = x + \frac{\pi}{3}$, then $\frac{\pi}{3} \leq t \leq \frac{7\pi}{3}$

Since $\frac{7\sqrt{3}}{16} < \frac{\sqrt{3}}{2}$, equation $\sin t = \frac{7\sqrt{3}}{16}$ $(\frac{\pi}{3} \leq t \leq \frac{7\pi}{3})$ has two real roots t_1 and t_2. $(t_1 < t_2)$.

We observe that $t_1 = x_1 + \frac{\pi}{3}$, $t_2 = x_2 + \frac{\pi}{3}$, then $t_2 = 2\pi + (\pi - t_1)$.

$t_1 + t_2 = \left(x_1 + \frac{\pi}{3}\right) + \left(x_2 + \frac{\pi}{3}\right) = 3\pi$

Sum of all real roots of $\sin(x + \frac{\pi}{3}) = \frac{7\sqrt{3}}{16}$ is

$x_1 + x_2 = 3\pi - \frac{2\pi}{3} = \frac{7\pi}{3}$

$\therefore p + q = 7 + 3 = 10$

244. ANSWER: D

$a_1 = 6, a_2 = 6 + 3, a_3 = 6 + 3 + 3^2, a_4 = 6 + 3 + 3^2 + 3^3,$

$\therefore a_3 = 45$

245. ANSWER: A

$y = \left(\frac{1}{3}\right)^x$ meets the line $y = 9$ when the x coordinate is -2, $\therefore A(-2,9)$

$y = \left(\frac{1}{9}\right)^x$ meets the line $y = 9$ when the x coordinate is -1, $\therefore B(-1,9)$

$\therefore$ Area of triangle OAB is $\frac{1}{2} \times 1 \times 9 = \frac{9}{2}$

246. ANSWER: E

$3^x - 3^{4-x} = 24$

$(3^x)^2 - 24 \times 3^x - 81 = 0$

$(3^x + 3)(3^x - 27) = 0$

$3^x = -3$ or 27

$3^x > 0$, hence $x = 3$

247. ANSWER: D

$-x^2 + 2ax - 6a < 0$

$x^2 - 2ax + 6a > 0$

$\Delta = 4a^2 - 24a$

$= 4a(a - 6) < 0$

$\therefore 0 < a < 6$ therefore $a = 1, 2, 3, 4, 5$

$\therefore 1 + 2 + 3 + 4 + 5 = 15$

248. ANSWER: A

$\log_n 4 \times \log_2 9 = 4 \log_n 3$

Let $4 \log_n 3 = m$ (m *is a natural number*)

$n = (3^4)^{\frac{1}{m}}$

$\therefore m = 1, n = 81$

$\therefore m = 2, n = 9$

$\therefore m = 4, n = 3$

Hence the sum of all possible values of n is

$81 + 9 + 3 = 93$

249. ANSWER: F

$\alpha + \beta = 24$

$k = \frac{\alpha+\beta}{2} = 12$

250. ANSWER: D

Let L_1 be the event that the salesman leaves his wallet in store 1. L_2 is the event that the salesman leaves his wallet in store 2.

$P(L_1|(L_1 \text{ or } L_2)) = \frac{P(L_1 \cap (L_1 or \ _2)}{P(L_1 \text{ or } L_2)}$

$= \frac{P(L_1)}{P(L_1 L_2' \text{ or } L_1'^{L_2})}$

$= \frac{\frac{1}{5}}{\frac{1}{5}+\frac{4}{5}\times\frac{1}{5}}$

$= \frac{5}{9}$

251. ANSWER: E

range=max-min

$23 = 37 - p$

$\therefore p = 14$

$IQR = q_3 - q_1$

$10 = q - 18$

$\therefore q = 28$

$\therefore p - q = -14$

252. ANSWER: C

$$s(t) = \int v(t)\, dt$$

$$= \int 3e^{2t} + 2t\, dt$$

$$= \frac{3e^{2t}}{2} + t^2 + C$$

Substitute $t = 0, s = 8$

$$8 = \frac{3e^0}{2} + C$$

$\therefore C = 6.5$

Therefore

$$s(t) = \frac{3e^{2t}}{2} + t^2 + 6.5$$

253. ANSWER: C

There are 90 integers to choose from. The minimum possible sum of its digits is $1 + 0 = 1$ and the maximum possible sum of its digits is $9 + 9 = 18$. The multiples of 7 in the range 1 to 18 are 7 and 14. Hence, we have to find for the number of positive integers between 10 and 99 that have sum of digits equal to 7 or 14.

The integers with sum of digits equal to 7 are 16, 25, 34, 43, 52, 61, 70 (total of 7), and integers with sum of digits equal to 14 are 59, 68, 77, 86, 95, (total of 5). Hence there are 12 integers out of 90.

$$\therefore \frac{12}{90} = \frac{2}{15}$$

254. ANSWER: E

$IQR = 7 - 2 = 5$

$upper\ inner\ fence = q_3 + 1.5(IQR)$

$= 7 + 1.5(5)$

$= 14.5$

255. ANSWER: A

$b = a + 1, c = a + 2, d = a + 3, e = a + 4$

From $a^2 + b^2 + c^2 = d^2 + e^2$,

$a^2 + (a + 1)^2 + (a + 2)^2 = (a + 3)^2 + (a + 4)^2$

$a^2 + a^2 + 21 + 1 + a^2 + 4a + 4 = a^2 + 6a + 9 + a^2 + 8a + 16$

$a^2 - 8a - 20 = 0$

$(a - 10)(a + 2) = 0$

Since a is positive, then $a = 10$

256. ANSWER: A

$k = 3,\ a = 2,\ b = 1$

$\therefore k \times a \times b = 6$

257. ANSWER: C

The two lines intersect when

$-\frac{1}{2}x = 2x - a \quad (x > 0)$

$-x = 4x - 2a$

$2a = 5x$

$x = \frac{2a}{5}$

$\therefore$ the area is $2\left[\frac{1}{2}(\text{base} \times \text{height}\right] = 2\left[\frac{1}{2}(a \times \frac{2}{5}\right]$

$= \frac{2a^2}{5}$

$\therefore \frac{2a^2}{5} = 40$

$a = 10 \ \ (a > 0)$

258. ANSWER: A

The car takes 10 minutes to travel from the point at which the van passes it until it arrives at Cambridge. Since the car drives at 40km/h and since 10 minutes equals $\frac{1}{6}$ hour, the car travels $\frac{40\text{km}}{\text{h}} \times \frac{1}{6}\text{h} = \frac{20}{3}$km in 10 minutes.

$\therefore$ the distance between the point where the vehicles pass and Cambridge is $\frac{20}{3}$km

Since the van travels at 50km/h it covers this distance in $\frac{203\text{km}}{50\text{km/h}} = \frac{2}{15}$h.

Now $\frac{2}{15}$h$=\frac{8}{60}$h which equals 8 minutes, hence the van arrives at Cambridge $10 - 8 =$ 2 minutes before the car.

259. ANSWER: F

Average height of Isaac and James is 175cm.

Average height of Isaac, James and Karl $= 1.04 \times 175 = 182$ (cm).

Sum of their heights $= 3 \times 182 = 546$ (cm)

Karl's height $= 546 - 2 \times 175 = 196$cm

260. ANSWER: C

i) solve $f(|x|) < \frac{8}{3}$ for $|x| < 5$

$\frac{4|x|}{5-|x|} < \frac{8}{3}$

$|x| < 2$

ii) solve $f(|x|) < \frac{8}{3}$ for $|x| > 5$

$\frac{4|x|}{5-|x|} < \frac{8}{3}$

$|x| > 2$

$|x| > 5$ (since $|x| > 5$)

Hence the set of solutions is $\{x < -5 \cup -2 < x < 2 \cup x > 5\}$

261. ANSWER: D

If two lines are parallel, they will not intersect unless they are the same line. ∴ two lines that have the same slope but different y-intersects cannot intercepts cannot intersect.

Similarly, two lines with different slopes always intersect at one point.

The six lines Max can graph can be broken into two sets of three distinct parallel lines. Each of the three lines with slope 1 intersects each of the three lines with slope -2 exactly once. ∴ $3 \times 3 = 9$ intersections.

We must check that none of the points have been counted more than once. (we need to have at least three of the six lines intersecting at the same point) There are only two possible slopes so among any three of the lines at least two must have the same slope. Therefore, if three of the lines intersect at the same point, then two distinct lines of equal slope intersect. This would mean that two distinct parallel lines intersect, which cannot happen.

Therefore, the nine points are distinct, so $n = 9$.

262. ANSWER: A

$\log_{x^2} y = 9 \log_y (x^2)$

$\frac{\ln y}{\ln(x^2)} = \frac{9 \ln(x^2)}{\ln y}$

$\frac{\ln}{2 \ln x} = \frac{18 \ln}{\ln y}$

$(\ln y)^2 = (6 \ln x)^2$

$\ln y = \pm 6 \ln x$

$\ln y = \ln\left(\frac{1}{x^6}\right)$ or $\ln(x^6)$

$y = \frac{1}{x^6}$ or x^6

263. ANSWER: B

$k = \frac{10}{3}$, so $\frac{6k}{5} - 2 = \frac{6}{5} \times \frac{10}{3} - 2 = \frac{60}{15} - 2 = 4 - 2 = 2$

264. ANSWER: C

Since $100 = 4 \times 24 + 4$, then 100 hours is 4 days and 4 hours.

The time 4 days before 7:00 am is also 7:00 am, and the time 4 hours earlier than this is 3:00 am.

$\therefore 3{:}00\ am$

265. ANSWER: A

When the line with equation $y = -2x + 7$ is reflected across a vertical line, the sign of the slop is reversed and becomes 2. $\therefore a = 2$

The point on the original line that has x-coordinate 3 has y-coordinate $y = -2(3) + 7 = 1$, hence point $(3,1)$ is on the original line.

When this line is reflected across $x = 3$, the point $(3,1)$ must also be on the reflected line. Substituting into $y = 2x + b$ gives $1 = 2(3) + b$ and so $b = -5$.

$\therefore 2a + b = 2(2) + (-5) = -1$

266. ANSWER: C

$1 + \frac{4|x|}{|x|+3} < 2$

$\frac{4|x|}{|x|+3} < 1$

$4|x| < |x| + 3$

$3|x| < 3$

$|x| < 1$

$\therefore -1 < x < 1$

267. ANSWER: F

$\log_k(8x - 2x^2) = 3$

$8x - 2x^2 = k^3$

$0 = 2x^2 - 8x + k^3$

$\Delta = b^2 - 4ac = 0$

$(-8)^2 - 4(2)(k^3) = 0$

$k = 2$

268. ANSWER: D

The total number of dots on the six faces is $1 + 2 + 3 + 4 + 5 + 6 = 21$. When the face lying on the table is x, the total number of visible is $21 - x$.

$21 - x > 19, x = 1$ or 2

$$\therefore \frac{1}{6} + \frac{1}{6} = \frac{1}{3}$$

269. ANSWER: E

A point of inflection occurs when $f''(x) = 0$, hence

$f''(x) = 3x^2 - 18x + 24 = 0$

$(x - 2)(x - 4) = 0$

$x = 2, 4$

270. ANSWER: E

m=full bottles of milk, s=full bottles of syrup. The volume of milk that Alex uses is $2m$ L and the volume of syrup is $1.4s$ L. For this ratio to equal 5:2, we need $\frac{2m}{1.4s} = \frac{5}{2}$ or $4m = 7s$.

Since 4 and 7 have no common divisor larger than 1, the smallest possible integers that satisfy this are $m = 7$ and $s = 4$. Thus, the volume (in litres) of chocolate beverage that can be made is $2 \times 7 + 1.4 \times 4 = 19.6$.

271. ANSWER: D

$5^a + 5^{a+1} = \sqrt{4500}$

$5^a(1 + 5^1) = 30\sqrt{5}$

$5^a = 5\sqrt{5}$

$5^a = 5^1 \times 5^{0.5}$

$5^a = 5^{\frac{3}{2}}$

$\therefore a = \frac{3}{2}$

272. ANSWER: E

Substitute $(a, 0)$ into the line,

$0 = a + 8$

$\therefore a = -8$

273. ANSWER: E

To find m

$f'(x) = 3e^{3x}$

$m = f'(0)$

$= 3e^{0x}$

$= 3$

The equation of L is

$y - y_1 = m(x - x_1)$

$y = 3x + 1$

274. ANSWER: D

Since $80 = 20 \times 4$, then to make $80 = 2 \times 4$ product B, it takes $20 \times 11 = 220$ product A. Since $220 = 44 \times 5$, then to make $220 = 44 \times 5$ product A, it takes $44 \times 18 = 792$ people.

$\therefore$ 792 people

275. ANSWER: D

First portion: $\frac{1}{3} \times 30 = 10\text{km}$

Second portion: $\frac{2}{3} \times 20 = \frac{40}{3}\text{km}$

$\therefore 10 + \frac{40}{3} = \frac{70}{3}\text{km}$

276. ANSWER: C

$f(y) = x$

$\sqrt{\frac{6+2y}{6-2y}} = x$

$\frac{6+2y}{6-2y} = x^2$

$3 + y = 3x^2 - x^2y$

$(x^2 + 1)y = 3x^2 - 3$

$y = \frac{3x^2-3}{x^2+1}$

$f^{-1}(x) = \frac{3x^2-3}{x^2+1}$

277. ANSWER: E

Possible pairs of outcomes: $6 \times 6 = 36$

$A = 1, B = 1,2,3,4,5,6$

$A = 2, B = 1,2,3,4,5,6$

$A = 3, B = 1,2,3,4,5,6$

$A = 4, B = 1,2,3,4,5$

$A = 5, B = 1,2,3,4$

$A = 3, B = 1,2,3$

$6 + 6 + 6 + 5 + 4 + 3 = 30$ pairs of outcomes

$\therefore \frac{30}{36} = \frac{5}{6}$

278. ANSWER: G

$2 = a(1^2) + b(1) + c$

$\therefore a + b + c = 2$

279. ANSWER: C

$2^{11} = 2048, 2^8 = 256$, then $2^{11} - 2^8 = 2048 - 256 = 1792$

$\therefore m^2 + n^2 = 11^2 + 8^2 = 185$

280. ANSWER: C

$\Delta = b^2 - 4ac = 0$

$16 - 8p = 0$

$\therefore p = 2$

281. ANSWER: E

Suppose x is ride downhill, y is ride on level road and z is ride uphill.

From town A to B:

$\frac{x}{24}+\frac{y}{16}+\frac{z}{12}=2$

From town B to A:

$\frac{x}{12}+\frac{y}{16}+\frac{z}{12}=2.25$

Add equations,

$\frac{x}{24}+\frac{y}{16}+\frac{z}{12}+\frac{x}{12}+\frac{y}{16}+\frac{z}{12}=4.25$

$\frac{x}{8}+\frac{y}{8}+\frac{z}{8}=4.25$

$\therefore x+y+z=34\text{ (km)}$

282. ANSWER: D

$f(x)=ag(x-h)+k$

$2(x-1)^2-8=a[6(x-h)^2]+k$

$2(x-1)^2-8=6a(x-h)^2+k$

$\therefore a=\frac{1}{3}, h=1, k=-8$

$\therefore 3a\times h\times k=-8$

283. ANSWER: B

First few terms of the sequence are

$$4, \quad 5, \quad \frac{5+1}{4} = \frac{3}{2}, \quad \frac{\frac{3}{2}+1}{5} = \frac{1}{2}, \quad \frac{\frac{1}{2}+1}{\frac{3}{2}} = 1, \quad \frac{1+1}{\frac{1}{2}} = 4, \quad \frac{4+1}{1} = 5,$$

$$\frac{5+1}{4} = \frac{3}{2}, \quad \ldots$$

Hence, a pattern is observed.

$1000 = 5 \times 200$

$\therefore$the 1000th term is equal to 5th term which is 1

284. ANSWER: D

$(2x+1)^4 = (2x)^4 + 4(2x)^3(1) + 6(2x)^2(1)^2 + 4(2x)(1)^3 + (1)^4$

$= 16x^4 + 32x^3 + 24x^2 + 8x + 1$

285. ANSWER: C

$$\binom{5}{2}(x^{5-2})(2^2) = 10(x^3)(4) = 40x^3$$

286. ANSWER: D

$$\log_3\left(1-\frac{1}{15}\right) + \log_3\left(1-\frac{1}{14}\right) + \log_3\left(1-\frac{1}{13}\right) + \cdots + \log_3\left(1-\frac{1}{8}\right) + \log_3\left(1-\frac{1}{7}\right) + \log_3\left(1-\frac{1}{6}\right)$$

$$= \log_3\left(\frac{14}{15}\right) + \log_3\left(\frac{13}{14}\right)$$
$$+ \log_3\left(\frac{12}{13}\right)$$
$$+ \log_3\left(\frac{11}{12}\right)$$
$$+ \log_3\left(\frac{10}{11}\right) + \log_3\left(\frac{9}{10}\right) + \log_3\left(\frac{8}{9}\right) + \log_3\left(\frac{7}{8}\right) + \log_3\left(\frac{6}{7}\right) + \log_3\left(\frac{5}{6}\right)$$

$$= \log_3\left(\frac{14}{15} \times \frac{13}{14} \times \frac{12}{13} \times \frac{11}{12} \times \frac{10}{11} \times \frac{9}{10} \times \frac{8}{9} \times \frac{7}{8} \times \frac{6}{7} \times \frac{5}{6}\right)$$
$$= \log_3\left(\frac{5}{15}\right)$$
$$= \log_3\left(\frac{1}{3}\right)$$
$$= -1$$

287. ANSWER: C

$$40nx^2 = \binom{n}{2}[1^{n-2}][(2x)^2]$$

$$40nx^2 = \left[\frac{n!}{2!\,(n-2)!}\right][4x^2]$$

$$40n = \left[\frac{n(n-1)}{2}\right][4]$$

$$20n = n(n-1)$$

$$0 = n(n-21)$$

$$n = 21$$

288. ANSWER: C

d =distance to travel

t =time passed from when she starts to travel

$$T - \frac{1}{2} = \frac{d}{20}$$

$$T + \frac{1}{2} = \frac{d}{12}$$

Add the two equations,

$$\frac{d}{20} + \frac{d}{12} = 2T$$

$$\frac{d}{15} = T$$

$\therefore$ if Clare travels at an average speed of 15 km/h, it will take her exactly T hours to travel $d\ km$

289. ANSWER: D

$$P(B|A) = \frac{P(A \cap B)}{P(A)}$$

$$= \frac{\frac{2}{5}}{\frac{2}{3}} = \frac{3}{5}$$

290. ANSWER: C

$$11^3 = 1331$$

291. ANSWER: C

$$2\pi r = 10\pi, r = 5$$

$$\therefore volume = \pi r^2 h = \pi \times 5^2 \times 4 = 100\pi$$

292. ANSWER: C

Asymptote of $y = 2^x + 5$ is $y = 5$.

$\therefore \log_3 x + 3 = 5$

$\log_3 x = 2$

$x = 3^2 = 9$

293. ANSWER: F

Slopes of AB and AC are equal.

$\frac{(-30)-(-8)}{9-5} = \frac{n-(-8)}{n-5}$

$\frac{-22}{4} = \frac{n+8}{n-5}$

$-22n + 110 = 4n + 32$

$n = 3$

294. ANSWER: C

$\sin 2x = -\frac{1}{\sqrt{2}}$

$2x = \frac{5\pi}{4}$ or $2x = \frac{7\pi}{4}$

$x = \frac{5\pi}{8}$ or $x = \frac{7\pi}{8}$

$\therefore \frac{5\pi}{8} + \frac{7\pi}{8} = \frac{12\pi}{8} = \frac{3\pi}{2}$

295. ANSWER: C

d m is the distance from point A to B, and w m/s is Lucy's walking speed. v m/s is the speed of the moving sidewalk.

$\frac{d}{w} = 45$ and $\frac{d}{v} = 90$

The amount of time that Lucy takes to walk with the moving sidewalk is $\frac{d}{v+w}$, since the resulting speed is the sum of walking speed and sidewalk speed.

$$\frac{d}{v+w} = \frac{1}{\frac{v+w}{d}} = \frac{1}{\frac{v}{d}+\frac{w}{d}} = \frac{1}{\frac{1}{90}+\frac{1}{45}} = \frac{1}{\frac{3}{90}} = 30$$

$\therefore$ 30 seconds

296. ANSWER: D

Length of the diagonal $= s + 1 = \sqrt{2}s$

$\therefore s = \sqrt{2} + 1$

Area of the square$= s^2 = 3 + 2\sqrt{2}$

297. ANSWER: E

Since $0 < a < 1$, $f(x) = a^x$ decreases. Hence the minimum is $\frac{5}{6}$ when $x = 1$ within the domain.

$a^1 = \frac{5}{6}$, $a = \frac{5}{6}$

$\therefore f(x) = \left(\frac{5}{6}\right)^x$

Within the domain, maximum is when $x = -2$,

$M = f(-2) = \left(\frac{5}{6}\right)^{-2} = \left(\frac{6}{5}\right)^2$

$$a \times M = \frac{5}{6} \times \left(\frac{6}{5}\right)^2 = \frac{6}{5}$$

298. ANSWER: C

$$4^{\sin^2 x} \times 2^{\cos^2 x} = 2\sqrt[4]{8}$$

$$2^{2\sin^2 x + \cos^2 x} = 2^{\frac{7}{4}}$$

$$2\sin^2 x + \cos^2 x = \frac{7}{4}$$

$$\sin^2 x + 1 = \frac{7}{4}$$

$$\sin^2 x = \frac{3}{4}$$

$$\sin x = \pm\frac{\sqrt{3}}{2}$$

$$x = \frac{1}{3}\pi$$

299. ANSWER: B

Number of ways to line up the card is $\frac{6!}{3! \times 2!} = 60$

Assume that two A cards are placed on both ends, then the number of ways to line up the 4 cards A, B, B, C is $\frac{4!}{2!} = 12$

Hence the probability is $\frac{12}{60} = \frac{1}{5}$

300. ANSWER: E

Range=23

$37 - 23 = p$

$p = 14$

IQR=10

$18 + 10 = q$
$q = 28$
$p - q = 14 - 28 = -14$

301. ANSWER: C

$\log_{3n} 675\sqrt{3} = \log_n 75$

$(3n)^{\log_{3n} 675\sqrt{3}} = (3n)^{\log_n 75}$

$675\sqrt{3} = 3^{\log_n 75} \times 75$

$9\sqrt{3} = 3^{\log_n 75}$

$3^{\frac{5}{2}} = 3 \log_n 75$

$\frac{5}{2} = \log_n 75$

$n^{\frac{5}{2}} = 75$

$n^5 = 75^2$

$n^5 = 5625$

302. ANSWER: C

$g(3) = a$

$f(a) = 3$

$a^3 + 5a + 3 = 3$

$a(a^2 + 5) = 0$

$a = 0$

$f'(x) = 3x^2 + 5$

$g'(3) = \frac{1}{f'(0)}$

$= \frac{1}{5}$

303. ANSWER: E

$x^2 - 4x - 5 = 0$

$(x - 5)(x + 1) = 0$

Roots are 5 and -1.

Roots of $x^2 + bx + c = 0$ are 25 and 1.

$-b = 25 + 1$

$b = -26$

$c = 25 \times 1 = 25$

$\therefore \frac{c}{b} = \frac{-25}{26}$

304. ANSWER: D

$\angle BOC = 360° - 50° - 90° - 90° = 130°$

Area of the sector is $\frac{130°}{360°}(36\pi) = 13\pi$

305. ANSWER: B

The function has maximum when $x = 2$. Hence the maximum is $y = \frac{1}{2-1} + 3 = 4$

306. ANSWER: A

$AC = \sqrt{AB^2 + BC^2} = \sqrt{676} = 26$

307. ANSWER: E

$(n+1)^2 - n^2 = 89$

$n = 44$

$n^2 = 1936$

308. ANSWER: B

$f'(x) = (x-2)(x-3)$

$f'(4) = (4-2)(4-3) = 2$

309. ANSWER: D

To get to $Q(-3,10)$ from $P(6,-2)$, we go 9 units left and 12 units up. $\frac{1}{3}$ of this would be 3 units to the left and 4 units up. $\therefore R(a,b) = (6-3,-2+4) = (3,2)$

$\therefore b - a = 2 - 3 = -1$

310. ANSWER: D

$$\frac{1}{a} - \frac{1}{b} = \frac{b-a}{ab} = \frac{\log_2 5}{\log_3 5} = \frac{\frac{\log 5}{\log 2}}{\frac{\log 5}{\log 3}} = \frac{\log 3}{\log 2} = \log_2 3$$

311. ANSWER: E

$a + (a+d) + (a+2d) = 15$

$\therefore a + d = 5$

$(a + 17d) + (a + 18d) + (a + 19d) = 12$

$\therefore a + 18d = 4$

Sum of 20 terms is $\frac{20}{2}(a + (a + 19d)) = 10(2a + 19d) = 10((a + d) + (a + 18d)) = 10(5 + 4) = 90$

312. ANSWER: B

$f'(x) = 6x - 2$

$f'(1) = 6 \times 1 - 2 = 4$

313. ANSWER: C

Height of the rectangle is k^2, as the vertex is the y-intercept.

$y = k^2 - x^2 = (k - x)(k + x)$, hence the x-intercepts are k and $-k$, making $AD = 2k$.

Perimeter of the rectangle is $48 = 2k^2 + 2(2k)$,

$k^2 + 2k - 24 = 0$

$(k + 6)(k - 4) = 0$

$\therefore k = 4, (k > 0)$

314. ANSWER: F

$\bar{x}_{Max,Jake,Anne} = \frac{x_1+x_2+x_3}{3}$

$\frac{x_1+x_2+x_3}{3} = 10.5$

$x_1 + x_2 + x_3 = 31.5$

$$\bar{x}_{Max,Jake,Anne,Kate} = \frac{x_1+x_2+x_3+x_4}{4}$$

$$\frac{x_1+x_2+x_3+x_4}{4} = 12$$

$31.5 + x_4 = 12 \times 4$

$x_4 = 48 - 31.5 = 16.5$

$\therefore 16.5\ seconds$

315. ANSWER: B

The amount of yellow paint is $0.8 \times 12 = 9.6$ pounds and the amount of red paint is $12 - 9.6 = 2.4$ pounds. For the new mixture to be 90% yellow, the amount of yellow paint is $9 \times 2.4 = 21.6$ pounds. $\therefore$ resulting orange paint has mass $2.4 + 21.6 = 24$ pounds

316. ANSWER: C

$y = 2\sqrt{x} + k$ passes (1,5) hence

$5 = 2\sqrt{1} + k$

$\therefore k = 3$

317. ANSWER: E

$\text{P(drives)} = \frac{5}{12}$

$\text{P(city A)P(drives|city A)+P(city B)P(drives|city B)} = \frac{5}{12}$

$p \times \frac{3}{4} + (1-p) \times \frac{1}{8} = \frac{5}{12}$

$\frac{5p}{8} + \frac{1}{8} = \frac{5}{12}$

$p = \frac{7}{15}$

318. ANSWER: F

Let n as number of sides of the regular polygon. The polygon has n vertices. A vertex will be a part of $n - 3$ diagonals (since a diagonal is a line segment joining a vertex to any non-neighbouring vertex).

There are $\frac{1}{2}n(n-3)$ diagonals in total.

$\therefore \frac{1}{2}n(n-3) = 90$

$n^2 - 3n - 180 = 0$

$(n - 15)(n + 12) = 0$

$n = 15\ (n > 0)$

319. ANSWER: E

Let the first term and the difference as a, since $a = d$

$a_n = a + (n-1)a = an$

$a_2 + a_4 = 2a + 4a = 24$

$a = 4$

$\therefore a_5 = 4 \times 5 = 20$

320. ANSWER: D

$V = 24\pi = \pi r^2 h$

$\therefore h = \frac{24}{r^2}$

321. ANSWER: F

$(x, 3)\phi(x, y) = (x^2 - 3y, xy + 3x) = (6,0)$

Hence $x^2 - 3y - 6 = 0$ and $xy + 3x = 0$

From the second equation, $x = 0$ or $y = -3$

If $x = 0$, from the first equation, $y = -2$

If $y = -3$, from the first equation, $x^2 = -3$ (not possible)

Hence, $(x, y) = (0, -2)$

322. ANSWER: A

$f(x) = \int 7x^2 - 32x\ dx$

$= \frac{7}{3}x^3 - 16x^2 + C$

$0 = \frac{7}{3}(2^3) - 16(2^2) + C$

$C = -\frac{56}{3} + 64 = \frac{136}{3}$

$\therefore f(x) = \frac{7}{3}x^3 - 16x^2 + \frac{136}{3}$

323. ANSWER: C

Ways of choosing 3 numbers is $\binom{6}{3} = 20$, considering that a, b, c are different numbers.

Once the numbers are chosen, there is only one way to assign them to a, b and c since $a < b < c$. Each time a die is rolled the possible number of combinations is $6^3 = 216$.

Hence the probability is $\frac{20}{216} = \frac{5}{54}$.

324. ANSWER: D

Area is $\int_0^2 6x(x-2)dx$

$= [-2x^3 + 6x^2]_0^2$

$= -16 + 24$

$= 8$

325. ANSWER: C

$f(y) = x$

$\sqrt{y-3} = x$

$y - 3 = x^2$

$y = x^2 + 3$

326. ANSWER: D

Mean is $\frac{(2)(10)+(24-2)(12)}{24} = \frac{284}{24} = \frac{71}{6}$

327. ANSWER: E

A circle with centre (a, b) and radius r has equation $(x-a)^2 + (y-b)^2 = r^2$

The circle has to be in the first quadrant and the centre (a, b) becomes (r, r).

$(x-r)^2+(y-r)^2=r^2$

Substituting (9,2),

$(9-r)^2+(2-r)^2=r^2$

$r^2-22r+85=0$

$(r-17)(r-5)=0$

$\therefore r=17$

328. ANSWER: B

$f(y)=x$

$\sqrt{y+7}=x$

$y+7=x^2$

$y=x^2-7$

329. ANSWER: A

$f'(x)=3px^2-q$

$2=3p(0)^2-q$

$\therefore q=-2$

It is given that $f(2)=12$

$12=p(2^3)++2(2)$

$8=8p$

$\therefore p=1$

$\therefore p\times q=-2$

330. ANSWER: F

Area of the cookie is $4^2\pi = 16\pi$ (cm^2)

Area of one chocolate chip: $0.4^2\pi = 0.16\pi$ (cm^2)

$k \times 0.16\pi = \frac{1}{4} \times 16\pi$

$k = 25$

331. ANSWER: C

$(g \circ f)(x) = g(f(x))$

$= g\left(\frac{x-2}{3}\right)$

$= 12\left(\frac{x-2}{3}\right) + 4$

$= 4(x-2) + 4$

$= 4x - 4$

$(g \circ f)(10) = a$

$4(10) - 4 = a$

$a = 36$

332. ANSWER: C

P(of different colours) $= 1 -$ P(of the same colour)

$= 1 - \left(\frac{8}{12} \times \frac{7}{11} + \frac{4}{12} \times \frac{3}{11}\right)$

$= \frac{16}{33}$

333. ANSWER: A

$f'(x) = 3kx^2$

$f'(2) = 3k(2^2) = 12k$

Slope of the normal to the curve is equal to $\frac{1}{6}$ hence

$-\frac{1}{12k} = \frac{1}{6}$

$k = -\frac{1}{2}$

334. ANSWER: E

For $\log_2 |x - 1|, x \neq 1$

$2\log_2 |x - 1| \leq 1 - \log_2 \frac{1}{2}$

$2\log_2 |x - 1| \leq 1 - (-1)$

$2\log_2 |x - 1| \leq 2$

$\log_2 |x - 1| \leq 1$

$\log_2 |x - 1| \leq \log_2 2$

$|x - 1| \leq 2$

$-1 \leq x \leq 3$

Hence, $x = -1,0,2,3$ $(x \neq 1)$

$\therefore 4$

335. ANSWER: B

$\int_1^x f(t)dt = x^2 - a\sqrt{x}$

Substitute $x = 1$

$$\int_1^1 f(t)dt = 0$$

$= 1 - a = 0,$

$\therefore a = 1$

$\therefore \int_1^x f(t)dt = x^2 - \sqrt{x}$

$\therefore \int f(t)dt = t^2 - \sqrt{t} + c$

And differentiate both sides of the given equation,

$f(x) = 2t - \frac{1}{2\sqrt{t}}$

Hence:

$f(1) = 2 - \frac{1}{2}$

$f(1) = \frac{3}{2}$

336. ANSWER: A

$P(A)$ =probability that the number of heads is equal to the number of tails

$P(B)$ =probability that coin is thrown 4 times

$P(A) = \frac{6}{36} \times \binom{4}{2} \times \left(\frac{1}{2}\right)^2 \left(\frac{1}{2}\right)^2 + \frac{30}{36} \times \binom{2}{1} \times \left(\frac{1}{2}\right)\left(\frac{1}{2}\right)$

$= \frac{1}{6} \times \frac{3}{8} + \frac{5}{6} \times \frac{1}{2}$

$= \frac{3+20}{48}$

$= \frac{23}{48}$

The probability that A and B happens together is

$P(A \cap B) = \frac{6}{36} \times \binom{4}{2} \times \left(\frac{1}{2}\right)^2 \left(\frac{1}{2}\right)^2$

$= \frac{1}{16}$

$P(B|A) = \frac{P(A \cap B)}{P(A)}$

$$= \frac{\frac{1}{16}}{\frac{23}{48}}$$

$$= \frac{3}{23}$$

337. ANSWER: B

$2Q(4) = 3Q(2)$

$2Q_0\left(1 - 2^{-\frac{4}{a}}\right) = 3Q_0(1 - 2^{-\frac{2}{a}})$

Let $t = 2^{-\frac{2}{a}}$, then since $a > 0,\ 0 < t < 1$.

$2(1 - t^2) = 3(1 - t)$

$2(1 - t)(1 + t) = 3(1 - t)$

$2(1 + t) = 3$

$t = \frac{1}{2}$

Hence $2^{-\frac{2}{a}} = 2^{-1}$

$-\frac{2}{a} = -1$

$a = 2$

338. ANSWER: E

$f(0) = 2^0 + 1 = 2$

$g(0) = -2^{-1} + 7 = \frac{13}{2}$

$\therefore A(0,2)$ and $B(0, \frac{13}{2})$

Hence $AB = \frac{13}{2} - 2 = \frac{9}{2}$

Equating $y = 2^x + 1$ and $y = -2^{x-1} + 7$,

$2^x + 1 = -2^{x-1} + 7$

$\frac{3}{2} \times 2^x = 6$

$2^x = 4$

$x = 2$

Since $f(2) = 2^2 + 1 = 5$, point C is (2,5)

Area of triangle $ACB = \frac{1}{2} \times 2 \times \frac{9}{2} = \frac{9}{2}$

339. ANSWER: D

$2 \sin^2 x + 3 \cos x = 3$

$2(1 - \cos^2 x) + 3 \cos x = 3$

$(\cos x - 1)(2\cos x - 1) = 0$

$\cos x = 1 \, or \frac{1}{2}$

$x = 0, \frac{\pi}{3}, \frac{5\pi}{3}$

Hence the sum of the roots is 2π.

340. ANSWER: A

Number of ways to pick 2 balls out of 6 balls is $\binom{6}{2} = 15$

Number of ways to pick two white balls is $\binom{2}{2} = 1$

$\therefore \frac{p}{q} = \frac{1}{15}$

$\therefore p + q = 1 + 15$

$= 16$

341. ANSWER: G

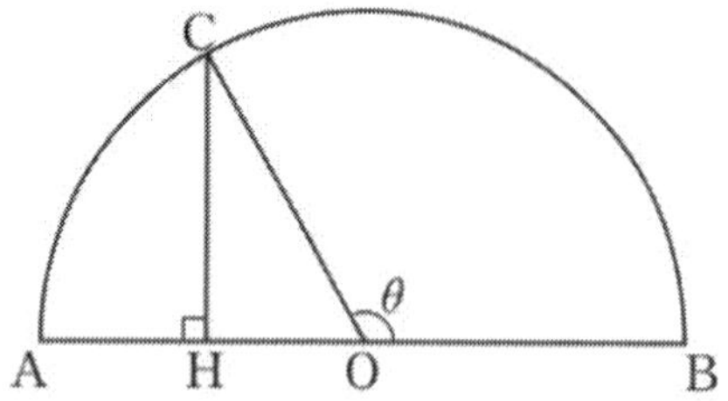

$OB = \frac{12}{2} = 6$

Let $\angle COB = \theta$, and considering $BC = 4\pi$

$l = r\theta$

We know that $l = 4\pi$

$l = 6 \times \theta = 4\pi, \theta = \frac{2\pi}{3}$

$\angle COH = \pi - \theta = \frac{\pi}{3}$

Since triangle CHO is a right-angle triangle and $OC = 6$,

$CH = OC \times \sin\theta$

$= OC \times \sin\frac{\pi}{3}$

$= 6 \times \frac{\sqrt{3}}{2} = 3\sqrt{3}$

Hence, $CH^2 = \left(3\sqrt{3}\right)^2$

$= 27$

342. ANSWER:D

$$\frac{\sqrt{32} + \sqrt{18}}{3 + \sqrt{2}} = a\sqrt{2} + b$$

$$= \frac{\sqrt{32} + \sqrt{18}}{3 + \sqrt{2}} \times \frac{3 - \sqrt{2}}{3 - \sqrt{2}}$$

$$= \frac{3\sqrt{32} + 3\sqrt{18} - \sqrt{64} - \sqrt{36}}{9 - 2}$$

$$= \frac{3(\sqrt{16}\sqrt{2}) + 3(\sqrt{9}\sqrt{2}) - 8 - 6}{7}$$
$$= \frac{3(\sqrt{16}\sqrt{2}) + 3(\sqrt{9}\sqrt{2}) - 8 - 6}{7}$$
$$= \frac{3(4\sqrt{2}) + 3(3\sqrt{2}) - 8 - 6}{7}$$
$$= \frac{12\sqrt{2} + 9\sqrt{2} - 14}{7}$$
$$= \frac{21\sqrt{2} - 14}{7}$$
$$= 3\sqrt{2} - 2 = a\sqrt{2} + b$$
$$\therefore a = 3, b = -2$$
$$\therefore a + b = 1$$

343. ANSWER: D

$$y = 9 - 4x - \frac{8}{x}$$
$$If\ P(2, y)$$
$$y = 9 - 4(2) - \frac{8}{2}$$
$$y = 9 - 8 - 4$$
$$y = -3$$
$$\therefore P(2, -3)$$

$$y = 9 - 4x - 8x^{-1}$$

$$\frac{dy}{dx} = -4 + 8x^{-2}$$

$$\left.\frac{dy}{dx}\right|_{x=2} = -4 + 8(2)^{-2}$$
$$\left.\frac{dy}{dx}\right|_{x=2} = -4 + \frac{8}{4}$$
$$\left.\frac{dy}{dx}\right|_{x=2} = -2$$

$$y - y_1 = m(x - x_1)$$
$$y + 3 = -2(x - 2)$$
$$y + 3 = -2x + 4$$
$$y = 1 - 2x$$

Hence the y intercept is (0,1)

344. ANSWER: C

$3x^2 + y^2 = 21 \quad (1)$
$5x + y = 7 \quad (2)$
$\text{Re} - \text{arrange (2) for } y: y = 7 - 5x$
Substitute value of y in (1)
$3x^2 + (7 - 5x)^2 = 21$
$3x^2 + (49 + 25x^2 - 70x) = 21$
$28x^2 - 70x + 49 = 21$
$28x^2 - 70x + 49 - 21 = 0$
$28x^2 - 70x + 28 = 0$
$2x^2 - 5x + 2 = 0$
$(2x - 1)(x - 2) = 0$
$x = \frac{1}{2}, x = 2$
Sub in (2): $y = 7 - 5x$
When $x = 2$
$y = 7 - 5(2)$
$y = 7 - 10$
$y = -3$
$\therefore x + y = 2 - 3 = -1$
When $x = \frac{1}{2}$
$y = 7 - 5\left(\frac{1}{2}\right)$
$y = 7 - \frac{5}{2}$
$y = \frac{9}{2}$
$\therefore x + y = \frac{1}{2} + \frac{9}{2} = \frac{10}{2}$

345. ANSWER: C

$y = (x - k)^2$
$y = x^2 + k^2 - 2xk$

$$\frac{dy}{dx} = 2x - 2k = 2x - 6$$
$2k = 6$
$k = 3$

346. ANSWER: B

First find the equation of the line passing through $(-1,3)$ and $(3,4)$

$$\frac{y - y_1}{y_2 - y_1} = \frac{x - x_1}{x_2 - x_1}$$
$$\frac{y - 3}{1} = \frac{x + 1}{4}$$
$4(y - 3) = x + 1$
$4y - 12 = x + 1$
$0 = x - 4y + 13$

You will notice that this line has the same gradient as the line with equation: $x - 4y - 21 = 0$. Hence, we know that we are trying to find the shortest distance between two parallel lines.

We must then find the perpendicular bisector passing through one of the known points:

Gradient $= \frac{4-3}{3-(-1)} = \frac{1}{4}$

Hence gradient of the perpendicular bisector is: -4

$y - y_1 = m(x - x_1)$
$y - 3 = -4(x + 1)$
$y - 3 = -4x - 4$
$y = -4x - 1$

We must know find its intersection with $x - 4y - 21 = 0$.

$x - 4y - 21 = 0$ & $y = -4x - 1$
Substitute the value of y

$x - 4(-4x - 1) - 21 = 0$

$x + 16x + 4 - 21 = 0$
$17x - 17 = 0$
$17x = 17$
$x = 1$
$y = -4(1) - 1$
$y = -4 - 1$
$y = -5$

$\therefore$ point of intersection: $(1, -5)$

We must find the length of the line segment joining the points (-1,3) and (1,-5)

$$d = \sqrt{2^2 + 8^2}$$
$$d = \sqrt{4 + 64}$$
$$d = \sqrt{68}$$
$$d = 2\sqrt{17}$$

347. ANSWER: G

$$\lim_{x\to 2}\left[\frac{1}{x(x-2)^2} - \frac{1}{x^2 - 3x + 2}\right].$$
$$= \lim_{x\to 2}\left[\frac{1}{x(x-2)^2} - \frac{1}{(x-2)(x-1)}\right]$$
$$= \lim_{x\to 2}\left[\frac{(x-1) - x(x-2)}{x(x-1)(x-2)^2}\right]$$
$$= \lim_{x\to 2}\left[\frac{(x-1) - x^2 + 2x}{x(x-1)(x-2)^2}\right]$$
$$= \lim_{x\to 2}\left[\frac{-x^2 + 3x - 1}{x(x-1)(x-2)^2}\right]$$
$$= \frac{1}{0}$$
$$= \infty$$

348. ANSWER: B

$y = p$ *and* $y = x^2 - x - 12$ intersect twice, with the line segment joining the points of intersection having a length of 9.

Hence when they intersect:

$p = x^2 - x - 12$

$x^2 - x - 12 - p = 0$ in the form $ax^2 + bx + c = 0$

Since we know that both intersections lie on y=p (where p is a constant) we know that the y coordinate will be the same at both points of intersection and only the x coordinate will vary by 9.

Therefore, we can consider this an application of roots of polynomials:
If $x^2 - x - 12 - p = 0$ has roots of α, β, we know that as the roots vary by 9, we can let

$\beta = \alpha + 9$.

Hence the roots can be: $\alpha, \alpha + 9$

We also know that:

$\sum \alpha = \alpha + \beta = -\frac{b}{a} = -\frac{-1}{1} = 1$
$\therefore \alpha + \alpha + 9 = 1$
$2\alpha + 9 = 1$
$2\alpha = -8$
$\therefore \alpha = -4$
$\beta = \alpha + 9$
$\therefore \beta = -4 + 9$
$\therefore \beta = 5$
You can now continue with finding the product of roots ($\alpha\beta$) in terms of p or alternatively you may notice:

$p = x^2 - x - 12$ has roots of -4 and 5
$p = (5)^2 - (5) - 12$
$p = 25 - 5 - 12$
$p = 8$
To verify:
$p = (-4)^2 - (-4) - 12$
$p = 16 + 4 - 12$
$p = 20 - 12$
$p = 8$
$\therefore p = 8$

349. ANSWER: A

$$\frac{\sqrt{a}}{\sqrt{a} + 2b} = \frac{2\sqrt{a} - b}{3a + b}$$

We know that the fraction is in its simplest form hence we can equate the numerators and the denominators:
$\sqrt{a} = 2\sqrt{a} - b \quad (1)$
$\sqrt{a} + 2b = 3a + b \quad (2)$
Rearrange (1) $\Rightarrow b = \sqrt{a}$

Substitute the value of b in (2)

$\sqrt{a} + 2(\sqrt{a}) = 3a + (\sqrt{a})$

$2\sqrt{a} = 3a$

$3a - 2\sqrt{a} = 0$

$\sqrt{a}(3\sqrt{a} - 2) = 0$

$a = 0 \ or \ \sqrt{a} = \frac{2}{3} \Rightarrow a = \frac{4}{9}$

$\therefore a = \frac{4}{9} \ (as \ a > 0)$

$b = \sqrt{a}$

$\therefore b = \sqrt{\frac{4}{9}}$

$\therefore b = \frac{2}{3}$

$\therefore ab = \left(\frac{4}{9}\right)\left(\frac{2}{3}\right) = \frac{8}{27}$

350. ANSWER: A

$y = \frac{x^4 - 3}{2x^2}$

$y = \frac{x^2}{2} - \frac{3}{2}x^{-2}$

$\frac{dy}{dx} = x + 3x^{-3}$

$\frac{d^2y}{dx^2} = 1 - 9x^{-4}$

$\frac{d^2y}{dx^2} = 1 - \frac{9}{x^4}$

$\frac{d^2y}{dx^2} = \frac{x^4 - 9}{x^4}$

351. ANSWER: D

First, sketch the graph to see which regions are required, and which are the possible negative regions.

Using the factorised form given, the roots of the equation are $x = -3, 0$ or 1.

It can be observed that it is a positive cubic, so the graph will look like this.

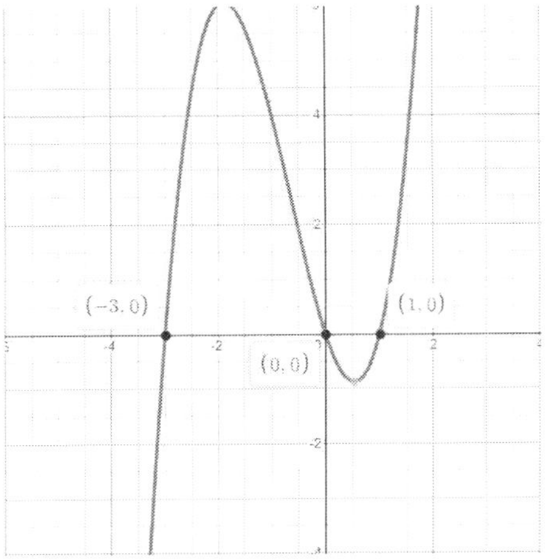

The two regions that need to be calculated are between -3 and 0, and 0 and 1.

This can be done using integration, so first expand the brackets to get $y = x^3 + 2x^2 + 3x$, and the two areas should be calculated separately.

The first area, $A = \int_{-3}^{0}(x^3 + 2x^2 + 3x)\,dx$

$A = \left[\frac{x^4}{4} + \frac{2x^3}{3} - \frac{3x^2}{2}\right]_{-3}^{0}$, expanding this definite integral gives

$A = 0 - \left(\frac{81}{4} - \frac{2}{3} \times 27 - \frac{3}{2} \times 9\right) = \frac{45}{4}$

Using the same method for the second area, we get

$A = \int_{0}^{1}(x^3 + 2x^2 + 3x)\,dx = \left[\frac{x^4}{4} + \frac{2x^3}{3} - \frac{3x^2}{2}\right]_{0}^{1} = \left(\frac{1}{4} + \frac{2}{3} - \frac{3}{2}\right) - 0 = -\frac{7}{12}$

However, since the area is negative due to the region being below the x axis, we must treat it as positive. Summing the two regions gives $\frac{71}{6}$.

352. ANSWER: B

To rewrite $\frac{2x^2+11x+12}{(x+3)(x+4)}$ in the required form, this requires simplifying the algebraic fraction, meaning the numerator needs to be rewritten. Using the ac method to factorise the numerator gives

$\frac{(2x+3)(x+4)}{(x+3)(x+4)}$. The fraction can now be cancelled down by removing the $(x+4)$ factor from the numerator and denominator.

The fraction can be written as $\frac{2x+3}{x+3}$, giving $a = 2, b = 3, c = 1, d = 3$, so $ab - cd = 3$

353. ANSWER: D

Given that the two tiles form regular polygons, this means that each interior angle is the same, as well as the side length of each. Therefore, the interior angle of Tile B is 60° because it is an equilateral triangle.

We know that the angle around a point is always 360°, and it can be observed that at one point, there are two interior angles of Tile A and one interior angle of Tile B.

Since it is a regular polygon, the interior angle of Tile A can be written as $\frac{180(n-2)}{n}$, where n is the side length.

An equation can be formed summing the three angles to 360.

$$\frac{180(n-2)}{n} + \frac{180(n-2)}{n} + 60 = 360$$

$\frac{180(n-2)}{n} + \frac{180(n-2)}{n} = 300$. Multiplying through by n and expanding the LHS gives

$360n - 720 = 300n$. Solving this linear equation gives $n = 12$

354. ANSWER: D

The key to this question is to manipulate the numbers into an algebraic term. Since the three numbers involved are 2014, 2015 and 2016, it would be easiest to place all numbers in terms of 2015.

Let $x = 2015$, and rewrite the expression as

$x^2 - (x + 1)(x - 1)$, notice the product is a difference of two squares. Expanding this gives

$x^2 - (x^2 - 1) = 1$

355. ANSWER: A

The easiest way to approach this question is to begin by forming an equation to find the value of n. Do this by using the definition of the mean, which is the sum of all values in a data set divided by the number of values added. The following equation can be set up

$n = \frac{17+23+2n}{3}$. By cross multiplying, and solving the consequential linear equation, you should get $n = 40$, meaning the sum of the digits is $0 + 4 = 4$.

356. ANSWER: C

Although the question may be worded differently, it is essentially asking for what value of x will the two functions be equal.

The easiest and quickest method for solving this would be to substitute each of the answers into both functions and finding which answer works for both functions. The answer will be 1.

Alternatively, it can be solved algebraically by equating the two functions as follows

$\frac{4x-20}{2} = (x + 3)(x - 3)$, simplifying the LHS and expanding the RHS gives

$2x - 10 = x^2 - 9$, this quadratic can be rewritten in the form

$x^2 - 2x + 1 = 0$, factorising the LHS gives

$(x - 1)^2 = 0$, giving $x = 1$

357. ANSWER: D

First, let the point at which lines AE and CD intersect be point F.

Since ABCD is a square, it follows that $\angle BCF = 90°$. Therefore, since angles on a line have sum $180°$, $\angle FCE = 90°$.

This means that in the triangles FCE and ABE, $\angle ABE = \angle FCE = 90°$. We can further see that $\angle BEA = \angle CEF$. These two facts would mean that the smaller triangle and larger triangle are mathematically similar. This allows us to set up the following ratio:

$\frac{FC}{AB} = \frac{CE}{BE}$.

since ABCD is a square, it means $AB = BC = 3$. It is given that $BE = 4$. Therefore $CE = BE - BC = 4 - 3 = 1$.

Substituting these values back into the previous ratio question gives

$\frac{FC}{3} = \frac{1}{4}$, which can be solved to give $FC = \frac{3}{4}$

Using the formula for the area of a trapezium, $\frac{1}{2}(a + b)h$, we get

$\frac{1}{2}\left(3\left(3 + \frac{3}{4}\right)\right)$ giving $\frac{45}{8}$

358. ANSWER: F

Firstly, to write $f(x) = 3x^2 + 6x + 1$ in the required form, we must complete the square, which is first done by factorising out he a from the first two terms, which gives

$3(x^2 + 2x) + 1$, then actually completing the square for the bracketed expression gives

$3((x + 1)^2 - 1) + 1$, which when simplified gives

$3(x + 1)^2 - 2$, where $p = 3, q = 1$ and $r = -2$,

This gives the value of $pq - r$ as 5

359. ANSWER: D

The key to this question is to understand what is happening and what is being asked. James bought a book on Friday for £5.50 which was 10% higher than normal.

This means $110\% = £5.50$, and this can be solved giving the normal price of the book (100%) to be £5.

Books on Saturday are reduced by 10% of their normal prices. Since 10% of £5, the price of the book on Saturday would be $5 \times 0.9 = 4.50$

360. ANSWER: E

This question involves conditional probability, and it is always helpful to draw a tree diagram.

On the first pick, since there are 4 rotten bananas, the probability he picks a rotten banana is $\frac{4}{x}$.

Given the second pick is also a rotten banana, we must remember that since there is no replacement, the total number of rotten bananas now is 3, so the probability become $\frac{3}{x-1}$.

The probability of picking two rotten bananas would be the product of these two branches in the tree diagram, which is $\frac{12}{x(x-1)}$, which can be equated to $\frac{1}{11}$ given in the question.

Equating these two gives $\frac{12}{x(x-1)} = \frac{1}{11}$, cross multiplying the fractions and simplifying gives the quadratic $x^2 - x - 132 = 0$, which can be factorised into

$(x + 11)(x - 12) = 0$, giving $x = -11 \; or \; 12$

Since x must be positive, it follows that there are 12 bananas in the box.

361. ANSWER: A

To solve this question, we must find the coordinates of the stationary point. A stationary point is a point on the curve when the gradient is 0, meaning we must differentiate.

$y = x^4 - 32x$

$\frac{dy}{dx} = 4x^3 - 32$, which we can equate to 0

$4x^3 - 32 = 0$, solving this gets $x = 2$

However, to then find the y coordinate, we must substitute this back into the original equation of the curve,

$y = 2^4 - 32 \times 4 = -48$, giving the sum of the coordinates to be

$2 - 48 = -46$.

362. ANSWER: E

This question again requires algebraic manipulation of a simple looking fraction. Since all the answers are given in the form of one fraction, it would be helpful to change $2017 - \frac{1}{2017}$

into one fraction.

$2017 - \frac{1}{2017} = \frac{2017^2 - 1}{2017}$, which was done using a common denominator.

It is important to be able to notice a difference of two squares which the numerator is,

so this can be rewritten as $\frac{(2017+1)(2017-1)}{2017} = \frac{2018 \times 2016}{2017} = E$

363. ANSWER: A

The question is asking to find the sum of an arithmetic series. Given the first few terms, it is easy to observe that the term-to-term rule is to subtract 5, and the starting term is 32.

Substituting these two values into the sum of an arithmetic series formula gives

$S_{50} = \frac{50}{2}\big(2(32) + (50 - 1)(-5)\big) = -4525$

364. ANSWER: C

To solve this question, we need to find the percentage change of the expression, meaning we need to know the value of the expression before and after.

The easiest way to do this would be to take arbitrary values of a, b, c and d before, and the easiest value would be to take them as 1. When we substitute 1 into the expression, we get $\frac{3}{2}$ as the value

Then, after the percentage increase, due to the multiplier, we can substitute each letter, which was taken to be 1, by 1.2, and simplify the new expression. This would initially give

$\frac{1.2^3}{2\times1.2} + \frac{3\times1.2^3}{3.6}$, this can be simplified because each fraction has common factors in both the numerator and the denominator.

$$\frac{1.2^3}{2 \times 1.2} + \frac{3 \times 1.2^3}{3.6} = \frac{1.44}{2} + 1.44 = 2.16$$

We now need to find the percentage change, which is $\frac{2.16-1.5}{1.5} \times 100 = 44\%$

365. ANSWER: C

The easiest way to solve these types of questions is to draw a sample space diagram, which shows all the possible outcomes. Then, count the number of desired outcomes, which in this case is getting a sum of 5, 6 or 7.

FIRST DIE

SECOND DIE	1	2	3	4	5	6
1	2	3	4	5	6	7
2	3	4	5	6	7	8
3	4	5	6	7	8	9
4	5	6	7	8	9	10
5	6	7	8	9	10	11
6	7	8	9	10	11	12

The total number of outcomes are 36, and the number of outcomes for getting a 5, 6 or 7 is 15.

Therefore, the probability is $\frac{15}{36} = \frac{5}{12}$

366. ANSWER: B

The area of a triangle is given by $\frac{1}{2}bh$, and since we know that the base is x, we now need to find the height.

Since the triangle is equilateral, it means that all the side lengths are equal to x, and we can draw another triangle to find the height. Halving the equilateral triangle leaves a right-angled triangle with base $\frac{x}{2}$ and hypotenuse x.

Using Pythagoras, we can get, $h^2 = x^2 - \frac{x^2}{4}, h^2 = \frac{3x^2}{4}, h = \frac{x\sqrt{3}}{2}$

Then, substituting this back into the equation for the area gives

$A = \frac{1}{2} \times \frac{x\sqrt{3}}{2} \times x = \frac{x^2\sqrt{3}}{4}$

367. ANSWER: D

The total number of outcomes for flipping a coin 4 times is 2^4, which is 16.

The total number of ways of getting 2 heads and 2 tails is 6,

HHTT, TTHH, HTHT, THTH, HTTH, THHT.

Therefore, the probability is $\frac{6}{16} = \frac{3}{8}$

368. ANSWER: D

If X is inversely proportional to the square root of Y, we can set up the following equation

$X = \frac{K}{\sqrt{Y}}$, where K is the constant of proportionality.

Given the values in the question, we can work out K.

$4 = \frac{K}{\sqrt{25}}$, solving this gives $K = 20$

Substituting the values for Y and K, we get

$X = \frac{20}{4}$, $X = 5$

369. ANSWER: D

To find the total surface area factor change, we need to calculate the surface area before and after.

A cube's surface is $6 \times$ the area of each face, which is $81cm^2$. This gives the surface area for the 9cm cube to be 486 cm^2.

The 9cm cube has a volume of $729cm^3$, and a 3cm cube would have a volume of $27cm^3$. This means that 27 smaller cubes can be made.

The surface area of the smaller cube is going to be $6 \times 3^2 = 54$. Since there are 27 cubes, this is a total surface area of $1458cm^2$.

Therefore, the scale factor is $\frac{1458}{486} = 3$

370. ANSWER: D

It is important to appreciate that for this question, x is between 0 and 1. When we think about what this means in relation to all the options, we find that e^x is the only answer that will be greater than 1.

The logarithm will yield a negative answer, whereas the two trigonometric functions will be have to be less than 1.

x^2 will only get smaller, since x is less than 1.

371. ANSWER: C

Candidates are very quick to think that since the speedometer is a hemisphere the angle 70mph will make may be 35° or 140°.

However, the case is that the upper bound of the speedometer is 200mph, so the proportion needs to be found. The proportion the speed takes is $\frac{7}{20}$.

To then find the angle it takes up, multiply this proportion by 180, giving 63°.

372. ANSWER: E

The function given is a binomial expansion, and it is required to find the coefficient of the x^2 term. Expand using binomial expansion rules

$f(x) = (2 - x)^5 = 2^5 + 5(2^4)(-x) + 5C2(2^3)(-x)^2 + \cdots$

The x^2 term is the third and the coefficient is $5C2 \times 8 = 80$

373. ANSWER: F

To solve this, equate the formulas for the volume and surface area of a sphere. Then, solve for the radius as follows.

$\frac{4}{3}\pi r^3 = 4\pi r^2$, since $r \neq 0$, we can divide through by r^2 and π

$\frac{4}{3}r = 4, r = 3$

374. ANSWER: E

The questions in which large and unnecessary calculations are needed always have easier ways to solve them. In this case, algebraic manipulation is needed, and you should quickly realise that $106^2 - 15^2$ is the difference of two squares. This can be rewritten as

$(106 + 15)(106 - 15) = 121 \times 91 = 11^2 \times 7 \times 13$

The greatest prime factor is therefore 13.

375. ANSWER: D

Certain questions will bombard you with information, and it is essential to go through each line carefully and highlight the important information, saving crucial time.

Since, Alexis is the youngest sibling, it is easier to assess the other siblings' ages relative to him. Let Alexis be a years old.

This would make Alexie be $3a$ years old, and Alex would be double of this, 6a.

Since the combined ages is 50, an equation can now be set up as follows

$a + 3a + 6a = 50$, solving this linear equation gives $a = 5$.

The difference in Alex and Alexis's age is $5a$, which is 25.

376. ANSWER: E

$\log(3x + 1) = 5$, since there is no specified base for the logarithm, we take it as base 10.

Using the definition for logarithms, we can derive an equation

$10^5 = 3x + 1$, solving this linearly gives $x = 33{,}333$

377. ANSWER: C

This question does involve calculating the exact values of base 10 logarithms, but instead use the information given logically. Since the numbers in question are 9 and 27, it would make sense to put them as powers of 3.

$\log 27 = 1.431$ can be rewritten in the form $\log 3^3 = 1.431$

Using the power law of logarithms, $3 \log 3 = 1.431$, from this we get

$\log 3 = 0.477$

Rewriting $\log 9$ gives $2 \log 3$, meaning the value of $\log 9 = 0.477 \times 2 = 0.954$

378. ANSWER: C

The initial price of the television is P. As always, let this original price be 100%. After increasing by 125%, this new price will be 225%.

It then decreases by 40%. To calculate 40% of the increased price, it is easier to first find 10%, which is $\frac{225}{10}$, which is 22.5%. You can obtain 40% by then multiplying this by 4 giving a 90% reduction. Therefore, the newest price, Q, $= 225 - 90 = 135$. Using the relationship given in the question to find K gives

$100K = 135$, dividing both sides by 100 gives $K = \frac{27}{20}$

379. ANSWER: B

A geometric series is a series that has the same ratio between each term that acts as a multiplier. This means we can set up the following equation

$\frac{2p+2}{p-2} = \frac{5p+14}{2p+2}$, then we can cross multiply and then solve for p. This will initially give

$(2p + 2)^2 = (5p + 14)(p - 2)$, then expanding the brackets gives
$4p^2 + 8p + 4 = 5p^2 + 4p - 28$, then simplifying gives the quadratic
$p^2 - 4p - 32 = 0$, which is then factorizable into
$(p - 8)(p + 4) = 0$, giving $p = 8$. It cannot be -4, because all the terms in the series are positive as stated in the question.

We can substitute this in the LHS of the equation above to find the common ratio, r, which is $\frac{18}{6} = 3$. The first term is $p - 2$, which is 6.

The 5th term will be $6 \times 3^4 = 486$.

380. ANSWER : A

Since $BD = CD$, triangle BCD must be isosceles, meaning that angle $DBC = DCB$.

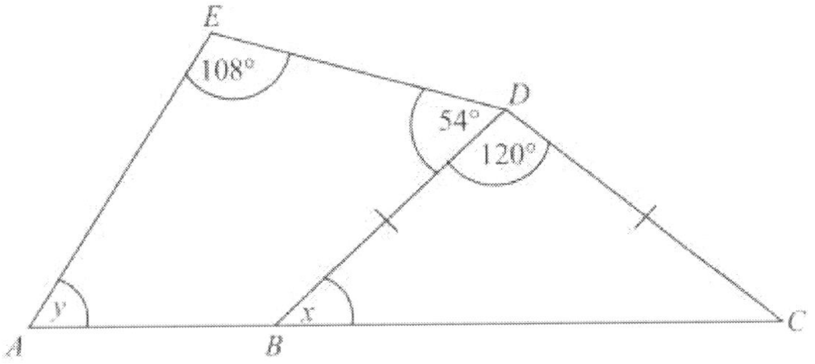

This can be calculated knowing that the sum of the angles in a triangle sum to 180. $DBC = x = \frac{180-120}{2} = 30$, this then means that angle $ABC = 150$, because angles on a straight-line sum to 180.

Therefore, $y = 360 - (150 + 54 + 108) = 48$, as the sum of the interior angles in a quadrilateral is 360°

$x + y = 78$

381. ANSWER: B

$\frac{x}{x+c} = \frac{p}{q}$, first cross multiply the fractions to get

$xq = p(x + c)$, then expand the RHS

$xq = px + pc$, then group together all the x terms on one side and then factorise

$x(q - p) = pc$, then divide both sides by $(q - p)$ giving

$x = \frac{pc}{q-p}$

382. ANSWER: E

This question is easiest to solve by setting up two different means for the two mini sets and then equating the two expressions together.

The mean of the first three numbers can be given by $\frac{15+5+}{3} = \frac{x+20}{3}$

The mean for the final 4 numbers can be given by $\frac{7+9+17+x}{4} = \frac{x+33}{4}$

Equating these two fractions gives $\frac{x+20}{3} = \frac{x+33}{4}$. Cross multiplying the two fractions gives

$4x + 80 = 3x + 99$, which can be solved linearly to give $x = 19$

383. ANSWER: A

The easiest way to find the right answer in multiple choice simultaneous equations is to substitute each answer into the equations and finding which option is correct. In this case, A is the right answer.

To solve it algebraically, it is easier to construct an equation in x as it is x that has the exponent in the first equation.
Rearranging equation 2 gives $y = 2 - x$, substitute this into the first equation, giving

$x^2 + 2(2 - x) = 12$, expanding and rearranging this gives the quadratic
$x^2 - 2x - 8 = 0$, factorise this to give $(x - 4)(x + 2) = 0$.

This means that $x = 2\ or\ 4$, remember to substitute these values back into one of the equations to find the values corresponded to y.

However, looking at the options, A is the only one who's x values are correct. Always be tactical during multiple choice and find ways to save time.

384. ANSWER: E

This question requires us to find the gradient at a fixed point on a curve. Therefore, it is helpful to first differentiate the function. This is easier by first rewriting the function as

$f(x) = 4x^2 + \frac{5-x}{x} = 4x^2 + 5x^{-1} - 1$, differentiating this gives

$f'(x) = 8x - 5x^{-2}$, then substitute $x = 1$ to find the gradient at P.

$f'(1) = 8 - 5 = 3$

385. ANSWER: C

The key to this question is to simplify the expression using index and surd laws.

$x^3\sqrt{2} \div \sqrt{\frac{32}{x^2}} = x^3\sqrt{2} \div \frac{4\sqrt{2}}{x}$

Dividing by a fraction is the same as multiplying its reciprocal, giving

$x^3\sqrt{2} \times \frac{x}{4\sqrt{2}}$, where the $\sqrt{2}$ can now easily cancel down, giving $\frac{x^4}{4}$.

386. ANSWER: D

$y = x^2$. The best way to approach this question, is to apply all the transformations to the turning point. This is because all the answers are in a completed square form, meaning knowing the final turning point will give you the correct answer.

First, we know that the turning point of $y = x^2$ is at the origin, $(0, 0)$. After the first translation, the turning point will move to $(7, 2)$.

The second step is where more careful attention needs to be paid. Reflecting in the line $y = 1$ means the x coordinate will stay the same but the y coordinate will be reflected.

Since, the y coordinate is currently 2, it is 3 vertical units away from the mirror line. Therefore, the reflected point will also be 3 units away but on the other side. $-1 - 3 = -4$

The final turning point has coordinates $(7, -4)$.

It is also important to realise that the reflected quadratic will be turned upside down, so it now has a negative coefficient of x^2. Using this, we know the new curve will have equation

$y = -(x-7)^2 - 4$

387. Answer: E

Firstly, it is easiest to rewrite $f(x)$ as $f(x) = 2x^{\frac{3}{2}} - 2x^{-\frac{1}{2}}$

Then, differentiate the function to get $f'(x) = 2 \times \frac{3}{2} \times x^{\frac{1}{2}} - 2 \times (-\frac{1}{2}) \times x^{-\frac{3}{2}}$, simplify this into

$f'(x) = 3x^{\frac{1}{2}} + \frac{1}{x^{\frac{3}{2}}}$, then substitute $x = 4$

$f'(4) = 3 \times 2 + \frac{1}{8}$

$= 6 + \frac{1}{8}$

$= \frac{49}{8}$

388. ANSWER: B

Using the facts about the roots of quadratics, we should know that the sum of the roots, α and β is $-m$.
Secondly, the product of the two roots is 1.

The equation given can be rewritten $\alpha\beta = \frac{1}{\alpha} + \frac{1}{\beta}$ as $\alpha\beta = \frac{\alpha+\beta}{\alpha\beta}$. Substituting what we know about the sum and product, we get

$1 = -\frac{m}{1}$, giving $m = -1$

389. ANSWER: B

This question should be solved using angle rules.

$\angle CBH = \angle GFH = 53°$, because corresponding angles are equal.

$\angle HFD = 180° - 53° = 127°$, because angles on a straight-line sum to 180.

$\angle AED = \angle HEF = 28°$, because vertically opposite angles are equal

Using the smaller triangle, FEH,

$\angle HEF + \angle HFD + x° = 180°$, because angles in a triangle sum to 180

$x = 180 - 127 - 28 = 25$

Hence the answer is 25°

390. ANSWER: F

$$A = \frac{25}{9}\pi = \pi r^2$$

$$\frac{25}{9} = r^2$$

$$r = \frac{5}{3}$$

As the circle touches the x axis at (4,0) and the radius is $\frac{5}{3}$, the centre of the circle, C is$\left(4, \frac{5}{3}\right)$

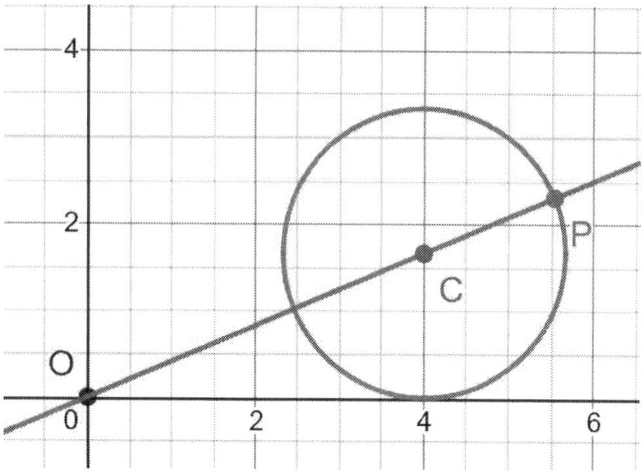

$$\therefore |OC| = \sqrt{4^2 + \left(\frac{5}{3}\right)^2}$$

$$|OC| = \sqrt{16 + \frac{25}{9}}$$

$$|OC| = \sqrt{\frac{144}{9} + \frac{25}{9}}$$

$$|OC| = \sqrt{\frac{169}{9}}$$

$$|OC| = \frac{13}{3}$$

$$|CP| = radius = \frac{5}{3}$$

$$|OP| = |OC| + |CP|$$

$$|OP| = \frac{13}{3} + \frac{5}{3}$$

$$|OP| = \frac{18}{3}$$

$$|OP| = 6$$

391. ANSWER: D

Firstly, many candidates may be puzzled since the quadratic is in terms of y and not x, but it is essentially applying the exact same processes.
To find the difference between the two, do the curve subtract the line, giving

$3(y-1)^2+4-7$, if we expand and simplify this, we get
$3y^2-6y+3+4-7=3y^2-6y$

This should then be integrated with the limits being the y values at which the line and curve intersect.
Finding the intercepts: $3(y-1)^2+4=7$, rearranging we get
$(y-1)^2=1$, remember now when we square root, there will be a positive and negative root, giving

$y-1= \pm 1, so\ y=0\ or\ 2$, now we can set up the definite integral to find the area

$\int_0^2(3y^2-6y)dy=[y^3-3y^2]_0^2$, expanding the definite integral will now give us

$8-12-0=-4$. Therefore, the area between the curve and the line will be 4, because areas cannot be negative.

392. ANSWER: C

This question requires us to use logical thinking and understand each person's statement in relation to the whole group.

It should be observed that Andy and Nick both have contradicting statement, as we know that only one person can be guilty. We can deduce therefore, that one of the pair must be the liar.

We should test both scenarios and see whose statement is able to match up with the rest of the group.

If we first assume that Nick is lying and Andy is telling the truth, it would mean that both Nick and Rathore are guilty, which goes against the information given in the question.

If we assume however than Andy is lying and Nick is telling the truth, Rathore is innocent, making Andy the only liar.

393. ANSWER: F

Since we know the total area of the trapezium, we can form an equation using the known formula in terms of x.

Area of the trapezium (A) can be expressed as $\frac{1}{2} \times x \times [(x-1)+(x+5)]$

$A = \frac{x(2x+4)}{2} = 120$ then after expanding, simplifying and rearranging, we can get the quadratic

$2x^2 + 4x = 240$, dividing through by 2 will give

$x^2 + 2x - 120 = 0$, factorising the quadratic gives

$(x-10)(x+12) = 0$

meaning, $\therefore x = 10$ $(x > 0)$

Since RS is $x + 5$, $RS = 15$

394. ANSWER: D

$\log\left(\frac{9}{14}\right) - \log\left(\frac{15}{16}\right) + \log\left(\frac{35}{24}\right)$. These 3 logarithmic terms can be simplified using the logarithmic addition and subtraction rules

$= \log\left(\frac{9}{14} \times \frac{16}{15} \times \frac{35}{24}\right)$

$= \log 1$

$= 0$

395. ANSWER: F

Since we know that $f(x)$ only has one real root, we can use the discriminant, $b^2 - 4ac$, to set up an equation in terms of k.

One real root means that the determinant is equal to 0, so

$144 - 4 \times k \times k = 0$

$36 = k^2$

$\therefore k = 6$ $(k > 0)$

396. ANSWER: B

The first step to solving this equation is to move all the x terms to one side and use the rules of logarithms, giving

$\log_6(x+3) + \log_6(x-2) = 1$, we can now combine the LHS using the additive law of logs.

$\log_6(x+3)(x-2) = 1$, using the definition of a logarithm, we can rewrite this as

$(x+3)(x-2) = 6$, this then becomes a quadratic that must be solved, so expand the LHS

$x^2 + x - 6 = 6$, rearranging gives

$x^2 + x - 12 = 0$, then factorise this into $(x+4)(x-3) = 0$, giving $x = -4 \text{ } or \text{ } 3$

However, x is not allowed to be -4, because the inside of a log cannot be negative.

Therefore, $x = 3$

397. ANSWER: D

Since we are not given any way to get the value of tan, it would be a good idea by expanding the RHS with the given rule.

$sinx = 2\left(sinx\, cos\frac{\pi}{6} + cosx\, sin\frac{\pi}{6}\right)$

Expanding and simplifying the RHS using the known values for sin and cos gives

$sinx = \sqrt{3}sinx + cosx$, rearranging to get sin and cos on separate sides gives

$sinx - \sqrt{3}sinx = cosx$, then factorising out $sinx$ from the LHS gives

$sinx(1-\sqrt{3}) = cosx,$ since we know that $tanx = \frac{sinx}{cosx}$, we can rearrange to get

$\frac{sinx}{cosx} = \frac{1}{1-\sqrt{3}}$, then the RHS needs to be rationalised by multiplying by the conjugate

$tanx = \frac{1}{1-\sqrt{3}} \times \frac{1+\sqrt{3}}{1+\sqrt{3}} = \frac{1+\sqrt{3}}{-2} = -\frac{1}{2}(1+\sqrt{3})$

398. ANSWER: C

Since we are given the mean of the 3 numbers, and the mean of the squares, we can find the overall sum.

Sum of numbers $= 6 \times 3 = 18$

Sum of squares $= 132 \times 3 = 396$

Let the three numbers be U_1, U_2 *and* U_3, and since it is an arithmetic sequence, there is a common difference, d.

Since U_2 is the number in the middle, it is easier to write the other two relative to this, so

$U_1 = U_2 - d$ and

$U_3 = U_2 + d$

We can form one equation using the sum of the three numbers

$U_1 + U_2 + U_3 = 18$, which can be rewritten in terms of U_2

$U_2 - d + U_2 + U_2 + d = 18$, simplifying this makes d cancel out, giving $U_2 = 6$

Now using the sum of the squares, we can write

$U_1^2 + U_2^2 + U_3^2 = 396$, then rewriting this in terms of U_2, knowing $U_2 = 6$

$(6 - d)^2 + 6^2 + (6 + d)^2 = 396$, expanding and simplifying all the brackets gives

$2d^2 = 288$, when solved $d = \pm 12$, it does not matter which root is taken because U_1 and U_3 will be the same either way.

The three numbers are therefore $-6, 6, 18$. The product of these three numbers is -648.

399. ANSWER: E

In questions like these, it is always helpful to draw a quick sample space diagram, and highlight the required outcomes, which in this case is a 4.

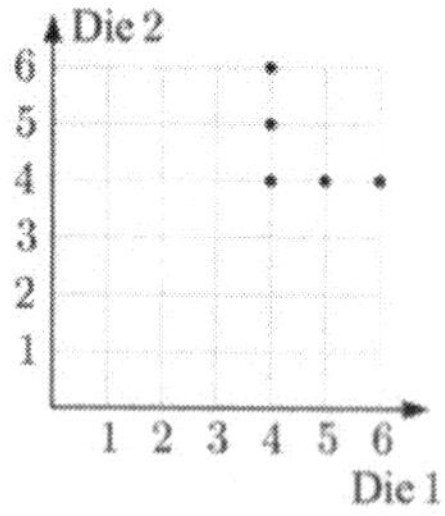

There are 36 different possible rolls, and 5 of these result in a 4 being the score. Therefore, the probability of rolling one 4 is $\frac{5}{36}$. Therefore, the probability of both Sally and Yangh scoring a 4 is $\left(\frac{5}{36}\right)^2 = \frac{25}{1296}$

400. ANSWER: A

Since we are not given any information about the triangle having a right angle, or the height,we should use the area formula for any triangle, $\frac{1}{2}absinC$, which is suggested from the information given.

Substitute the side and angle into this formula to get

$A = \frac{1}{2} \times 4x \times (8 - 3x) \times sin60$, expanding and simplifying this gives

$A = 8\sqrt{3}x - 3\sqrt{3}x^2$, since we now need to find the maximum area, let us differentiate the area with respect to x.

$\frac{dA}{dx} = 8\sqrt{3} - 6\sqrt{3}x$, since we want to maximise the area, we need to find the value for x,

for which $\frac{dA}{dx} = 0$.

$8\sqrt{3} - 6\sqrt{3}x = 0$, dividing through by $\sqrt{3}$ gives

$8 - 6x = 0$, so $x = \frac{4}{3}$. Substituting this into the previous formula for the area gives

$A = \frac{32\sqrt{3}}{3} - \frac{16\sqrt{3}}{3} = \frac{16\sqrt{3}}{3}$

Essay Guide

The second section of the ECAA requires you to write an essay based on a given extract. The new ECAA exam now gives candidates 1 hour for the essay as opposed to previously where candidates were only given 40 minutes. This would suggest admissions tutors are placing more emphasis on a candidate's ability to construct a logical and powerful essay.

Unfortunately, you are not given any choice in the essay topic. Since there is no set specification for this part of the exam, it is essential that you are well versed with current affairs and the economics behind them. Although doing Economics at A-Level is not a prerequisite to apply, we would suggest that people who are studying it should have a broad and in depth understanding of the course, allowing this knowledge to be brought into the essay. Alternatively, students who are not formally studying economics at school should have a good understanding of the general topics covered, such as supply and demand, international trade, and government policies.

The essay component of the exam is not marked out of a certain number like section 1 (out of 40) but is given a grade between 1.0 and 9.0 on its overall quality. The key factors that examiners will assess your essay are knowledge, analysis, evaluation and quality of writing. Note that the quality of writing is given a separate grade from A to E. The essay component allows admissions tutors to assess candidates ability to discuss different problems and areas in economics which is a key skill that is required in the Economics course at Cambridge.

A common misconception to many candidates is that Section 2 is much less important than section 1, which leaves candidates preparing much less for this part. Strong preparation for the essay has 2 very important benefits. Whilst firstly giving you a good score in this component, it can also significantly expand your knowledge base, enabling you to perform and analyse question further in the interview stage. Therefore, we would definitely suggest not neglecting this component but actually preparing and practising hard for it.

How to Prepare for Section 2

Preparation for section 2 can be split into two separate phases. The first phase, we suggest starting in July and early August, and this phase is the learning phase. This mainly comprises of getting confident with A-Level/IB Economics specifications. Whilst the first year of the course should be fresh in your minds, it is definitely worth going ahead and learning the key topics of the second year. This would include international trade, poverty and inequality for example. This is because the exam can throw any question at you, so it is important to cover all the bases in terms of knowledge.
Secondly, it is not just the academic side of economics that you should be comfortable with, but also the practical reality side of it. This includes having an in depth understanding of

various issues and affairs occurring around you every day. This at minimum should include Brexit, the COVID pandemic and government policies.

The second phase of preparation is practising. A lot of candidates get complacent at this stage and neglect this part. After having accumulated all your knowledge and understanding of the school course and current affairs, it is time to finally get pen on paper and start writing. The majority of candidates prefer to just plan essays instead of writing them, believing that it is the same. However, actually writing the essay in full enables you to practise more skills which is essential. In the latter stages nearing the exam, once you are more confident with your writing, it would be more appropriate to plan essays if time is a constraint.

How to write the essay

Essay writing is a skill and with this guide, we hope that you too can hone this skill and show off your writing ability in the exam.

Firstly, we must emphasise that the essay is not meant to be a collection of hundreds of ideas, where you are just showing off your knowledge. Instead, writing an academic essay involves laying out a coherent and logical set of ideas and formulating these into an argument.

Essays are often considered to be linear, meaning they follow one idea at a time, such that the order of the ideas follows a clear chain of analysis and make the best possible sense to the reader.

Structuring the essay

Essays in general do not have to follow a set structure but we would suggest following similar extended structure to that followed in school. This is set as follows:

- Introduction
- Argument 1
- Counterargument 1 (Evaluation)
- Argument 2
- Counterargument 2 (Evaluation)
- Argument 3
- Counterargument 3 (Evaluation)
- Conclusion

A well-structured essay enables your arguments to unfold.

Introduction

A strong introduction paragraph is very important in writing an essay, as it dictates the reader's attention throughout the rest of the essay. You will have often heard the saying that "you only get one chance to make a first impression, and the introduction serves

The purpose of the introduction is to set up your argument and let the reader know what is to be expected in the consequent paragraphs. The introduction allows you to set a background for the consequent paragraphs as well as set your viewpoint which you will then be arguing for.

Main Body

Following the introduction comes the main body of your essay which actually answers the question. This is where you should bring your knowledge and understanding of the subject. The key to the main body is to make sure your essay follows a clear chain of analysis in an easy-to-understand manner for the reader, almost like a story.

First, begin with your main point and it is important to start with a topic sentence. This means starting your paragraph explicitly stating the point you're making in direct relation to the question. This point should then be explained in detail going through each step, and it is very effective to use a PEE approach to each paragraph. This is point, example and explanation. Therefore, it is very important to read around the subject, as including your own knowledge and examples can be very effective in building up a convincing argument.

After your first point has been built and analysed, it becomes important to immediately evaluate it, which means coming up with counterarguments. It is essential that you give the same importance to the evaluation of the essay as you do the main arguments. Successful evaluations involve finding the key flaws or inaccuracies in your previous points and suggesting reasons why they may not necessarily be the case. This allows you to consider the opposite viewpoint and allows your essay to be balanced and give arguments from both perspectives. This argument then counterargument duo should be followed 2-3 times, allowing you to bring in a wide range of points onto the table, demonstrating good analysis and evaluative skills to the examiner.

Conclusion

The conclusion is a very important part of the essay, as it serves as a summary to your main arguments and evaluations. It is crucial that the conclusion presents your overall stance on the question, and most importantly, answers it.

Many candidates decide to bring in a new idea at this stage, believing that it allows them to show off even more knowledge. However, this is very debatable, as in more cases than not, can take away quality from your essay. We would recommend that only if you have a strong and interesting point to bring it up briefly at this stage. However, if it does not add anything to your breadth or depth of the essay, then your essay is more powerful without.

General Points

The use of topic sentences is essential in each paragraph. It allows the reader to understand what they will be getting into right from the outset. Remember the examiners will be reading hundreds of different scripts and if they must try hard to decipher your points, it will not sit well with them.

Use specialist economics terminology as much as possible. However, this does not mean littering your essay with complicated words that have no relevance to the question or the point you're making. Effective vocabulary can indicate to the reader that you understand the economic applications behind the questions and can use terminology correctly.
Bring as much of your own knowledge into your essay as possible. Although a passage is provided, many weaker candidates will rely too heavily on this, and their essay will be limited in external points. Therefore, it is important to read widely and bring in your own case studies. This can show to the examiner that you are a serious candidate who genuinely does have an intellectual curiosity.

Since the exam is 1 hour long, we would suggest underlining the key points that you are likely to use in your essay. This saves a lot of time whilst writing as you do not need to be scouring the passage again for the kye phrases.
We would definitely recommend spending a brief few minutes after having read the passage to plan your essay. There time constraint has been reduced, allowing you to plan your thoughts clearly on paper. The best candidates are the ones who plan before rather than jumping straight into it and giving a sub par essay.

Practise Essay Questions

1. Using the article and your own knowledge, explore whether negative interest rates are an effective solution during a pandemic.

What Happens When the Fed Lowers Interest Rates?

Congress has tasked the Federal Reserve with keeping the economy on track by managing U.S. monetary policy. The Fed has a long list of tools at its disposal to accomplish this job, and at the top of the list are interest rate cuts.

The Fed's Open Market Committee (FOMC) meets eight times a year to discuss the economy and examine whether to change its monetary policy strategy. Depending on the state of growth, inflation and employment, the FOMC can decide to increase or decrease the federal funds rate, also referred to as the federal funds target rate—or leave the interest rate benchmark unchanged. This rate has far-reaching implications for many of the interest rates consumers and businesses pay on money they borrow and savings they may hold.

"The Fed will cut interest rates when it feels like employment and inflation are too low and it wants to incentivize borrowers to consume and invest more quickly," says Christopher Burns, vice president, investment strategist for Greenleaf Trust, in Kalamazoo, Mich. When consumers have access to less expensive credit, they tend to buy more goods and services, driving more economic activity. Meanwhile, businesses are able to more easily finance their operations, which can help boost employment and the overall economy.

Zero Interest Rate Policy and QE

eval

The trouble with interest rate reductions is that eventually the Fed runs out of room to cut rates further. Once the fed funds rate has been cut to zero, there's nowhere else to go. Central banks in Europe and Japan have experimented with negative interest rates that effectively penalize people for not spending money, but the Fed has consistently shied away from this possibility.

Instead, once rates are at zero, the FOMC turns to other policy tools to keep increasing the supply of money and credit in the economy. Since the Great Recession, its weapon of choice has been quantitative easing (QE). This involves purchasing securities on the open market in an attempt to further increase the supply of money and drive more lending to consumers and businesses.

Impact on the Stock Market

Data suggests that stock markets don't perform especially well in the wake of Fed interest rate cuts. But remember, the Fed cuts interest rates to increase the amount of money available in the economy and spur economic growth. In other words, when the Fed moves to cut rates, economic projections are already looking bleak.

This lines up with data collected by Nick Maggiulli, the chief operating officer for Ritholtz Wealth Management LLC. Maggiulli has graphed the performance of the S&P 500 for one year after each of the 29 Fed rate cuts from 1994 to March 2020 and found that returns held steady in the immediate aftermath of the cuts, but after a year were down approximately 10%.

This is not terribly surprising since the FOMC deploys rate cuts to deal with an economic crisis that is either imminent or already upon markets. The same forces that drive the economy into recession, then, are ones that also drive stock markets lower.

Impact on Bonds

Fed rate cuts are designed to lower interest rates throughout the economy and make it cheaper to borrow money. As a result, newly issued debt securities offer lower interest rates to holders while existing debt that carries higher interest rates may trade at a premium—that is, prices in the secondary market may rise. Entities that issue callable bonds may choose to refinance the securities and lock in lower rates.

"In recent years, low interest rates have increased the need to look elsewhere for returns and/or income, including stocks, real estate, alternative funds and more," says Ryan P. Johnson, director of portfolio management and research for Buckingham Advisors, an Ohio-based investment advisory firm. Especially in the aftermath of the Covid-19 crisis, "the Fed has committed to low rates, which makes it more difficult to earn yield on bonds without taking a considerable amount of increased credit risk."

Impact on Consumer Lending

The steeper the Fed rate cut, the more impact it can have on the cost of consumer credit, for things like certain types of mortgages, auto loans and credit cards. Cuts to the fed funds rate have the most immediate impact on short-term loans, such as credit card debt and adjustable-rate mortgages, which feature floating interest rates that fluctuate regularly with market interest rates.

The Bottom Line

While it's understandable that consumers react to lower interest rates by taking on more debt, leveraging low rates to consolidate higher-interest rate loans, their investment strategies shouldn't change too much after the Fed slashes interest rates.

"Reactionary investment actions are rarely great ones," says David D'Eredita, founder of Rise Private Wealth Advisor, in Tucson, Ariz. "Changes to the economic environment really shouldn't be the catalyst for your investment changes. Changes in your own needs and time horizons should."

Article: "What Happens When The Fed Cuts Interest Rates?" By Brian O'Connell, Ben Curry, published by Forbes, June 2021
https://www.forbes.com/advisor/investing/fed-cuts-interest-rates/

2. Using the article and your own knowledge, explain whether the UK should adopt a free trade or protectionist approach after Brexit.

Protectionism vs. free trade in the UK

The UK government's official stance is to "champion free trade, fight protectionism and remove barriers at every opportunity". This approach to negotiations with overseas would-be trading partners is, of course, expected as the UK seeks strategic partnerships and alliances after the conscious decoupling with the EU. However, the government has simultaneously passed a series of protectionist-focused new laws, and there have been public calls from British businessowners for increased government intervention in order to protect British businesses and industry.

Post-Brexit trading landscape

Some may have envisioned Brexit as an opportunity to protect and promote UK home-grown businesses and trade; others may view being freed from EU regulation and trade agreements as a step toward establishing Britain as an independent global proponent of free trade. In an impending era of post-Brexit Britain (and an economy impoverished by the effects of the coronavirus crisis) and the government identifying the maintenance of London as the HQ of European FinTech and innovation as a top priority, one can probably expect further protections for goods and services of UK origin, in both the public and private sectors. As the UK government forges ahead with negotiating free trade agreements with foreign nations, while simultaneously trying to stimulate the COVID-19 battered economy and protect the livelihoods of the nation, a balance must be struck. Free trade and protectionism are not mutually exclusive. It will be crucial to ensure that the legal regime in the UK preserves its commitment to multilateral trade and fosters the City of London's well-earned reputation for welcoming new investment and innovation on a truly global scale.

Calls for increased government involvement

The unprecedented reliance by the private sector on the government during the COVID-19 pandemic and the various lockdowns imposed has been extraordinary in terms of scale and duration. The diverse stimulus package implemented by the UK government to address the economic impact of the coronavirus (including the UK Coronavirus Job Support and Retention Schemes, establishment of the Future Fund scheme and Bounceback loans for start-ups and small businesses, tax and business rates reliefs for affected sectors) has united the public and private sectors in a common goal: to rebuild the UK economy and consumer confidence. It is interesting to note the calls for increased government involvement in dealmaking, such as the proposed $40bn takeover of Cambridge-based company ARM Holdings by NVIDIA. Hermann Hauser, co-founder of

ARM, has publicly expressed concern that British jobs will be lost overseas. Intriguingly, Mr Hauser has implored the government, via an open letter to prime minister Boris Johnson, to either block the deal, impose legally-binding job guarantees for all ARM employees in the UK or has alternatively recommended that ARM be floated on the London Stock Exchange (LSE) as a British company with a 'golden share' (to be issued to the government) in order to protect national economic security and protect tech sovereignty. The UK government has typically been reluctant to intervene in commerce or private business deals, unless it is on the grounds of protecting public interest or national security.

New controls of foreign investment on national security grounds

On 11 November 2020, the UK announced new powers pursuant to the National Security and Investment Bill 2020 (NSI Regime) which will allow the government to screen takeovers and investments by foreign buyers in a range of industries from defence and technology to energy, transportation and communications (including a proposal to intervene retrospectively in certain circumstances). These powers mirror those adopted by an increasing number of countries around the world to guard against foreign direct investment (FDI) in strategic sectors – and reflect growing protectionist tendencies amid increasing concern about the ability of foreign companies (often with state backing) to acquire critical infrastructure and assets.

These powers are intended to "modernise government's powers to investigate and intervene in potentially hostile foreign direct investment". The government hopes that these new rules will stimulate foreign inward investment by providing legal certainty and transparency to investors and businesses, while also increasing the number of sectors subject to national security review.

New merger control powers in public interest cases

In an effort to address concerns about protecting the public interest, new competition laws have also come into force which grant the government the power to intervene or impose conditions on a takeover or merger of a business in order to protect financial stability, media plurality, national security (it should be noted however that the NSI Regime, once implemented, will replace the secretary of state's ability to scrutinise takeovers and mergers which give rise to a national security consideration under the Enterprise Act 2002, as amended), or if in response to a public health emergency (this category was added in response to the COVID-19 outbreak).

The government's focus on the burgeoning UK tech industry and enhanced regulation and protection for this sector are apparent from the lowering of the threshold at which the secretary of state may intervene or scrutinise completed or potential mergers or takeovers in three subsectors of technology crucial to protecting national security, namely artificial intelligence (AI), cryptographic authentication technology and advanced materials. However, the impact on foreign inward investment is likely to be limited as the Competition and Markets Authority (CMA) or secretary of state interventions only apply in limited scenarios where safeguarding the public interest is paramount.

Protectionism: transatlantic comparison

The UK has traditionally been far less bullish in protecting its homegrown creations and inventions, compared to the US. The US already maintains a far more comprehensive review regime for FDI and continues to bolster its export controls, particularly on emerging and foundational technologies, in order to protect its technology advantage both domestically and in conjunction with its allies and partners.

In the realm of FDI, the broadening of the authority of the Committee on Foreign Investment in the United States (CFIUS), pursuant to the August 2018 passage of the Foreign Investment Risk Review Modernization Act (FIRRMA), has enabled CFIUS to better address national security concerns arising from certain types of investments and transactions that were previously outside of its jurisdiction, specifically non-controlling investments by foreign parties into certain US businesses involved in critical technology, critical infrastructure or sensitive personal data, as well as certain real estate transactions. This has given CFIUS even greater power to review for national security considerations investments involving foreign governments, particularly through state-owned enterprises, as well as acquisitions involving cutting-edge or foundational technologies, and when such concerns cannot appropriately be mitigated, to require that they be blocked or unwound. Meanwhile, as part of the National Defense Authorization Act for Fiscal Year 2019, the US Congress enacted the Export Control Reform Act of 2018 (ECRA), which grants the Bureau of Industry and Security (BIS) of the US Commerce Department greater authority to establish appropriate controls, including interim controls, on the export, reexport, or transfer (in-country) of 'emerging' and 'foundational' technologies that are essential to US national security. While the rulemaking process remains ongoing, BIS has already identified a number of representative categories of technology for which additional export controls may be required to protect national security, including in biotechnology, AI and machine learning technology, additive manufacturing, advanced materials, and advanced surveillance technologies. In addition, the US has issued a flurry of new export control measures in just the last few months aimed at preventing foreign adversaries, notably China and Russia, from acquiring US technology that could be used in development of weapons, military aircraft or surveillance technology, particularly through civilian supply chains or under civilian-use pretenses.

These measures have been further enhanced in an 'America First' campaign that has been at the forefront of the Trump administration's agenda, aimed at protecting US industry and creating a level playing field for American workers. 2021 looks set to herald a new era for the US, in the form of the Biden/Harris administration – it will be interesting to see to what extent this rhetoric shifts.

Concluding remarks

Just one year ago it would have been impossible to predict an almost global economic shutdown in 2020, but as Britain looks ahead to life post-COVID-19 and post-Brexit, the government will be seeking to strike a balance between rebuilding the nation's businesses and weakened economy, and establishing an independent global trading power to be reckoned with.

The influence of the practices of the US and other key allies on the UK's new proposed FDI regime can already be seen and will likely continue to shape the narrative as the government moves forward with establishing trade deals in the new world order. The overriding message is clear: Britain is open for business, not exploitation.

Extract adapted from "Protectionism vs. free trade in the UK". By Matthew Levitt, SJ Beaumont and Jason Wilcox, published by Financier Worldwide, January 2021.

https://www.financierworldwide.com/protectionism-vs-free-trade-in-the-uk#.YPyzAY5KguU

3. Using the article and your own knowledge, compare and contrast price and non-price competition amongst the supermarket industries. You must conclude as to the most effective policies.

Supermarket deliveries: how UK services stack up for price and choice

Supermarket delivery services boomed during the coronavirus lockdown and many households who had not previously had their groceries brought to their door are now committed online shoppers. With more slots available, and the past few weeks bringing changes to Tesco's delivery charges and Ocado's switch from Waitrose to M&S, it could be a good time to review your choice. We look at what's on offer and who does it best.

Best for price

Industry magazine the Grocer has tracked prices every week on 33 goods at Asda, Morrisons, Sainsbury's, Tesco and Waitrose for almost 20 years.

Its price check for the week ending 28 August named Morrisons as the cheapest, with a basket of 33 goods costing £81.81, and Asda just behind. Across the year the two chains tended to come top of the table for prices – except when the Grocer had a guest appearance from Lidl, Aldi or Iceland. On these occasions, the guests seriously undercut the traditional chains.

For example, the basket of 33 goods (the precise basket items change each week) on 17 January this year cost only £44.53 at Lidl, compared with £51.13 at Asda and £57.21 at Tesco.

Finding a delivery slot

When Guardian Money set up accounts at the supermarkets from an address in central London and searched for the next available delivery slot, Co-op was best, giving us a slot on the same day in only three hours' time. Aldi was good, too, although that was its deal with Deliveroo on a limited range of items and currently only at relatively few of its stores. Tesco and Sainsbury's offered us next-day delivery slots, while Asda was a two-day wait. Ocado had no slots available for the next five days and Morrisons and Waitrose were only a little better. Amazon Fresh took the wooden spoon: it wasn't able to offer us a slot at all. Note, of course, that this was only one test on one address – it is likely to vary enormously elsewhere.

Delivery charges

Waitrose is delivering for free if you spend more than £60 (it will soon fall to £40), which means that while you may pay more for groceries you can save on delivery. Iceland is also cheap, with free delivery if you spend more than £35.

Tesco charges a flat-rate £4.50 for any slot. The others operate a demand-led system, with Sainsbury's, for example, charging £6-£7 for Saturday and Sunday morning deliveries but only 50p at quiet times, such as Wednesday evenings.
While most supermarkets promise your groceries will be with you within a one-hour slot, Asda is still at two hours, as is Iceland.

Buy a delivery pass – if you can find one
Asda's deal is best – £55 to cover delivery for a year. Unfortunately, it is not available at the moment as it is still tackling high demand. At £60 a year, Sainsbury's is the cheapest you can buy now. Amazon' offers free delivery – but only if you are a Prime member, costing £7.99 a month or £79 a year.

The challenge from Amazon
Amazon Fresh brings goods from Morrisons, Booths and Whole Foods Market. It currently delivers only in London and other parts of the south-east but there are plans to roll it out to more of the UK. We could not get a slot but its free delivery offer, if you are an existing Prime customer, plus Morrison's prices, will no doubt prove popular.

More equitable and sustainable deliveries?
This week Co-op launched a home delivery trial with Pinga to cover parts of east London. Pinga claims: "We use minimal packaging, most of our people are on bicycles and we pay them fairly." Its website promises delivery workers £10 a task. Under the Co-op deal, shoppers can pick 25 items from their local store and have them delivered within 90 minutes at a delivery charge of £2.99.
It is not the only delivery app for smaller baskets of groceries delivered locally. Chop Chop app works with Sainsbury's and promises a 60-minute delivery on a minimum spend of £15 (maximum 20 items) with a £4.99 delivery fee.

Article: "Supermarket deliveries: how UK services stack up for price and choice", by Patrick Collinson, published by the Guardian, September 2020.

https://www.theguardian.com/money/2020/sep/05/supermarket-deliveries-best-uk-services-price-choice-covid

4. Given the information in the text and your own knowledge, explore three policies governments should use to effectively combat climate change.

US's Yellen urges better coordination on carbon policy

VENICE, July 9 (Reuters) - U.S. Treasury Secretary Janet Yellen called on Friday for better international coordination on carbon-cutting policies to avoid trade frictions, days before the European Union is due to unveil a controversial carbon border tax.

The EU's carbon border adjustment mechanism (CBAM) would impose levies on the carbon content of imported goods in an effort to discourage "carbon leakage", the transfer of production to countries with less onerous emission restrictions.
Speaking as G20 finance ministers met in Venice, Yellen said there were multiple paths to achieve the emissions cuts needed to tackle climate change besides explicit carbon-pricing.
"It's important that any carbon border adjustment system focus on the degree to which a country's climate policies reduce emissions, and hence carbon content, rather than focus only on explicit carbon pricing," Yellen told a climate tax forum.

"Recognizing the different paths countries are taking to address climate change could help avoid policy measures to address carbon leakage that inadvertently create new international risks and spillovers," she added.

Yellen said countries in the club of G20 large economies would need to make significant public and private investments and take "difficult economic decisions" to achieve the goals of decarbonizing their economies by mid-century.

Approaches could include regulatory restrictions and emissions standards, direct public investments, public subsidies to incentivize private investments, and carbon markets.
The Biden administration is pursuing major public investments to decarbonize the U.S. power and transportation sectors, she said.

This is different from the EU's plans to unveil on July 14 the world's first levy on carbon imports as part of a package of legislation to cut net greenhouse gas emissions by 55% by 2030 from 1990 levels.

Levies will reflect benchmark prices on the EU's emissions trading system (ETS),the largest carbon market in the world. But EU trading partners doubt the scheme will reduce emissions and think it could act as a protectionist tool.

French Finance Minister Bruno Le Maire, speaking at the same G20 forum, called for a global minimum price for carbon emissions in the absence of a single global price.
"I think that a global floor could be a very good starting point to have all the G20 member countries committing on carbon pricing," Le Maire said.

COST BURDEN ON POOR

Developing countries expressed caution in proceeding with a one-size-fits all approach, noting that the economic burden for low-income people will be high.

Mexican Finance Minister Arturo Herrera said, for example, that the gasoline cost burden for Mexican families, of which more than half live below the poverty line, is 5% of disposable income, more than twice the 2% level in the United States.

A cornerstone of Mexico's approach to emissions reduction will be more investment in clean public transportation, Herrera said.

Yellen suggested coordination such as taking a common approach to climate-related data and financial disclosures through groups like the Financial Stability Board, and using the G20 finance track's Sustainable Finance Working Group as a forum to discussed proposed climate pricing measures.

She also said the Biden administration was still considering a range of other carbon reduction policies, including some that would put an "implicit price" on carbon emissions, and provide a point of comparison to other countries' carbon prices.
She did not provide details of these measures but Biden administration officials have said they would consider carbon border adjustment measures.

Article: "US's Yellen urges better coordination on carbon policy", by David Lawder, published by Reuters, July 2021.

https://www.reuters.com/business/sustainable-business/g20-countries-can-take-several-paths-cut-carbon-emissions-yellen-says-2021-07-09/

5. Using the article and your own knowledge, explore the various policies to reduce smoking consumption to maximise public health and the economy.

Tobacco taxation – a win for public health, a win for revenue and a win for the economy overall

A new tobacco tax manual recently released by WHO, confirms that the most cost-effective, mechanism for reducing tobacco consumption is a significant increase in excise taxes that leads to price increases. Although this evidence on the effectiveness of tobacco taxation is irrefutable, it remained the least implemented of the MPOWER measures (designed to support implementation of the WHO Framework Convention on Tobacco Control) in 2018 globally.

Even more concerningly, in many low- and middle-income countries over the past decade cigarettes have become more, rather than less, affordable. This could be due to many countries setting rates at insufficient levels and increasing them too infrequently, while others still use complex and inefficient taxation structures.

Tobacco taxation in the WHO European Region

Tax represents more than 75% of the retail price of the most popular brand of cigarettes in 25 out of 53 countries of the European Region. The fact that over half of countries in this region levy taxes below the best-practice level is a missed opportunity to raise funds for tobacco control and the health sector in general.

Moreover, a great disparity between cigarette retail prices was observed in 2018, with the price of a 20-cigarette pack of the top-selling brand varying from Int$ 1.82 in Belarus to Int$ 18.81 in Turkmenistan. Cigarettes have also become more affordable in 2 countries, while 13 countries had seen no trend change in affordability since 2008. Strengthening tobacco taxation will help European Region countries to bring about substantial reductions in tobacco use and the health and economic harms it causes.

WHO technical manual on tobacco tax policy and administration

Tobacco taxes work. This is why the industry invests so much money and effort in opposing tax increases and effective tax policies. Policy-makers, finance officials and others involved in tobacco tax policy development must not succumb to industry pressure and need to follow the facts when deciding on tax reform. The WHO manual provides all the information needed to make the right decisions at each step of the process – from designing, evaluating, implementing and administering tax policy to refuting industry attacks and ensuring the right support for tax policy change among legislators and the broader population.

Building back better with tobacco taxation

Fiscal policies can also be a key factor in addressing the socioeconomic consequences of the COVID-19 pandemic. Interventions such as tobacco taxation should be part of a comprehensive strategy to build back better. Indeed, as the new report shows, raising tobacco taxes is a SMART policy: it Saves lives; Mobilizes resources; Addresses health inequities; Reduces burdens on health systems; and Targets tobacco use, a major risk factor for noncommunicable diseases.

Article: "Tobacco taxation – a win for public health, a win for revenue and a win for the economy overall", published by the World Health Organization

https://www.euro.who.int/en/health-topics/disease-prevention/tobacco/news/news/2021/7/tobacco-taxation-a-win-for-public-health,-a-win-for-revenue-and-a-win-for-the-economy-overall

6. Using the article and your own knowledge, explore policies that could be effective in mitigating brain drain in developing countries.

Brilliant Strategy to reverse the Malaysian brain drain

Many people lament the brain drain in Malaysia. It's bad, and it's getting worse. I've children of my own who could be part of the drain (err, that doesn't sound quite right).

A brain drain sucks because when brains leave, they leave behind the no-brains. Being lighter, for not having any brains, no-brains rise to the top, displacing whatever brains are left. Like cream in milk. Or maybe scum in a pond. One of those.

Efforts have been made to stop the flow of brains leaving the country. This includes enticing Malaysians who've left to return through the "Malaysia My Second Home But Now My First" programme.

But none of these efforts have worked out. We brought back people by the hundreds, while we still lose people by the hundreds of thousands.

Some of the brain drain is a result of unavoidable geoeconomic reality. Rich countries steal the best talent from poorer countries. Look at the number who left India for greener pastures. If only they'd remained, India would ... still be where it is today. Nothing would've changed.

It's not just about holding on to the brains, but also giving them the environment to thrive. Otherwise, we're just processing them like commodities for export to rich countries, but, unlike commodities, getting nothing back in return.

America doesn't seem to suffer from a brain drain, so it's difficult to explain the bout of silliness there over the last few years. Maybe they suffered instead from drain brain, but your guess is as good as mine.

Malaysia had been pursuing a brilliant alternative strategy – give our young people bad education so their brain won't have any brains! Then they'd never leave the country; unless one day they leave for Indonesia to work as housemaids or plantation workers.

You can't really tell people that's your actual strategy though. Somebody may lodge a police report against you. Then you'd have to lodge a counter report and hire lawyers and all that stuff. Messy.

But you can dress up your strategy by calling it the National Education Policy, NEP. Engage an expensive consulting firm to write the policy white paper, and play songs about it on RTM non-stop. A no-brainer.

OK, back to today. This is still the strategy, and is constantly being renewed and refreshed every few decades. But now I'm suggesting a new strategy that is totally original and brilliant.

The problem with brain drain is not the actual brains that go away, but the brains left behind. The Brain Ratio, popularly called the "B" number, is ideally 1.0. Now it's at 3.7, meaning for every brain remaining in the country, 3.7 brains have left.
As an emergency measure, we could do a brain lockdown (BMCO) so no brains would ever leave its district or state or much less the country. Sure, some celebrities and politicians would violate that, but we are talking about brains, OK?

We can also vaccinate against brain drain. But we'd need to vaccinate at least 70% of the population before we reach herd mentality. And by some accounts, we may have reached herd mentality decades ago even without vaccines.

We should use the Chinese vaccine Sinowhack, which has been proven to create herd mentality in China. The religious authorities will certify it halal for Muslims. Indians can take it with whiskey, while Chinese can get it from the non-halal counters at supermarkets.
My suggestion on how to reach a "B" number of 1.0 is incredibly simple – encourage the no-brains to leave the country too! For every 3.7 brains that leave the country, we should encourage 3.7 no-brains to leave the country as well.

In reality, some fellow citizens are already working hard to achieve the "B" number of 1.0 by voluntarily leaving the country and living off their bank accounts in Singapore, Dubai or Switzerland.

But that number is relatively small. Only the Malaysian Anti-Corruption Commission (MACC) knows the actual number. And given these are classified as the "C" people, they won't really affect the "B" number anyway.

We must turn the process into a bilateral government-to-government arrangement and set up a GLC to manage it. We should appoint as chairman a politician who's an expert in the New Education Policy, and who understands the "B" number well, and perhaps is on MACC's "C" list too.

Let's start by exporting some deputy ministers to Singapore. We have a few hundred (so I was told) whereas Singapore is really thin on deputy ministers. They can have some of ours. Or, all of ours actually.
We can even offer some full ministers to go as deputy ministers! Singapore is actually jealous that we have so many ministers while they don't. So kiasu lah our neighbours!

We may even be able to throw in some prime ministers, current or past, too...
We can send some religious teachers to Indonesia and Bangladesh. We've been net importers of their religious teachers – it's time we address that negative balance of teachers.

They're fellow Muslims and I'm sure they'd appreciate our gesture.
Indonesia will be a breeze for our exports because their language is almost identical to Malay. Bangladesh isn't a problem either because many there already speak Malay.

We can also export religious enforcement officers to Indonesia. That country is awash with deviant Islamic teachings. They're letting non-Muslims there wantonly breach Islamic copyrights on such words as Allah and Tuhan. This must stop.

We've many "B" experts (who are also on the "C" list) who've built global expertise using bilateral country relationships, Swiss bank accounts and bags of cash. They just need to be incentivised to focus on this new national priority.

And these people, instead of being based in Malaysia, can base themselves overseas, further helping to reverse the brain drain and lower the "B" number (and "C" number too) further.
In the worst case, if the target countries are recalcitrant, we can even put our "B" exports in boats and smuggle them through the borders at night. We have lots of expertise in that. Lots of boats too.

A win-win for Malaysia, no? Malaysia shouldn't have a choice of only either brains or drains.

Extract adapted from: "Brilliant Strategy to reverse the Malaysian brain drain", by Adzhar Ibrahim, published by Free Malaysia Today, June 2021.

https://www.freemalaysiatoday.com/category/opinion/2021/06/20/brilliant-strategy-to-reverse-the-malaysian-brain-drain

7. Using the article and at least 2 economic models of your choice, explore the extent to which economics should be determined by mathematical models.

No, Economics Is Not a Science

Economists have faced a deluge of negative press in the past few years, ranging from criticisms over the failure to forecast the financial crisis, to the more recent disbelief over the granting of the Nobel Prize in Economics to three economists, two of whom hold views that can be said to be polar opposites. Indeed, the reputation of mainstream economics—specifically macroeconomics—is arguably at its worst since the formation of the field in the 1930s, with the advent of the Great Depression. This state of affairs prompted Raj Chetty, a professor of economics at Harvard, to author a defense of the field in 'The New York Times,' titled "Yes, Economics Is a Science."

It seems as though economics is fighting for its right to stay in the exclusive group of fields deemed worthy enough to be called "science," where subjects such as physics, chemistry, and molecular biology reside comfortably. Some instead opt to call economics, along with psychology and sociology, a "social science"—a vague term, often blurred with humanities, which is neither here nor there. Nevertheless, the underlying implication behind this battle is that to be a "science" is to be credible.

I don't agree.

First and foremost, I don't agree at all that economics is a science. Let me preface this by saying that I am concentrating in economics, and have the utmost respect for the field. Let me also clarify that when I say "economics" throughout this article, I primarily mean macroeconomics—microeconomics is an entirely different beast. While the two are intrinsically related, the methods of experimentation are so drastically different that the two can hardly be subject to the same criticisms.

Merriam-Webster's definition of science is "a study of the natural world based on facts learned through experiments and observation." What physics and chemistry and molecular biology have in common is that the building blocks of what they observe and experiment with don't change. Such is the natural world. But what is the building block of economics? People. Economics does not study any unit smaller than a collection of people. And human behavior can never be absolutely predicted or explained—not if we wish to believe in free will, at any rate.

In fact, in a strict sense, economics does not even follow the scientific method. Engrained in the scientific method is the process of testing hypotheses with repeatable, falsifiable, and parameter-controlled experiments. Unfortunately for the field of economics, there are certain non-trivial barriers to experimentally tanking the Czechoslovakian economy over and over while controlling for interest rate levels. Oftentimes, the best economists can do is sit back and pore through the data given to them—data that is muddled by changing cultural standards, changing technological innovations, and changing time periods, among other factors.

All of this is not to say that I disapprove of economics, or think it illegitimate in any way—quite the opposite, actually. I believe that economics is a crucial field that directly impacts most everyone on this planet, perhaps more so than any other subject. The discovery of the Higgs-Boson made headline news around the world and has been heralded as one of the greatest triumphs of mankind's collective intellect in history, but the Higgs-Boson has very little bearing, if any, on the daily lives of people. On the on the other hand, ill-timed economic austerity measures in Britain caused a very real, and very noticeable effect nearly immediately, setting the backdrop for the 2011 London riots.

This direct influence economics has on the individual lives of people stems from the fact that economics is, at its heart, a very person-centered and normative field of study. It is unique in the sense that economics fuses quantitative data and modeling with qualitative judgments; unlike in physics or chemistry, economics appends an implied "therefore..." statement to its conclusions. Economists' findings that expanded insurance coverage increased lifespans and reduced costs lent implicit support to the Affordable Care Act—a law that will affect tens of millions of Americans.

Economics is not a science in the way that physics or chemistry is a science. Yet, this is not something to be lamented. Economics is not, and will never be, at the stage where models can precisely predict the day on which a financial crisis will start before it happens, but this is not due to the lack of legitimacy of the field; instead, it is due to the inherently unpredictable sphere of study in which economics operates. People are not atoms—and this is exactly why economics is immediately relevant.

What this means is that all of us—and the press in particular—should cease treating economics as though it were a science. We need to understand that economics is attempting to neatly model a very messy world.

Do not expect clean answers.

Extract adapted from: "No, Economics Is Not a Science", by Alan Wang, published by The Harvard Crimson, December 2013.

https://www.thecrimson.com/article/2013/12/13/economics-science-wang/

8. Given that wealth inequality is a persistent problem in the UK, using the article and your own knowledge, explore the efficacy and effects of the imposition of a wealth tax.

<u>A Mansion Tax Is An Idea Whose Time Has Come</u>

More than at any other point in recent history, a mansion tax is an idea whose time has now come. However, significant barriers remain to define and execute this idea effectively. Even the label 'mansion tax' is a magnet for controversy and political opposition. This essay will outline the reasons why taxing the most expensive properties will be increasingly important for generating revenue and for addressing inequality. It will also explore the barriers to effective implementation and offer a solution based on reforming existing property taxes instead of just imposing a single new tax on high-priced properties.

The case for increasing the taxation of high-value properties
All forms of taxation will need to be reviewed as the country faces its largest decline in annual GDP in 300 years and record levels of national debt, each a direct result of the Covid-19 pandemic. In addition, structural issues such as healthcare and social provision for the UK's ageing population, and climate change, will put further pressure on government finances.

Under this review, taxes on wealth must become a priority to tackle rising inequality. A recent ONS study reveals that the richest tenth of the UK population saw their wealth rising at more than three times the rate of that of the poorest 10%. The same study reports that property contributes more than a third (35%) of all wealth held in the UK.

An increasing proportion of this property wealth is generated from inheritances. The Office for Tax Simplification reports that out of 591,197 deaths, only 21,850 estates paid inheritance tax in the 2018/19 financial year. These taxes are disproportionally paid by middle-income earners who do not use trusts and other avoidance strategies that are now standard among the wealthy. The untaxed transfer of wealth to the next generation accelerates social inequality. Large homes and land holdings are widely viewed as an unfair intergenerational tax management system for the richest in society.

Effective tax rates are also higher for income from work versus income from wealth. Researchers at the LSE and Warwick University found that for the 2015/16 tax year, the average person with £10 million in taxable income and capital gains paid an effective tax rate of 21%, much less than the tax paid by people living solely from a £30,000 salary.

Similarly, a study by City University of income and taxation in the period between 2011 and 2018 concluded that while job income was taxed at an average of 29.4%, wealth from house-price increases and pensions had been taxed at just 3.4%. The author says that there may be an untapped resource of an additional £174 billion if income and wealth effective tax rates were aligned.

One important way to address revenue shortfalls and inequality would therefore appear to be a new tax on the most expensive properties, ie. 'mansions'. This would have the added advantages of impacting only a small proportion of the population and normalising higher taxes on unearned income.

Execution challenges of a mansion tax If it were that simple, of course, it would probably have been done already. So what are the key barriers that must be overcome if a mansion tax is to generate significant revenues while also impacting inequality?

Transparency of property prices and value

For a mansion tax to function effectively, there must be a visible price/value point that makes it clear which homes are 'mansions' and which ones are not. This is important because recent purchase and sales data is only available for a limited number of properties. Council Tax bands are progressive but are still based on 1991 house prices. Valuations based on these outdated rates can be challenged, but very few people do so.

An updated, fair and clear evaluation system covering all higher value properties would need to be established by the Government's Valuation Office for a mansion tax to work. The issue of transparency is so fundamental that it could be considered a deal-breaker for a mansion tax if no valid system is put in place ahead of implementation. The question must be asked: is this possible?

Annual tax versus one-off payment

Unfortunately, there is no simple solution to the question of whether a mansion tax should be a one-off payment or an annual charge. An annual mansion tax payment is likely to generate more revenue in the long term than a one-time payment at the time of the transaction. This does reduce the spending power of the property owner, although this is less likely to impact the very wealthy. Annual taxes may also hit cash-strapped groups such as mortgage holders and pensioners as described below.

Thresholds

A mansion tax payment threshold would have to be low enough to encompass a sufficient number of homes to generate significant revenues, but would also need to avoid penalising people with lower overall wealth. For example, in areas such as London and the Southeast, where house prices are highly inflated compared to the rest of the country, many people own expensive homes but may not be financially secure due to large mortgages. Similarly, pensioners who bought homes a long time ago at very low prices may have since seen the value of their homes skyrocket while they remain on low incomes. Both of these groups would struggle to pay an annual property tax. However, these groups could easily pay higher capital gains tax at the time of sale or through the inheritance tax paid on their estates.

Cliff edges and distortion

Regardless of what threshold is set for a mansion tax, it will inevitably become a cliff edge and distort buyer and seller behaviours. Homes valued around the threshold will gravitate in price to just below the threshold to avoid incurring the tax. In some cases, people may choose to rent out their property instead of selling it. Others may choose to hold property within a trust structure to minimise taxation.

A study of New York's mansion tax, established in 1989, highlighted that the extra 1% imposed on the transaction of properties valued at over $1 million led to an estimated elimination of 0.7% of the total transactions and created bunching of prices below and above the threshold6 . Interestingly, the original flat rate has since been replaced with progressive rates up to a maximum of 3.9% on properties of $25 million or more.

Ease of avoidance

A fundamental characteristic of inequality is that the wealthy have access to expert advisors and the financial flexibility that allow them to avoid taxes, regardless of the structure of these taxes. If a mansion tax becomes payable on £2 million houses, the wealthy may easily buy three homes valued at £700,000 to avoid the tax. This disincentive for the wealthy to own fewer, more expensive homes could lead to an inflated housing market.

The way forward: Reform all existing property taxes

As demonstrated above, there are many barriers to the effective implementation of a mansion tax, despite the indisputable need for just such a tax on higher value properties. There are enough potential implementation pitfalls for a mansion tax to become just like inheritance tax, ie. to make no real impact on inequality.

A more pragmatic approach would therefore be a systematic reform of all forms of property taxation with the goal of impacting the top 10% of properties. This end-to-end reform of several property taxes, including stamp duty, council tax, capital gains and inheritance tax, will minimise the challenges and limitations for each individual measure because they could be managed as a whole. The use of digital tools for assessment, calculation and payment will need to be at the heart of reform. Tax simplification and ease of payment will encourage and enable payment and compliance.

This reform of property taxes must identify opportunities to reduce costly avoidance measures to increase both revenues and fairness. A gradual phasing out of trusts and complex tax mechanisms would be an obvious, albeit controversial step to take. They have no place in a society that is serious about tackling inequality.

Economists like Thomas Piketty have long argued that equality is bad for everyone, including the rich. While a hard core may never accept the logic of this argument, it is an idea that is no longer considered radical. At Davos this year, an international group of wealthy individuals calling themselves the Patriotic Millionaires lobbied for higher taxation on wealth. Changing perceptions on inequality should result in stronger support in the future for more progressive taxes on all wealth, including so-called 'mansions'.

Extract adapted from: "A Mansion Tax Is An Idea Whose Time Has Come", by Marco Minasi-Smith, published by the Royal Economics Society, 2020.

https://www.res.org.uk/uploads/assets/bd95a6cb-6608-4534-87de76af25e9401d/Marco-Minasi-Smith-essay.pdf

9. Using the article and your own knowledge, explore the effects a maximum wage would have on poverty, inequality and the economy.

Maximum wage' would fund pay rise for low earners

More than half of the public (54%) would support the introduction of a 'maximum wage' in order to tackle excessive executive pay packets and redistribute wealth among the workforce.

According to a report by think tanks Autonomy and the High Pay Centre, the UK has the ninth most unequal labour market in the OECD, the extent of which has been revealed by the employment issues created by the Covid-19 pandemic.

"As the UK economy buckles and growth crawls to a halt, the government – and business leaders – need to consider mechanisms by which existing cash in the labour market can be more equally distributed, so as to save livelihoods and industries. Wage caps are a powerful instrument to do this," the Paying for Covid: capping excessive salaries to save industries report says.

"In the aftermath of the pandemic, with many businesses operating at reduced capacity, it seems highly likely that the UK economy will be much smaller than previously envisaged for a considerable period of time, with profound implications for living standards. Changes to individuals' material incomes and wealth are determined by the level of economic growth, and/or changes to the way existing resources are distributed.

"Therefore, it seems likely that significant falls in incomes and living standards will occur unless better methods of redistributing existing resources are found. Without this, the UK faces a major struggle to protect as many jobs and livelihoods as possible."

Redistributing the salaries of the top 1% of earners would fund pay rises for 9 million low and middle income earners, the report finds.

Alternatively, a government-mandated maximum wage of £100,000 would redistribute the cash equivalent of more than 1 million jobs and would mean that organisations would not have to make mass redundancies in order to survive, as their top earners would be receiving less.

This would increase the annual median salary of middle and low income earners by £3,535 and would only negatively affect 2.85% of workers in the UK, the report claims.

"Recent estimates have suggested that the top 1 per cent of UK earners now receive around 17% of total incomes, up from just 6% at the beginning of the 1980s. The pay of top executives illustrates the extent to which very high earners are increasingly capturing a larger and larger share of available pay," says the report.

"While consistent data is difficult to come by owing to varied quality of disclosures, research suggests that the average FTSE 100 CEO [with a median salary of £3.6m] is now paid around 126 times the average UK worker, compared to 'only' 58 times in 1999."

A poll carried out by Survation for the report found that a cap of £100,000 was the most popular option when respondents were asked what the fairest maximum wage would be. Some 31% support a wage cap at this level.

Overall, 69% of respondents support maximum wages of either £100,000, £200,000 or £300,000.

To provide an £11 per hour wage to every worker in the arts, entertainment and recreation industries – where wage inequality is considered to be significant – only 0.64% of earners (or 2,000 people) would need to have pay caps of £251,760.

However, it adds that wage redistribution at an economy-wide level might be difficult to achieve. One option could see top-earners wages redistributed via direct taxation and transfer – in the form of social security payments, for example – while another could involve reforms to employment or business regulations that result in employers paying low paid workers more and high paid workers less.

The report estimates the possible impact using data from UK-listed companies. For example, BP pays at least £126,085 to their top quarter of UK employees, while the bottom quarter earn less than £19,108. It claims redistributing just 3% of the top earners' pay would mean a £3,783 pay rise for the bottom quarter of employees.

Extract adapted from: "Maximum wage' would fund pay rise for low earners", by Ashleigh Webber, published by Personnel Today, October 2020.

https://www.personneltoday.com/hr/maximum-wage-would-fund-pay-rise-for-low-earners-and-save-industries/

10. Using the article and your own knowledge, explore the differences between quantitative easing and interest rates, and their relative effectiveness in the aftermath of the pandemic.

Bank of England set to stay split on QE after inflation jump

LONDON, June 21 (Reuters) - Britain's top central bank officials look set to remain divided this week over whether to pull the plug on their 875 billion-pound ($1.2 trillion) government bond purchase programme, after inflation hit its highest in nearly two years.

Bank of England chief economist Andy Haldane was alone in May when he voted to halt the quantitative easing (QE) bond purchases in August once they reached 825 billion pounds.

Economists expect Haldane to retain this stance when the BoE announces its latest policy decision on Thursday and are looking to see if others on the Monetary Policy Committee join him.

Haldane has ramped up his anti-inflation rhetoric ahead of what will be his final MPC meeting before leaving the BoE. In early June he described the policy outlook as the most dangerous since sterling dropped out of the European Exchange Rate Mechanism in 1992.

May's consumer price inflation came in above the BoE's and other economists' forecasts at 2.1%, the first time it had surpassed the BoE's 2% target since July 2019. Some economists now see inflation exceeding 3% later this year versus BoE forecasts of 2.5% for the end of 2021.

"Stronger growth, labour market and inflation data, thus far, should tilt next week's policy statement in a slightly more hawkish direction," Deutsche Bank economist Sanjay Raja said.

Although British inflation is below the 5% last recorded in the United States, and its post-COVID recovery is less advanced, financial markets expect the BoE to begin raising rates before the U.S. Federal Reserve - a historically rare sequence.

"The BoE is not aiming to overshoot the (inflation) target, like the Fed," said Bank of America economist Robert Wood, who now predicts a first rate rise in Britain in May 2022. Interest rate futures price in the BoE's main interest rate rising to 0.25% from its current 0.1% by June 2022, a turnaround from early 2021 when the BoE was viewed as more likely to cut rates below zero.

Gertjan Vlieghe, normally one of the more dovish BoE policymakers, said last month he expected rates would need to rise in late 2022 if the economy grew as expected.

But most economists polled by Reuters still expect the BoE to start raising rates only in 2023.

FAST GROWTH

Britain's economic growth in April was the fastest since July 2020 as "non-essential" shops, pubs and restaurants reopened after widespread vaccinations.
But plans for a further easing on June 21 have been delayed by four weeks due to the fast spread of a new coronavirus variant.

Economic output in April was still almost 4% below pre-pandemic levels after a near 10% slump in 2020, and 1.7 million people - 7% of employees - were relying on government furlough support at the end of May.

Uncertainty about what happens to them when furlough support stops at the end of September is a key reason why most BoE policymakers are not expected to change policy.

Also, the BoE has described energy prices and other factors pushing up prices as "transient".

Inflation spikes in Britain after the 2008 financial crisis did not trigger 1970s-style wage-price spirals due to the weak bargaining power of many workers, and public inflation expectations have fallen.

Bank of America's Wood also said reducing asset purchases now risked weakening their future power.

"Voting to end QE early would undermine the QE tool, since it works in part by being a credible signal that rates will be lower for longer," he said.

Extract adapted from: "Bank of England set to stay split on QE after inflation jump", by David Milliken, published by Reuters, June 2021.

https://www.reuters.com/world/uk/bank-england-set-stay-split-qe-after-inflation-jump-2021-06-21/

11. Examine the extract from the essay 'Characteristics of a Circular Economy' by economist John Maynard Keynes (1930) below. Based on this extract, complete the task below

- **Explain what is meant by the basic economic problem, referring to its relevance in the present day.**
- **Discuss the extent to which Keynes' predictions have come true in the past 100 years.**

Economic Possibilities for our Grandchildren - John Maynard Keynes

Let us, for the sake of argument, suppose that a hundred years hence we are all of us, on the average, eight times better off in the economic sense than we are to-day. Assuredly there need be nothing here to surprise us.

Now it is true that the needs of human beings may seem to be insatiable. But they fall into two classes – those needs which are absolute in the sense that we feel them whatever the situation of our fellow human beings may be, and those which are relative in the sense that we feel them only if their satisfaction lifts us above, makes us feel superior to, our fellows. Needs of the second class, those which satisfy the desire for superiority, may indeed be insatiable; for the higher the general level, the higher still are they. But this is not so true of the absolute needs – a point may soon be reached, much sooner perhaps than we are all of us aware of, when these needs are satisfied in the sense that we prefer to devote our further energies to non-economic purposes.

Now for my conclusion, which you will find, I think, to become more and more startling to the imagination the longer you think about it.

I draw the conclusion that, assuming no important wars and no important increase in population, the economic problem may be solved, or be at least within sight of solution, within a hundred years. This means that the economic problem is not – if we look into the future – the permanent problem of the human race.

Why, you may ask, is this so startling? It is startling because – if, instead of looking into the future, we look into the past – we find that the economic problem, the struggle for subsistence, always has been hitherto the primary, most pressing problem of the human race – not only of the human race, but of the whole of the biological kingdom from the beginnings of life in its most primitive forms.

Thus we have been expressly evolved by nature – with all our impulses and deepest instincts – for the purpose of solving the economic problem. If the economic problem is solved, mankind will be deprived of its traditional purpose.

Will this be a benefit? If one believes at all in the real values of life, the prospect at least opens up the possibility of benefit. Yet I think with dread of the readjustment of the habits and instincts of the ordinary man, bred into him for countless generations, which he may be asked to discard within a few decades.

Extract adapted from "Characteristics of a Circular Economy" by John Maynard Keynes.

12. Examine the Article below from the Conversable economist blog. Based on this extract complete the task below:

- **Explain the potential risks of a rise in income inequality.**
- **Discuss the extent to which income inequality impedes economic growth.**

Does Inequality Reduce Economic Growth: A Skeptical View

Those who find the rise in income inequality over the last few decades to be concerning, like me, can find themselves facing the "so what?" question. Is my concern over rising inequality an ethical or perhaps an aesthetic judgement, and thus a personal preference where economics really doesn't have much guidance to offer? Faced with this possibility, the temptation arises to claim the following syllogism: 1) We have experienced greater inequality, which is undesirable. 2) We have experiences slower economic growth, which is undesirable. 3) Therefore, greater inequality causes slower economic growth.

A variety of studies have undertaken to prove a connection from inequality to slower growth, but a full reading of the available evidence is that the evidence on this connection is inconclusive. For example, the OECD has recently published a report called "In It Together: Why Less Inequality Benefits All," and Chapter 3, titled "The Effect of Income Inequality on Economic Growth," offers an OECD analysis seeking to connect the two. But before presenting the new study, the OECD report has the honesty and forthrightness to point out that the full body of literature on this subject is inconclusive as whether such a relationship even exists--and if so, in what direction the relationship goes.

The report first points out (pp. 60-61 that as a matter of theory, one can think up arguments why greater inequality might be associated with less growth, or might be associated with more growth. For example, inequality could result less growth if: 1) People become upset about rising inequality and react by demanding regulations and redistributions that slow down the ability of an economy to produce growth; 2) A high degree of persistent inequality will limit the ability and incentives of those in the lower part of the income distribution to obtain more education and job experience; or 3) It may be that development and widespread adoption of new technologies requires demand from a broad middle class, and greater inequality could limit the extent of the middle class.

In passing, it's worth noting that the first reason falls into the category of "frustrated people killing the goose that lays the golden eggs." In other words, finding a correlation between rising inequality and slower growth could be a sign of dysfunctional responses to the rise in inequality.

On the other side, inequality could in theory be associated with faster economic growth if: 1) Higher inequality provides greater incentives for people to get educated, work harder, and take risks, which could lead to innovations that boost growth; 2) Those with high incomes tend to save more, and so an unequal distribution of income will tend to have more high savers, which in turn spurs capital accumulation in the economy. The report doesn't mention a third hypothesis that seems relevant in a number of developing economies, which is that fast growth may first emerge in certain regions or industries, leading to greater inequality for a time, before the gains from that growth diffuse more widely across the economy.

Given the competing theoretical explanations, what does the actual evidence say? The OECD writes (pp. 61-62):

The large empirical literature attempting to summarize the direction in which inequality affects growth is summarised in the literature review in Cingano (2014, Annex II). That survey highlights that there is no consensus on the sign and strength of the relationship; furthermore, few works seek to identify which of the possible theoretical effects is at work. This is partly tradeable to the multiple empirical challenges facing this literature.

The report then goes on to discuss issues like: 1) variations in estimation methods, including whether the analyst looks at one country over time, multiple countries at a point in time, or multiple countries over time, along with the statistical tools used; 2) in many countries around the world, the data on income distribution is not measured well, not measured consistently over time, and not measured in ways that are easily comparable to other countries; 3) in empirical studies the already-weak data on inequality is often boiled down into a single number, like a Gini coefficient or a ratio between those in the 90th and 10th income percentiles, a simplification that might miss what is happening; 4) the connections between income inequality and growth might differ across groups of countries (like high-income and low-income countries), and looking at all countries together averages out these various effects; and 5) whether (and how) the researcher should take into account factors like the extent of progressive taxation and redistribution, the extent of financial markets, or the degree of economic and social mobility over time.

There's an old saying that "absence of evidence is not evidence of absence," in other words, the fact that the existing evidence doesn't firmly show a connection from greater inequality to slower growth is not proof that such a connection doesn't exist. But anyone who has looked at economic studies on the determinants of economic growth knows that the problem of finding out what influences growth is very difficult, and the solutions aren't always obvious. For example, the OECD study argues that inequality leads to less investment in human capital at the bottom part of the income distribution. If this result holds up in further study, an obvious answer is not to focus on inequality directly, but instead to focus on additional support for human capital accumulation for those most in need.

There are a few common patterns in economic growth. All high-income countries have near-universal K-12 public education to build up human capital, along with encouragement of higher education. All high-income countries have economies where most jobs are interrelated with private and public capital investment, thus leading to higher productivity and wages. All high-income economies are relatively open to foreign trade. In addition, high-growth economies are societies that are willing to allow and even encourage a reasonable amount of disruption to existing patterns of jobs, consumption, and ownership. After all, economic growth means change.

On the other hand, it's also true that fast-growing countries around the world, either now or in the past, show a wide range of levels and trends of inequality, as well as considerable variation in the extent of government regulation and control, patterns of taxation and redistribution, structure of financial sector, and much more. Consider the pattern of China's fast economic growth in recent decades, with rising inequality and an evolving mixture of private initiative and government control. At least to me, China looks like a situation where growth is causing inequality, not where inequality is slowing growth. It may be that the question of "does inequality slow down economic growth" is too broad and diffuse to be useful. Instead, those of us who care about both the rise in inequality and the slowdown in economic growth should be looking for policies to address both goals, without presuming that substantial overlap will always occur between them.

Extract adapted from "Does Inequality Reduce Economic Growth: A Skeptical View" By Timothy Taylor. May 2015

https://conversableeconomist.blogspot.com/2015/05/does-inequality-reduce-economic-growth.html?m=1

13. Examine the Article below from the conversable economist. Based on this extract complete the task below:

- **Explain the economic consequences of the overconsumption of sugary soft drinks.**
- **Discuss the extent to which the introduction of a tax on sugary drinks would be the most effective means of preventing obesity.**

A Soft Drinks Tax?

The October 2011 issue of Choices, published by the Agricultural and Applied Economics Association, has a set of six short readable articles on the subject: "Should Soft Drinks Be Taxed More Heavily?"

The case for taxing soft drinks--or as some of this literature puts it, SSBs (sugar-sweetened beverages)-- is based on a hope that taxes on sugary beverages would reduce obesity and improve public health. Jason Fletcher cites some striking evidence (citations omitted here and throughout): "Soft drink consumption has increased by almost 500% in the past 50 years, and recent data suggest it represents 7% of overall energy intake in adults and often larger proportions in children ... a 16% share of calories in youth ages 12-19 and 11% in children ages 2-11." Carlisle Ford Runge, Justin Johnson, and Carlisle Piehl Runge write: "U.S. sugar-sweetened sodas account for one-half of the increase in caloric consumption over the past 25 years, and are the largest source of added sugars in the average diet ..."

Reducing calories by a small amount, if sustained continually, would bring down weight. Fletcher again: "We know that soda consumption is an important share of total consumption, and ample evidence suggests that maintained reductions in consumption of approximately 100 calories per day—less than a can of soda—could halt weight gain for 90% of the population ..."

Jason P. Block and Walter C. Willett cite a number of studies which estimate a price elasticity of demand for soda, often finding estimates in the range of .7 or .8--that is, a 10% rise in the price of the soda would lead to a decline of 7 or 8% in the quantity consumed.

The main counterargument is that when people cut back on soda or soft drinks, they don't switch to drinking water. Instead, most of them will shift to other equally caloric beverages, including cheaper brands of soft drinks, sugary fruit waters, and juices or milk. As a result, calorie intake won't drop. Fletcher one more time: "[T]here is now ample research that examines the association between the level of state soft drink taxes—or soft drink prices—and obesity rates and found no effect. ... [W]hile individuals in states with higher soda taxes have lower soda consumption, these individuals completely offset the reductions in calories from soda by consuming other high-calorie beverages, such as milk and juice. This evidence is consistent with the view that individuals demand calories each day, and if the price increases on one mechanism of attaining calories (soda) then individuals shift their consumption relatively easily to satisfy their demand."

There is also some evidence that there may be mildly positive health effects from a soda tax, but at best, the empirical evidence that an SSB tax would improve health is questionable and uncertain. Indeed, it may be that those who most need to lose some weight are also the group who would be most likely to substitute toward other caloric drinks.

Even if a sugar-sweetened beverage tax didn't reduce obesity, it might have some side benefits. For example,
Runge, Johnson, and Runge have an essay titled: "Better Milk than Cola." Their point is that drinking milk or orange juice provides some other nutrients, even if the calorie count is the same, rather than just empty sugar. There may be dental health benefits, too.

Is there a way to make sugar-sweetened beverage taxes into a more useful policy tool? There are a number of possibilities. First, an obvious possibility would be to have higher taxes on sugar-sweetened beverages, and to focus them on those beverages in particular, not on all soft drinks. Block and Willett point out that "the inflation-adjusted price of soda has declined by as much as 48% over 20 years."

At present, lots of states apply their sales taxes to soft drinks. But usually such taxes are not specific to sugar-sweetened beverages vs. diet or low-calorie drinks. In addition, such taxes are not usually very large, and so are unlikely to have much effect on behavior. Here is Frank J. Chaloupka, Lisa M. Powell, and Jamie F. Chriqui (citations omitted): "[V]ery few governments, including seven U.S. states, levy small taxes that are unique to soft drinks and other non-alcoholic beverages, and almost none of these, including the few state taxes, apply only to sugar-sweetened beverages. However, most governments do impose their value added or sales taxes on a variety of beverages, with about two-thirds of U.S. states levying sales taxes on carbonated soft drinks. Again, none of these differentiate sugar-sweetened from unsweetened or artificially sweetened beverages. Given the low sales tax rates in the United States, these taxes add very little to retail prices, on average accounting for less than 5% of the tax inclusive price." A true SSB tax would presumably focus on sugar-content or calorie count.

A number of the essays point out that there may be interactions with public information campaigns or advertising and a soda tax. For example, publicity about the soda tax might help to make the tax salient in the minds of the consumers, so that they react to it more strongly. Publicity about healthier alternatives might also help in making healthier substitutions. Joshua Berning points out that soft drink companies spend tens of milllions each year on television advertising for top brands, which certainly suggests that advertising can influence choices. It also suggests that a tax on sugar-sweetened beverages could be undercut or offset by changes in advertising strategy.

One concern sometimes raised about a tax on sugar-sweetened beverages is that if people switch to diet soda, that might also have some negative health effects. However, studies of health effects of drinking diet soda need to account for two-way causality: that is, it may be that drinking diet soda causes poor health, or it may be that those who are already in poor health are more likely to drink diet soda. Block and Willett write: "When all of these studies are considered together, it appears that many, if not all, of the apparent adverse effects reported for artificially sweetened beverages may be due to reverse causation—individuals may switch to artificial sweeteners because of weight gain or blood glucose abnormalities. The studies that properly account for possible reverse causation, by using longitudinal data on subjects over time and controlling for dieting behaviors and weight, find no clear association between artificially-sweetened beverage consumption and metabolic risk."

The final essay, by Robbin Johnson, offers a counterargument to the idea of a soft drink tax. He points out that there are lots of contributors to obesity: "spending too much time sitting down watching screens; a physical environment that promotes vehicle use rather than walking; competition for the dining-out dollar that leads to larger portion size; lack of access to healthy foods or individualized portions; advertising messages promoting processed, calorie-dense foods; genetic factors; hormonal or other metabolic causes; use of medicines that contribute to weight gain; emotional needs that encourage overeating; quitting smoking; sleeping too little or too much; and aging." Most advice about weight loss and good health is about taking responsibility for moving toward an overall healthy lifestyle, not about identifying certain foods as "bad foods" and taxing them.

A "bad foods" tax, after all, would probably also focus on potato chips, french fries, snacks, candies, desserts, and processed meat, along with sugar-sweetened drinks, A "bad lifestyles" tax would tax or subsidize all sorts of actions. Leave aside the practical difficulties of designing and administering a bevy of such taxes. The conceptual insight is that these taxes would affect many foods and actions that are not bad for your health if done in moderation. There is something of a mismatch between a bevy of taxes to micromanage food and lifestyle choices for the average person, and the goal of discouraging the minority who are obese from overconsuming.

Extract adapted from "A Soft Drinks Tax?" By Timothy Taylor. December 2011

https://conversableeconomist.blogspot.com/2011/12/soft-drinks-tax.html

14. Examine the essay below from conversable economist blog. Based on this extract complete the following tasks:

- **Explain the ways in which the COVID-19 pandemic has impacted Global Supply Changes.**
- **Discuss the likelihood of Global Supply Chains making a swift recovery after the COVID-19 pandemic.**

Are Global Supply Chains Going to Bounce Back?

As the pandemic eventually wanes, a major question is what economic patterns will bounce back. Pol Antràs argues that global supply chains are likely to bounce back. His argument comes in two parts: they they have bounced back before after the Great Recession of 2007-2009; and the large multinational firms that have made a long-term investment in these global supply chains will not quickly change their plans. Here are his comments from an interview with Luis Garicano, "Is globalisation slowing down?" The interview appears in a recent e-book book by Luis Garicano: Capitalism After COVID: Conversations with 21 Economists (June 2021, CEPR Press). Here's Antràs:

One reassuring thing is that, contrary to expectations, trade flows and international exchanges have recovered.

A big chunk of world trade is associated with a few hundred companies that are large and that have complex global value chains. When the crisis came and things came to a halt, they didn't reorganise things massively. For example, they didn't start changing suppliers very dramatically, so that when things went back to normal, they could scale up again easily. We saw that from previous studies that looked at the Great Recession or previous studies that looked at the Asian financial crisis. These are large shocks. But even when those very large shocks happen, very often we don't see international links being broken up. It's very complex to set up value chains, so people tend to stick together and try to ride it out. The current crisis may have led companies to reassess what they should be doing – maybe they should move out of China and set up plants in their own country – but when they crunch the numbers, they may realise that it's very expensive to build new plants, new equipment. There are such economies of scale that it's very costly to move things around.

I must confess, you might remember back in 2008 and 2009 when the crisis was starting ... That was probably the first time I was talking to the press. I was all sure of myself, and was warning that the recession would lead to depressed trade flows for the next five to ten years. Because it's so hard to create those links, if the crisis breaks them up you can't expect things to reappear quickly. But six months later, I was looking like a fool because things picked up very quickly.

I had missed that firms are not dumb. Firms realise that resetting value chains is very costly, so they hold together. If the supplier was in trouble, they would extend the line of credit just to keep things alive so that when things go back to normal, they can scale up. When, a couple of years later, people started looking at the microdata, what we call the extensive margin, the trade links did not move much. It was all an intensive margin – shut down and then back up. For the current covid crisis it's a bit early to tell, but Asier Minondo (2020), a Spanish economist, has looked at Spanish data and found that things have recovered very quickly because the adjustment has been 95% of the intensive margin.

So I do think that it takes very large and persistent shocks to lead to a reorganisation of production, not even a Great Recession is enough. Policy shocks that are likely to persist are going to lead to this. But Covid to me, and especially at this point, looks like something that in a year we're out of it.

Extract adapted from "Are Global Supply Chains Going to Bounce Back?" By Timothy Taylor. July 2021

https://conversableeconomist.wpcomstaging.com/2021/07/05/are-global-supply-chains-going-to-bounce-back/

15. Examine the essay from the conversable economist blog. Based on this extract complete the following tasks:

- **Explain the ways in which Automation may be beneficial.**
- **Discuss the extent to which the USA's tax code encourages automation over employment.**

Does the US Tax Code Favor Automation Over Jobs?

Imagine a company that is considering two possible ways to improve efficiency and productivity. One is to pay for many of its employees to go through a training program to learn new sets of useful skills. The other is to pay for new equipment that will replace many of the employees. Daron Acemoglu, Andrea Manera, and Pascual Restrepo argue that the US tax code tends to favor the second option. The technical version of their argument, "Does the U.S. Tax Code Favor Automation?" is published in most recent Brookings Papers on Economic Activity (Spring 2020, a short readable overview of the paper is also available at the link). They write (citations and footnotes omitted):

The most common perspective among economists is that even if automation is contributing to declining labor share and stagnant wages, the adoption of these new technologies is likely to be beneficial, and any adverse consequences thereof should be dealt with appropriate redistributive policies (and education and training investments). But could it be that the extent of automation is excessive, meaning that US businesses are adopting automation technologies beyond the socially optimal level? If this were the case, the policy responses to these major labor market trends would need to be rethought.

There are several reasons why the level of automation may be excessive. Perhaps most saliently, the US tax system is known to tax capital lightly and provide various subsidies to the use of capital in businesses. In this paper, we systematically document the asymmetric taxation of capital and labor in the US economy in the US tax system labor is much more heavily taxed than capital. ...

Mapping the complex range of taxes in the US to effective capital and labor taxes is not trivial. Nevertheless, under plausible scenarios (for example, depending on how much of healthcare and pension expenditures are valued by workers and the effects of means-tested benefits), we find that labor taxes in the US are in the range of 25.5-33.5%. Effective capital taxes on software and equipment, on the other hand, are much lower, about 10% in the 2010s and even lower, about 5%, after the 2017 tax reforms. We also show that effective taxes on software and equipment have experienced a sizable decline from a peak value of 20% in the year 2000.3 A major reason explaining this trend in capital taxation is the increased generosity [of] depreciation allowances ...

I should emphasize that this paper is part of an ongoing research effort by these authors to think about interactions between automation and jobs. I have blogged about a previous entry in this line of research in "Is Something Different This Time About the Effect of Technology on the Labor Market?" (May 6, 2019). I discussed there a paper by Daron Acemoglu and Pascual Restrepo titled "Automation and New Tasks: How Technology Displaces and Reinstates Labor."

In that paper, they suggest a framework in which automation can have three possible effects on the tasks that are involved in doing a job: a displacement effect, when automation replaces a task previously done by a worker; a productivity effect, in which the higher productivity from automation taking over certain tasks leads to more buying power in the economy, creating jobs in other sectors; and a reinstatement effect, when new technology reshuffles the production process in a way that leads to new tasks that will be done by labor. In this model, the effect of automation on labor is not predestined to be good, bad, or neutral. It depends on how these three factors interact.

In that context, the authors of the current paper suggest the theoretical possibility of an "automation tax," defined as "a higher tax on the use of capital in tasks where labor has a comparative advantage." They would combine this with a lower tax on other forms of capital, as well as on labor. In my own words, they are proposing that the tax code encourage the kind of automation that complements what workers do in a way that leads to sharp increases in productivity and output, but that the tax code not encourage the kind of automation that mostly just replaces workers with a real but only modest cost savings for the employer.

Of course, it's reasonable to note that a theoretical economic model can just create variables for these two kinds of automation, while a real world policy might face some difficult challenges in distinguishing between them. Still, the authors are trying to break out of a binary choice where automation is viewed as always good or always bad, and automation is instead being viewed as a range of choices that include automation that is more likely to be job-destroying or more likely to be job-creating. It feels to me like a potential distinction worth investigating.

Extract adapted from "Does the US Tax Code Favor Automation Over Jobs?" By Timothy Taylor. March 2020

https://conversableeconomist.wpcomstaging.com/?s=Does+the+US+Tax+Code+Favor+Automation+Over+Jobs%3F

16. Examine the extract below from the conversable economist. Based on this extract, complete the following tasks:

- **Explain the significance of the US Dollar in the global Economy.**
- **Discuss the extent to which the COVID-19 pandemic has affected the US-Dollar.**

The US Dollar in the Global Economy

The US dollar remains the preeminent global currency. The Committee on the Global Financial System describes the network of international US dollar funding and some of the tradeoffs in "US dollar funding: an international perspective" (June 2020, CGFS Papers No 65).

The two left-hand red bars in this table show the US share of global trade and the US share of the global economy. The other blue bars show the role of the US dollar in cross-border loans, international debt securities, foreign exchange transaction volume, official foreign exchange reserves, invoicing of international trade, and payments made through the international network (mainly but not all banks) called SWIFT.

The CGFS report goes into considerable detail on the role of the US dollar in each of these areas. But here's an overview of pluses and minuses for the world economy:

Global economic and financial activity depends on the ability of US dollar funding to flow smoothly and efficiently between users. The broad international use of a dominant funding currency generates significant benefits to the global financial system, but also presents risks. Benefits arise from economies of scale and network effects, which reduce the costs of transferring capital and risks around the financial system. At the same time, financial globalisation, coupled with the dominant role of the US dollar in international markets, may have led to a more synchronised behaviour of actors in the global financial system, at least in part because many international investors and borrowers are exposed to the US dollar. As a consequence, it is possible that shocks stemming from US monetary policy, US credit conditions or general spikes in global risk aversion get transmitted across the globe. These dynamics increase the need for participants to manage the risk of a retrenchment in cross-border flows.

In short, having a currency that can be widely used around the global economy–whether directly or as a fallback whenever needed–is a huge benefit. But one tradeoff is that many players in global markets around the world are dependent on having access to a continuing supply of US dollars (say, to make payments or repay loans). This may not be a problem in many cases–for example, perhaps the party in question has a US dollar credit line at a big bank. But many other parties around the world may not have direct access to US dollars when needed.

In addition, when someone who is in an economy that doesn't use US dollars promises to make payments in US dollars, there is always a danger that if exchange rates shift, that payment may become more difficult to make.

And also in addition, if there was for whatever reason a shortage of US dollar financing for the global economy as a whole, the problems would hit in all kinds of locations and markets all at once. Because of the global dependence on US dollars, any actions of the Federal Reserve or the US banking authorities can have outsized and unexpected effects on the rest of the global economy. As a policy response, the Federal Reserve has set up "swap lines" with a number of central banks around the world, where the Fed agrees in advance to swap US dollars for the currency of that central bank during a time of crisis, so that the other central bank, in turn, could make sure those US dollars were available in its own economy.

Problems along these lines arose during the global financial crisis from 2007-2009, and again during the crisis in European sovereign debt markets in 2010. Although the main focus of this report is an overall perspectives on international US dollar funding, it does include some discussion of how these issues erupted in March 2020 as concerns over COVID-19 erupted. Financial and corporate actors around the world had an increased desire to hold US dollars, as a safety precaution in uncertain times. The foreign exchange value of the dollar appreciated about 8% in a couple of weeks. Those who had been planning to trade in US dollars or borrow in US dollars, around the world, found that it was more difficult and costly to do so. The report notes:

The prospect of a severe economic downturn drove a significant increase in demand for US dollar liquidity. Many businesses around the globe, anticipating sharp declines in their revenues, sought to borrow funds (including US dollars) to meet upcoming expenses such as paying suppliers or servicing debts. US dollars were in particularly high demand given the dollar's extensive international use in the invoicing of trade, short-term trade finance and long-term funding ... Faced with uncertainty about how large such needs would be, many firms, as a precaution, chose to draw on any source of US dollar funding they could obtain.

The activities of NBFIs [non-bank financial institutions] also appear to have contributed to strong demand for US dollar liquidity. In recent years, non-US insurers and pension funds have funded large positions in US dollar assets by borrowing US dollars on a hedged basis ... The appreciation of the US dollar meant that these NBFIs in some jurisdictions were required to make margin payments, potentially adding to demand for US dollar funding. ...

At the same time, US dollar funding became much more difficult to obtain in global capital markets as suppliers of funding shifted into cash and very liquid assets. ...

Finally, EMEs [emerging market economies] that raise US dollar funding have faced particular strain. Over the past decade, corporations, banks and sovereigns in EMEs had issued large volumes of US dollar debt securities, partly owing to a shift away from bank-intermediated funding ... The pandemic has seen fund managers substantially shift their portfolios away from US dollar bonds issued by EME borrowers ... At the same time, many EME governments and corporations have an increased demand for funding (across currencies), owing to fiscal expansions and sharply lower revenues, including from commodity exports. Together, these pressures have contributed to a spike in US dollar bond yields for EME sovereigns and corporations ...

The US Federal Reserve worked with central banks around the world to make sure that the flow of US dollar financing was only hindered in a way that gave it a reasonable chance to adjust, not harshly interrupted. With the widespread use of the US dollar around the world, and the interconnections of the world economy, the Fed has little choice but to accept some responsibility for the availability of US dollars not just in the US economy, but around the world.

Extract adapted from "The US Dollar in the Global Economy" By Timothy Taylor. July 2020

https://conversableeconomist.wpcomstaging.com/2020/07/13/the-us-dollar-in-the-global-economy/

17. Examine the extract below from the conversable economist. Based on this extract, complete the following tasks:

- **Explain the circumstances under which high levels of government debt may arise.**
- **Discuss the extent to which the consequences of high levels of government debt.**

High Government Debt: A Bang or a Whimper?

Watching the travails of the euro area in the last few years, it seems as if the negative consequences of high government debt are likely manifest themselves with a bang: that is, a scenario in which investors fear that the debt will not be repaid, and thus begin demanding much higher interest rates for being willing to hold the debt, which then makes it impossible for the government to repay. Rounds of financial panic alternating with recrimination follow, while the economy of the country flounders. In a roundabout way, this scenario is oddly comforting for Americans, because there is no sign in the financial markets (and remember, financial markets look toward future interest rates, not just current rates) that U.S. Treasury debt is anywhere near to experiencing a surge in its perceived riskiness.

But in the Summer 2012 issue of my own *Journal of Economic Perspectives*, Carmen M. Reinhart, Vincent R. Reinhart and Kenneth S. Rogoff offer a different scenario in "Public Debt Overhangs: Advanced-Economy Episodes since 1800." They argue that very high levels of government debt can also lead to a debt-without-drama situation in which interest rates rise little or not at all, and no deep financial crisis occurs--but the economy nonetheless suffers a prolonged slowdown in its long-term growth rate.

They begin by collecting the available data on advanced economies from 1800 to 2011, and found 26 situations in which the ratio of gross government debt/GDP in a certain country exceeded 90% for at least five years. U.S. government debt passed the gross debt/GDP ratio in 2010, but because it has not remained in that zone for five years, the current U.S. debt experience is not included in their group of 26 examples. They point out many patterns in this data, but here, I would emphasize three:

- When the government debt/GDP ratio climbs above 90%, it tends to remain there for awhile. They find only a few examples where the 90% ratio was reached that lasted less than five years--mainly cases of wartime debts that declined quickly after the war. As they note: "the 26 episodes of public debt overhang in our sample had an average duration of 23 years." Some countries had multiple lengthy episodes of high government debt. "For example, since 1848 (when the public debt data is available), Greece leads the way with 56 percent of the debt/GDP ratio observations above 90 percent."

- "However, we find that countries with a public debt overhang by no means always experience either a sharp rise in real interest rates or difficulties in gaining access to capital markets. Indeed, in 11 of the 26 cases where public debt was above the 90 percent debt/GDP threshold, real interest rates were either lower, or about the same, as during the lower debt/GDP years."
- "Consistent with a small but growing body of research, we find that the vast majority of high debt episodes—23 of the 26— coincide with substantially slower growth. On average across individual countries, debt/GDP levels above 90 percent are associated with an average annual growth rate 1.2 percent lower than in periods with debt below 90 percent debt; the average annual levels are 2.3 percent during the periods of exceptionally high debt versus 3.5 percent otherwise." The cases of high debt/GDP ratios and fast growth are typically cases of a bounceback from postwar rebuilding.

In discussing how government debt might lead to slower growth, there is a challenging problem of determining cause and effect. It is possible that high government debt leads to reduced growth, perhaps by leading to lower levels of domestic investment as government borrowing soaks up the available financial capital. (The authors do not have long-term data on investment levels to test this hypothesis.) But it is also possible that a country with slow economic growth might find it easier to build up excessive government debt and harder to muster the economic resources or political decision-making to reduce that debt. In all of these scenarios, high government debt and slow growth accompany each other--but which is the cause and which is the effect?

Reinhart, Reinhart, and Rogoff cite a number of studies using different groups of countries over different time frames, along with statistical approaches that seek to clarify the question of cause and effect (for example, instrumental variables, generalized method of moments estimation, measuring growth with five-year averages that are determined by other variables and thus not subject to feedback effects, fitting data to an endogenous growth model, and the like). They find:

"We would not claim that the cause-and-effect problems involved in determining how public debt overhang affects economic growth have been definitively addressed. But the balance of the existing evidence certainly suggests that public debt above a certain threshold leads to a rate of economic growth that is perhaps 1 percentage point slower per year. In addition, the 26 episodes of public debt overhang in our sample had an average duration of 23 years, so the cumulative effect of annual growth being 1 percentage point slower would be a GDP that is roughly one-fourth lower at the end of the period. This debt-without-drama scenario is reminiscent for us of T.S. Eliot's (1925) lines in "The Hollow Men": " This is the way the world ends/Not with a bang but a whimper." Last but not least, those who are inclined to the belief that slow growth is more likely to be causing high debt, rather than vice versa, need to better reconcile their beliefs with the apparent nonlinearity of the relationship, in which correlation is relatively low at low levels of debt but rises markedly when debt/GDP ratios exceed the 90 percent threshold. Overall, the general thrust of the evidence is that the cumulative economic losses from a sustained public debt overhang can be extremely large compared with the level of output that would otherwise have occurred, even when these economic losses do not manifest themselves as a financial crisis or a recession. ..."

"This paper should not be interpreted as a manifesto for rapid public debt deleveraging exclusively via fiscal austerity in an environment of high unemployment. Our review of historical experience also highlights that, apart from outcomes of full or selective default on public debt, there are other strategies to address public debt overhang including debt restructuring and a plethora of debt conversions (voluntary and otherwise). The pathway to containing and reducing public debt will require a change that is sustained over the middle and the long term. However, the evidence, as we read it, casts doubt on the view that soaring government debt does not matter when markets (and official players, notably central banks) seem willing to absorb it at low interest rates—as is the case for now."

Extract adapted from "High Government Debt: A Bang or a Whimper?" By Timothy Taylor. August 2012

https://conversableeconomist.wpcomstaging.com/2012/08/08/high-government-debt-a-bang-or-a-whimper/

18. Examine the extract below from Donald Marron's blog post. Based on this extract, complete the following tasks:

- **Explain the mechanisms through which carbon taxes help to reduce the external costs of air pollution.**
- **Discuss what is the most effective useage for revenue generated from Carbon taxes.**

How Should We Use the Revenue from Taxing Carbon?

Tax reformers want to cut business and personal taxes. Budget hawks want to reduce future deficits. Environmental advocates want to invest in clean energy. Progressives want to expand the social safety net. And so on.

How should we make sense of these competing ideas? In a new policy brief, we suggest a framework for thinking through these options. We identify four basic uses of carbon tax revenues:

1. Offset the new burdens that a carbon tax places on consumers, producers, communities, and the broader economy;
2. Support further efforts to reduce greenhouse gas emissions;
3. Ameliorate the harms of climate disruption; or
4. Fund public priorities unrelated to climate.

Each has merit, especially as part of an effort to build a political coalition to enact and maintain a carbon tax. But some ideas have more merit than others.

On both policy and political grounds, it makes sense to use carbon tax revenue to soften the blow on lower-income households and coal workers and their communities. Doing so will require only a small fraction (15 percent or so) of carbon tax revenue, leaving substantial resources for other purposes.

Recycling revenue into broader cuts in personal and business taxes also has particular merit. It can help offset the economic burden of the carbon tax and facilitate pro-growth tax reforms. By assuaging concerns that a carbon tax is just another way to expand government, moreover, revenue recycling may be essential to enacting a tax. However, requiring strict revenue neutrality also has downsides. Some policy goals, such as assistance to displaced coal workers, could be better pursued by spending the money directly, rather than indirectly through the tax system.

Policymakers should approach other uses of carbon tax revenue with more caution. For instance, they should be careful in using revenues to try to cut emissions further. A well-designed carbon tax would do a good job reducing greenhouse gas emissions, so additional policy initiatives should focus on filling in gaps—reducing emissions the tax may miss. Merely duplicating efforts—e.g., supporting clean electricity facilities—would not be cost effective. Indeed, policymakers could roll back tax credits for solar and wind power and other subsidies and mandates that a sizable carbon tax would make redundant. That would free up resources to pursue other, more beneficial goals.

Policymakers should be similarly cautious about tightly linking revenue to specific new spending, whether climate-related (e.g., coastal protection) or not (e.g., new highways). Earmarking risks overspending on any one line item, deploying resources inefficiently, and fueling concerns that the tax would become a slush fund for politicians' pet projects.

Decarbonizing the economy requires long-term solutions. Many emissions-reducing investments involve large expenditures on long-lived capital, such as power plants and industrial facilities. A carbon tax package that businesses and people believe will endure will be more environmentally successful than one that people think may not survive the next election.

In Australia, for instance, a carbon tax that took effect in 2012 was repealed just two years later, an object lesson in how highly partisan climate policies can be rescinded by future governments. Policymakers should thus give special attention to identifying revenue uses that build ongoing support for a carbon tax.

Extract adapted from "How Should We Use the Revenue from Taxing Carbon?" By Donald Marron. February 2016.

https://dmarron.com/2016/02/23/how-should-we-use-the-revenue-from-taxing-carbon/

19. Examine the extract below from Ed Dolan's blog post. Based on this extract, complete the following tasks:

- **Explain how demographic factors affect India's growth.**
- **Discuss the extent to which other factors are most significant in enhancing India's growth.**

India's Secret Weapon in its Economic Race with China

The eclipse of the G7 by the G20 puts the spotlight more than ever on India and China as the economic superpowers of the future. So far, China has the lead, but India has a secret weapon that will carry it into first place by the end of the century. What exactly? Widely spoken English? That helps India's service sector, but it is not decisive. Democracy? True, democracies outperform authoritarian regimes on average. It is no coincidence that 17 of the G20 are functioning democracies, but China is hanging in there as an exception to the rule. No, the real secret weapon that will carry India into the lead is demographics.

It is not just that sometime around 2030, India's total population will become larger than China's. Total population is an ambiguous factor in prosperity, as those of us know who were raised on the intellectual sparring of Julian Simon and Paul Ehrlich. On the one hand, people are a country's most valuable resource; on the other hand, badly managed population growth can overtax other resources and leave a country populous but impoverished. Rather than total population, it is the inner dynamics of population growth, in particular, the evolution of the dependency ratio, that will make the difference for India and China.

The total dependency ratio is the ratio of the nonworking population, both children and the elderly, to the working age population. Low-income countries with fast population growth have high dependency ratios because they have lots of children. Rich countries with slow population growth have high dependency ratios because they have many retirees. In between these two states, countries go through a Goldilocks period when the working age population has neither too many children nor too many parents to support. The dependency ratio reaches a minimum, and growth potential reaches a maximum. The following chart shows the dynamics of the dependency ratio for India and China, with the United States included for comparison.

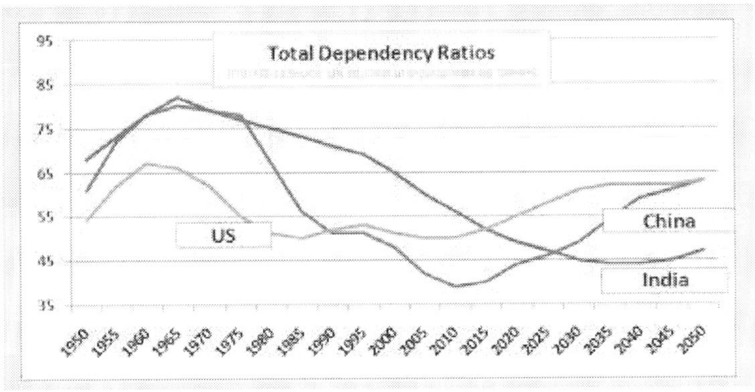

As the chart shows, India is just entering its Goldilocks period while China, like the United States, is already leaving. Furthermore, The dip in the Indian chart is more gradual and longer-lasting than the corresponding dip for China. For the next several decades, China will be tacking into the wind while India still has its spinnaker up. Chinese economic growth will slow, while India's, assuming a supportive policy environment, will edge past it.

What explains the difference in population dynamics? The answer can be found in the evolution of the total fertility rate in the two countries. (Total fertility is a measure of the number of children born to a representative woman over her lifetime.) China's total fertility rate dropped from almost six in 1965-70 to under three just a decade later. The famous one-child policy, introduced in 1978, contributed to the decline, but it was already well underway before that. By 1990-95, China's fertility rate had dropped below the replacement mark of about 2.1. In India, by contrast, the decrease in total fertility from six to three took 30 years to accomplish, and fertility is not expected to drop to the replacement rate until sometime in the coming decade. To switch metaphors, China slammed on the brakes, leaving big skid marks, while India made a more prudent deceleration. Furthermore, as Adam Wolfe, among others, has pointed out, China's official data may understate the true rate of decline in fertility, and therefore understate the future demographic drag on the country's growth.

There is nothing inherently wrong with slow, or even negative, population growth, but the transition to it is not easy to manage. The United States is not doing a particularly good job, as we know from the wrenching debate over the impact of social security and Medicare on the budget deficit. China is not doing well either. It has not yet found a social safety net to replace the long-vanished "iron rice bowl" of the Maoist era, and social insecurity, in turn, contributes to other imbalances in its economy. India, too, is not not exactly a Swedish-style paradise for the young and the old, but at least it has more time to get its act together.

In short, India, by all indications, is likely to be the world's largest economy at the end of the 21st century. It appears that President Obama knew what he was doing when he endorsed India for a permanent seat on the UN security council during his recent South Asia visit. He wasn't just maneuvering to put together a coalition to contain China, as some commentators suggested. Instead, he was backing the probable winner in the global economic race.

Extract adapted from "India's Secret Weapon in its Economic Race with China" By Ed Nolan. November 2010.

http://dolanecon.blogspot.com/search?q=India%27s+Secret+Weapon+in+its+Economic+Race+with+China

20. Examine the extract below from the Reuter's Article. Based on this extract, complete the following tasks:

- **Explain two reasons why Sudan has a large debt burden.**
- **Evaluate the effectiveness of the IMF's debt relief for Sudan.**

Sudan approved for debt relief, $2.5 billion funding by IMF

June 29 (Reuters) - Sudan received approval from the International Monetary Fund on Tuesday for relief on more than $56 billion in debt and new IMF funding of $2.5 billion over three years.

The IMF has accepted the East African country into the Highly Indebted Poor Countries (HIPC) initiative based on the country's commitment to macroeconomic reforms, it said, meaning Sudan can finally access debt forgiveness and new funds. Sudan is the penultimate candidate for the IMF-World Bank programme and by far the largest debt holder.

Now at the programme's "decision point," Sudan will see its external debt drop to about $30 billion relatively soon. It will then fall to $6 billion when Sudan achieves irrevocable debt relief after an estimated three years, at the "completion point," IMF mission head Carol Baker said.

Analysts said the HIPC decision came unusually quickly, a product of international goodwill toward Sudan's civilian leaders sharing power with the military during a fragile political transition and acknowledgement of rapid, painful economic reforms.

"It's not over yet but this is a really significant milestone on the country's path to a more prosperous future," said Ian Clark, partner at legal firm White & Case, which is advising the government on debt restructuring through the HIPC with financial adviser Lazard.

Deepened by decades of isolation and sanctions, Sudan's economic crisis includes inflation approaching 400%, shortages of basic goods and services and a spike in food insecurity.

Recent economic reforms include the removal of fuel subsidies and a sharp exchange rate devaluation under an IMF-monitored programme required to enter HIPC.

Another condition for accessing HIPC was removal from the U.S. list of state sponsors of terrorism, achieved last year after Sudan agreed to provide compensation to victims of attacks and normalize relations with Israel.

"This is a big day for Sudan and reaffirms that all the efforts and sacrifices of the Sudanese people are recognized and rewarded," Prime Minister Abdalla Hamdok said in a statement.

NO PANACEA

Under Omar al-Bashir, ousted as president after a popular uprising in April 2019, Sudan accumulated massive arrears, or unpaid interest and penalties, that grew to account for 85% of the country's total debt. Its power-sharing deal is due to last until the end of 2023.

Sudan is still calculating its full debt, but in a March report the IMF said the country owed $19 billion to Paris Club countries and the same to non-Paris Club countries, including Kuwait, Saudi Arabia and China as of the end of 2019. Its large commercial debts of at least $6 billion are roughly matched by what it owed to multilateral organisations.

Sudan's arrears to the World Bank and African Development Bank were settled earlier this year, and the IMF announced on Tuesday that its arrears were also resolved with help from a French bridge loan.

Next month, the Paris Club will decide on the proportion of debt it will forgive, expected around 70%, and a comparable agreement is expected to apply to other creditors, subject to individual negotiations.

The HIPC programme has been far from a panacea: Three of its graduates – Ethiopia, Zambia and Chad – are currently applying for debt relief under the G20 common framework programme launched in 2020. Others such as Mozambique and Congo have also been forced to restructure.

NEW FINANCING

The $2.5 billion in new funding is a combination of grants and cheap loans that the IMF calls an "extended credit facility." This will provide Sudan much needed direct financing but requires that Sudan push ahead with reforms also required for permanent debt relief.

Some $1.4 billion of the total was dispersed immediately, the IMF said, in order to repay France. The remainder will be disbursed over the next 39 months.

"We are looking to make space for private sector-led growth to create jobs," including by reducing the country's need to print money, said Baker.

Sudan must demonstrate it has achieved macroeconomic stability and improved governance and that it has used the new "fiscal breathing space" to reduce poverty, finance ministry senior adviser Magdi Amin told Reuters. Khartoum cannot fall back into arrears on its remaining debt for the relief to be made permanent, he added.

That is crucial for Sudan's over-burdened government, which Baker said inherited reserves at less than a week's worth of imports from the Bashir regime. It routinely struggles to import fuel, causing frequent power cuts.

The IMF estimated in April that Sudan needs more than $7 billion in external financing over the next two years.

The reforms so far have caused food and transportation costs to surge, forcing Sudanese people to make sacrifices. There are frequent protests, including demonstrations planned on Wednesday.

"It's imperative that (the government) communicate properly to the population ... on this so people don't look up and just see the pain," said Jonas Horner, Sudan analyst at the International Crisis Group.

Extract adapted from "Sudan approved for debt relief, $2.5 billion funding by IMF" by Nafisa Eltahir, Karin Strohecker and David Lawder for Reuters. June 2021

https://www.reuters.com/world/africa/sudan-crosses-last-hurdle-towards-debt-relief-sudanese-official-2021-06-28/

Congratulations!

We sincerely hope that you have found this guidebook helpful in your preparation for the ECAA. Having done all the maths questions and practised the essays should now place you in a strong state and should hopefully give you enough confidence to do well.

It is now essential you begin to do practise papers under strict time conditions to mimic the conditions in the real exam, and doing timed tests enables you to challenge yourself and assess your current standard.

We understand that many of you will be busy with the other stages of your application regarding personal statement, predicted grades and interviews, so would like to remind you of the other services offered by Frontier Education:

- Personal Statement Guidance
- Mock Interviews
- Tutoring for Mathematics, Further Mathematics and Economics for A and AS level

Once again, please feel free to contact us regarding any queries or questions not limited to the ECAA but general guidance regarding academics and University preparation.

frontiereducation2021@gmail.com

Alternatively feel free to connect with Sachin Sarin or Thapan Reddibathini via LinkedIn.

We would finally very much appreciate if you could leave us a review on Amazon where you purchased this book to make sure others can benefit in the same way in following years.

On a final note, we wish you the best of luck in your application to Cambridge and other Universities!

Printed in Great Britain
by Amazon

67616866R00226